AG 20 '93			
AP 29 '94			
AP 30 '96			
MY 24 '96			
AP 27 00			
OC 11 01			
MR 25 02			
AP 15 02			
SE 25 02			

DEMCO 38-296

POLITICAL
ISSUES
DEBATED

third edition

POLITICAL
ISSUES
DEBATED

an introduction to politics

HERBERT M. LEVINE

Prentice Hall, Englewood Cliffs, New Jersey 07632

Library of Congress Cataloging-in-Publication Data

Levine, Herbert M.
    Political issues debated : an introduction to politics / Herbert
M. Levine. -- 3rd ed.
        p.   cm.
    Includes bibliographies and index.
    ISBN 0-13-685124-X
    1. Political science.   I. Title.
JA66.L46   1990
320--dc20   89-15987
                                                                  CIP

Editorial/production supervision and
   interior design: Marina Harrison
Copyeditor: Ann Hofstra Grogg
Cover design: 20/20 Services, Inc.
Manufacturing buyer: Peter Havens

© 1990, 1987, 1982 by Prentice-Hall, Inc.
A Division of Simon & Schuster
Englewood Cliffs, New Jersey 07632

Printed in the United States of America
10 9 8 7 6 5 4 3 2 1

ISBN   0-13-685124-X

Prentice-Hall International (UK) Limited, *London*
Prentice-Hall of Australia Pty. Limited, *Sydney*
Prentice-Hall Canada Inc., *Toronto*
Prentice-Hall Hispanoamericana, S.A., *Mexico*
Prentice-Hall of India Private Limited, *New Delhi*
Prentice-Hall of Japan, Inc., *Tokyo*
Simon & Schuster Asia Pte. Ltd., *Singapore*
Editora Prentice-Hall do Brasil, Ltda., *Rio de Janeiro*

FOR MARVIN MAURER

Contents

II   FORMS OF GOVERNMENT   33

3   Democracy and Dictatorship   35

III   IDEOLOGY   67

4   Liberalism, Conservatism, and Fascism   69

14 International Politics: Instruments and Constraints   279

Preface

When college students become involved in politics, it is often because issues are of vital concern to them. At times these issues may directly affect their lives, such as a decision by government to register young people for the draft or to send them to war; or, less seriously, to increase their tuition at state-supported universities. At other times, moral considerations compel college students to become involved in issues of vital concern to others, such as ending *apartheid* in South Africa or eliminating capital punishment.

This book focuses on issues in the hope that the excitement of politics, which comes from its subject matter and the controversy it generates, will interest students to learn more about politics. To that end, the book deals with subjects of great complexity and importance, such as the purpose of government, the reality of democracy, the nature of communism, the poverty of distant nations, and the prospects of ending the arms race. The book examines twenty-six issues, some of longstanding concern, such as the relationship between interest groups and the public interest, the possibility of participatory democracy, and the superiority of the British parliamentary system over the American presidential system of government. Other issues are of more recent relevance, such as whether television news has a unique impact on public opinion, whether America is a fascist society, and whether the West should redistribute its wealth to Third World countries.

The issues have been selected because of their controversial character. The intent of the author is to introduce subjects that will stimulate student interest in the study of politics. Background information is provided for each chapter. This material is designed to present the subject matter to students so that they will have the facts necessary to understand the debates. The length of the background information varies considerably, since the amount of information included depends upon the breadth of the subject matter considered in the debates. A list of Recommended Readings at the end of each chapter provides additional sources that students may consult in order to develop their understanding of an issue. Questions are offered to encourage a discussion of the issues, and Key Terms are cited to focus attention on important concepts and definitions.

The purpose of the book and the nature of the format dictate an approach to the subject matter that is not methodologically rigorous. It is the belief of the author that students must first become interested in politics before they concern themselves with methodological matters.

The debate approach offers several educational benefits. First, students who are accustomed to believe in the truthfulness of the printed word will be encouraged to use their own critical talents, since opposing viewpoints are presented. Second, the debate format is a useful way for students with a limited background in politics to become interested in the subject matter of politics. Third, the instructor will have many possibilities in lecturing and giving assignments. Lectures can be presented that highlight the background information or take one or both sides of a debate. Classroom participation can be encouraged by dividing the class into groups that argue different sides of an issue.

A debate format is not without problems, however. First, students may be encouraged to think that there are only two sides to every argument, when often there are several worthy of consideration. Second, a certain amount of information about politics, which ordinarily is included in an introductory course, may have to be left out or treated briefly. The

instructor must determine how to minimize the risks through lectures and class discussions.[1]

The third edition of *Political Issues Debated* has retained the structure and most of the debate topics of the second edition. Three new debates deal with the significance of the economic and political reforms instituted by Soviet leader Mikhail Gorbachev, the controversy over the decline of U.S. power, and the effectiveness of economic sanctions as an instrument of foreign policy.

The material in all chapters has been updated and revised in order to present additional information and to refine arguments. In some cases, separate Questions and Recommended Readings are supplied for debate issues in addition to those covering general subject matter.

ACKNOWLEDGMENTS

In preparing the third edition of this book, I had the professional help of several people in both the academic and publishing communities. I am grateful to them for their assistance.

The editorial consultants for the book were Professor David W. Dent, Towson State University; and Professor David M. Wood, University of Missouri/Columbia.

Karen Horton was the political science editor, and Marina Harrison was the production editor. Ann Hofstra Grogg was the copyeditor.

Although I had the assistance of many people, I accept full responsibility for any mistakes that may appear in the book.

---

[1] For a discussion of the merits of the debate format in the American Government course, see Charles W. Dunn, "Using Debates to Teach American Government," *News for Teachers of Political Science*, 26 (Summer 1980): 11, 20–21.

POLITICS, GOVERNMENT, AND NATIONS

What government is and what government does are of interest to many people concerned with goals, such as physical security, economic well-being, health, and education. In the twentieth century, governments throughout the world have grown in the services they perform to achieve those goals and the numbers of people who provide those services. People differ about the priority of these goals and about the allocation of resources. Government plays a prominent role in setting public priorities and in allocating scarce resources.

Chapter 1 discusses the way in which people attempt to achieve their goals through public policy. Politics and government are defined before consideration is given to the necessity of government.

Chapter 2 focuses on nations, which have become a battleground for political activity. Distinctions are made between nations and states. Debates are centered on nationalism: its divisiveness, its tendency toward war, and its obsolescence.

chapter 1

Politics and government

WHAT IS POLITICS?

The term *politics* has many definitions and many uses. To some it is a disparaging word. "He got his job through politics" might mean that "connections" rather than "competence" was the reason for his selection to a position. Along somewhat similar lines, a *politician* is distinguished from a *statesman* to the extent that the politician is concerned with catering to the interests of a narrow constituency while the statesman serves the interests of the country.

Not everyone, however, has used *politics* and *politician* in a derogatory manner. It is essential when defining a term with such emotional connotations to find suitable objective ways to describe it. Recognizing that the term **politics** has many varied definitions, we shall use it to mean subjects dealing with (1) the state, (2) power, and (3) public policy.

The State

Politics has been traditionally concerned with the state. The term *politics* is in fact derived from the Greek word **polis,** which means city-state or organized community. As used in this chapter, the state is a legal entity that is equivalent to a country. In this regard the United States is a state. So, too, are France, Spain, and more than 160 countries throughout the world. This causes some confusion to Americans who are accustomed to thinking of regional units of their country as states, for example, California, Louisiana, and New Jersey. These are, however, equivalent to provinces or districts in other countries. We shall define a **state** as a political entity that possesses people, territory, a government, and sovereignty.[1]

---

[1] See Chapter 2 for a more elaborate description of states and nations.

People. Every country possesses people, who may vary in religion, race, language, and ethnic composition. When people identify with others who live within the state, they constitute a nation. Nations are discussed in Chapter 2. Here it is only necessary to point out that the number of people who reside within states varies considerably. Liechtenstein, one of the world's smallest states, has a population of twenty-eight thousand people, and the People's Republic of China, the world's most populous state, contains more than one billion people.

Territory. Every state contains a specific piece of territory that distinguishes it from other states. That bounded geographical area may be in one continuous land unit, or it may be separated by other states or large bodies of water. The United States contains among its regional units Alaska and Hawaii—both of which are separated by vast distances from their continental base. States vary in size as they do in population. The Soviet Union, occupying one-seventh of the world's surface, is the largest state in the world. States such as Malta and Singapore are among the smallest. Some states are so small—either in area or population—that they are known as **microstates.**

Government. **Government** is the social organization that has authority to rule the state. Government is, however, different from other social organizations, such as a family or group. It makes laws that affect all the people within its territory. Its rules are binding upon the people whether they wish to be bound by such rules or not. Institutions other than government, such as churches, village elders, and companies, have made rules binding upon their members in the past and do so now. Today, however, such institutions tend to be limited in authority to a segment of a society rather than applicable to the entire society.

One of the most important features of government is that it is the only social organization that has the legal authority to use force. To be sure, groups ranging from "organized crime" to vigilantes use physical coercion in an unauthorized manner—which is to say that they resort to violence—but such an application of violence by these groups or individuals is regarded as illegal.

Among the major sources of instability in the world today is the conflict over which group of people should constitute a government of a state. The problem of maintaining **authority** (the establishment of formal power) and **legitimacy** (the acceptance of authority) is a major difficulty of our times. Northern Ireland, Israel, and Lebanon provide recent examples of guerrilla warfare resulting from rival claims to government authority and legitimacy.

Sovereignty. The term **sovereignty** means total legitimate power. It was first used in the sixteenth century by the French political philosopher Jean Bodin. As originally conceived, the term meant that the monarch had total authority to make rules for all the people within the kingdom. In more recent centuries, however, the term has been applied to government's authority rather than the monarch's authority.

The state, then, is the legal entity containing all these elements of people, territory, a government, and sovereignty. Although the state had its origins in antiquity, its modern form arose in Europe between the fourteenth and seventeenth centuries. Powerful monarchs, such as Louis XIV of France and Elizabeth I of England, centralized power in the state. The power of the monarchs declined from the eighteenth century on—in some cases violently through revolution and in other cases peacefully through the establishment of popularly elected institutions—

so that the state in the twentieth century is quite different from what it was in the seventeenth century.

Today, students of politics concern themselves with the state. Many are interested in the principal institutions of the state, such as the legislature, the executive and bureaucracy, and the judiciary (see Chapters 11 and 12). In practice, however, the role of these institutions is often not sharply circumscribed, and how each institution operates in a state varies on the basis of tradition and the realities of power. In focusing on the state, students of politics are also concerned with the relationships between the central government and its regional units (see Chapter 10).

Power

Although students of politics have been concerned with the institutions of the state, such interest is only a partial preoccupation of their research. One could not hope to understand how American government works, for example, by looking solely at the political institutions of the president, Congress, the courts, and the regional governments. Nor, for that matter, could one hope to understand how the Soviet political system functions by looking only at its formal institutions of state power.

Students of politics consequently are concerned with power. **Power** is the ability to influence people to do things they may not want to do. In this context, power may (but need not) have anything to do with government. When a criminal threatens a person with physical injury unless he or she complies with the criminal's demands, that is power. A teacher's pledge to give high grades to students for superior academic work is another kind of power that students disregard at their peril. Power carries with it a sanction: in the case of the criminal, physical safety; in the case of the teacher, a grade.

In every society power is distributed unevenly among its members. Power is derived from different sources, such as information, wealth, force or violence, position, and organization. In international relations, for example, precise information about the strength of an adversary's armed forces is of enormous significance to a state. Wealth may not buy happiness, but it may be used to gain political power. The knowledge that the police may legitimately use force to stop a motorist is a deterrent to speeding. The use of violence by terrorists, moreover, has influenced the behavior of diplomats as much as airline passengers. A formal position, such as governor, judge, or teacher, carries with it power for those affected by its decisions. A small, well-organized conspiratorial organization, as the Russian revolutionary V.I. Lenin observed, may have much more power than a weak association of the disorganized masses.

In the context of politics as power, politics is, to use political scientist Harold Lasswell's expression, the study of who gets what, when, and how.[2] Politics arises from the fact that the goals of human endeavor, such as health, economic security, prestige, and jobs, are limited. More people want such goals than are available.

Politics, then, can determine who at a hospital can be treated with a rare but vital medicine, who in a university becomes a tenured professor, who in a philanthropic organization becomes humanitarian of the year, and who in a corporation becomes chief executive officer. In none of these cases does the process of selection involve a government decision.

---

[2] Harold Lasswell, *Politics: Who Gets What, When, and How* (New York: Peter Smith, 1950).

Public Policy

In addition to the application of the term *politics* to the state and to power, *politics* is used to refer to **public policy**—the laws, rules, regulations, and decisions that governments make about particular subjects. In modern societies government has come to play an increasing role in allocating resources. Government may improve the quality of health of some citizens through supporting programs to increase the number of doctors, mandating immunization, and financing public hospitals. It may promote the economic security of some individuals by setting minimum wages, imposing tariffs and quotas, or granting monopolies. It may enhance prestige by giving recognition to the contributions that people have made to society. It may provide jobs by appropriating funds to employ people who seek work. To be sure, the beneficiaries of government may vary. Some people may be taxed so that others may benefit. Government, moreover, may engage in programs that do not achieve the purposes for which they have been established. Whether for good or evil, government has the authority to allocate scarce resources—the prizes of politics.

Students of politics, then, are concerned with how government decides to allocate scarce resources. In this regard, they seek to understand the behavior of individuals and groups who demand from government such prizes as recognition, economic resources, health, and welfare.

In contrast, government may make demands upon individuals and groups. When President John F. Kennedy said in his inaugural address, "Ask not what your country can do for you; ask what you can do for your country,"[3] he was suggesting that self-sacrifice be a part of citizens' obligations to their country. Most political leaders demand that some expression of civic consciousness be demonstrated by the people who benefit from living in the community. This expression may take the form of jury duty, military service, or loyalty to the state.

Political systems differ as to what is the proper relationship between the state and the people. Some dictators argue that the individual is subservient to the state. Those people who are committed to democracy, however, contend that the state should be subservient to the individual (see Chapter 3). For our purposes, it is essential to note that politics involves the study of how resources are authoritatively allocated in society.

---

[3] Quoted in "Text of Kennedy's Inaugural Outlining Policies on World Peace and Freedom," *New York Times*, January 21, 1961, p. 8.

ISSUE

Government plays such a prominent role in our lives that we find it difficult to imagine a society existing without it. In our contemporary period, government is an active participant in promoting military security, encouraging economic well-being, and extending welfare benefits.

The record of government's success in these areas is mixed, however. The support for government is also mixed. Ancient Greeks saw the state and government as a natural and necessary part of human experience, and modern liberals generally approve of government (see Chapter 4). There is, however, a tradition in Western thought that has viewed government in hostile terms. **Anarchists** look upon any authority, and particularly the state, as essentially harmful to people. More recently, **libertarians,** a group which believes that individual liberty is paramount and that the state is an oppressive institution, have made the strongest objections to government. Some socialists, moreover, perceive that government under certain conditions is evil because it is an instrument of oppression against the masses of people (see Chapter 5). Is government, then, an institution that is avoidable?

1/YES   IS GOVERNMENT AVOIDABLE?

Government has such a pervasive presence in society that most people regard it as a natural phenomenon, like the air they breathe. After all, they ask, who else but government can furnish the essential prerequisites of a community, such as order, security, and welfare?

From the city-state of ancient Greece to the superstate of the modern world, however, government has been marked by two horrendous features: (1) its enslavement of people, and (2) its suppression of societal needs. Wherever government has been established—whether it called itself democratic, monarchial, aristocratic, or communist—there human beings have suffered.

Enslavement of People. People ought to be free to do what they want to do provided they do not harm others. Governments, however, have been established for the purpose of both preventing people from doing what they want to do and encouraging them to cause injury to others. Such an accusation can be substantiated when we consider murder and theft.

Most of us condemn the acts of murderers and thieves. If a person takes another person's life, that act is quite properly condemned as a heinous crime. So, too, is the taking of another person's property. If a thief enters somebody's home and steals a television set, stereo equipment, and other valuable items, most of us would agree that the individual should be apprehended, compelled to return the stolen property, and punished.

Those actions that are condemned as contemptible when committed by individuals, however, are often condoned when committed by government. By definition, government is the only institution in a society that has the legitimate right to exercise force and to make binding rules upon all individuals who reside within its jurisdiction. Government, conse-quently, can legitimately kill and steal.

Governments have had much experience and success in killing. Since government alone possesses the legitimate right to use force, it has often exercised this right through foreign wars. Government takes young men away from their homes and puts them into military service, often against their will. It tells them that it is an honor to engage in violence against the government's foes. The greatest mass murders in history, such as those resulting from the saturation bombing of Dresden and the dropping of atomic bombs on Hiroshima and Nagasaki in World War II, were government-ordered acts, as have been many other acts of war throughout the ages.

Even wars employing conventional weapons take a heavy toll on life. By July 1988, for example, an eight-year war between Iran and Iraq had left 1 million dead, 1.7 million wounded, and 1.5 million in flight as refugees, and had cost $400 billion, according to some estimates.[4]

Government, too, kills within its own juris-diction. It establishes a criminal justice system that enforces its will against those who do not abide by the rules it determines. It puts down rebellions that challenge the governing authorities.

Government also engages in constant theft. It does not label as theft its acts of taking people's property forcefully; instead, it calls these acts taxation. Taxation is taking money that has been duly earned by an individual and spending it for purposes that benefit either government or others. Often the justification for such theft is that society benefits when government redistributes income or concocts programs ostensibly aiding the poor and the

---

[4] Fox Butterfield, "8-Year Gulf War: Victims But No Victors," *New York Times*, July 25, 1988, p. A1.

disadvantaged. Such an argument, however, is ludicrous, as it is based on the notion that the government, rather than the people, is the better judge of society's needs. Is it not, then, proper to call anyone who kills, a murderer, and anyone who steals, a thief—whether that "anyone" is an individual or government? We think so, unless one adopts a double standard of justice.

Societal Needs. Government acts in ways that are detrimental to social well-being. Among the most important elements of such well-being are physical protection, economic security, and welfare. In all of these areas, government has shown that it is not only incapable of achieving these societal goals but rather that its existence is a real hindrance to achieving them.

Billions of dollars are spent each year for police protection, yet crime—particularly violent crime—remains high. Government has established so many restrictions on people's liberty that the police must devote their attention to punishing offenders of victimless crimes rather than pursuing real, hardened criminals. Why should government interfere in the private lives of its citizens? If an individual wishes to use drugs, see a pornographic film, or engage the services of a prostitute, why should the government try to enforce its own vision of morality?

In nearly every country in the world, however, government is involved in devoting considerable resources to curbing victimless crimes. It is no wonder, then, that murderers, looters, and thieves are not apprehended, given the misdirection of government expenditures. It is no surprise either that people have come to rely on private rather than public security services for their physical protection. The growth of private detective services, private police personnel, and private television surveillance is a reflection of the failure of the government to protect life and property of the citizenry.

Like physical protection, economic security is a societal goal. Wherever government intervenes, however, it inhibits rather than enhances such security. Such a poor economic record is seen from government's direction of the economy and from government's own industrial management.

In an attempt to "do good," government offers all kinds of economic benefits to favored groups. It institutes a variety of programs designed to favor one group of citizens at the expense of others. It offers subsidies to farmers, import quotas for domestic firms facing competitive foreign products, and bailouts for inefficient businesses. Instead of allowing market forces to operate and, consequently, bring prices down, it interferes to keep prices high. Such intervention harms consumers, who are penalized through high prices.

In many countries, moreover, government itself has taken over control and management of industries. When government becomes the employer, mismanagement can be guaranteed. The United States Postal Service is but one case in point. It is inefficiently run. Any private company wishing to compete with the government's monopoly of mail delivery is prevented from doing so because the government has determined that it does not want any competitors—at least for the delivery of regular mail. Such lack of competition has meant constantly rising prices for first-class mail. Special-interest users of mail, such as producers of books and magazines, are subsidized so that their rates are kept low while ordinary people must pay for these subsidies either with higher mailing rates or higher taxes.

What is true for the United States Postal Service is true for other industries managed by government as well. If government obtains a monopoly in any field, there is no competitive reason why it must operate that industry in an efficient manner. Government's inefficiency, consequently, means rising prices to the ordinary citizen.

Government, too, has failed to promote welfare. The term *welfare* connotes many things. In this context, we mean not *relief,* but rather services such as health care, education, and housing.

An individual ought to be free to go to any doctor he or she chooses. The increased role of government in matters of health care, however, has meant that in many countries not only is the choice of doctors severely restricted but also the quality of health care is poor. Public hospitals are generally inferior to private hospitals. Talented young men and women are deterred from entering careers in medicine, moreover, because of government controls on doctors' salaries. The quality of medical care, consequently, is kept poor. In Great Britain, a country that has **socialized medicine** (government control of medical care), people have to wait for years, in some cases, to have operations because of a shortage of medical facilities.

Education is another of government's failures. In the United States, for example, the costs of public education are rising. More money is spent for public school education than ever before, yet the reading ability of students—a major factor in how well students perform—is poor. Parents are often so frustrated with the large classes, crime in the schools, and the poor quality of education their children are receiving that they take their children out of the public schools and send them to private schools. Such an action constitutes double taxation, since the parents pay taxes for schools that will not be used by their children as well as pay tuition to private schools. Attempts to strengthen private schools are resisted by the public school teachers and administrators so as to restrict private choice.

Good housing, too, has been wrecked by government. Government is responsible for poor housing in many ways. When inflation occurs (largely because of government spending), government institutes rent controls. The effect of rent controls is to reduce the profits of landlords. If landlords have profits, they reinvest those profits into new housing construction. Because of government interference, however, landlords use whatever money they make in more profitable nonhousing enterprises in which the return on investment is high.

Government programs involving public housing, moreover, cause many social problems. Government puts up skyscrapers that often become crime ridden. The major beneficiaries of public housing are not the poor, but rather the well-to-do, such as property developers and promoters.

The cases of health care, education, and housing show that when government intercedes, its ostensible generosity and caring are misdirected. Government should avoid messing up people's lives, and the well-being of society will then prevail.

Alternatives to Government. Government, then, is an encumbrance placed upon society. It is self-serving and inefficient. If we recognize government's inadequacies, we can begin to look for an alternative: the elimination of government and the restoration of power to the people. Instead of government, people can decide for themselves how they wish to solve their problems. They can build their own homes, educate their own children, and provide for their own health care.

Those who favor government, however, say that such a society is utopian. Such partisans of government have a paternalistic attitude toward people. They believe that people are incapable of providing for these essential needs of physical protection, economic security, and welfare. We have already shown that government has not been able to achieve those goals and that in many cases people are paying double taxation to provide for some of them, such as police protection and education. It is time now to eliminate government intervention and restore the people's control of their own lives.

1 / NO   IS GOVERNMENT AVOIDABLE?

In modern times we are so often conscious of the weaknesses and evils of government that we neglect the positive contributions government makes to society. The existence of government is a natural consequence of the increasingly complex nature of human relationships that exist in society. A society without government is neither desirable nor possible.

It is certainly true that throughout history some governments have enslaved their people and pursued policies which hindered, rather than helped, society in achieving some of its vital objectives, such as physical protection, economic security, and welfare. The more notorious examples in this century alone include Adolf Hitler's persecution and mass extermination of the Jewish people, Joseph Stalin's liquidation of millions of people in the Soviet Union, and Pol Pot's massacre of his own Cambodian citizens. There are, however, many governments that have found such actions to be reprehensible and have acted to extend the range of freedom for their people. They have served their citizens well. Let us look more closely at the *Affirmative*'s charges that government acts to enslave its people and to thwart societal needs in order that we may more properly evaluate the record of government.

Enslavement of People. Although government uses force and collects taxes, it is misleading to view such behavior as murder and theft. Government, to be sure, has the legal monopoly to use force. It is unrealistic to assume that without government there would be no use of force or that private individuals could be expected to cope with dangers to their security.

Much of the criticism directed against government is based on the notion that human beings are essentially good but that government makes them bad. Is such a view valid? We think not. Are human beings more or less likely to break the law in the absence of government? To answer that question, we should imagine what would happen if the police went out on strike permanently. Is it not reasonable to assume that there would be more looting, mugging, and other violations of persons and property than would occur with the presence of government?

The *Affirmative* argues that conscription is evil because it violates individual liberty. Such a view overlooks the character of a political system. In some political systems, such as democracies, the government is responsive to popular wishes (see Chapter 3). If duly elected officials determine that an armed force is needed to protect the people of a nation and decide that conscription is the best form of military organization, then government is acting in ways the people themselves would choose. It is wrong to think that because government creates an army it is acting in a manner contrary to popular wishes.

Taxation could possibly be regarded as theft if the money raised from taxes were used for the benefit of the government. Tax money is more often used, however, for the benefit of society as a whole. People demand services, such as education, housing, welfare, and police security, and they expect government to provide them. To do so, they understand there must be taxes. If they did not believe that government should provide these services, they could—in democracies at least—vote the spenders out of office and replace them with nonspenders.

It is certainly true that taxpayers' revolts have occurred from time to time. For the most part, however, these revolts have been directed at the level of taxation rather than at the principle that government has a right and duty to impose taxes to achieve social objectives. Taxation, consequently, is not theft; it is the taking of funds from individuals to secure legitimate objectives.

It is wrong, too, to regard the very existence of government as an obstacle to human freedom. There are many cases in which government has been responsible for expanding human freedom. The government of the United States, for example, was in the forefront of human freedom when it used its power on behalf of black people and against such private racist organizations as the Ku Klux Klan and the White Citizens Council. That same government, moreover, has extended the freedom of women against acts of discrimination in the free market.

Societal Needs. Government has acted in many cases to provide physical protection, economic security, and welfare for its people. Police forces throughout the world do provide protection to people. Much attention is paid to the failures of police agencies, rather than to their successes. If, in spite of large expenditures on police protection, there is still much crime, that situation is not the fault of the police but is rather the result of social and economic factors beyond the control of the police.

Government has been blamed for establishing, as criminal, acts that should not properly be so designated. Specifically, laws relating to prostitution, drugs, and pornography are cited. It is wrong to argue, however, that these are "victimless crimes," because these crimes do produce victims and because society has a right to determine for itself what are its fundamental values. Government should assist society in maintaining those values.

Should adolescent girls be encouraged to

engage in prostitution? In a totally free society without any government regulation, such a freedom would be assured. Does not common sense, however, dictate that there should be severe penalties imposed on those who entice young women into the world of prostitution? We think so.

Drugs, moreover, are harmful to human health. What good is it to say that human beings should be free to do as they wish if, as a result of such freedom, people become incapable of exercising their drug-damaged brains? When government imposes regulations against the possession and sale of drugs, it is acting in a way that most people approve. Fighting against drugs is a pressing social need.

One need not agree with the extremes of censorship rules to favor restrictions on pornography. Should a pornographic movie house be permitted next door to a church? Only the most extreme advocate of freedom would say so. Society has a right to impose certain restrictions on pornography as it seeks to maintain its traditional values. Government becomes society's agent when it acts in this manner.

Government involvement in the economy is a necessity when it serves society's needs. Public benefits to health, security, and fair play require a government role in the economy, for example.

Individual entrepreneurs may manufacture products that cause illness to unsuspecting consumers. In many countries of the world, food processing is supervised by government to assure that the products measure up to health standards. If cost becomes the single most important factor in the processing of foods, then, quite conceivably, cost saving could be induced by sacrificing health standards. Government establishes health agencies to prevent that from happening.

In the past private companies cared little about water or air pollution. They disposed of chemical wastes in ways that poisoned the air and the rivers. It became essential for government to intervene to make certain that people would not be injured by dangerous chemicals, which could produce long-term genetic defects and even death.

Government is essential to provide security for people. If poor people must pay for their own private security forces, then they will surely suffer the harshness of what will be, for them, a lawless society. The police must serve rich and poor alike in any just society, and economic affluence should not be the criterion for people's safety.

Fair play, too, requires government intervention in the economy. Minority groups and women have long been subjected to discrimination in paid employment. In the United States, for example, blacks, Jews, Catholics, Hispanics, Chinese, American Indians, and women have been denied corporate positions not because they lacked competence but rather because companies would not hire them for important jobs. Such discrimination is morally reprehensible. Theoretically, a person who experiences discrimination is free to find another job. In fact, however, the person may be relegated to an inferior position everywhere because of patterns of discrimination in the corporate world. Government should provide an opportunity for a redress of grievances, for the sake of justice.

Government's involvement in the economy, then, can be beneficial to society. So, too, is government's role in promoting the welfare of society, such as in matters of health care, education, and housing.

It is certainly true that some mismanagement and unwise decisions have characterized public health matters, but the principle of government involvement in health is a good one. Thanks to public immunization programs supported by government research and money, for example, some illnesses have been virtually eliminated, smallpox and polio being two prominent examples.

Government involvement in health care is based upon the principle that society should provide health care to anyone who is unable to afford it. If an individual develops a serious handicap because of reasons beyond his or her control, that person should be able to receive medical care. Elderly people particularly experience illness at a time in their lives when they may no longer be capable of working. Are the elderly to be discarded like so much garbage after they have reached their "golden" years? To be sure, people should save for a rainy day, but in many cases they cannot prepare for every contingency. Some forms of medical treatment, moreover, require more money than they could possibly save. How else should elderly people be helped but with government support?

Many of the government programs for sick people have benefited them (and, incidentally, made them economically productive people in society because of their restored health). We may properly object to the bad management practices under socialized medicine, and attempts should be made to improve medical services rendered to the people. We should, however, recognize that people are in better health because they are permitted to obtain medical service at public expense than would be the case if they could not afford to pay for such care.

Public education in many countries has been an outstanding success. Millions of people have moved up the economic ladder because of the educational opportunities opened up to them, not only at the elementary school level but also at secondary schools and universities.

It is certainly true that public schools are not always the perfect educational institutions they should be and that they often do not succeed in enhancing social mobility. Many of the charges against public education are not, however, valid. When critics of public education point to declining reading scores and the rise of crime within the schools as evidence for their case, they are providing misleading information.

A major reason for the low reading scores and the rise of crime in the public schools is the rise of private schools. Public schools must accept every child: the bright and the dull, the sick and the healthy. More affluent parents have an alternative of sending their children to private schools. If they would only send their children to public schools, the reading score average of the public school would increase. No doubt crime would decrease with the infusion of more serious students, as adequate resources would be provided to control crime.

Government has played a positive role with respect to housing, too. Without rent controls, private, greedy landlords would take advantage of any situation to gouge tenants with exorbitant increases in rent. People would then be "free" to find luxury apartments at high rentals, but that quest would result in the denial to themselves and their families of many other essentials of well-being.

As far as public housing is concerned, it is often better than the rat-infested housing it replaced. It is certainly true that big-time property developers take advantage of public housing programs, but that is not a sufficient argument against public housing. Public housing still offers benefits to those who cannot find adequate private housing. If the public housing units are run poorly, it is because not enough money is appropriated for the maintenance of public housing. *More* government, not less, would be the solution to the problem of poor housing.

Government, then, can be a force for good. The cases of health care, education, and housing show that although government does have weaknesses, it is a vital force in serving societal needs.

Alternatives to Government. People who talk about a society without government are offering utopian solutions to real problems. Given the complex nature of society, human beings through voluntary associations could not cope with the essential needs of society. Government has at times been oppressive. Oppression, however, is not a necessary ingredient of government. How government, in fact, can be made responsive to popular needs is a matter to which we should devote our attention (see Chapter 3).

KEY TERMS

Anarchists

Authority

Government

Legitimacy

Libertarians

Microstates

Polis

Politics

Power

Public policy

Socialized medicine

Sovereignty

State

QUESTIONS

1. Who would be harmed and who would be hurt if the state were dissolved? Why?
2. What functions that government performs could be better performed by private individuals? Why?
3. What functions that private individuals perform could be better provided by government? Why?
4. Should government regulate pornography? Why?
5. What effect would the abolition of government have on war? Why?

RECOMMENDED READINGS

ALMOND, GABRIEL A., and G. BINGHAM POWELL, eds. *Comparative Politics Today: A World View.* 4th ed. Boston: Scott Foresman/Little, Brown, 1988. A study of comparative politics.

CRICK, BERNARD. *The American Science of Politics: Its Origins and Conditions.* Berkeley: University of California Press, 1959. Reprint. Westport, Conn.: Greenwood Press, 1982. A study of the development of political science.

————. *Socialist Values and Time.* London: Fabian Society, 1984. A defense of socialism.

DAHL, ROBERT A. *Modern Political Analysis.* 4th ed. Englewood Cliffs, N.J.: Prentice Hall, 1984. A study of politics.

————. "Power." *International Encyclopaedia of the Social Sciences* (1968), 12:405–15. An introduction to the subject.

FERNS, H. S., and K. W. WATKINS. *What Politics Is About.* London: Sherwood Press, 1985. A basic introduction to politics.

FRIED, MORTON H. "The State: The Institution." *International Encyclopaedia of the Social Sciences* (1968), 15:143–50. An overview of the subject.

FRIEDEN, KARL. "Public Needs and Private Wants." *Dissent* 34 (Summer 1987): 317–25. An argument against the stereotype of government as inefficient.

HARRINGTON, MICHAEL. *The Next Left: The History of a Future.* New York: H. Holt, 1987. A vision of a socialist future.

LASSWELL, HAROLD. *Politics: Who Gets What, When, and How.* New York: Peter Smith, 1950. An examination of politics as the study of influence and the influential.

LUKES, STEVEN, ed. *Power.* New York: New York University Press, 1986. A collection of articles analyzing power.

MACHAN, TIBOR, ed. *The Libertarian Reader.* Totowa, N.J.: Rowman and Littlefield, 1982. Essays on libertarianism.

NARVESON, JAN. *The Libertarian Idea.* Philadelphia: Temple University Press, 1988. An analysis of libertarianism.

NEWMAN, STEPHEN L. "The Chimeras of 'Libertarianism': What's behind This Political Movement?" *Dissent* 34 (Summer 1987): 308–16. A critique of libertarianism.

SOMIT, ALBERT, and JOSEPH TANENHAUS. *The Development of American Political Science: From Burgess to Behavioralism.* Enlarged ed. New York: Irvington Publishers, 1982. A description of the development of the political science discipline.

WATKINS, FREDERICK M. "State: The Concept." *International Encyclopaedia of the Social Sciences* (1968), 15:150–57. A survey.

WOODCOCK, GEORGE. *Anarchism: A History of Libertarian Ideas and Movements.* Cleveland: Meridian Books, 1962. A study of anarchism.

chapter 2

Nations

If we have to start over again with another Adam and Eve, then I want them to be Americans and not Russians, and I want them on this continent [North America] and not in Europe.[1]

When United States Senator Richard Russell uttered these words during a debate on military preparedness, he was criticized for his belief in a patriotism bordering on madness. What difference does it make, his critics asked, what the nationality is of the last two survivors of a nuclear holocaust that destroyed the lives of billions of people?

However farfetched the notion of preserving nationality after a nuclear catastrophe may be, the hazards of nationality are widespread in the world. An example from the South Atlantic is illustrative of the dangers.

---

[1] Quoted in the *New York Times*, January 22, 1971, p. 43.

In the first week of April 1982, Argentine military forces seized control of the Falkland Islands, a possession of Great Britain, in a bloodless strike. Until that action, the world had little reason to suspect that the Falkland Islands—a small archipelago in the South Atlantic located approximately three hundred miles east of Argentina at its southernmost point—would be the scene of war between Argentina and Great Britain. True, the Falkland Islands, under British control for 150 years, had been a source of contention between the two countries, but diplomatic negotiations about the future of the islands had been progressing until recently.

Britain responded to the Argentine military operation with military actions of its own in an effort to retake the islands. By the time the fighting was over, the war had claimed the lives of about 960 combatants and had cost the belligerents billions of dollars.

At the core of the dispute between the

two countries was the principle of nationalism—pride in the people and territory of one's country. In this instance of nationalism, the British claimed that the inhabitants of the islands were British and that Great Britain had legal rights because of discovery by British explorers, settlement by British people, and principles of international law. The Argentines claimed that their Argentine forebears had been illegally evicted from the islands in 1833 and that the islands legally belonged to Argentina. In evaluating the contending viewpoints, one writer determined that the claims on both sides "are based on historical facts that are by turns vague, confused and disputed."[2] Such ambiguity in status did not deter the government and people of each side from rousing the symbols of patriotism.

Some observers in Britain, Argentina, and elsewhere regarded the entire affair as absurd, a relic of ancient tribal loyalties and a triumph of insanity over reason. How else to explain the vast costs for protecting approximately 1,700 people on the islands? Other observers, however, noted that this was but one in a series of conflicts brought on by nationalism.[3]

Whatever one's view of the Falkland Islands dispute, there is general agreement that nationalism has become one of the most important political forces of our times. So dynamic is this force that it has swept through every continent and influenced every major political ideology. An understanding of nationalism, then, is essential to evaluate one of the most important influences on political stability and change in states and governments today.

In this century nationalism has been expressed in a variety of forms—from acts of violence to demonstrations of cooperation. At its worst, nationalism is the basis of the expansion of a country into the territory of others. Adolf Hitler's attempt to unite German-speaking people under Nazi rule is but one of many examples. In more recent times acts of terrorism have been performed in the name of nationalism. Urban guerrillas, proclaiming the nationalisms of Croatia, Palestine, and other places, have hijacked airplanes and held innocent passengers as hostages.

Nationalism, however, is not only an expression of war and violence. For many men and women in the world, it is an association of different groups in a common effort. To be sure, conflict is often a characteristic of nationalism, but in some countries—such as the United States, Switzerland, and India, for example—diverse **ethnic groups** (people possessing characteristics that distinguish them from other groups)[4] have, albeit with major exceptions, worked in relative peace and harmony.

Historians, philosophers, political scientists, and policy makers differ about the meaning of nationalism. The term *nation* derives from the Latin verb *nasci*, meaning "to be born." Originally, *nation* referred to a group of people born in the same area of the world, although no limit on the basis of the size of territory was associated with the term. Today, **nation** refers to a group of people who identify with a state. **Nationalism** may be defined as an ideology in which a people, regardless of their race, class, or religion, feel that they have more in common with each other than they have with other people and give their highest loyalty to a state or to part of a state that may

[2] Peter Calvert, "Sovereignty and the Falklands Crisis," *International Affairs* (London) 58 (Summer 1983): 405.

[3] Accounts of the Falkland Islands dispute may be found in ibid., pp. 405–13; and in H. E. Chehabi, "Self-Determination, Territorial Integrity, and the Falkland Islands," *Political Science Quarterly* 100 (Summer 1985): 215–25.

[4] See Benjamin Akzin, *State and Nation* (London: Hutchinson University Library, 1964), pp. 30, 46.

eventually become a separate state.

In discussing nationalism we deal with some difficult concepts. As we shall see, the world is not an ethnically "tidy" place. That is to say, ethnic groups have moved around in the world because of war, economic factors, discrimination, and personal reasons. In only about 10 percent of the countries of the world do ethnic boundaries of a single ethnic community coincide with state boundaries. As a result there are sizable communities of Germans in Austria as well as Germany, of Indians in East Africa as well as India, and of Italians in the United States as well as in Italy.

In Chapter 1 the term *state* is defined as a political entity that possesses people, territory, a government, and sovereignty. When we talk about a state, we are, then, referring to a *political* or legal entity. A state may or may not contain people who feel especially attached to other members of the state. The term **nation-state** is sometimes used to mean a political institution combining the concepts of nation (an anthropological notion) with state (a legal idea).

Examples of giving one's highest loyalty to the state are varied. It means that an American citizen of German descent would fight for the United States in a war against Germany, or that a British capitalist would terminate a commercial relationship with an Italian capitalist if their two countries were at war, or that a French factory worker would rather support a French capitalist than a Dutch factory worker.

In the twentieth century nothing seems more natural than that a Greek citizen should feel a stronger attachment to Greece than to Turkey, or that a French citizen should feel especially loyal to France; but this feeling of attachment to the state is of rather recent vintage, dating only from the late eighteenth century. The contrast between the prenational and national periods is striking. In medieval times, to be identified as a religious heretic was regarded as one of the most heinous crimes, a category that in the twentieth century is reserved for a traitor to one's country. In the first half of the eighteenth century, moreover, a foot soldier felt no attachment to his own state but fought for any monarch who paid him. The soldier found nothing extraordinary about switching allegiance from the army of one country to the army of its rival. Today, such activity is regarded as treason, punishable by death or imprisonment.

Historically, nationalism is only one of many group loyalties that people have held. In the past people have given allegiance to forms of social and political organization other than the nation, such as a tribe or clan. In ancient Greece, people respected their *polis*, or city-state, but citizenship was restricted. Certainly the citizens of Athens, one of the most important of the Greek city-states, felt no special attachment to the Athenian slaves. Although empires of antiquity ruled over people of diverse ethnic backgrounds, there was no universal attachment to the empire comparable to the popular loyalty directed by the nation today.

In medieval Europe, people showed loyalty to a variety of entities: a guild, a village, a province, a region, and a church. There was little sense of camaraderie among people of diverse classes, that they had more in common with each other than they had with peoples of other regions. A French, Prussian, or Croatian lord felt that his horse was more a part of his "nation" than were the peasants who worked his lands. In the period prior to the French Revolution, the "nation" was sometimes identified with the ruling class—the sovereign and the aristocracy.

Although forerunners of the nation go back at least to ancient times, nationalism as a force stems mostly from the period of the French Revolution in the late eighteenth century. It began in Western Europe and North America and has moved gradually to include the peoples of the entire world.

Throughout the centuries, many explanations have been put forward to describe the origin and continuation of nations. One of these is that God created the nation. Although much attention has been given to the idea that the Jewish people trace their nationality to God's Will, American, German, and French writers have made similar claims for their own nation. Another explanation is that of the conservative eighteenth-century writer Edmund Burke, who contended that the nation was formed from mystical forces linking past to future generations.[5]

Most scholars today, however, argue that a variety of factors has contributed to creating a feeling of nationalism, although not every factor was involved in shaping national consciousness in each case. The most important features include common political system, territory, enemy, language, history, people, religion, economy, and culture.

POLITICAL SYSTEM

It is often the case that a common political system serves as a basis for building nationalism. In this sense, the state precedes the nation. First a legal entity, the state, is created, and then a feeling of nationalism develops within the context of the state.

In seventeenth- and eighteenth-century Europe, strong states existed for the most

---

[5] For these and other explanations, see Boyd C. Shafer, *Nationalism: Interpreters and Interpretations*, 2d ed. Publication 20 (Washington, D.C.: Service Center for Teachers of History, 1963), pp. 5–6. For a discussion of recent interpretations of nationalism, see Ernst B. Haas, "What Is Nationalism and Why Should We Study It?" *International Organization* 40 (Summer 1986): 707–44, and the books mentioned in Haas's article.

part without a popular national consciousness. So lacking was a feeling of nationalism in this period that monarchs transferred territory with diverse ethnic populations without taking into account the ethnic composition of the people included in the transfer. In the late nineteenth and twentieth centuries, however, such transfers were less likely to occur.

Jordan is an example of how national boundaries were shaped by a common political system. There was no Jordanian nationalism in the sense of a Jordanian people in existence when Jordan (then known as Transjordan) was created after World War I. Its boundaries were shaped largely by the major colonial powers in the Middle East—Britain and France— rather than through the assertion of a Jordanian national consciousness. Once the political entity of Jordan was created, however, Jordanian national consciousness emerged.

What was true for Jordan was also true for other British colonies in Asia and Africa. The British created the basis of political integration through the maintenance of law and order, administrative unity, social and political values, a common English language, and fiscal and economic integration. Nationalism emerged within the political units that Great Britain had created.

The process by which a common political system can serve as a basis of nationalism is clear. First, a political system creates laws governing the people who reside within a geographical area. Then, as certain forces such as war or industrialization mobilize a society, a feeling of nationalism arises out of the common political system.

TERRITORY

Nationalism is associated with a particular territory, although the boundary lines of states have often shifted. Common territory is often distinguished by peculiar geographical configurations. The Pyrenees Mountains, for example, provide a natural barrier between France and Spain, and the English Channel separates France from Great Britain.

Nationalism is the fusion of the idea of a group unity with a particular territory. Even when territories were under foreign rule, as in the cases of Poland for two centuries and Palestine for two thousand years, the national ideal was tied to specific geographical regions.

ENEMY

Nothing may unite a people more quickly than attack by a hostile power. Divisions along class, regional, and ideological lines may disappear if there is a sense of danger from outside forces. For example, when Napoleon's armies moved forward from France to the rest of continental Europe in the early nineteenth century, a feeling of resistance and unity emerged against the invading forces in some cases. Spanish and Russian nationalism, particularly, grew in response to the foreign danger.

Just as invasion and mobilization sparked feelings of nationalism in Europe in the early nineteenth century, so, too, did similar actions mark the African and Asian experience in the twentieth century. During the world wars European powers such as Great Britain and France took into their armies people from their colonies. Once Africans and Asians were mobilized and trained in military skills, it was only a matter of time before they used those skills against their colonial mentors. After the world wars were over, the colonial peoples perceived their imperial rulers as foreigners and enemies. Colonial peoples tended to unite across ethnic and regional lines against the European power. In this way a common enemy united a people. After the imperial power was defeated, however, fragmen-

tation and civil war often characterized the political life of the former colonial people in their newly independent country.

LANGUAGE

People who speak the same language communicate with each other more easily and often than with people who speak other languages. Language is thus a feature that serves to distinguish or separate one group of people from another. The fact that the people of France speak French and the people of Spain speak Spanish means that unless people from each of these countries are bilingual, they will tend to communicate and associate with people who speak the same language. Similarity of language, consequently, may lead to a feeling of nationalism: a solidarity among people who can literally understand each other. Language, however, may become an instrument of introducing competitive national symbols, as French served in promoting a sense of separatism in the Canadian province of Quebec in past years.

HISTORY

The fact that people share a common history over a long period of time is an important force strengthening nationalism. For example, the English people developed their institutions over centuries and feel that they have more in common with each other than they have with other people. Since the thirteen American colonies had in many cases a similar history brought on by more than one hundred years of British rule, a sense of nationalism among the colonial Americans was created as well.[6]

---

[6] Although the term *Americans* can refer to people from North or South America, it is used here to mean people from the United States.

Every people have their own heroes, sometimes from legendary sources, and their own historical memories. Often, however, the historical events they remember are selected carefully to nurture a sense of nationalism rather than to portray internal differences. Recollections of American history, for example, often reflect the "melting pot" idea, in which people from all over the world emigrated to the United States and developed American values. The racial, ethnic, and religious conflicts that characterized American history are often downgraded or avoided in the national memory, not by historians but rather by the writers of more popular accounts of American history. It has been well said that "a nation is a group of persons united by a common error about their ancestry and a common dislike of their neighbors."[7]

PEOPLE

Every nation is composed of a people, although the number of people constituting a nation varies. Sometimes a people is made up of different ethnic groups. It is often difficult to recognize a people, since we tend to ignore some characteristics and pay attention to others.

Race, however, is one element used often to distinguish a people. Although the black people of South Africa speak many languages and come from different ethnic backgrounds, many of them feel a sense of black nationalism that unites them in opposition to the government of white-ruled South Africa. In spite of efforts by the Portuguese to integrate the native Africans living in the colonies of Angola and Mozambique, a black consciousness developed in opposition to the Portuguese.

---

[7] Karl W. Deutsch, *Nationalism and Its Alternatives* (New York: Knopf, 1969), p. 3.

Racial and ethnic similarities have often been used in distinguishing one people from another. For the most part, however, the concept of a people is a psychological one. In effect, a people is any group that thinks of itself as a unique community. People with similar racial characteristics have sometimes chosen to identify with different states. Conflict between black African nations, such as marked the relationship between Uganda and Tanzania for many years, is a case in point.

RELIGION

Religion is a factor that can contribute to a sense of nationalism. The Jewish people have had an ancient religious history that has been a source of a sense of solidarity. Although the Jewish people were expelled from Palestine for a period of nearly two thousand years, the Jewish religion has been essential to the creation and continuation of the Israeli nation. Religion was the basis for the establishment of the state of Pakistan, with its predominantly Muslim population, out of British India with its predominantly Hindu population.

ECONOMY

Economic factors have also served to unify nations. The tearing down of tariff barriers and the strengthening of commercial ties among the thirteen states of the United States after the defeat of the British in the American Revolutionary War helped to unite people into one nation. Similar patterns of economic cooperation appeared in other countries.

There seems to be a relationship between the rise of industrialism and the emergence of nationalism, although it is not clear that the former is a cause of the latter. Preindustrial society was generally characterized by limited movement of people either geographically or socially, and by relative separation of government from the daily lives of the masses of people. In contrast, industrialization may be looked upon as a component of **modernization,** which is the application of technology by extensive social interdependence, organization, literacy, social mobility, and other factors.[8] The Industrial Revolution produced vast social upheavals in which people moved from the countryside to the cities, causing social, economic, and psychological disruptions in their lives. Industrial society required that people of diverse racial, religious, and social backgrounds work together for a common purpose. The nation provided the conditions of military security and economic unity under which industrialism could flourish. Previous forms of social organization—tribes and empires, for example—could not provide those conditions.

The exact relationship between economics and nationalism is most controversial. Marxists believe that nationalism will disappear and that it has no real basis for existing once the socialist revolution

occurs (see Chapter 5). Other political advocates have had different ideas of the role of economics in nation building. However difficult they may be to measure, economic factors undoubtedly have been important in shaping nations.

CULTURE

The idea of nationalism is often the creation of intellectuals who give expression to a **culture,** which may be defined as a core of traditional ideas, practices, and technology shared by a people. The German philosopher Johann Gottlieb Fichte heralded a German nationalism. Theodore Herzl, a Hungarian Jewish journalist, became the founding father of **Zionism,** a philosophy that identifies the Jewish people with a homeland in Palestine. The concept of a Pakistani nation separate from India was mostly a creation of a group of intellectuals in the 1930s.

Nationalism also has roots in the cultural traditions of ordinary people through their customs, songs, and style—all are factors that have strengthened nationalism. To the extent that the state increased its power over society in the past two centuries, national symbols of culture have often been encouraged. Public schools in the nineteenth and twentieth centuries also became promoters of cultural unity.

---

[8] Claude E. Welch, Jr., ed., *Political Modernization: A Reader in Comparative Political Change* (Belmont, Calif.: Wadsworth, 1967), p. 2.

ISSUES

Because of its continued impact on society, nationalism remains a controversial ideology and political movement. Its defenders see it as a force for unity; its detractors condemn it as a force for divisiveness and war.

Three principal questions arise prominently in dealing with this subject: (1) Is nationalism divisive? (2) Does nationalism lead to war? (3) Is the nation-state outmoded in the twentieth century?

2/YES   IS NATIONALISM DIVISIVE?

Nationalism is divisive because of its ambiguity and its **ethnocentrism**—belief that one's group or nation is of universal importance. With nationalism so pervasive, it is almost inevitable that the world should remain chaotic.

Ambiguity. The ideal model of a nation, according to political scientist Rupert Emerson, is "a single people, traditionally fixed on a well-defined territory, speaking the same language and preferably a language all its own, possessing a distinctive culture, and shaped to a common mold by many generations of shared historical experience."[9] The problem, however, is that no such nation ever existed.

The elements that go into making each nation are often vague and varied. For example, a common political system may include peoples of diverse languages and culture. Switzerland and the Soviet Union are two cases in point. Switzerland is composed of three major ethnic groups: French, German, and Italian. One could logically break up the Swiss nation, dispersing parts of it to France, East or West Germany, and Italy. The Soviet Union is composed of about twenty different nationalities and recognizes more than one hundred ethnic groups or "peoples." The Soviet Union, however, would not be likely to permit the secession of an ethnic group under Soviet control.

There are many separate nations that speak the same language. British playwright George Bernard Shaw once commented that the Irish and English are separated by the same language.

Wars, dynastic marriages, discovery, territorial purchases, migrations of peoples, and historical accident have all contributed to creating a world in which peoples have become scattered in such a way as to prevent the construction of neat categories clearly distinguishing nations. Hardly any land in Europe

exists that did not once belong to a neighboring state. The legacy of such territorial change is a residue of ethnic minorities all over Europe. German populations can be found in Austria, Poland, and Switzerland. Italian people are located in Yugoslavia and Austria. Greeks inhabit Cyprus as well as Greece.

There are, moreover, few natural frontiers in the world, such as the Alps and Pyrenees Mountains. Many a country could, with the logic of geography, be made into two or more nations. The Mississippi River and the Rockies could be regarded as natural frontiers, yet neither of these topographical barriers has prevented the United States from becoming one nation. The Nile River, moreover, unites rather than divides Egypt.

Geographical proximity became one basis for the Argentine claim to the Falkland Islands. But if such closeness is the central feature governing self-determination, then the Channel Islands would have to revert to France, St. Pierre and Miquelon to Canada, the Dodecanese to Turkey, Bernholm to Sweden, and the Canary Islands to Morocco.[10]

Clearly, then, the components of nationalism are quite diverse. There is no objective way to distinguish one nation from another, and this ambiguity often leads to rivalry of people for the same piece of territory.

Ethnocentrism. Although there is no clear-cut definition of what constitutes a nation, a more serious component of the divisive quality of nationalism is the ethnocentrism it produces. So powerful is nationalism that many of the values that people acquire derive from the nation-state. Americans, for example, are taught at an early age to respect national authority. They attend public schools and study their national heritage. They learn the national anthem and the pledge of allegiance. From cradle to grave, Americans as well as people from all over the world discover that the nation is the strongest symbol of loyalty.

---

[9] Rupert Emerson, *From Empire to Nation: The Rise to Self-Assertion of Asian and African Peoples* (Cambridge, Mass.: Harvard University Press, 1967), p. 103.

[10] Chehabi, "Self-Determination, Territorial Integrity, and the Falkland Islands," p. 221.

People, consequently, think of themselves in national terms, such as Americans, Italians, Kenyans, or Japanese. They emphasize those characteristics that separate them from other people. Such a preoccupation with what separates people is basically harmful to the global community.

What is really important is not what separates people but, rather, what unites them. Human beings everywhere have similar needs: personal happiness, physical safety, and economic security. Since the world is composed of *people,* not the abstract and unreal national designations of Americans, or Russians, or Chinese, a disservice is done to humankind by these national labels. Without the ideology of nationalism Americans would feel the same sense of compassion when a famine appears in sub-Saharan Africa, causing death and illness to Africans, as they do when they learn that Mississippi River floodwaters have taken the lives of Americans. Nationalism is partially responsible for a people's insensitivity to the needs of other peoples of the world.

2/NO   IS NATIONALISM DIVISIVE?

Ambiguity. Nationalism may indeed be an ambiguous concept, but that ambiguity has not necessarily promoted divisiveness among people. In terms of the evolution of nationalism we can see that nationalism has served in many cases as a force that unites rather than divides people. There are many illustrations of this point. The United States began as thirteen states along the Atlantic seaboard. At the time of its independence from Great Britain, it had a population of about 3 million people. Today, the United States is composed of fifty states containing more than 254 million people with many diverse ethnic groups. Even Hawaii, which has a minority Caucasian population, is entirely integrated into the American nation. The American ideal is one of the "melting pot."

The United States is not a unique case. One can cite Germany, too. In the nineteenth century Prussia became the champion of German unity. Prussia was able to strengthen that unity through creation of the North German Confederation in 1866. A few years later, in 1871, Germany became a unified country, incorporating many states into one nation. Italy, too, was composed of many principalities that united into a single Italy. For the peoples of Africa and Asia the nation represents not a force of disintegration, but rather one uniting the many diverse and smaller ethnic or tribal groups into a larger political unit.

The unifying element of nationalism may best be seen by examining its economic aspects. Although the components that help shape a nation are diverse, it is clear that there is a relationship between the emergence of nationalism and the rise of the modern industrial state. As indicated above, to a considerable extent the underlying ideal behind industrialism and nationalism is similar: namely, that people should work together for some common effort.

Peaceful relations among diverse groups within a nation must exist if the political system is to become strong and integrated. There must also be a basic respect for law and a feeling that the rules are equitable for all members of the nation.

Industrial development requires many of the same things. There can be no economic development without peace. No one will invest money in building a factory if social tensions are so great that the factory is in danger of being blown up. If industrial society is to progress, moreover, the best talent—regardless of race, gender, or religion—must be obtained. To be sure, discrimination has marked hiring practices in industrial societies, but often at the expense of economic development.

The emergence of the nation-state in Europe served to strengthen economic development in a variety of ways. It produced internal order through its control of the armed forces. It established tariffs, which strengthened the domestic market. It gave incentives to industries in the form of subsidies and grants to economic development.

Many Third World countries in Africa and Asia today are experiencing similar benefits from the nation. Some of these states have unusual difficulties because of their enormous poverty and scarce resources. The nation-state often is helpful in devising planning instruments to manage these scarce resources and the economy generally. To the extent that many of these new nations can get people from varying ethnic groups to work together for a common effort, to that degree will there be an improvement of the economy. The destruction of the nation-state would, then, undermine economic development.

Although much has been said about the divisiveness of nationalism with references made to secessionist groups agitating for self-determination, it is important to keep in mind that most states have been able to control or contain these militant groups. In spite of the behavior of militant nationalist groups, including Basques, French Canadians, Corsicans, Armenians, Puerto Ricans, and others, states have rarely been destroyed in the past quarter-century as a result of nationalist agitation. This might suggest that nationalism is not as divisive as its critics contend.

Ethnocentrism. There is a difference between attachment to one's political community and intolerance toward others. Patriotic symbols unite diverse people. Loyalty to one's country does not necessarily mean indifference to other loyalties of religion, class, or profession.

Patriotic Americans who collect money for the relief of famine-stricken Ethiopians are as compassionate to their fellow human beings outside of this country as they are to Americans in distress. Sensitivity to the downtrodden and the oppressed is not suppressed merely because individuals feel especially loyal to their country.

Chew Sock Foon, a specialist in ethnic studies, argues that in multiethnic states ethnic identity is compatible under certain conditions with national loyalty. She contends that if a government pursues congruent public policies designed to implement the core supraethnic values, such as official recognition and encouragement of minority languages *and* tolerance for the cultures of all resident ethnic groups, "then national identification might well be heightened, even as ethnic identification persists at significant levels."[11]

---

[11] Chew Sock Foon, "On the Incompatibility of Ethnic and National Loyalties: Reframing the Issue," *Canadian Review of Studies in Nationalism* (Prince Edward Island) 13 (Spring 1986): 7.

3 / YES   DOES NATIONALISM LEAD TO WAR?

Because of the realities of power, nationalism has often led to bitterness and war. Economic and military interests take precedence over considerations of nationalism, and the legacy of such priorities is conflict.

The problem of the conflict between national and other considerations became particularly acute during the Versailles Peace Conference that was organized to settle the future of the defeated powers after World War I. The victors had their own military security and economic interests, and when these goals conflicted with the principle of national self-determination, then the latter principle was denied, compromised, or minimized. The effects of the peace settlement that resulted had much to do with the evils of the next two decades. The nationality question of the German minorities in Europe was an important factor contributing to the coming of World War II.

The Versailles Treaty illustrates the difficulty of applying the principle of nationalism when other considerations are important. One major example deals with Czechoslovakia. The peace treaty created Czechoslovakia but based its territorial configuration on factors other than ethnic homogeneity. Had Czechoslovakia been created to unite the northern Slav peoples previously under Austro-Hungarian rule, it might have become a more politically viable state. Western political leaders, and Czechs and Slovaks themselves, however, believed that a large section of Bohemia containing 3.1 million Germans would allow the country to be militarily secure and economically viable. A further complication was that the new country had 750,000

Hungarians in Slovakia and Ruthenia plus 460,000 Ukrainian peasants with loyalties outside of Czechoslovakia.[12]

In addition to producing political mayhem at Versailles, the principle of nationalism portended political chaos ahead. The revolutionary impact of the principle of national self-determination, in which every people has its own state, was clearly recognized during the immediate post–World War I years. Robert Lansing, Woodrow Wilson's secretary of state, criticized the principle as "loaded with dynamite." He added:

It will raise hopes which can never be realized. It will, I fear, cost thousands of lives. In the end it is bound to be discredited, to be called the dream of an idealist who failed to realize the danger until too late to check those who attempt to put the principle in force. What a calamity that the phrase was ever uttered! What misery it will cause.[13]

Even in the post–World War II period, the principle of national self-determination led to enormous problems. The struggle against Western imperialism was made in the name of national self-determination. "Algeria for the Algerians," "Nigeria for the Nigerians," "Angola for the Angolans," and similar nationalist slogans became the battle cries of the opponents of French, British, and Portuguese imperialism. It became increasingly difficult for Western countries, particularly democracies, to continue colonial rule for many reasons. One of the factors that contributed to the decline of Western imperialism, however, was the moral appeal to national self-determination. How could Western policy makers challenge with conviction the principle of national self-determination that they themselves had asserted on behalf of their own nation-states and their European allies?

Once they had achieved freedom from colonial rule, however, the newly independent countries of Africa and Asia faced challenges from among their own people. These countries themselves were not homogeneous but were, rather, **multinational states**—composed of diverse ethnic groups that are included in identifiable geographic regions. When the "nations" within these states called for separation on the principle of national self-determination, they were opposed by the very governments that had previously used the principle against their former colonial masters.[14] In that manner they were following in the footsteps of the European experience. When Poland achieved independence from Russian, German, and Austrian rule in 1919, it had to defend that independence against the German, Ukrainian, and White Russian minorities within its borders. These minorities constituted one-third of the entire population.[15]

Nigeria experienced a severe civil war, which may have cost the loss of more than one million lives, after the Ibos, one of the three largest ethnic groups in the country, sought independence as the Republic of Biafra in 1967. The Bengalis of East Pakistan successfully seceded from Pakistan to establish Bangladesh. More often than not, however, the smaller ethnic groups within the newly independent states have not succeeded in achieving independence and forming separate states.

Such restiveness is played upon by the United States and the Soviet Union as superpowers in their own struggles and for their own purposes. Nationalism, as both American President Woodrow Wilson and Soviet leader V. I. Lenin early recognized, is a powerful political force. It is not only a powerful force, but one so disruptive of international order that it should be eliminated from the face of the earth.

Political leaders who inculcate values of loyalty to the nation often cannot draw the line between patriotism and chauvinism. **Patriotism** is love of country. **Chauvinism** is excessive, almost obsessive, patriotism and may best be illustrated in this toast by American Admiral Stephen Decatur in 1816: "Our country! In her intercourse with foreign nations may she always be in the right; but our country right or wrong." One wit may have been on much sounder footing when he cited the Decatur

---

[12] See Glen St. J. Barclay, *Twentieth Century Nationalism* (New York: Praeger, 1971), p. 26.

[13] Robert Lansing, *The Peace Negotiations: A Personal Narrative* (Boston: Houghton Mifflin, 1921), pp. 97–98.

[14] See Walker Connor, "Self-Determination: The New Phase," *World Politics* 20 (October 1967): 30–53.

[15] Hans Morgenthau, "Nationalism: Dilemma," in *Nationalism and International Progress,* ed. Urban G. Whitaker, Jr., rev. ed. (San Francisco: Chandler, 1961), p. 180.

toast as the moral equivalent of "My mother, drunk or sober!"

Once the values of nationalism are put forward, it is difficult to draw limits. It is but a short step from saying, "My country is different from yours," to proclaiming, "My country is better than yours." Nationalism, consequently, has produced wars of **irredentism** (national agitation by an ethnic group opposed to foreign rule and demanding incorporation into a country with a similar ethnic composition), wars of imperialism, and wars of self-determination. Major examples of nationalism turning warlike and expansionist in this century are Adolf Hitler's Germany and Benito Mussolini's Italy. Both dictators espoused ideologies that revered the nation-state. Mussolini stressed the classical Roman heritage of Italy as the basis for expansion into Ethiopia. Hitler heralded the superior German nation or race as the justification for expansion into the countries of Europe. Nazism and Italian fascism (see Chapter 4) were logical outgrowths of the age of nationalism.

Even if the fascist examples of Italy and Germany are not considered, nationalism and *total* war seem to have emerged at the same time. In the eighteenth century, monarchs conducted wars fought by professional soldiers, and it was possible to distinguish between a soldier and a civilian. Even during periods of warfare, citizens of the belligerent countries could travel to the enemy states. Wars were thought to be the province of governments and armies, rather than the people. With the emergence and strengthening of nationalism in the nineteenth and twentieth centuries, the character of war changed to include not only the armed forces but also the civilian population. In essence, the age of nationalism became the age of total war and affected every sector of society, separating the peoples of each country and obliterating the distinction between soldier and civilian. Now the enemy became entire peoples, consequently enlarging the battlefield to include factories and even apartment complexes.[16] Nationalism has made war more devastating and should, therefore, be brought to an end.

---

[16] See Edward Hallett Carr, *Nationalism and After* (London: Macmillan, 1968), pp. 26–27.

3/NO   DOES NATIONALISM LEAD TO WAR?

Critics who berate nationalism as a force for war overstate their case: (1) they ignore the many factors that cause conflict; and (2) they do not see that the nation-state is a stepping stone to a larger political organization.

Causes of War. In addition to promoting peace within a country, nationalism can create a pattern of cooperation and peace rather than war among nations. In fact, this idea stems from the heyday of European nationalism. In the nineteenth century the Italian liberal Giuseppe Mazzini was only one among many liberals in Italy and elsewhere who believed that a world organized on the principle of national self-determination would be a peaceful world. The reason for war, the Italian nationalist contended, was an absence of national self-determination; when every people have their own nation, then there will be no further basis for conflict.

Woodrow Wilson, another liberal, also believed in national self-determination, although he had hoped to apply it to Europe rather than to the colonial world. A world organized under the principle of one nation, one state, he believed, would provide a sufficient basis for peace. He urged that the League of Nations be organized under such a principle.

Because of the attention given to wars based on the national principle, many people have equated wars with nationalism. It is important to remember that people were slaughtering each other long before the emergence of the nation-state. In the Thirty Years War, fought in the seventeenth century, it is estimated that 30 percent of the German people were killed. In that instance religious difference was a strong causal factor of violence.

People kill for many reasons, among which are psychological maladjustment, ethnic differences, religious commitment, and ideological fervor. In fact, many observers contend that there are more people killed in internal than in external wars. About 500,000 people were killed in Indonesia in 1965 in an internal nonnational conflict. Millions of Soviet citizens were put into slave-labor camps in the 1930s. Many of these people were liquidated by the Soviet leader Joseph Stalin not because of considerations of nationalism but rather because of the need to maintain power for a privileged class—or possibly because Stalin was insane.

There is no reason to believe that the nation-state, consequently, is the cause of turmoil. Long before the nation appeared, human beings killed each other. Nationalism as a force has been unfairly criticized for many of the wars and acts of violence in the past few centuries. For whatever its defects, nationalism has been more beneficial than harmful to the global community.

Stepping Stone. Political institutions are in a constant state of flux. They exist because of some important economic or social need. Throughout most of recorded history, there has been no feeling of nationalism. Is it not plausible to believe that the nation-state is not permanent but is, rather, a necessary step toward some higher form of political association? And does not the higher form constitute a wider community in which people will live in cooperative relationships?

For many people the nation-state represents a higher association than they had been accustomed to, for example, family, tribe, city-state, or feudal unit. Many Americans in the late eighteenth century identified with their smaller state units, with Georgia or New York; today, they think of themselves more as Americans than as Georgians or New Yorkers. Mil-

itary and economic power, moreover, has been transferred to a considerable extent from local and regional sources to a larger national unit.

Cannot we assume that at a certain stage of economic development, countries will abandon their national aspirations for some larger political unit in the manner of the American experience? The European Community clearly is an illustration of this trend and furnishes evidence of remarkable change. For about nine centuries the French and Germans prepared war against each other, but they have now stopped thinking along these lines. In the words of one scholar of nationalism: "For the first time in many centuries Western Europe is now a pluralistic security community in some ways comparable to Scandinavia. This is a change of large potential implications."[17]

The **European Community** (or **Common Market)** is an organization of European countries that includes France and West Germany and is committed to reducing tariff barriers and stimulating trade among the member nations. It is a political institution that makes binding rules governing the member states. Although the European Community has had problems of political integration, it continues to have the support of its members. A European parliament in which the people of each member country directly elect their own representative is a sign of an evolutionary, peaceful transformation beyond the nation-state. It may well be the case that as the countries of the world climb upward on the industrial ladder, they, too, will follow the advanced industrial nations of the Common Market, abandoning their narrow national attachments for some larger regional groupings.

_____
[17] Deutsch, *Nationalism and Its Alternatives,* p. 35.

4/YES   IS THE NATION-STATE OUTMODED IN THE TWENTIETH CENTURY?

Perhaps a case can be made for the past existence of the nation-state system. The military and economic reasons for the emergence of nations have already been pointed out. What is clear, however, is current military, economic, and environmental factors make the nation-state outmoded.

Up to the end of World War II, military power was dispersed among many countries. In the past few centuries no single state has become so powerful as to conquer all others. To be sure, the great disturbers of the peace—Louis XIV, Napoleon, Kaiser Wilhelm, and Adolf Hitler—have all been crushed by alliances of states. Great Britain, acting as the balancer in a world in which military strength was dispersed among several great powers, was able to throw its naval forces to the other side when it appeared that one state was becoming too strong.

In 1945 the nuclear age was born. The American atomic bombs dropped at Hiroshima and Nagasaki were a thousand times more powerful than the large, conventional bombs used in World War II. Today, nuclear weapons are available that are millions of times more powerful than the conventional bombs of World War II.

Nuclear weapons are far more dangerous than conventional weapons not only because of their immediate effects but also because of their long-term consequences. Most of the larger nuclear weapons not only destroy valuable property and millions of lives but also produce radioactive clouds that move across the world, descending as rain on neutral countries. These radioactive clouds containing poisonous chemicals such as strontium 90 and cesium 137 can cause death, cancer, and genetic damage.

For a period of four years the United States was the only country to possess these weapons, but the nuclear monopoly was broken by the Soviet Union in 1949. By 1989 membership in the nuclear club had grown to include Great Britain, France, the People's Republic of China, and India. It is widely reported that Israel possesses these weapons although it has not tested them. Pakistan and South Africa are believed to be close to producing nuclear weapons. Estimates of up to fifty more states joining the nuclear club by the year 2000 are frequently made by military experts.

The knowledge of how to construct these weapons is readily available, and the raw materials they require are relatively easy to acquire. There is significant evidence that the cost of producing these weapons is declining. The cruise missile, for example, is capable of traveling a distance of up to two thousand miles with a payload of two hundred kilotons.[18] Such a payload represents more than ten times the strength of the atom bomb detonated at Hiroshima, which took the lives of seventy-eight thousand people. The cost of this weapon,

moreover, may be low enough that relatively poor countries can develop a strategic nuclear capability. As more countries move into the industrial and postindustrial ages, it is quite clear that proliferation of nuclear weapons is a foregone conclusion. The danger of nuclear proliferation is the greatest threat to the survival of civilization.

The United States and the Soviet Union have enough nuclear weapons to destroy civilization as we know it. A nuclear exchange between the superpowers would, no doubt, involve many, if not all, the countries of the world. In short, unlike any other time in history, one country can destroy the world.

For the first time ever, weapons have become so powerful as to make the nation-state obsolescent. The cannons that destroyed feudal castles paved the way for the modern state. Is it not clear that nuclear weapons can be perceived as being so dangerous as to pave the way for world government? Since in the nuclear age there is no such thing as military security in any traditional sense of the term, is it not clear that the nation-state today is a detriment to the global community and must be abolished along with the idea of nationalism, or separateness of one people from another?

Economic arguments support the military realities of our times that oppose the continuation of the nation-state. In a less complex era, it was easier to talk about a country's self-sufficiency. In an industrial and postindustrial world, there is a much greater interdependence among states.

Complex societies need raw materials to support their national machinery. Oil, particularly, is a vital component of a modern society. Without oil, the economies of countries would die, causing severe unemployment and social unrest. Advanced industrial societies need to import that oil primarily from the Middle East, South America, and Africa, if they are to strengthen their economies. In turn, the oil-producing countries need the sophisticated technologies and know-how of the advanced societies in order to modernize their economies.

Countries are more and more dependent on each other for goods and expertise. Trade between the Western countries and the Eastern European communist world, for example, has been increasing rapidly. French and Italian automobile companies are helping the Soviet

---

[18] A kiloton is the equivalent of one thousand tons of TNT.

Union to produce automobiles. Japanese technicians offer their expertise in countries throughout the world. The development and strengthening of the multinational corporations, such as International Telephone and Telegraph (ITT), Ford Motor Company, and International Business Machines (IBM), moreover, are further demonstrations of interdependency.

The multinational corporations have already demonstrated the decaying quality of the nation-state. **A multinational corporation** (MNC) is a large enterprise with offices and/or branches in numerous countries conducting business operations across state lines. MNCs in many cases have resources exceeding those of most countries. Faced with restrictions imposed by a country, many MNCs can move their operations to another country. The nation-state, consequently, is at a disadvantage in dealing with the MNC. The existence of MNCs makes the creation of transnational political institutions essential if goods and services are to be produced for the benefit of the people of the world, rather than for the benefit of the few engaged in private enterprise.

Tariff barriers, import controls, and restrictions on the flow of labor from one country to another all impede the rapid economic development that would be advantageous to all. The development of the European Community is an indication of the necessity for transcending boundary lines. The nation-state is now an impediment to economic development and must be abolished.

Although military and economic factors alone are sufficient arguments against nationalism, environmental reasons, too, contribute to the necessity of condemning the nation-state principle. If more than 160 countries in the world continue to pursue their own selfish interests, harmony will not result. The pollution of oceans, rivers, and seas caused by the reckless dumping of waste material can only be controlled by actions transcending nation-states. Similarly, the destruction of rain forests in one country may contribute to global ecological disaster.

The nation-state, then, is obsolete. Military, economic, and environmental factors have contributed to the weakening of the nation-state and the strengthening of newer, transnational institutions.

4 / NO   IS THE NATION-STATE OUTMODED IN THE TWENTIETH CENTURY?

For all the talk about how the nuclear age has made the nation-state irrelevant, it is important to remember that no country has used nuclear weapons in war since 1945. Deterrence rather than defense has become the cornerstone of nuclear policy. Deterrence is based on the recognition that there would be no winner in a nuclear war, a thought sufficient to prevent a country from going too far in making demands on an adversary. The possession of nuclear weapons by independent states, consequently, may serve the cause of peace.

It is important to remember, too, that nuclear weapons are not the only component of military force. Conventional wars have been fought even in this nuclear age. Formal or informal alliances of independent states have been successful in protecting South Korea and Zaire. Traditional alliances based on military

support can serve to enhance the security of many people.

The notion that changes in military technology are bringing about a transformation in the state's traditional independence is based upon a false assessment of the independence of states in the conduct of war. Commenting on European states, Anthony D. Smith notes that in the past they nearly always acted in concert and few were strong enough to "go it alone." Recognizing the possible exceptions of Prussia-Germany and Napoleon's France in this assessment, he observes that few states had the wealth, skill, and leadership to convert temporary military power into political hegemony. He adds:

The "wars of states" and the "wars of nations" of the eighteenth and nineteenth centuries were carried on within a tight framework of interdependent polities just as today's superpower blocs are locked into a similar geopolitical balance. If today's nation-states can no longer act as "world policemen" (if they ever did so), several of them can still defend their own political interests, by force if necessary, as recent examples in Chad or the Falklands make clear.[19]

From an economic point of view, it is clear that the nation-state is not outmoded. There is nothing about the nation-state system that requires two states not to cooperate. Indeed, Canada and the United States are great trading partners, as are Japan and the United States. The multinational corporation has been able to work within the context of the nation-state system as an instrument of economic development.

Much has been made of the power of the MNCs. It is true that MNCs are powerful economic institutions, but nation-states have been able to exercise control of them. Some of the MNCs are vulnerable because they have huge fixed investments in mineral development and buildings that they cannot pick up and move from one country to another. They and other less vulnerable MNCs have been forced to make accommodations to the demands of nation-states, such as in the employment of host nationals, the reinvestment of part of their profits in host countries, and joint ventures in which the state has significant financial shares. The nation-state shows no sign of eroding because of the MNC challenge.

Much has also been said about the interdependence of nations along economic lines. The real story, however, has not been interdependence but increasing economic independence. The Arab oil embargo of 1973 stimulated energy-hungry countries to become independent of foreign energy supplies. Indeed, the American program was named Project Independence. Western European countries and Japan rushed into all kinds of research and production efforts to avoid dependence upon foreign oil.

There is sufficient evidence to indicate that the control of the state over its economy is increasing rather than decreasing. Twentieth-

century improvements in communications and public administration have facilitated collecting taxes, imposing tariffs, and regulating private companies, for example.

The system of separate states, moreover, has not necessarily meant that states cannot cooperate in solving environmental problems. Because the states of the world have worked together in health matters, smallpox—a dreaded disease that decimated communities for centuries—has been eliminated from the face of the earth. Many countries have entered into agreements about nuclear wastes, health, and pollution—all within the context of the nation-state system. It is foolish to change a system when it works.

Like the achievement of security and economic well-being, the achievement of human freedom is one of the great problems of our times—a problem that concerns citizens of every country in the world. In the twentieth century totalitarian political philosophies (see Chapter 3) have threatened to rule the world. Communism is one of the more important examples of totalitarianism.

Communism is discussed in Chapter 5. For our purposes it is important to note that communism as an ideology is nothing more than a modern version of classical Russian expansionism, as true of Russian czars as of Soviet commissars. When at the conclusion of World War II, the army of the Soviet Union found itself in occupation of considerable parts of Eastern Europe, the Soviet leader Joseph Stalin established communist governments sympathetic to him. According to basic communist philosophy, there is supposed to be no conflict among people under communist rule. The only basis for conflict, according to communist theory, is economic differences between classes. So long as capitalism is eliminated and communist regimes are established, it is impossible to have conflict among communist countries.

But nationalism has served to weaken Soviet Communist party control of Soviet society. From its very beginnings in 1917, Soviet leadership made accommodations to the nationality principle in the forms of the federal system (see Chapter 10) and limited cultural autonomy. Soviet leaders hoped that the Communist party would provide a powerful unifying force in which ethnic nationalism would converge diverse nations and nationalities in a supra-

[19] Anthony D. Smith, "History and Liberty: Dilemmas of Loyalty in Western Democracies," *Ethnic and Racial Studies* (London) 9 (January 1986): 44.

national Soviet state. The hope has not been realized, as nationalist agitation continues to be expressed in the Soviet Union in the Baltic republics, the Ukraine, Georgia, and among the Crimean Tatars.[20] The riots and demonstrations by Armenians in Nagorno-Karabakh in 1988 are another example of nationalism encountered by the Soviet government in Soviet borders.

Soviet leaders also had to deal with the nationality problem in its relations with other communist states. Under Stalin the idea of communist solidarity was used as a subterfuge to rid the communist states of governments hostile to Stalin, whether real or imagined. The communist countries of Eastern Europe were treated in the same manner that Western imperialist powers had dealt with their colonies, with the exception that the West often permitted dissent and protest movements to form so long as these were done peacefully. According to Stalin, the nonviolent protests of Soviet or other Eastern European dissidents would not only be crushed but would go unnoticed since they would not be reported by Western journalists, who would be barred from covering the stories.

But nationalism undermined Stalin's all-embracing communist ideology. First, Josip Broz Tito, the Yugoslav leader, challenged Soviet domination and later called for national roads to communism. Other signs of nationalism appeared, destroying the pretense of universal communist solidarity. In 1953, East Berlin riots were put down by Soviet forces. In 1956, the Hungarian people rose in opposition to Soviet domination. In that same year there were demonstrations in Poland. Perhaps more severe challenges to the ideology of universal communism came from Mao Zedong's People's Republic of China. Mao denounced the claim of the Soviet leaders that the Soviet Union was the leader of the communist world, and fighting, subsequently, erupted along the Sino-Soviet border. The movement by trade unions in Poland in the 1980s for greater freedom was partly a rejection of Soviet domination of that country. In Afghanistan, rebel forces con-

tinued to fight a communist regime imposed by Soviet military power. Relying on the help of some countries, most notably the United States and Pakistan, the rebels succeeded in inflicting enough damage to compel the Soviet Union to withdraw its forces from the region by 1989, thus undermining the existing communist regime there.

Nationalism has been a more powerful force than communism. Nationalism has, consequently, contributed to the erosion of a totalitarian political ideology.

Nationalism serves not only to weaken global totalitarianism but also to strengthen freedom and dignity. Particularly to the peoples of Africa and Asia who have been under colonial rule, the idea of nationalism implies a dignity that was lacking in the old colonial world. In the nineteenth and early twentieth centuries many people in the West regarded themselves as superior people. Some thought about their responsibilities to "take up the white man's burden" or "civilize" the non-Western peoples.

The victors in World War I had no desire to liberate their own colonies. They established a system of **mandates** (countries held in trust by advanced industrial countries) that applied exclusively to the colonies of the vanquished European powers. Even as late as 1945, Charles de Gaulle, leader of the French forces, and British Prime Minister Winston Churchill proclaimed that victory over fascist imperialism did not mean that the French and British colonies would become independent.

For many of the peoples of Africa and Asia, then, nationalism became associated with independence from colonial rule. It meant an end to racial discrimination and the notion of a superior Western people. Representation at the United Nations put the new countries on a par with the more industrially advanced states. The principle of **sovereign equality,** in which all states are equal in law, characterized the voting procedure at the General Assembly of the United Nations and was an important element of self-respect. With the influx of newly independent countries into the United Nations in the 1950s and 1960s, the major powers were compelled to court the favor of the former colonies. Today both African and Asian countries often actually vote in opposition to their former colonial rulers. All of this has worked

---

[20] See Gail W. Lapidus, "The Nationality Question and the Soviet System," in *The Soviet Union in the 1980s,* ed. Erik P. Hoffman, *Proceedings of the Academy of Political Science* 35, no. 3 (1984): 98–112.

to provide a sense of dignity for the leaders and people of new states.

The nation-state, then, has demonstrated that it is a viable institution. It retains its military and economic effectiveness. It serves, moreover, as a force for human freedom.

KEY TERMS

Chauvinism

Common Market

Culture

Ethnic groups

Ethnocentrism

European Community

Irredentism

Mandates

Modernization

Multinational corporation

Multinational states

Nation

Nation-state

Nationalism

Patriotism

Sovereign equality

Zionism

QUESTIONS

1. What are the factors that help create a feeling of nationalism?
2. What are the problems of trying to structure the world under the principle "one nation, one state"?
3. Create a case study in which a particular territory has been claimed by different parties, such as the Falkland Islands, Northern Ireland, Israel, or Kashmir. Make a case for one side on the basis of what you know about nationalism.
4. Does the nation create the state or does the state create the nation?
5. What effect would the elimination of nationalism have on world politics?

RECOMMENDED READINGS

AKZIN, BENJAMIN. *State and Nation.* London: Hutchinson University Library, 1964. A study of the relationship between the political phenomenon of the state and the ethnic phenomenon of the nation.

BRIMELOW, PETER. *The Patriot Game: Canada and the Canadian Question Revisited.* Stanford, Calif.: Hoover Institution Press, 1986. A study of Canadian nationalism.

BROWN, SEYOM. "The World Polity and the Nation-State System: An Updated Analysis." *International Journal* (Toronto) 39 (Summer 1984): 500–28. An argument that the nation-state, although strong, is declining in power.

CHEHABI, H. E. "Self-Determination, Territorial Integrity, and the Falkland Islands." *Political Science Quarterly* 100 (Summer 1985): 215–25. An assessment of the Falkland Islands controversy in terms of the principle of national self-determination.

COBBAN, ALFRED. *The Nation State and National Self-Determination.* London: Collins, 1969. A revised and updated version of an earlier work presenting a history and political analysis of national self-determination.

COMMITTEE ON INTERNATIONAL RELATIONS OF THE GROUP FOR THE ADVANCEMENT OF PSYCHIATRY. *Us and Them: The Psychology of Ethnonationalism.* Report 123. New York: Brunner/Mazel, 1987. An examination of the psychology of ethnicity.

DEUTSCH, KARL W. *Nationalism and Its Alternatives.* New York: Knopf, 1969. An analysis of how the problems of nationalism are developing in the contemporary world.

————. *Nationalism and Social Communication: An Inquiry into the Foundations of Nationality.* 2d ed. Cambridge, Mass.: MIT Press, 1966. A theory relating nationalism to social communication.

EMERSON, RUPERT. *From Empire to Nation: The Rise to Self-Assertion of Asian and African Peoples.* Cambridge, Mass.: Harvard University Press, 1967. An analysis of nationalism in Asia and Africa with attention to the philosophy and history of nationalism in the West.

FOON, CHEW SOCK. "On the Incompatibility of Ethnic and National Loyalties: Reframing the Issue." *Canadian Review of Studies in Nationalism* (Prince Edward Island) 13 (Spring 1986): 1–11. An argument that ethnic identity may be compatible under certain conditions with national loyalty in multiethnic states.

GRODZINS, MORTON. *The Loyal and the Disloyal: Social Boundaries of Patriotism and Treason.* Chicago: University of Chicago Press, 1956. An examination of loyalty and disloyalty.

GUSTAFSON, LOWELL S. "The Principle of Self-Determination and the Dispute about Sovereignty over the Falkland (Malvinas) Islands." *Inter-American Economic Affairs* 37 (Spring 1984): 81–99. An assessment of the Falkland Island dispute.

HAAS, ERNST B. "What Is Nationalism and Why Should We Study It?" *International Organization* 40 (Summer 1986): 707–44. A review of four books on nationalism.

HAYES, CARLTON J. H. *Essays on Nationalism.* New York: Macmillan, 1926. A classic book by one of the leading scholars on nationalism.

————. *Nationalism: A Religion.* New York: Macmillan, 1960. A summing up of the author's research on nationalism with special attention to Europe.

JAMES, ALAN. *Sovereign Statehood: The Basis of International Society.* London: Allen and Unwin, 1986. A rigorous analysis of sovereign statehood in the modern international system.

KEDOURIE, ELIE. *Nationalism.* 3d ed. London: Hutchinson University Library, 1966. An analysis of nationalism.

KELLER, BILL. "Soviet Union's Ethnic Minorities Find Little Room at Top." *New York Times,* April 3, 1988, sec. 4, p. 3. An article on Soviet ethnicity today.

KOHN, HANS. *The Idea of Nationalism: A Study in Its Origins and Background.* New York: Collier Books, 1967. A historical treatment of nationalism.

LAPIDUS, GAIL W. "The Nationality Question and the Soviet System." In *The Soviet Union in the 1980s,* ed. Erik P. Hoffmann. *Proceedings of the Academy of Political Science* 35, no. 3 (1984): 98–112. An argument that the nationalities problem in the Soviet Union is a continuing one.

MILLER, J. D. B. "The Sovereign State and the Future." *International Journal* (Toronto) 39 (Spring 1984): 284–301. An argument that the sovereign state shows vitality and will probably continue to do so.

MORROW, LANCE. "Israel: At 40, the Dream Confronts Palestinian Fury and a Crisis of Identity." *Time* 131 (April 14, 1988): 36–40, 43–44, 46–47, 49–50. A retrospective of Israel.

PFAFF, WILLIAM. "On Nationalism." *New Yorker* 63 (May 25, 1987): 44, 47–48, 50, 52–54, 56. As assessment of American foreign policy in the context of contemporary nationalism throughout the world.

SHAFER, BOYD C. "Debated Problems in the Study of Nationalism." *Canadian Review of Studies in Nationalism* (Prince Edward Island) 11 (Spring 1984): 1–19. An overview of the major problems of nationalism.

SMITH, ANTHONY D. *The Ethnic Origins of Nations.* New York: Basil Blackwell, 1987. An analysis of the premodern roots of nationalism.

WHITE, PHILIP L. "What Is a Nationality?" *Canadian Review of Studies in Nationalism* (Prince Edward Island) 12 (Spring 1985): 1–23. A historical investigation of the concept of nationalism.

part II

FORMS OF GOVERNMENT

Political systems may be compared in many ways in order to understand their relationship to the level of citizen participation in political affairs, the establishment of a just society, and the kinds of policies that a government produces. In ancient Greece, for example, Aristotle classified government in terms of the number of people who ruled and whether that rule was for the benefit of the polity or for the benefit of the political rulers themselves.

Other distinctions have been made throughout the ages between arbitrary government and constitutional government, rule by intellectuals and rule by the masses, and monarchy and republic. In the twentieth century a prominent distinction in classifying governments is made between democracy and dictatorship. Chapter 3 deals with defining and debating issues concerned with such a distinction.

chapter 3

Democracy and dictatorship

The problem of distinguishing democracy from dictatorship lies in the fact that popular support of the term *democracy* is so widespread today that it is rare to find a government that openly supports dictatorship as an ideal. Instead, the tendency is for governments to call themselves democratic although they may act in ways that are contrary to the traditional meaning of the term *democracy*.

The defense of democracy is so broad as to appear in nearly all bands of the political spectrum. Communists herald their system as an expression of democracy. Conservatives condemn as violations of democracy the suppression of dissent in the communist countries of the Soviet Union, Cuba, and East Germany. Liberals complain about the absence of or restrictions on democracy in countries like Chile and Taiwan, where, freedom of participation in electoral activity has been prevented or impeded. Capitalists acclaim the free enterprise system as an example of democracy, and socialists argue that only with socialism can there be real democracy. Terrorists hijack planes, bomb buildings, and assassinate elected officials in the name of democracy. Many of those who praise democracy denounce dictatorship but differ markedly about whom they regard as dictators.

In order to understand the controversy, it is essential to examine the different meanings of the terms *democracy* and *dictatorship*. Afterward, issues that highlight the character of and differences between democracy and dictatorship will be explored.

DEMOCRACY

Democracy is literally derived from two Greek words: *demos*, meaning "the people," and *kratein*, meaning "to rule." **Democracy** is popular sovereignty, or rule by the people, and it is a form of government distinguished from rule by a king or queen (**monarchy**), rule by a hereditary nobility (**aristocracy**), rule by the most educated, rule by the elders, and rule by religious leaders. To say that democracy means rule by the people, however, does not reveal enough about the meaning of democracy. For a better explanation, it is necessary to look at three of the principal uses of the term *democracy:* participatory (direct) democracy, representative (indirect) democracy, and economic democracy. These are by no means the only forms of democracy, but they are among the most prominent.

Participatory Democracy

Participatory democracy, or **direct democracy,** is a form of government that emphasizes three features: (1) popular participation, (2) majority rule, and (3) political equality. It has its origins in Athenian experience, which was different from the form of government that many Americans today regard as their own democracy. The major differences reflect geography, participation, and the relationship between citizen and state.

Democratic rule today generally involves a community containing millions of people scattered throughout large geographic regions. The democracy of the United States, for example, governs a transcontinental territory of more than 250 million people. In the fifth and fourth centuries B.C., Athens was a city-state (*polis*) with a population of from 300,000 to 400,000 people—about the same number of people as in Omaha, Nebraska, in 1989—and a territory of about one thousand square miles—roughly the size of Rhode Island. Since many Athenian citizens knew each other, spoke the same language, shared political, religious, moral, and cultural values, and constituted a small political unit, there was a good deal of mutual trust and a real sense of community among them.

Political participation in ancient Athens involved only citizens—that is, male property owners. Women, slaves, youth, and foreigners were excluded from citizenship. The citizens in Athens constituted a minority of the population of the city-state—only about 20,000 to 40,000 men, according to most estimates.

Citizens were expected to participate actively in the actual making of laws, administration of laws, and dispensing of justice. The political institutions of the day—the Assembly, Council, and juries—were set up in such a way as to give the greatest scope for citizen participation. There was no permanent governing unit in the sense in which today the United States has a Congress and a president charged with the responsibility of making and enforcing laws. All Athenian citizens were expected to play a political role. Rotation in office at one- or two-year intervals and selection by lot for those offices were designed to enhance participation by all citizens rather than by a permanent governing group of representatives. There were no elections, since elections were regarded as aristocratic devices of choosing "the best people" instead of placing government in the hands of the people.[1]

In ancient Athens, moreover, there was no distinction between state and society. Citizens, consequently, possessed no rights against certain acts of the state. The Greek city-state encompassed political, social, and cultural life. In theory, there were no limits on what actions the state could take against its citizens. In fact, however, there was more freedom in Athens for citizens than in undemocratic Greek city-states of ancient times and in many political systems of later centuries. Varying controversial opinions were offered at the As-

---

[1] See M. I. Finley, *Democracy Ancient and Modern* (New Brunswick, N.J.: Rutgers University Press, 1973), pp. 19–20.

sembly, and even those people who disagreed with the fundamental principles of Athenian democracy were free to voice their own beliefs. For example, the philosopher Plato established his own school in Athens, the Academy, where he taught for a generation. His views were critical of traditional Athenian beliefs and values, yet he was free to advocate his ideas.

The system of decision making was based on majority rule. A majority of the citizens present at an assembly or jury decided on matters within their jurisdiction and punished individuals as they so chose, sometimes brutally. Majority rule itself was based on the principle of **political equality,** or one person, one vote, as it is referred to today, in which each person's vote is counted equally.

In the contemporary world, participatory democracy in the Athenian sense is virtually nonexistent on the national level. There are, nevertheless, certain practices of participatory democracy that are found in contemporary political systems. The **New England town meeting,** in which the citizens of a small town get together to decide policy for the town, is one example of the contemporary participatory approach. Swiss cantons have similar practices. The Israeli *kibbutz* (agricultural commune) is yet another example of participatory democracy. Jury duty in courts, in which ordinary citizens judge the legal cases, continues in modern democracies, although professional judges preside.

Direct participation in law making exists on a national level, but its scope is rather confined. The **referendum,** in which the people of a political unit— sometimes national and at other times regional—are asked to decide directly on an issue, is one example. In American states and cities, bond issues, involving the authorization of bonds to raise money for the construction of schools and hospitals, are often considered in this manner. Even Great Britain, which does not

have a referendum tradition, conducted the first referendum in its history in 1975 on the desirability of remaining in the European Community.

Another example of direct democracy is the **initiative,** in which citizens can propose legislative or constitutional changes by filing of formal petitions to be acted upon by either the legislature or the entire electorate.

In the 1960s and 1970s, advocates of participatory democracy directed their attention to **decentralization** (whereby the authority to make certain decisions is transferred from a central source to smaller or local units) and the direct involvement of amateurs in decision making.[2] A key slogan became "power to the people," which to the advocates meant taking power away from the nation's elected public officials and transferring it to the "grass-roots" level. It was this emphasis on participatory democracy that characterized the radical groups known as the New Left.

Participation is also a feature of decentralization in the workplace. In the 1980s some advocates of participatory democracy focused their attention on worker involvement in decision making. In this regard Yugoslavia established a system of workers' councils in which workers contributed to decision-making processes affecting their own work. These councils give workers some control of policy in factories in such matters as plant expansion and the distribution of profits. Western capitalists and socialists have at times allowed for greater participation by workers in deciding how to solve production problems.

---

[2] Terrence E. Cook and Patrick M. Morgan, eds., *Participatory Democracy* (San Francisco: Canfield Press, 1971), p. 4.

Representative (Indirect) Democracy

Participatory democracy is at least possible in small communities, but is it possible in large political entities? That is a question that will be considered. What is important at this point, however, is that with the emergence over the past few centuries of political communities containing diverse ethnic, religious, and racial groups, larger numbers of people, and more sophisticated economies, a different kind of democracy has developed: representative democracy.

A representative democracy, or indirect democracy, possesses some of the features of direct democracy but is different in some important ways. Characteristics that are somewhat similar are popular participation, political equality, and majority rule. Representative democracy is different from direct democracy in that it is a system of representative government based on free elections and a system of limitations on state activity (constitutionalism).

Representative democracy is based on the principle of popular sovereignty. Although modern representative democracy requires popular participation, the scope and form of that participation are different from Athenian democratic practices in two ways. First, the number of people included in the political community is larger. Today, representative democracies claim maximum popular participation and have extended the right to vote to include everyone except criminals, youth, the insane, and noncitizens. Modern representative democracies, moreover, are characterized by **pluralism**: the existence of a variety of associations that are autonomous, or independent from government domination.

Second, although most citizens play no direct role in making laws (with the exception of engaging in such practices as deciding on referenda and initiatives), other forms of political participation are permitted. Some citizens join interest groups for the purpose of influencing elected officials and appointed bureaucrats to act in particular ways. Citizens also work in political campaigns in order to support candidates who favor their views. They conduct meetings, write pamphlets and articles, take out newspaper advertisements, and hold peaceful demonstrations—all with the goal of influencing policy.

In modern representative democracies, the principle of political equality remains, but various devices have been used to prevent a complete realization of this goal. In many countries, Great Britain and the United States being examples, representation has at various times been based on a geographic region rather than population. In England, a system of "rotten boroughs" developed in which it was possible for one member of Parliament to represent a few hundred people while another member represented hundreds of thousands of people. A somewhat similar (but less extreme) system of **malapportionment** (in which legislative districts contained unequal numbers of people) worked also in the United States to the detriment of the heavily populated areas and to the well-being of people in rural areas. Some legislative bodies do not recognize the principle of political equality in their systems of representation. The United States Senate, for example, consists of two senators per state regardless of the size of population, because the men who wrote the Constitution intended that senators represent the states rather than the people. Gradually, however, the worst evils impeding political equality have been eliminated, and today most democratic systems operate under the principle of political equality.

Majority rule is applied both in deciding who the law makers will be and whether or not bills become laws. The majority principle has sometimes been bypassed even in these areas. In some instances (usually important matters), a two-thirds or three-fourths vote is necessary to enact laws or constitutional amendments. Legislative devices, such as the **filibuster** (in which United States senators can talk a bill to death by preventing a vote from being taken) or the tying up of a bill in committee, can prevent a majority from deciding law. **Judicial review** (in which a court can declare any act of the legislature or the executive as unconstitutional) can also thwart the will of the majority. The principle of majority rule, however, is generally the accepted norm in representative democracies.

Although popular participation, political equality, and majority rule are adapted with variations from the Athenian experience, representative democracy in contemporary practice presents two new components: a system of representation based on free elections conducted at specified periods and constitutionalism.

Indirect democracy is based on the principle of representation. Differences exist as to what representation means; that is, whether it means a mirror image of the population, a reflection of the groups who elected the representative, or a trustee relationship in which the elected official decides issues on the basis of his or her conscience. What is generally agreed, however, is that the representative is elected in competition with one or more people for the same office, that the election is for an agreed maximum period of time, and that if the official is defeated for office, he or she turns over that office in a peaceful manner to the winner of the election.

Constitutionalism may mean many things, but in the context of representative democracy it means that the acts of government are limited—even if these acts clearly represent majority wishes. Constitutionalism is fundamental to liberal ideas (see Chapters 4 and 7). Liberalism is a political philosophy that makes a distinction between society and the state.

According to liberal theorists, individuals possessed natural rights before the state was established. Governments are created by people to protect people's rights.

Some writers argue, consequently, that there is a conflict between democracy and liberalism. According to them, democracy means majority rule *without limitations.* The majority may decide anything, even to deny rights of political participation to the minority. A "tyranny of the majority" is, thus, consistent with democracy. Liberalism, however, assumes that there are limits to what the majority may decide. The majority is not free to suppress freedom of speech and assembly, for example. It is this concern with individual liberty that ties representative democracy to liberalism, so that the phrase **liberal democracy** is often equated with representative democracy.

Still other writers argue that rights need not be justified according to a belief in liberalism. They contend that a system based on popular participation and political equality assumes that people should be free to participate in the political process and that, regardless of their views, they should be allowed to try to organize majorities. A political system that suppresses freedom to participate, consequently, cannot be classified as democratic. Rights, according to this view, are inherent in democracy.

Both the argument based on liberalism and the argument based on democracy, then, accept the view that there are limits to what the majority can do.

In summary, recognizing that the definition is not without its critics, we will use the phrase **representative democracy** (or **indirect democracy**) to mean a system of government characterized by popular participation in the political process, political equality, majority rule, representative government based on free elections, and constitutionalism.

Economic Democracy

Participatory democracy and representative democracy are generally referred to as *political democracy*. The basic premise about political democracy is that government can do whatever it wishes *and remain democratic* so long as its duly elected officials act in accordance with approved methods. In principle, at least in the minds of some supporters of democracy in its political form, all that democracy signifies is a *method* by which majorities (either the people directly or their representatives) make decisions affecting public policy.

In the past century growing attention has been given to broadening the understanding of democracy beyond method. What does it matter, some partisans have asked, if people can vote but the effect of voting makes no real difference in the quality of their lives? According to this line of reasoning, voting may make no difference because government may exclude certain economic decisions from its consideration. To the extent to which a free enterprise economy allows private individuals to make economic decisions that create conditions of inequality of wealth, then many people—most notably, the poor, the unemployed, and the targets of racial, religious, and gender discrimination—will be losers in the political process. These people would vote, but their vote would not change their dismal situation.

Those who contend that democracy should be more than a method use the phrase **economic democracy** to specify a system of government that distributes the material resources of society so as to maximize equality and improve the quality of life for the masses of people. People who support economic democracy call for government programs to minimize inequalities: programs such as the redistribution of income from the wealthy to the poor, public education to give poorer people who do not attend private schools equal opportunities to learn, and government-sponsored health-care laws to provide all people with the benefits of health care regardless of their income.

Attention to economic equality has raised the issue among democrats of the relationship between liberty and equality. Most supporters of democracy argue that democracy means liberty *and* equality. Some writers argue, however, that liberty and equality are inherently conflicting principles. If liberty means freedom to do what one wishes without interference from the state, then efforts to redistribute income are a denial of liberty. Other writers contend, however, that the two principles are not inconsistent. They argue that the standard of living in representative democracies is generally higher than it is in other forms of government. Low-income people live well in representative democracies, and the affluence of the few does not depend upon the poverty of the many. In fact, there is a large middle class in representative democracies.

Two prominent groups support economic democracy: social democrats (or democratic socialists) and communists. Although these groups are described more fully in Chapter 5, here we indicate that social democrats argue that democracy requires *both* the features of political democracy *and* economic democracy. They favor free elections, a free press, freedom of speech, and pluralism, but they also support the welfare state.

Communists contend that economic democracy is *the only* element of democracy. By economic democracy they mean the abolition of the free enterprise system and the installation of a socialist economy. Political democracy, in their view, is a sham, since it is capitalists who really control the system. Communists do not, consequently, support free elections, a free press, freedom of speech, and pluralism.

Although the use of the phrase *economic democracy* is associated with socialism and communism, the linking of the character of an economy to a political system is not exclusive to those ideologies. Some advocates of the free enterprise system regard the character of an economy as a feature of democracy, but they focus on economic freedom. They hail **democratic capitalism** as a system that combines economic freedom with political freedom. Without economic freedom, they contend, political freedom is unlikely.[3]

DICTATORSHIP

Today most people live in political systems that do not possess attributes of liberal democracy—namely, representative government, majority rule, political equality, and constitutionalism. It is important to understand the political system in a variety of these undemocratic governments in order to see the contrast between democracy and dictatorship.

Like the term *democracy* dictatorship encompasses different meanings.[4] Many words have been associated with dictatorship, and it is useful to clarify related concepts such as dictatorship, autocracy, absolutism, despotism, tyranny, authoritarianism, and totalitarianism.

Dictatorship may be broadly defined as a political system of arbitrary rule by an individual or small group that is not constitutionally responsible to the people or their elected representatives. Dictatorship is derived from a practice of ancient Rome in which extraordinary power was entrusted to a single leader for a term of no more than six months to promote public order or guarantee military security in a situation of great emergency. At the conclusion of the stipulated period, the dictator would relinquish his power, and constitutional government would be restored. In many respects, this practice is similar to modern **crisis government,** in which extraordinary powers are temporarily given to an elected official to meet an obvious danger. The power given to Winston Churchill in Great Britain during World War II is an example of crisis government. Elections were suspended in Britain during that war. Once the war against Germany was won, however, elections were held (and Churchill's government was defeated).

Autocracy is rule by an individual who governs without constitutional limits. **Absolutism** is a system in which one or more persons govern with unlimited powers. **Despotism** refers to rule by an absolute leader governing for himself rather than for the common good. **Tyranny** means a system of government in which laws are made for the benefit of those who govern rather than for the common good.

Authoritarian Government

Terms such as *autocracy, absolutism, despotism,* and *tyranny* remain imprecise, although it may be said that they all connote dictatorship. Two modern forms of dictatorship, authoritarian and totalitarian, deserve attention as contemporary dictatorships.

The term *authoritarian* is derived from the word *authority,* which has been defined as the establishment of formal power (see Chapter 1). A police officer in a free society, consequently, has the authority to make an arrest when someone is committing a crime. *Authoritarianism* refers to a belief in a political system that emphasizes authority and tradition instead of

---

[3] See, for example, Michael Novak, *The Spirit of Democratic Capitalism* (New York: Simon and Schuster, 1982). For a critique of democratic capitalism, see Samuel Bowles and Herbert Gintis, *Democracy and Capitalism: Property, Community, and the Contradictions of Modern Social Thought* (New York: Basic Books, 1986). Economic freedom and the market economy are discussed in Chapter 5.

[4] See Franz Neumann, *The Democratic and the Authoritarian State: Essays in Political and Legal Theory* (Glencoe, Ill.: Free Press, 1957), p. 235.

individual liberty.[5] An **authoritarian government** is based on principles hostile to democracy, such as rule by a select few, suppression of opposition, and reliance on physical coercion rather than law.

Rule by a Select Few. Any government—authoritarian or not—is rule by a select few, but authoritarian government limits its ruling elite very narrowly and does not permit free elections that would allow new leaders to come to power. In an authoritarian system the government is responsible to itself rather than to the general public. This is not to say that authoritarian regimes are not responsive to change and do not take into account the principal groups that make up the political system. Most governments, in some ways at least, reflect the interests of the dominant groups of society lest they be toppled from power. The scope of the opposition in authoritarian regimes, however, is limited, and the opposition's political behavior is confined to a narrow range, as determined by the ruling few.

Suppression of Opposition. Authoritarian regimes fear opposition that may culminate in a new government. They often act to restrict the opposition in many ways. They may declare any opposition political party illegal and may in fact imprison those party leaders; shut down newspapers and magazines that print stories unflattering to the regime; censor books that they believe to be dangerous to the government; persecute students and faculty members who meet to challenge the existing political and social order; and break up peaceful protests and imprison the leaders of protest groups.

Physical Coercion. Authoritarian re-

---

[5] Michael R. Curtis, "Dictatorship," *Encyclopedia Americana* (1979), 9:82.

gimes often display the symbols of their strength: the army and the secret police. In many authoritarian countries the leader himself is a military officer, such as was the case with Antonio Salazar in Portugal, Anastasio Somoza in Nicaragua, and Francisco Franco in Spain. The army and the secret police support the regime at home and abroad. The secret police use techniques varying from assassination and torture to economic pressure and psychological threats to stop potential dissidents from engaging in activities hostile to the regime.

Authoritarian regimes emphasize the need for order rather than the quest for liberty. They usually justify their actions in terms of the benefit to the people and rely on the symbols of democracy, such as elections, but these elections are rigged to benefit the government. The paradox of dictatorship in authoritarian and other forms is that the government seeks popular support but suppresses dissent.

Authoritarian leaders may want to change society by bringing on rapid industrial development, but they do not indoctrinate the people with a particular ideology pervading all aspects of their lives. The late shah of Iran is cited as an example of an authoritarian leader. He relied upon the army and Savak (a brutal secret police) for his rule. He actively sought to eliminate any opposition to his rule through ruthless means.

Totalitarian Government

In the twentieth century a form of dictatorship that is often regarded as new has appeared: totalitarian government. The prototypes of the totalitarian state are Joseph Stalin's Soviet Union and Adolf Hitler's Germany (see Chapters 4 and 5). Benito Mussolini's Italy is often cited as an example of a totalitarian dictatorship in part because Mussolini coined the phrase *totalitarian state* to describe his rule in Italy. Mussolini's state, however, was never really in the same league as Stalin's or Hitler's. Carl J. Friedrich and Zbigniew K. Brzezinski, two leading scholars of **totalitarian government,** define its central features, which may be summarized as follows:

- **Ideology.** An elaborate ideology covers all aspects of life, and everyone in the society must adhere to it. The ideology is directed at producing a "perfect society," a utopia.
- **Single Mass Party.** A single party is usually led by one man, the dictator, and constitutes a small part of the population (up to 10 percent). The party promotes the prevailing ideology and is typically superior to or completely intertwined with the government.
- **Terror.** A secret police uses terror to prevent any challenge to ruling authorities. Terror is applied to restrict and prevent dissident activity within the party and by groups outside the party.
- **Control of Mass Communication.** The government controls the entire media. No independent media sources are permitted.
- **Control of the Armed Forces.** The weapons of war and the armed forces are under near-complete government domination.
- **Central Direction of the Economy.** The government dominates the entire economic system.[6]

Some writers contend that there is a qualitative difference between authoritarian and totalitarian systems. Their argument is as follows: Authoritarian leaders impose a dictatorship and are content to rule. So long as individuals and groups do not challenge the government, they are generally left alone. In contrast, totalitarian leaders, while accepting the fundamental practices of authoritarianism, go beyond authoritarianism and seek to change the character of human beings. For example, Stalin promoted "the new Soviet man" who would behave in accordance with communist ideology. In totalitarian systems everything must be subordinated to the prevailing ideal, and the regime is not only concerned with the way citizens behave politically but with what they *think* as well. Hence, government emphasizes ideological orthodoxy and indoctrination in education, economics, culture, athletics, and science.

According to Friedrich and Brzezinski, there have been precursors to totalitarianism, such as the dictatorships of ancient Greece, of which Sparta was a leading example, and the Oriental despotisms, but these were *totalist* rather than totalitarian. That is, they lacked the technological underpinnings that made modern totalitarianism possible. Without a modern technology, the scholars contend, it is not possible to maintain control over the armed forces, impose total terror, and centralize the direction of the economy; nor is it easy to induce active participation of the masses in the goals of the dictator.

Some authors criticize the concept of totalitarianism as a useful category to describe certain kinds of dictatorship. They argue that most modern dictatorships—whether they be communist, fascist, or military—have similar goals. These could include the strengthening of the autonomy of the state, the destruction and integration of existing political institutions and structures, and the quest for popular legitimacy and support. They contend that even Stalin's Soviet Union and Hitler's Germany were really authoritarian.[7]

These authors assert that the single party in both cases was never monolithic, for example. Even Friedrich and Brzezinski refer to autonomous units, or "islands of separateness," such as the family, the

---

[6] Carl J. Friedrich and Zbigniew K. Brzezinski, *Totalitarian Dictatorship and Autocracy,* 2d ed. rev. by Carl J. Friedrich (New York: Praeger, 1965), p. 22.

[7] See William S. Allen, "Totalitarianism: The Concept and the Reality," in *Totalitarianism Reconsidered,* ed. Ernest A. Menze (Port Washington, N.Y.: Kennikat Press, 1981), pp. 97–106.

church, the army, the professions, and ethnic groups that maintain their separate identity in spite of the dictatorial pressures to impose uniformity.

Critics of the concept of totalitarianism argue further that use of the term tends to blur the many differences between the two most prominent totalitarian systems. Although Stalin's communist and Hitler's Nazi systems were dictatorships, they differed in terms of political philosophy and supporters[8] (see Chapters 4 and 5). Communism purported to be rational and scientific. It sought the abolition of the state and the creation of a classless society. To the extent that it believed in rapid industrialization, it was revolutionary. Totalitarian nazism, in contrast, was irrational, antiscientific, and if it had a utopia at all, it was certainly different from the communist utopia. It revered the state, the nation, and a superior race. To the degree that it was anti-industrial and antiurban, it was in conflict with the professed goals of communism. The Nazis drew their main strength from the lower middle class and the military, whereas the communists drew from the intelligentsia and the working classes.

Critics of the concept of totalitarianism contend, furthermore, that the term is no longer applicable to the contemporary communist world. Stalinist-type terror is rare in most communist states today. Dissidents are harassed and some are imprisoned, but not all are treated in the same manner. Dissident criticism within the Soviet Union is heard in the West—something which would not have been permitted in Stalin's day. Also, there are more foreign visitors traveling to communist countries and more contact with the West than before. Even censorship

does not have the same heavy hand that it had under Stalin. These critics would not argue that communist countries are democracies, but rather that the old model of totalitarianism is useless in describing the current communist scene.

Although the critics of totalitarianism have made telling points, particularly in arguing against scholars who attempt to describe all communist governments as totalitarian, there remains much that is useful in the concept. It serves as a model that some dictators seek to achieve. Totalitarianism, consequently, connotes something qualitatively different from authoritarianism despite imprecisions in describing the actual political behavior in any political system.

THE FUTURE OF DEMOCRACY

Advocates of representative democracy are not of a single mind on the future of democracy. Some see the forces of democracy improving in the world, while others are more pessimistic and imagine that, over the long term, dictatorship is more the wave of the future.

As we have seen, it is difficult to engage in a discussion about democracy because *democracy* lacks a universally accepted definition. It is also the case that even when there is agreement about a definition of say, *representative democracy*, there are problems in applying the features of democracy to concrete situations. Some observers look upon democracy as a continuum, with some countries showing acceptance of all of its prominent features and some getting good marks in only some of them.

Recognizing the difficulties, we may still want to look at the long-term prognosis of democracy. Democracy has been most successful in the West—in North America and Western Europe in particular—and in some countries of other continents, such as Japan, India, and Australia. In

---

[8] Michael Curtis, "Retreat from Totalitarianism," in *Totalitarianism in Perspective*, ed. Carl J. Friedrich, Michael Curtis, and Benjamin R. Barber (New York: Praeger, 1969), pp. 109–110.

the West of the post–World War II era, the trend has been steadily toward democracy. Dictatorships have been replaced by democracies in Spain, Portugal, and Greece. The defeated European Axis powers—Germany (more particularly the Federal Republic of Germany) and Italy—are now full-fledged members of the democratic community. Japan, the third major Axis power, has a political system with strong democratic institutions.

Most of the states that have achieved independence in Africa and Asia since the end of World War II are dictatorships—with rule by a military leader, a one-party system, or a monarch. In Latin America, the record is mixed. Some Latin American countries have succeeded in adopting democracy only to have the system overturned by a dictator from military or civilian ranks. Democracy in Costa Rica and Venezuela seems to be strongly entrenched, but Chile, which was a democracy, was under military rule from the early 1970s until 1989. Although elections have been promised by the end of 1989, a democratic future for Chile remains uncertain. El Salvador has been only partly successful in establishing democracy. By 1989, its democratic institutions were at best fragile and at worst disappearing. Cuba has one of the worst records of human rights violations in the Western hemisphere, and the Marxist government in Nicaragua suppresses its political opposition and the press.

The communist world has shown some signs of adopting some of the features of democratization, although the significance of the changes is a subject in dispute (see Chapter 5). The Soviet Union has instituted or is about to institute both political and economic reforms, including tolerance of a greater amount of freedom of expression, the competition in local elections, and more openness in society. Some Eastern European countries, moreover, have taken some similar steps. Still, there is no movement by the Soviet leadership or by any communist country to accept the full panoply of features that characterize Western democratic political systems.

The movement toward democracy and the frequent reverses in this century suggest that democracy is a vulnerable system. As indicated above, democracy is, with the exception of the ancient Athenian system, a recent development. Dictatorships in one form or another were the typical political system throughout most of history. It is easy to see why democracies are rather fragile political structures. They depend on a variety of cultural, economic, and political factors that are not always prevalent.

From a cultural point of view, democracy requires a tolerant community. The people who lose in elections must not fear that the winners will persecute or liquidate them. In a presidential election in the United States, for example, the people who vote for the losing candidate do not worry that the incoming president will imprison them or close down the offices of the losing parties, major and minor.

Such tolerance is not taken for granted elsewhere. Violence between Christians and Muslims in Lebanon and between the Tamils and Sinhalese in Sri Lanka is intense because of basic distrust. It is difficult for hostile ethnic or religious groups in a single political entity to cooperate. The stable democracy of India is, however, a shining example of how ethnic and religious differences can function within a single political system—although there is occasional communal violence. Still, India encompasses five hundred former kingdoms, sixteen languages, more than fifteen hundred dialects, six major religions, and countless other divisions. It has also much poverty, high illiteracy, and a population explosion. Yet its democratic institutions seem firmly entrenched, as it has now forty years of experience with periodic elections, an independent judiciary, a free press, and an apolitical military.[9]

Democracy also depends upon favorable economic conditions. Observers as far back as Aristotle noted the importance of a large middle class in maintaining a stable constitutional system. Where a society is polarized into rigid class structures, with a few people owning or controlling all the wealth and the overwhelming masses languishing in poverty, then democracy is difficult to establish and maintain.

Setbacks to democracy occur during periods of adverse economic conditions, such as depression and hyperinflation. While a booming economy can satisfy all groups, since an expanding "economic pie" means that even a smaller share might still be larger, a declining economy pits one group against the other, for one group's gain is another group's absolute loss. The rise of nazism in Germany in the 1930s owes much to the tensions and chaos generated by hyperinflation.

Even with an expanding economic pie, democracy may be vulnerable if the economic demands made by different groups are so great that the government is not able to meet them. Since candidates tend to get elected to public office on the basis of what they have done or can do for different groups, they make promises that are costly to keep and may contribute to inflation, thus undermining the government's stability.

Democracies are vulnerable, too, because of political factors such as foreign policy. As we discuss more fully in Issue 9, democracies may lose their freedom by conquest. Hitler's Germany destroyed democracy in France and other Western European countries. But democracy can also be destroyed through militarization required to meet an external threat, since in wartime normal democratic freedoms are more readily dispensed with. Napoleon was the first modern military leader to use his position as a military leader to create a dictatorship. More than a century later, the philosopher Bertrand Russell warned that if Great Britain militarized to meet the threat of a militarized Germany, it might become the mirror image of its enemy. This view is also associated with Harold Lasswell, who coined the phrase "garrison state" to mean a state that is militarized to such an extent that its citizens lose their freedoms.

For these reasons, we may well need to be cautious in assessing the future of democracy. Yet political leaders are not without resources in meeting the challenges. They may adapt political procedures to the needs of local conditions, for example. In this regard political scientist Arend Lijphart notes, for example, that majority rule is only one model of democracy and may not be applicable to all conditions. Another model is **consociational democracy,** in which "majority rule is replaced by joint consensual rule." In such a system the working principles are "grand coalitions, mutual veto, proportionality, and segmental autonomy."[10] Consociational systems are appropriate to societies that are sharply divided.

Governments in representative democracies, moreover, have had some successes in limiting government spending. When citizens are faced with rising interest rates, increasing inflation, growing unemployment, and more taxes, they have often voted for candidates who wanted to limit government spending.

Some governments have been able to maintain their security and their democratic systems at the same time. To be sure, great stresses are placed on democratic institutions in wartime or in periods of war preparedness. But for Great Brit-

---

[9] "Passage to Democracy," *New Republic* 197 (September 7, 1987): 7.

[10] Arend Lijphart, "Majority Rule Versus Democracy in Deeply Divided Societies," *Politikon*, 4 (December 1977): 118.

judgment of the more affluent members
society.[12] If all citizens voted, then the re
resentatives would enact laws that would cat
more to the needs of the poor and the di
advantaged.

Some observers contend that nonvoting
an expression of happiness with the existii
state of affairs. But as Frances Fox Piven ai
Richard A. Cloward observe, "No one h
satisfactorily explained why 'the politics
happiness' is so consistently concentrat
among the least well off."[13]

Information. So long as polling groups ha
concerned themselves with public opinic
there has been realization that the masses
people lack information on important politii
issues.[14] Even when people give a Yes or I
answer to a pollster, the response to follo
up questions usually reveals a great ignoran
of details.

Lacking information, the masses depend
the experts who control information and w
manipulate the choices available to the peop
What can a janitor tell a military officer abc
weapons' technology? How does a factc
worker (in contrast to a professional ecor
mist) understand the intricacies of the mor
supply, the balance of payments, or the r
tional debt? Clearly, the masses of people a
dependent upon the experts who rule.

Manipulation. Ordinary people can be ea
ily swayed through scientific marketing tec
niques. Selling political candidates and p
grams is as scientific today as selli
automobiles and soaps. Professional mari
research experts use clever techniques to s
their political "products." Given the public
resources available to President John F. Ki
nedy, for example, the American people I
came enthralled with a program to send a m
to the moon within a decade. On reflecti
however, many ordinary citizens preferred t

more dangerous combat zones—are more
likely to be from poor and minority groups,
while members of the middle and upper classes
are often deferred because they are engaged
in "sensitive work" needed for the defense
effort. Even programs purporting to serve the
poor work, in fact, for the benefit of the affluent: contractors, realtors, bureaucrats with high
salaries, and stockholders. Democracies,
moreover, get involved in neocolonial wars
halfway around the world not because the
people want war but because war serves the
interests of the ruling few.

Representative democracies offer the appearance and not the reality of true, democratic government. Low voting turnout, widespread ignorance of political information, and
elite manipulation of the masses demonstrate
that representative democracies represent the
interests of the powerful few rather than the
people.

DEMOCRACIES REPRESENT
THE POWERFUL FEW
PEOPLE?

such as free trade, illegality of trade unions,
and weak government to give strength to a
free enterprise economy. In 1867, most urban
workingmen were given the franchise, a right
extended to rural workingmen in 1884. With
the inclusion of the working classes into the
electorate, the **welfare state,** (in which government promoted programs dealing with education, health, social security, and welfare)
became a reality.

Every advanced industrial democracy has
become a welfare state in spite of the holding
of public office by leaders calling themselves
conservatives or liberals. The support that
masses of people give to low-cost housing,
public education, and inexpensive health care
shows up in the welfare laws of countries such
as Sweden, the United States, Belgium, Holland, and Switzerland. What forces the political
leaders to move in the direction of the welfare
state is the fear that large segments of the
voting public will vote for an opposing candidate who promotes and delivers more of
what people want.

[12] E. E. Schattschneider, *The Semisovereign Peo
A Realist's View of Democracy in America* (Hinsd
Ill.: Dryden Press, 1975), p. 103.

[13] Piven and Cloward, *Why Americans Don't V
p. 13.

[14] See Angus Cambell, Philip E. Converse, W
ren E. Miller, and Donald E. Stokes, *The Amer
Voter* (New York: John Wiley, 1960).

The direct effect of voting on social and political matters can also be seen. So long as black people were excluded from participation in the American political process, there was no need for elected public officials to be responsive to their needs. When blacks were assured that they could exercise their freedom to vote without intimidation, the elected public officials responded to the realities of political power.

This transformation may be seen in the person of George Wallace, an arch segregationist of the 1960s. As governor of Alabama, he was a national leader opposing the federal government's intervention to end racial discrimination in America and the symbol of resistance to civil rights laws. When he ran for governor again in 1982, many years after blacks in the South had been enfranchised, he successfully courted the black vote by promising to support laws and appoint officials favorable to black people. After his victory, he carried out his promises.

Laws are a reflection of popular will on the local as well as the national level. In predominantly fundamentalist Baptist areas, for example, local laws ban the sale of alcohol and theaters are forbidden to show X-rated movies. In areas where alternative life-styles are accepted, laws opposing gay rights, nude bathing, and pot smoking have either been struck down or liberalized. Clearly, when government acts in such a manner, it is reflecting the prevailing views of the political community. The record shows that democracy works to reflect the will of the people.

If some people do not vote, it should not be assumed that democracy is not working or that the people feel they are powerless. Many people choose not to vote because they are *satisfied* with the way things are going or because they find some views of each candidate to be worthy. The existence of **cross-pressures,** in which a voter who belongs to several groups does not vote because some of his or her views are reflected by one candidate and some by the other, indicate not that the voter is alienated. On the contrary, cross-pressures are evidence that candidates in a democracy seek votes from diverse interests.

Even those who choose not to vote are often regarded as potential voters by the contending campaigners in an election. It is true that voters exercise more influence than nonvoters. Even nonvoters, however, can become voters in the event an issue becomes important enough. The fact that so much legislation benefiting disadvantaged, poor, or uneducated people (many of whom do not vote) has been enacted in the Western democracies reveals that the weak are not ignored. Indeed, the record of Western democracies shows that the causes of the weak are often taken up by the people who are educated members of the middle class, especially those with higher university education.

Finally, it is not necessarily the case that nonvoters differ significantly in political preferences from voters in a manner that works against the poor and disadvantaged. In their study of the presidential election of 1972, Raymond E. Wolfinger and Steven J. Rosenstone show that demographic variables, such as education, family income, age, marital status, and ethnic background, are significant in voting or not voting. Their evidence demonstrates that voters constitute a distorted sample of society. They note, however, that with the exception of party identification, the political differences between voters and nonvoters were small. They find that voters are not disproportionately hostile to social welfare policies. Differences are also small between voters and nonvoters on social issues, such as abortion, legalization of marijuana, and women's equality. Wolfinger and Rosenstone determine that both liberals and conservatives are slightly overrepresented at the polls, at the expense of moderates and people who say they have no ideological tendency. "As long as attitudes on issues are so weakly related to social class and race," they conclude, "the poor and minorities will find enough allies to avoid political weakness in proportion to their own voting rates."[15]

The authors observe that for the election they studied, political cleavages do not parallel income, race, and age differences. If in the future that will not be the case, they say, the consequences of variation in turnout will be felt in the fate of policy proposals. This study of the 1972 election suggests, however, that

---

[15] Raymond E. Wolfinger and Steven J. Rosenstone, *Who Votes?* (New Haven: Yale University Press, 1980), pp. 109–11.

nonvoting may not result in policies that are harmful to the poor and the disadvantaged.[16]

Information. It is certainly true that many people are uninformed about government. But many people are informed. Citizens of democracies may not have the time to understand the ramifications of each and every issue, but they certainly do concern themselves with the issues most important to them. Veterans, for example, know a good deal about government programs benefiting veterans. The same applies to workers who know about occupational safety laws, to business people who know about taxes, and so on.

People affected by decisions, moreover, often join groups whose leaders inform them about what government is doing. Many people, consequently, receive their information in this manner and keep informed on issues through their group leaders.

Those who emphasize the lack of information of the masses and the dominance of the experts misunderstand the relationship between the expert and the masses. A janitor does not have to know the intricacies of weapons' technology to know that a war is being won or lost; battlefield casualties speak clearly on this point. A factory worker does not have to understand about the money supply, the balance of payments, or the national debt to know that the economy is experiencing inflation; a visit to the supermarket will reveal this immediately. What democracy means, then, is not that the masses of people have expertise, but rather that they evaluate the work of the experts.

Manipulation. The view that ordinary people are easily manipulated cannot be substantiated. Are people so stupid that they cannot recognize their true interests? Millions of dollars might be spent on proclaiming the virtues of a commercial product, but the consumers soon know if the product is good or bad. Corporations with enormous funds and marketing research techniques have gone bankrupt because they could not convince consumers as to the desirability of their products. The wizards of soda pop in Atlanta were

certain in 1985 that Americans would happily switch to the new Coca-Cola™ after a media blitz would entice them with images of a new magic liquid formula. The expensive campaign fizzled, as Americans demanded and received a return to the old Coke (renamed Classic Coke™).

Ordinary people may make mistakes (as experts do), but it is incorrect to confuse expertise with wisdom. Wisdom is a quality available to the well-informed and the poorly informed alike.

The view that an elite actually governs for its own interest in a representative democracy is not correct in the sense that elite theorists have asserted. The Marxist case in particular is historically inaccurate. Democratic government is not a capitalist dictatorship. Capitalists did not want trade unions to form and to have power, but these organizations of workers did form and do have power in every Western democracy. Capitalists resisted the welfare state with its demands for high taxes. They also opposed government regulations protecting workers from industrial accidents and from substandard wages. They fought the environmental protection laws requiring them to introduce costly machinery to eliminate or reduce pollution. They battled the laws passed on behalf of consumer protection. If a capitalist elite rules the Western democracies, it is acting in a noncapitalist manner. Perhaps it is the capitalists, rather than the ordinary people, who do not know what their true interests are!

Nor is there validity to the arguments of the non-Marxist elite theorists, such as Michels, Mosca, and Pareto. Although there is variation in what each says, the gist of their argument is that democracy is impossible, rulers rule as they see fit, and there is an ultimate separation of interests between the rulers and the ruled.

Although clearly the leadership of some organizations in the democracies has acted in the manner the elite theorists describe, such is not the case in most organizations. If individuals are not happy with their leaders, they can vote to change them or they can leave those private associations and join others.

At the government level voters are free to vote for opposition parties. In those instances in which the parties come too close together, new parties form to reflect the views of those

---

[16] Ibid., p. 114.

who feel excluded from representation. When the Republican and Democratic parties in the 1880s ignored the pleas of the farmers and workers for reform, for example, the Populist party was established. The Democratic party adopted the platform of the Populist party in 1896 and thus effected a realignment of the parties.

When the elitists argue that democracy is impossible, what they really mean is that participatory democracy is impossible. This, however, is another matter. What we contend here is that representatives do reflect popular judgment, and the evidence is clear for this assertion.

6 / YES   SHOULD REPRESENTATIVE DEMOCRACIES REPRESENT THE JUDGMENT OF ELECTED LEADERS RATHER THAN THE PEOPLE?

Democracy has been described by some writers as a system of government that expresses the common will of a political community. Such a description is labeled the classical formulation of democracy by economist Joseph A. Schumpeter. Specifically, he characterizes the classical view as

that institutional arrangement for arriving at political decisions which realizes the common good by making the people itself decide issues through the election of individuals who are to assemble in order to carry out its will.

Schumpeter challenges the view that democracy means government *by* the people in the same sense that the people as an entity decide issues through their elected representatives. According to Schumpeter, the people do not hold definite and rational opinions about every individual question of public policy, and they do not, consequently, give effect to this opinion "by choosing 'representatives' who will see to it that that opinion is carried out."[17]

Schumpeter suggests that a different definition of democracy, one that conforms to the democratic world as it in fact exists, is appropriate. He proposes a reversal of the classical relationship between leaders and the people. The role of the people in a democracy is not to make policy but to produce (elect) a national executive or government. Democracy as it exists, then, can be defined as a *method:*

"that institutional arrangement for arriving at political decisions in which individuals acquire the power to decide by means of competitive struggle for the people's vote." So long as interest groups and political parties are free to compete in the political process and so long as contending members of the political elite abide 'by the "rules of the game" (rigorous adherence to constitutionalism), a system is democratic. In this view, popular participation is limited to accepting or rejecting the people who are to rule them.[18]

Political scientist Robert A. Dahl has built upon this perception of democracy put forward by Schumpeter. In so doing, he is one of the exponents of pluralism. Dahl prefers to use the term **polyarchy,** meaning the rule of multiple minorities, to describe representative democracy as we know it in practice.[19] Dahl argues that Western democracies are characterized not by majority rule but by minorities rule. Not all groups are interested in every aspect of public policy, he asserts. In Western democracies, individual groups have an ability to influence laws and administrative actions through their involvement in the specific policy areas for which they have special concern. Religious groups, consequently, exercise influence over religious matters, educational groups over education, and so on. Democracy, according to Dahl, does not mean majority. rule, but rather a system in which "all the

---

[17] Joseph A. Schumpeter, *Capitalism, Socialism, and Democracy,* 3d ed. (New York: Harper and Brothers, 1950), p. 250.

[18] Ibid., pp. 269, 285.

[19] Robert A. Dahl, *After the Revolution? Authority in a Good Society* (New Haven: Yale University Press, 1970), p. 78.

active and legitimate groups in the population can make themselves heard at some crucial stage in the process of decision."[20] What distinguishes democracy from dictatorship, then, is that democracy is government by *minorities* and dictatorship is government by *a minority*.[21] According to Dahl, a polyarchy, in contrast to a dictatorship, greatly extends "the number, size, and diversity of the minorities whose preferences will influence the outcome of governmental decisions."[22]

Many other social scientists have supported this interpretation that focuses on elites rather than the masses of people. It is neither necessary nor desirable that popular participation be massive for democracy to exist. In fact, too much popular participation will cause instability that may threaten the viability of the democratic system itself.

In this regard, sociologist Seymour Martin

Lipset notes antidemocratic tendencies in lower-class groups. He finds from data from a number of countries that such groups have been supporters of demagogues such as Adolf Hitler and Senator Joseph McCarthy. The lower strata may be more liberal in support of welfare state measures, higher wages, graduated income taxes, and trade unions, he asserts, but they are more intolerant than the rest of society on civil liberty matters.[23]

Lipset and other social scientists, consequently, find that there are advantages of stability that assist the system in contemporary representative democracies. The upper-activist strata tend to be more tolerant than the rest of society and are more committed to preserving the "rules of the game" by which a democracy is governed. This is not to say that popular participation is detrimental to stability; but too much participation may undermine the possibility of governing effectively and coherently. So we can see that representative democracy should represent the judgment of elected leaders rather than the people.

---

[20] Robert A. Dahl, *A Preface to Democratic Theory* (Chicago: University of Chicago Press, 1956), p. 137. See also pp. 145, 150.

[21] See Jack Lively, *Democracy* (New York: St. Martin's Press, 1975), p. 20.

[22] Dahl, *Preface to Democratic Theory*, p. 133.

---

[23] Seymour Martin Lipset, *Political Man: The Social Bases of Politics* (Garden City, N.Y.: Doubleday/Anchor, 1963), p. 92.

6/NO — SHOULD REPRESENTATIVE DEMOCRACIES REPRESENT THE JUDGMENT OF ELECTED LEADERS RATHER THAN THE PEOPLE?

Democracy should require maximum participation of the people rather than reliance on elected leaders. We base our case on three points: (1) voting power is not a sufficient democratic resource of the people; (2) participation in politics has a positive impact on the personality of the participants and, consequently, on the stability of the democratic system; and (3) greater participation will produce better laws.

Voting. Voting power is influential only at the time that citizens cast their ballots. Citizens exercise their voting power only once every few years and, thus, relinquish to representatives power and authority to do what they wish once they are in office.

Many people do not participate in the political process because they come to feel that their vote is not important. Constitutional arrangements in representative democracy create impediments to popular rule, as the examples of an overpowering bureaucracy and an imperial judiciary in the United States attest. Laws are sometimes written in a vague manner, allowing bureaucrats discretion to interpret them. Judges who do not even have to compete in elections are able through statutory or constitutional interpretation to prevent popular will from being implemented, moreover. It is no wonder that many citizens do not vote.

Voting does not mean much in reflecting the wishes of the masses, and that is why there has been a decline in the percentage of voters casting ballots. What political scientist Benjamin R. Barber notes about the United States may also be applied to other countries: "In a country where voting is the prime expression of citizenship, the refusal to vote signals the bankruptcy of democracy.[24]

Participation should mean more than voting. It should include active popular involvement in the discussion of political issues as well as a direct voice in making decisions about laws and policies. Citizens cannot be expected to vote if they do not think of themselves as involved in all aspects of the political process.

Personality and Stability. More popular participation in government is desirable because of the effect it has on the character of people and, consequently, on the stability of the democratic system itself. To the extent that the individual participates in the political process, he or she develops those qualities of character that are healthy for the individuals themselves and for the community.

Mass participation signifies a sense of community. Civic action helps to generate a feeling of involvement, commitment, and obligation. When people participate actively in all facets of the democratic process, their self-esteem and self-confidence grow. Elitists who argue for limited mass participation ignore the beneficial consequences of participation on the character of citizens.

Much has been made of the antidemocratic tendencies of people who do not participate actively in the political process. Elitists fear these tendencies, but they fail to recognize the democratizing spirit that participation generates. If people are encouraged to participate, they will become more familiar and supportive of the democratic rules of the game. As Ronald M. Mason observes, "These rules of the game would include tolerance of differing opinions, protection of minority rights, and other libertarian principles."[25] We should not believe, then, that the enlargement of participation

brings a greater susceptibility to dictatorship.

The effect of participation on character in a democracy is political stability. People who do not participate in the political process feel alienated from the community. They then become easy prey for demagogues, who enflame their frustrations and feelings of powerlessness and encourage undemocratic practices. Nonparticipants will be treated shabbily by political leaders. They will, consequently, lose self-esteem and become hostile to the system that rejects them.

In this regard, John Stuart Mill wrote, "The most important point of excellence which any form of government can possess is to promote the virtue and intelligence of the people themselves."[26] A political system is important, consequently, not only because of the laws it produces but also because it produces better people.[27] That is why maximum popular participation is necessary in a democracy.

Laws. The elitist view is essentially a *status quo* position concerned with the maintenance of the system rather than with expansion of democratic ideals. The result of the elitist view is that masses of people are unrepresented. As indicated previously, the more advantaged groups tend to participate in the political process. The poor and the disadvantaged, consequently, remain either unrepresented or underrepresented.

Greater participation produces better laws. Widespread popular involvement in politics assures that more voices are heard, more viewpoints expressed, and more government responsiveness to the people that government is committed to serve.

Perspectives on democracy that minimize popular participation give support to a continuation of policies favorable to the more affluent members of a society. The fact of a large nonvoting population in Western democracies, particularly the United States, signifies nothing more than a sickness of democracy.[28]

[24] Benjamin R. Barber, *Strong Democracy: Participatory Democracy for a New Age* (Berkeley: University of California Press, 1984), p. xiii.

[25] Ronald M. Mason, *Participatory and Workplace Democracy: A Theoretical Development in Critique of Liberalism* (Carbondale, Ill.: Southern Illinois University Press, 1982), p. 40.

[26] John Stuart Mill, *Representative Government* in his *Utilitarianism, Liberty and Representative Government* (London: J. M. Dent and Sons, 1910), p. 193. The book was originally published in 1861.

[27] Lively, *Democracy*, p. 132.

[28] Schattschneider, *Semisovereign People*, p. 96.

7/YES   IS PARTICIPATORY DEMOCRACY DESIRABLE?

Supporters of elements of participatory democracy come from a variety of viewpoints. Liberals favor more participation from the poor and the disadvantaged when they call for reform of the system. Conservatives urge greater "local control" on occasions. Anarchists and the New Left make participatory democracy a cornerstone of their political philosophies. Although it is difficult to come up with a single political philosophy tying these groups together, we can support some of their main arguments in favor of participatory democracy.

Participatory democracy is both necessary and possible. Participatory democracy is necessary because big government organizations are not able to understand the problems and needs of the people they ostensibly serve. In this regard, there is something wrong when transportation policy is made by people who do not ride public transit; when education policy is made by people who send their children to private schools; and when war policy is made by people who are themselves too old to fight.

So poorly does government function in representative democracies that it is often said that present-day systems are ungovernable. If nations and regional units in representative democracies are ungovernable, it is because the masses of people have not been able to participate actively in decision making. How else to explain that billions of dollars are spent for education, and yet many students are poor readers; that billions are spent for welfare, and yet the welfare problems become worse; and that billions are spent to fight crime, yet urban neighborhoods are unsafe?

There is much opportunity for greater popular participation in all sectors of government and society. At the national level, referenda should be put forward so that the people themselves can decide some issues of concern to them.

Popular participation can be encouraged particularly in regional and local matters. In addition to more use of referenda, the New England town-meeting approach to local problems can be expanded. Other forms of popular participation can be broadened through community boards, neighborhood councils, local school boards, and other units of civic action at the neighborhood level.

There should be greater citizen participation in organizations. For example, in Yugoslavia, "worker control" allows for greater participation in management decision making, and this feature should be copied elsewhere. Universities, too, can have more participation from their principal constituents—students and faculty. Students can play a role in hiring a faculty and in curricula. Teachers can participate in deciding administrative issues.

Why shouldn't the poor be consulted about poverty programs, since they are the people who are affected by government decisions about poverty? Why shouldn't the people who live in a neighborhood decide whether or not their community should be broken up so that a new civic center can be built where their homes now stand? Why shouldn't young people be asked if they really want to fight in Grenada or Nicaragua? These are legitimate questions raised by critics of democracy in its representative form, thus suggesting that there is merit in the participatory model of democracy.

7/NO   IS PARTICIPATORY DEMOCRACY DESIRABLE?

Modern society is too complex for widespread popular participation in government. Even dedicated and conscientious law makers do not have the time to read and comprehend the words in every bill introduced in the legislature. There must be a division of labor in a democracy in which the experts read and interpret the issues and inform the masses about the best options. All democracy requires is that the people choose officials who understand the issues and debate them openly.

Group leaders understand the issues. It is their responsibility to understand them. Clearly, a labor leader in a democracy monitors all legislation dealing with labor matters and reports back to union members. A leader of a feminist group considers every administrative action pertaining to women's rights and informs the members of the feminist association. In the real world of the last quarter of the twentieth century, specialization demands that the masses of people work through their leaders.

Ordinary people do not have time to participate in the political process in the way that group leaders do. As political scientist Gerald Pomper notes, "Voters have too many pressing tasks, from making money to making love, to follow the arcane procedures of government."[29]

Besides, if the masses of people become so heavily involved in politics, then the system would become so politicized as to lead to great social tensions. Because most people are concerned with their private rather than their public lives, governments are able to work effectively.

The problems of modern society, moreover, cannot be solved by participatory democracy schemes of the modern type. Decentralization cannot cope with the problems of environmental protection (in which poisonous chemicals from one area of a country are used in other areas of the country), the well-being of the economy (in which matters affecting a national market must be decided from a central source), or war (with its global connotations). Decentralization is irrelevant to these and other matters.

Finally, when we really take a close look as to what some supporters of decentralization mean by participatory democracy, we can see that in actual fact they often really do not mean "power to the people" but rather transferring power from one group of leaders to another. When segregationists in the United States called for local control in deciding racial issues, what they meant was that local segregationists rather than central government integrationists should decide policy. When community-action leaders ask for participation by the poor, what they really mean is participation by the more politically active leaders who live in the community and speak in the name of the poor. In the name of participatory democracy, then, many sins are committed in which power is given to an unrepresentative few.

---

[29] Gerald Pomper, "The Contribution of Political Parties to Democracy," in *Party Renewal in America*, ed. Gerald Pomper (New York: Praeger, 1980), p. 7.

8/YES   DOES DEMOCRACY PRODUCE WORSE GOVERNMENT THAN DICTATORSHIP PRODUCES?

We need to go no further than to read the morning newspapers to see that democracy produces bad government. We can see every day that democracy creates a government of poor leadership, corruption, and inefficiency.

Leadership. The masses of people are envious of superior people and seek lackluster leaders to govern. It is no accident, then, that democracies choose leaders of no outstanding qualities or accomplishments.

Because leaders must respond to popular whims, democracies subject themselves to leadership by **demagogues:** leaders who rely on highly emotional and usually irrational appeals to receive the immediate approval of the masses rather than to serve the needs of the country. It is no wonder, then, that democracies have their share of demagogues like the late Huey Long and Joseph McCarthy.

Particularly in a modern, complex society, we need knowledgeable people to run the government. Specifically, we need experts who understand the technical intricacies of the problems of our society rather than leaders adept at pandering to mobs. We may ask ourselves, for example, if before expert doctors perform an operation, they must consult with patients, orderlies, nurses, and janitors in the hospital about the proper surgical techniques. Shouldn't the doctors, because of their many years of experience in the study of medicine, be entitled to perform the surgery as they deem fit? Similarly, we would not regard it as rational for the passengers of a ship to tell the captain how to run the ship. In a comparable way, it is foolish to expect the masses of people to select expert leaders when they do not know the first thing about governing.

In a democracy even leaders of great ability must pander to popular tastes and are not free to act in the public interest because of the democratic reverence of equality. The people of a country are not equal in intelligence, strength, or character. By enshrining the principle of equality, men and women of great ability are leveled to the standards of the mediocre. In political campaigns, for example, they must travel to the "grass roots" and engage in such ridiculous tasks of leadership as wearing Indian headdresses, eating kosher hotdogs, and dancing Polish dances, none of which has anything to do with good government.

The principle of equality is dangerous to the well-being of society because of the leveling tendencies of society. In a dictatorship, people trained for leadership and excellence receive the prizes a polity has to distribute: political leadership, social prominence, and economic prosperity. In a democracy, in contrast, the masses demand *equality of results* rather than *equality of opportunity.* Those concerned with results oppose talent and ability and are not satisfied if they are left out of top positions. They demand redistribution of income to their own class, and they destroy the incentive of more qualified, intelligent, and innovative people. They ask for **affirmative action** programs in which government can demand that citizens create special recruitment opportunities for minorities and other groups which have previously suffered from discrimination. These programs are no more than an egalitarian attack against merit. The masses of the mediocre, consequently, vote only for those officials who pass laws giving the mediocre advantages that they do not deserve. The result is a society of the mediocre, of unprofessional professionals: teachers who

cannot teach, doctors who know little about medicine, and lawyers who do not understand law. Paradoxically, such a society is detrimental to the masses of people who are dependent upon poorly qualified teachers, doctors, and lawyers. How would any sane human being feel about the prospect of undergoing brain surgery by a surgeon who flunked Brain Surgery 101 in medical school but was given a medical license anyway because of egalitarian pressures?

Corrupt Government. Corruption in democracies is widespread. "To the victor belong the spoils," said Andrew Jackson on coming to the presidency as a "people's candidate." That slogan has been made acceptable at the highest and lowest levels in democracies. The corruption denoted by the Watergate affair implicated not only cabinet figures but the president of the United States as well. Illegal campaign contributions to the Committee to Reelect the President (CREEP) were given by big corporations in return for political favors. Watergate signified not only financial corruption but the abuse of power by both the president and many of his appointed advisers.

At the regional and local levels, moreover, corruption is widespread. Payoffs to police to allow criminals to engage in drug sales, prostitution, and gambling are a matter of common knowledge. As government has become big at all levels, it has accumulated more rewards to distribute—contracts, tax law enforcement, and jobs—and the scope of corruption has expanded accordingly. The democracies of West Germany, Italy, the United States, and Japan, for example, have in recent years received prominent attention because of major acts of corruption by leading political figures.

Inefficiency. Although a case can be made that government itself is inefficient, it is clear that democratic governments in particular are highly inefficient. Too many bureaucratic agencies and interest groups must be consulted and enticed in a democracy. So slow is the laborious process of criticism and debate, moreover, that inefficiencies are bound to result. There is no central authority with the strength to break through the maze of obstacles to action.

Road construction, for example, must be approved by the political leaders from areas not actually involved. The result in this and other policies is duplication and administrative overlapping—two features of an inefficient system. In a dictatorship, in contrast, someone at the top can cut through the red tape and get things moving.

8/NO   DOES DEMOCRACY PRODUCE WORSE GOVERNMENT THAN DICTATORSHIP PRODUCES?

To be sure, democracy has some weaknesses, and these are often pointed out by supporters of dictatorship. The criticisms about democracy producing bad government are weak, however, when a close examination is made of the data. We may best think of democracy in the same way that the late French entertainer Maurice Chevalier thought about old age at a time in his life when he was old, "Old age is all right," he said, "especially when you consider the alternative." We can say, then, that in spite of the imperfections, democracy produces good government. We can deal with the issues raised by the *Affirmative.*

Leadership. The argument that bad leaders are chosen by an ignorant electorate is wrong because it confuses the relationship between leaders and people and also because it is factually incorrect. It is certainly true that the masses of people are poorly informed about issues, but this does not mean that they are stupid or that they are unwise. To begin with, ordinary people have common sense and wisdom and are aware of the consequences of government laws and policies. A political leader may say, for example, that a government will soon win a war, but ordinary people know the daily battle casualties and the economic costs of pursuing victory. They can make a sound judgment based on the costs and sacrifices.

Ordinary people in democracies, moreover, have often chosen great leaders possessing intellect and judgment. American presidents such as Abraham Lincoln, Theodore Roosevelt, and Woodrow Wilson have made outstanding contributions to good government. Thomas Jefferson was one of the most brilliant of American presidents and showed excellence as a political leader, architect, musician, and philosopher. Other democracies, too, have produced outstanding leaders: Benjamin Disraeli and Winston Churchill in Great Britain, and Georges Clemenceau and Charles de Gaulle in France, for example. The masses of people have not shown hostility to excellence in political leadership. The fact that so many experts are recruited for high-level administrative posts is a reflection of this popular support of expertise.

Dictatorships have produced their share of demagogues and leaders who lacked expertise. Adolf Hitler purged the universities of their eminent scientists. Joseph Stalin liquidated many competent leaders, some of whom were even loyal communists. Both these leaders and other dictators brought their countries to ruin or near-disaster. The record of democracies is better.

Much has been made of the egalitarian evils of democracy. It is essential to note, however, that there is much confusion about democracy. The main egalitarian component of democracy is *political equality;* that is, each person's vote should be counted equally. That concept is based on a respect for the individual. Proponents of democracy contend quite properly that regardless of talent, intelligence, and ability, every individual has a right to be an active participant in the political process and make whatever contributions he or she deems desirable.

It is certainly true that the people—whether they be disadvantaged, poor, or sometimes unqualified—have made demands on democratically elected officials, but this is often because of the past history of discrimination and deprivation and not because of a desire to reward the unworthy.

Dictatorships do not, in fact, bring the "best" people to positions of eminence. Let us take a look at authoritarian aristocracies as a case in point. In European countries of the seventeenth and eighteenth centuries, aristocratic rule dominated the political system. It was the landed gentry who actually ruled. Were these people "the best"? Certainly the aristocratic system produced people of great merit in politics, science, and the arts. It also, however, produced incompetents who only maintained their positions because of their privilege, not their abilities. We can look at the officer corps of the aristocratic armies as a case in point. To be an officer in the army it was essential to be of the nobility. Any relationship between military competence and royal blood was often a mere happenstance. In the nineteenth century, in contrast, the aristocratic barriers to the officer corps were removed in many countries and military careers were thrown open to talent. Where an openness of competition was permitted, the quality of armies improved.

Corrupt Government. Like the charge of poor leadership, the accusations by antidemocracy advocates about corruption are oversimplified. It is certainly true that corruption exists in democracies, but the nature of the democratic system is such as to minimize it. A political system reflects a social system; and if the character of a people is corrupt, no government can improve it.

The features of a democracy, however, make it likely that corruption will be minimized. Constitutional democracies require open and responsible government. Part of the oldest traditions of these constitutional democracies is the right of a legislator to inquire of the government (through its responsible cabinet minister, for example) about impropriety in office. A free press, moreover, makes it possible for corruption to be exposed. A reporter in a free society seeks the acclaim—perhaps even a Pulitzer Prize or its foreign equivalent—for uncovering a scandal involving political leaders. In reporting the information leading to the revelations about Watergate, Bob Woodward and Carl Bernstein were continuing a long tradition of independent journalism. It is no wonder, then, that elected officials of all political persuasions—from liberal Democrats to conservative Republicans—have criticized the overzealousness of the press.

Dictatorships do not permit Woodwards and Bernsteins to roam around government corridors in search of information about government wrong-doing. Graft, corruption, and abuse of power exist even when unreported, however. Without the constraints imposed by a free society—an independent legislature and a free press, for example—corruption is likely to get out of hand. Reports of corruption in dictatorships, such as Iran under the shah, Nicaragua under Anastasio Somoza, and Germany under Hitler, have been documented after the fact. It is wrong to believe that democracies have more corruption because they publicize their own evils.

Inefficiency. The notion that dictatorships are efficient is a myth. Supporters used to comment that at least Benito Mussolini made the trains run on time and Hitler got the economy moving again to point out the achievements of dictatorship. Dictatorships, however, are often inefficient. Hitler's political and economic system seemed to many to run like a well-oiled machine. In fact, however, the Nazi regime displayed tremendous inefficiency as government agencies overlapped in authority and competed against each other.[30] Hitler's minister of armaments and munitions, Albert Speer, claimed that Hitler was too frightened to call upon the German people to make the same kinds of sacrifices as those demanded by Franklin D. Roosevelt and Winston Churchill of the American and British people, respectively. As a result, Speer observed, the German war effort could not be mobilized to the greatest efficiency.[31]

The inefficiency of dictatorships is also inevitable because of the relationship between the dictator and subordinates. Dictators want their immediate subordinates to be good—but not too good—lest the dictators be no longer needed to save the nation. The dictator of a country must seem to be indispensable and so must purge associates who are achieving too much eminence. Subordinates, consequently, are reluctant to make decisions that the dictator may envy or may not like. There is a press toward decision making at the top. The mere volume of decisions that must be made forces incessant delays pending consideration by the dictator. Instead of delegating power, dictators concentrate it into their own hands and make government that is inefficient. Dictatorships, then, do not produce better government than democracies.

------

[30] See H. R. Trevor-Roper, *The Last Days of Hitler*, 3d ed. (New York: Collier Books, 1962), p. 64.

[31] Albert Speer, *Inside the Third Reich*, trans. Richard and Clara Winston (New York: Macmillan, 1970), p. 214.

9 / YES ARE DICTATORSHIPS BETTER ABLE TO DEAL WITH FOREIGN POLICY THAN ARE DEMOCRACIES?

Whatever may be said on behalf of democracy in a domestic political context, certainly there is no good case to be made for democracy in matters pertaining to the conduct of foreign policy and national security. The sanctity of the national interest in foreign policy, the requirements of war, and the need to maintain secrecy in a dangerous global setting all point to the weaknesses of democracy.

National Interest. The conduct of foreign policy requires the highest attention to the protection of the national interest. Now, as in earlier centuries, national security is the paramount feature of national interest and affects citizens of a state regardless of class, religion, or race. As such, political leaders must take whatever actions are essential to protect that security.

There are many possible goals for a nation to pursue in the conduct of foreign policy: economic, ideological, or military, for example. Only a political leader who does not have to suffer the political constraints imposed by democracy can act properly to serve the security interests of the state.

In the realm of foreign policy, political leaders have been hamstrung by popular legislatures and the popular press. Each of these institutions has injected popular sentiment into foreign policy deliberations and has forced policy makers to act in ways detrimental to the national interest. The passion to engage in modern "holy wars" is difficult to resist, for example. The "yellow press" encouraged wars of imperialism, moreover. American conduct in promoting the Spanish-American War of 1898 is a case study of popular interference in the conduct of foreign policy.

The present day provides more examples of national security harmed by other goals. From a security point of view, it can be argued that the United States should pursue closer relations with the Republic of South Africa. South Africa contains needed resources, a strategic location, and markets for American business. Yet the foreign policy of the United States toward South Africa is strained because of the role of black and liberal American groups

whose focus is on destroying South Africa's minority white rule and the practice of racial segregation.

We have no praise for the undemocratic and racist government of South Africa. Granted that South Africa acts in an immoral way and should be condemned, but the United States has no business being the guardian of liberty for the entire world. South Africa has been America's ally in three wars: World War I, World War II, and the Korean War. It has allowed American naval ships to refuel in its ports, and it has leased naval bases to the United States. However much we may detest its internal system, we must support South Africa. We have no guarantee that a new government created from the black majority, moreover, will be as supportive of American interests as is the present government. By putting pressure on American *elected* officials to undermine the government of South Africa, black groups are acting in ways detrimental to American security.

A similar charge could be made against American support for Israel. To be sure, the Jewish people suffered a cataclysmic fate as a result of Nazi brutality. About six million Jewish people—men, women, and children— were liquidated in Nazi extermination camps in the Holocaust. One may sympathize with the Jewish people but still oppose the creation of a Jewish state of Israel because of the security interests of the United States. Even when Israel was created, it was recognized that the creation of a Jewish state in an ocean of Arab states would be a disaster for stability in the Middle East. American Secretary of State Dean Acheson warned President Harry Truman of the dangers to American security. Truman acted quickly, however, to recognize and aid Israel, and U.S. security interests have suffered ever since. The most vital aspect of the Middle East as far as American security is concerned is oil. By supporting Israel, the United States jeopardizes the access of the West to Arab oil. This point was vividly brought home during the October War of 1973, in which Israel fought her Arab neighbors. The Arabs cut off the oil flow to the West, causing economic disarray. Although Western dependency on Arab oil has decreased, still Arab countries remain vital to America's security interests. Yet the United States cannot afford to alienate its American Jewish population because of the political effect on elected officials.

There is nothing unique about the Jewish influence in the conduct of American foreign policy. Catholic groups have influenced United States foreign policy toward Spain and toward the Soviet Union. Irish-Americans have also attempted to influence American policy toward Northern Ireland. In all of these cases, the effects of such democratic pressures—however high-minded they may seem—have been to harm the security interests of the United States for the benefit of other objectives often hostile to national security.

War. Statesmen who are trained for leadership are less susceptible to the passions of either war or peace. They are able to put events into proper perspective. Democracies, in contrast, require the firing up of people's minds and hearts if citizens are to go voluntarily to war. There is a need, consequently, to engage in propaganda and to make entire nations appear to possess inhumane characteristics. And so the Germans were referred to as Huns during World War I, for example, recalling the bellicose Germanic ancestors of modern Germany. Once such popular forces of agitation are released, it is difficult for statesmen to engage in moderation or to bring a war to its end. Commenting on how democratic war increases emotionalism in war compared to dynastic wars of earlier centuries, writer Hoffmann Nickerson notes, "It has been well said that the grenadiers of Maria Theresa did not have to be told that Frederick the Great was a Sodomite, or those of Frederick that Maria ate babies."[32]

Similarly in democracies, when the mood is for peace, it is difficult to get the country to prepare for war or to engage in military acts deemed vital to national security. Great Britain in the 1930s may be used as an example. Public opinion was hostile to rearma-

ment in spite of the rearmament of Germany under Adolf Hitler. The British government was weak in responding to Hitler's expansionist policies because of popular opposition to military measures. If British leaders could have acted without the democratic pressures, the country would have been better able to cope with the dangers to national security.

War, too, reveals yet another limitation of democracy. Because so many people have to be consulted—legislators, administrators, and opinion leaders—it is difficult to engage in war in defense of the national interest. Legislatures have constantly acted in a fashion detrimental to the purely military conduct of a war. As commanding general during the American Revolution, George Washington suffered from constant investigations by the Continental Congress. The congressional Committee on the Conduct of the War restricted Abraham Lincoln in a similar way in the Civil War.

Secrecy. One of the great weaknesses of democracy in foreign policy and national security policy has to do with the openness of democracy. Members of Congress reveal classified information harmful to the national security when that information serves their own interests, whether personal, political, or ideological. A free press embarrasses the government by disclosing in advance any secret military operations or "hush-hush" activities deemed vital to the national interest. All that an enemy of a democracy has to do is to read the daily newspaper, study published government debates, and question the participants, and he or she then can determine much about a democracy's foreign policy. The publication of the classified *Pentagon Papers* by *the New York Times* in 1971 is but one example of a democracy revealing its own secrets.

A dictatorship can keep secrets from a democratic adversary. Its agents can operate at home and abroad without fear that some journalist interested in winning a reporter's trophy will publish a list of names and addresses of intelligence agents. A dictator's secret police, moreover, have great discretionary powers in serving the national interest. Why should a democratic country put itself at such a disadvantage? As Soviet exile Alexsandr Solzhenitsyn indicated, democracies can be suicidal when it comes to protecting their legitimate foreign policy needs.

---

[32] Hoffmann Nickerson, *The Armed Horde, 1793–1939: A Study of the Rise, Survival and Decline of the Mass Army* (New York: G. P. Putnam's Sons, 1940), p. 12.

Alexis de Tocqueville, the great French observer of the American political scene, noted in his monumental *Democracy in America* (1835) the weaknesses of democracy in the conduct of foreign policy. His words are as true today as they were when the book was published:

A democracy finds it difficult to coordinate the details of a great undertaking and to fix on some plan and carry it through with determination in spite of obstacles. It has little capacity for combining measures in secret and waiting patiently for the result. Such qualities are more likely to belong to a single man or to an aristocracy. But these are just the qualities which, in the long run, make a nation, and a man, too, prevail.[33]

---

[33] Alexis de Tocqueville, *Democracy in America*, ed. J. P. Mayer and Max Lerner, trans. George Lawrence (New York: Harper and Row, 1966), p. 211.

9/NO   ARE DICTATORSHIPS BETTER ABLE TO DEAL WITH FOREIGN POLICY THAN ARE DEMOCRACIES?

Although we do not attribute to democracy any divine wisdom, we can appreciate democracy best by putting it in perspective. Democracy is not only good for domestic policy, but it serves foreign policy interests equally well.

National Interest. It is certainly true that democracies have suffered reverses in foreign policy. It is not true, however, that national security either must be or is more likely to be undermined in a democracy than in a dictatorship. First, it is not always true that dictators act in the security interests of their countries. They, too, are subject to ideological pressures and occasionally even to insanity. Communist China under the control of Mao Zedong pursued policies designed to isolate the People's Republic of China internationally. It seems clear in retrospect that Mao's policies were detrimental to the security interests of his country. When Pol Pot, the leader of the communist Khmer Rouge, came to power in Cambodia, he proceeded to butcher his own people, a horror that can be compared to the Nazi elimination of the Jews. As a result of this genocide, Cambodia left itself vulnerable to attack by another country, Vietnam.

Second, national security is a difficult concept to identify. It is often associated with the school of foreign policy known as *Realpolitik,* which focuses on power considerations as a guide to policy making. *Realpolitik,* or **realism** as it is also called, is often contrasted to **idealism,** which is concerned with other considerations, such as human rights, economic development, and welfare. Often, however, idealism is far more "realistic" about foreign policy than is realism. As World War II came to an end, for example, "realists" like Winston Churchill and Charles de Gaulle believed that Western imperialism could resume operations in Africa and Asia. It was the idealist Franklin D. Roosevelt who accurately foresaw the clamor for national self-determination in Africa and Asia and the consequent decline of Western colonialism. What is good for the security interests of a country, therefore, is best determined by the give-and-take of debate that characterizes a democratic society.

Third, there are other objectives besides security that nations may properly pursue. The goals of foreign policy are not necessarily contradictory to each other. It may be true, for example, that the security interests of a country may require it to ally itself with a dictatorship. The domestic pressures of the democracy toward liberalization of the dictatorship may work to the betterment of both the security interests of the democracy and the increasing popular support of the dictatorship. Let us examine the case of Iran as an example. Iran, under the leadership of the shah, was a dictatorship complete with secret police and persecution of a free press. The shah did little to broaden the base of support but relied instead on the police, the army, and a thin segment of Iranian society. Once faced with a rising opposition, he lacked strong and wide support. The shah's government, which had been so friendly to the United States, was toppled and replaced by a government more neutralist in its foreign policy. American power, consequently, suffered a loss of influence in the Persian Gulf.

In commenting on the affair a year after the

fall of the shah, former Secretary of State Henry Kissinger told a group of reporters that if the United States had to do it over again, it should have put pressure on the shah to broaden his base of support. Had the political pressures in the United States been strong enough to compel the administration to apply its influence on the Iranian government, the shah might possibly have retained power, and the position of the United States in world affairs would have been stronger. There is an analogy today with South Africa. It is only a matter of time before white rule is toppled. The United States should get behind the forces of change now so that when a black government is in power in South Africa, it will be friendly toward the United States.

We should keep in mind the success of the United States in rallying around Corizon Aquino in toppling Ferdinand Marcos as leader of the Philippines in 1986. By backing Aquino the United States was able to win the support of a popular and democratic government rather than suffer the opprobrium of propping up a corrupt and unpopular leader. A stable and democratic Philippines, consequently, serves the security interests of the United States.

War and Secrecy. If foreign policy, in general, can benefit from democracy, the same can be said about the conduct of war. People who live in democracies have been willing to temporarily give up certain freedoms during periods of war. Many Western democracies in World War I and World War II, for example, engaged in practices ranging from suspending elections to censoring the press. Once the wars were over, however, it was business as usual for the democracies.

Democracy, moreover, has much to contribute in the conduct of a war. War requires the cooperation of the people who fight them, so that if there is no means by which popular sentiment can be expressed, then the prospects for victory may be dimmed. The tactics of British and French generals in World War I called for massive frontal assaults against superior enemy firepower, for example, and resulted in the loss of millions of lives. It was duly elected political figures, such as David Lloyd George and Winston Churchill in Great Britain and Georges Clemenceau in France, who forced the professional military leaders— the experts—to rethink the tactics they had

adopted. Similarly, it was duly elected political leaders who complained that the United States could not win the Vietnam War it fought in the 1960s and 1970s. Had there not been an outlet to voice disapproval with the war, even more casualties would have been experienced by both Vietnam and the United States.

One other example of democratic rule in matters pertaining to war concerns weapons systems. We often think, incorrectly as it turns out, that dictatorships make good decisions about armaments since they can more readily cut through red tape. Closer examination of dictatorial conduct of war, however, reveals top-heavy development and bungled decision making. Adolf Hitler, for example, shunned development of jet aircraft and delayed production of ballistic missiles, both of which appeared too late in the war to serve the Nazi cause.

The democratic United States established a good record in developing new weapons, as the case of the atomic bomb illustrates. When scientists told Franklin D. Roosevelt about the possibility of building the atomic bomb, Roosevelt was receptive to the idea. It has been argued that had Roosevelt not supported the development of this new super-weapon, no doubt the scientists would have tried to convince Congress and the press. In a dictatorship, there would have been little recourse to such independent sources of decision making. A comparison of the two systems shows that democracy possesses strengths in weapons procurement, an area vital for national security.

The record of dictators in the conduct of war, moreover, is not as good as the record of democratic leaders. Hitler's decision to move heavily into the Soviet Union and his orders for German troops not to withdraw led to a destruction of Germany's Sixth Army at Stalingrad. The case of Joseph Stalin as a war leader is equally instructive. Soviet leader Nikita Khrushchev revealed (although long after Stalin had died) that Stalin was responsible for great military disasters in World War II, which he attributed to "Stalin's annihilation of many military commanders in the years 1937– 41."[34] Clearly, the war record of dictatorships

―――――――
[34] Robert Conquest, "De-Stalinization and the Heritage of Terror," in *Politics in the Soviet Union:*

is marked by bad decisions. To be sure, democracies, too, make errors, but there is no case to be made for the overwhelming superiority of dictatorships in the conduct of war.

The record of U.S. foreign policy in the decades since the end of World War II suggest that de Tocqueville was wrong about the qualities of democracy in the conduct of foreign policy. As political analyst Josef Joffe observes:

In the decades of the postwar era the United States not only executed a "vast design" by singlehandedly erecting a new order on the ashes of the old; it also "persevered" in spite of serious obstacles, to use Tocqueville's terminology.

Joffe cites the accomplishments by the United States during this period: the building of a global trading system, a global monetary system, an interlocking security system, and initially, at least, a global institution (the United Nations) dominated by the United States. Joffe adds that the United States did not lack the "patience" of a long-term policy. A tough con-

tainment policy of the United States toward the Soviet Union lasted for at least a quarter century.[35]

It is possible, then, to conclude that it was not de Tocqueville, but another foreign observer of the American scene—James Bryce—who accurately described the role of democracy in the conduct of foreign policy. He wrote in his *Modern Democracies* (1921):

In a democracy the People are entitled to determine the Ends or general aims of foreign policy.

History shows that they do this at least as wisely as monarchs or oligarchies, or the small groups to whom, in democratic countries, the conduct of foreign relations has been left, and that they have evinced more respect for moral principles. . . .

Whatever faults modern democracies may have committed in this field of administration [foreign policy], the faults chargeable on monarchs and oligarchies have been less pardonable and more harmful to the peace and progress of mankind.[36]

---

[35] Josef Joffe, "Tocqueville Revisited: Are Good Democracies Bad Players in the Game of Nations?" *Washington Quarterly* 11 (Winter 1988): 164.

[36] James Bryce, *Modern Democracies* (New York: Macmillan, 1921), 2:283.

---

7 *Cases*, ed. Alexander Dallin and Alan F. Westin (New York: Harcourt, Brace and World, 1966), p. 48.

KEY TERMS

Absolutism
Affirmative action
Aristocracy
Authoritarian government
Autocracy
Consociational democracy
Constitutionalism
Crisis government
Cross-pressures
Decentralization
Demagogues
Democracy
Democratic capitalism
Despotism
Dictatorship
Direct democracy
Economic democracy
Elite
Filibuster
Idealism
Indirect democracy

Initiative
Judicial review
Kibbutz
Liberal democracy
Malapportionment
Monarchy
New England town meeting
Oligarchy
Participatory democracy
Pluralism
Political equality
Polyarchy
Realism
Realpolitik
Referendum
Representative democracy
Repressive tolerance
Totalitarian government
Tyranny
Welfare state

QUESTIONS

1. Is student participatory democracy possible in a college? What might be the strengths and weaknesses of such an approach?
2. What effect would the denial of constitutional freedoms in representative democracy have on economic democracy?
3. If there is an elite that rules in representative democracies, what influence do the masses have on it?
4. What role should experts play in public policy matters in democracies?
5. What are the strengths and weaknesses of dictatorship?
6. Why do dictatorships perish?
7. Why do democracies perish?
8. Do civil liberties strengthen or weaken a democracy? Why?
9. Is the distinction between authoritarianism and totalitarianism meaningful? Why?
10. What are the strengths and weaknesses of democracies in their conduct of foreign policy?
11. What are the consequences to democracy of greater popular participation in political affairs?

RECOMMENDED READINGS

ARBLASTER, ANTHONY. *Democracy*. Milton Keynes, England: Open University Press, 1987. A brief introduction to the subject.

ARENDT, HANNAH. *The Origins of Totalitarianism*. New ed. New York: Harcourt, Brace and World, 1966. A philosophical treatment of totalitarianism.

BACHRACH, PETER. *The Theory of Democratic Elitism: A Critique*. Boston: Little, Brown, 1967. An argument asserting the view that many twentieth-century social scientists who study democracy ignore the necessity of greater political participation by the masses of people.

BARBER, BENJAMIN R. *Strong Democracy: Participatory Democracy for a New Age*. Berkeley: University of California Press, 1984. A democrat's criticism of liberal democracy.

CLINTON, DAVID. "Tocqueville's Challenge." *Washington Quarterly* 11 (Winter 1988): 173–89. An assessment of democracy in the conduct of U.S. foreign policy.

CURTIS, MICHAEL. *Totalitarianism*. New Brunswick, N.J.: Transaction Books, 1979. A brief analysis of totalitarianism.

DAHL, ROBERT A. *Dilemmas of Pluralist Democracy: Autonomy vs. Control*. New Haven: Yale University Press, 1982. An argument that organizations should possess some autonomy, and at the same time they should be controlled.

———. *A Preface to Democratic Theory*. Chicago: University of Chicago Press, 1956. An analysis of polyarchy as a modern form of representative democracy.

———. *A Preface to Economic Democracy*. Berkeley: University of California Press, 1985. An examination of the relationship between political democracy and economic democracy.

FINLEY, M. I. *Democracy Ancient and Modern*. New Brunswick, N.J.: Rutgers University Press, 1973. An examination of democratic Athens and the relevance of Athenian democracy to the contemporary world.

FRIEDRICH, CARL J., and ZBIGNIEW K. BRZEZINSKI. *Totalitarian Dictatorship and Autocracy*. 2d ed. rev. by Carl J. Friedrich. New York: Praeger, 1965. A landmark book on totalitarianism.

GLAZER, NATHAN. "Nazis and Soviets." *New Republic* 193 (July 8, 1985): 15–16. A discussion of the relevance of totalitarianism as an analytical concept.

GRAHAM, KEITH. *The Battle of Democracy: Conflict, Consensus and the Individual*. Totowa, N.J.: Barnes and Noble Books, 1986. An analysis of democratic theory.

GREGOR, A. JAMES. *The Ideology of Fascism: The Rationale of Totalitarianism*. New York: Free Press, 1969. A philosophical assessment of fascism.

JOFFE, JOSEF. "Tocqueville Revisited: Are Good Democracies Bad Players in the Game of Nations?" *Washington Quarterly* 11 (Winter 1988): 161–72. An assessment of the strengths and weaknesses of the United States as a democratic country in the conduct of foreign policy.

KORNHAUSER, WILLIAM. *The Politics of Mass Society.* New York: Free Press, 1959. A case favoring the existence of independent elites and groups as a prerequisite for democracy.

KRAUTHAMMER, CHARLES. "Divided Superpower." *New Republic* 195 (December 22, 1986): 14, 16–17. An assessment of the conflict between the status of the United States as a superpower and the preservation of democratic institutions.

———. "The Price of Power." *New Republic* 196 (February 9, 1987): 23–25. An assertion that there is a conflict between democracy and foreign policy.

LAQUEUR, WALTER. "Is There Now, or Has There Ever Been, Such a Thing as Totalitarianism?" *Commentary* 80 (October 1985): 31–39. A survey of the research on totalitarianism. See also "Letters from Readers: Totalitarianism." *Commentary* 81 (February 1986): 2, 4–6.

LIPSET, SEYMOUR MARTIN. "The Expansion of Democracy" [Speech delivered on July 24, 1987]. *Vital Speeches of the Day* 53 (October 1, 1987): 748–51. An assessment of the future of democracy.

LIVELY, JACK. *Democracy.* New York: St. Martin's Press, 1975. An evaluation of analytical and empirical theories of democracy.

MENZE, ERNEST A., ed. *Totalitarianism Reconsidered.* Port Washington, N.Y.: Kennikat Press, 1981. Differing perspectives on totalitarianism.

MILBRATH, LESTER W., and M. I. GOEL. *Political Participation: How and Why Do People Get Involved in Politics?* 2d ed. Chicago: Rand McNally, 1977. A major work synthesizing many studies on political participation.

PATEMAN, CAROLE. *Participation and Democratic Theory.* Cambridge, England: Cambridge University Press, 1970. A critique of contemporary theories of democracy.

PENNOCK, J. ROLAND. *Democratic Political Theory.* Princeton, N.J.: Princeton, N.J.: Princeton University Press, 1979. An evaluation of democratic theory.

REVEL, JEAN-FRANCOIS, with BRANKO LAZITCH. *How Democracies Perish*, trans. William Byron. Garden City, N.Y.: Doubleday, 1984. An argument that Western democracies are vulnerable to totalitarian manipulation.

RUBIN, BARRY. *Modern Dictators: Third World Coup Makers, Strongmen, and Populist Tyrants.* New York: McGraw-Hill, 1987. An explanation of why dictatorships have formed in the Third World.

SARTORI, GIOVANNI. *The Theory of Democracy Revisited.* Vol. 1: *The Contemporary Debate;* Vol. 2: *The Classical Issues.* Chatham, N.J.: Chatham House, 1987. A major work in democratic theory.

SCHATTSCHNEIDER, E. E. *The Semisovereign People: A Realist's View of Democracy in America.* New York: Holt, Reinhart & Winston, 1960. Reprint. Hinsdale, Ill.: Dryden Press, 1975. A critique of modern empirical theories of democracy and a call for greater participation in the American political system.

SCHUMPETER, JOSEPH A. *Capitalism, Socialism, and Democracy.* 3d ed. New York: Harper and Brothers, 1950. Part IV contains a critique of the classical theory of democracy.

TULLOCK, GORDON. *Autocracy.* Dordrecht, The Netherlands: Kluwer Academic Publishers, 1987. An inquiry into the nature of dictatorships.

WALKER, JACK L. "A Critique of the Elitist Theory of Democracy." *American Political Science Review* 60 (June 1966): 285–95. A description of how democracy works.

WIESELTIER, LEON. "Democracy and Colonel North." *New Republic* 196 (January 26, 1987): 22–25. A case for the relevance of democracy in the conduct of foreign policy.

See also Recommended Readings in Chapters 4 and 5.

IDEOLOGY

In political life ideas play important roles. When during World War II, for example, Germany experienced reverses on the battlefield, Adolf Hitler continued to divert enormous resources from military purposes toward the implementation of Nazi policy to liquidate the Jews. The appeal of liberal values to some Western intellectuals, moreover, led them to urge America into the war against Germany in 1939 and 1940 when only Europe was ablaze in war.

The political ideas that influence people and events are diverse and are used to justify acts of liberty and slavery, free enterprise and socialism, war and peace, and strong government and weak government. When these ideas are put into a coherent structure to describe, explain, predict, and justify political behavior, they are known as **political ideology.**

Ideology is more than a collection of political beliefs, which are unsystematic preferences individuals hold about poli-

tics. Ideology, rather, is an entire system of ideas that is designed to guide behavior. Often, consequently, ideology is a pattern of ideas that some individuals hold as a matter of fundamental conviction.

Political ideologies serve different purposes in a political system. They are sometimes used to legitimize the system of political rule. In every modern political system a few people rule the many. When the masses of people accept the way the rulers come to power and exercise their power, then the government is said to be a **legitimate government.** Governments find great difficulty in sustaining their rule only by force, so they must rely on popular support to be effective. An ideology that shows wide popular support for the basis of rule, consequently, allows for government to act effectively.

Another purpose of ideology in a political system is to legitimize the interests of various groups in the society. Individuals who benefit from weak government, for example, sometimes promote an ideology like classical liberalism, which justifies weak government (see Chapter 4). Individuals who benefit from strong government, in contrast, sometimes favor socialism or communism (see Chapter 5). Not all who espouse an ideology, however, do so for their own immediate economic benefit.

Another function of ideology is to undermine the legitimacy of a political system. In the age of imperialism, for example, the ideology of nationalism undermined colonial rule (see Chapter 2). When V. I. Lenin became leader of the Soviet Union, moreover, he established an international communist organization, the Comintern, and asserted that henceforth communists throughout the world had a legitimate right to overthrow noncommunist regimes (see Chapter 5).

Ideology is important in a political system because of its influence on public policy through laws and executive actions. Ideological concerns have much to do with the stability of political systems and the relationship between individuals and the state.

Part III examines a few of the most influential ideologies of the past two centuries: liberalism, conservatism, fascism, capitalism, socialism, and communism. They are by no means the only important ideologies, but they do reveal some of the more vital political ideas of our times and suggest some important contemporary issues.

chapter 4

Liberalism, conservatism, and fascism

The ideologies of liberalism, conservatism, and fascism have been among the most powerful political ideologies guiding the conduct and beliefs of statesmen, political philosophers, and ordinary citizens. Although liberalism and conservatism owe more to the eighteenth and nineteenth centuries and fascism more to the twentieth century, they are discussed together here because of the contrasts they show and the issues they raise.

LIBERALISM

The terms *liberal* and *liberalism* are labels used in describing not only political but other matters as well. In politics, **liberalism** today connotes certain values, such as a commitment to individual freedom, an opposition to militarism, and a support of the welfare state. *Liberal*, however, is also used as a synonym for "generous," as in the portions of food offered at a

restaurant; for "reformist," as in reforming church hierarchy by including women in the clergy; or for "experimental," as in trying new forms of educational techniques.

Any understanding of liberalism requires a knowledge of its origins. In this regard, liberalism is a political philosophy that originated in the latter part of the seventeenth century and remains strong today, although its tenets have been somewhat modified. In the seventeenth century, however, it presented a challenge to the rule of government based on the theory of the **divine right of kings**—the belief that the monarch exercises authority by gift from God. Liberals sought to limit the power of the state and to maximize the rights of the individual against arbitrary rule.

The seventeenth-century English writer John Locke was the foremost early exponent of the liberal ideal. Positing a **social contract,** in which government is created with the consent of the governed as a means of combining individual freedom with the benefits of social cooperation, Locke established the foundation of liberalism. In Locke's view, individuals in a state of nature lived harmoniously but voluntarily chose to establish a government. Other social contract theorists such as Thomas Hobbes and Jean-Jacques Rousseau differed with Locke's view about the character of the society and the nature of the social contract. But Locke's social contract is most clearly associated with liberalism and influenced government not only in England but also in the United States, France, and other countries.

The views that Locke and later exponents of liberalism put forth between the seventeenth and nineteenth centuries are often referred to as **classical liberalism,** as distinguished from its later, twentieth-century version. As a doctrine and political program, classical liberalism developed most fully in England in the period between the Glorious Revolution of 1688 and the Reform Act of 1867. Although there were many differences among classical liberals, the central tenets of classical liberalism are: the preservation of individual liberty is the primary concern of any polity; human beings by nature are good; reason will solve problems; progress can be expected; equality of opportunity is desirable; people are the same everywhere; government is a dangerous but necessary evil; and the free market economy will produce the best social order.

Individual Liberty

Liberalism has always regarded individual liberty—whether in politics, economics, or religion—to be the primary concern of any polity. Institutions that might endanger that liberty—government, churches, and the army—must be restrained. John Stuart Mill, one of the leading nineteenth-century liberals, emphasized individual liberty in his writing. Modern liberals often look to the writings of Mill for insights in the defense of liberty.

Human Nature

To liberals, human beings are by nature good. Locke depicted men in the state of nature as essentially free and decent. They choose government, according to Locke, to take care of basic minimal needs that each could not deal with alone—in other words, as a convenience—but the basic character of human beings remains constantly good.

Reason

Liberals understand that there remains much conflict in the world. War, terrorism, and crime exist, but liberals attribute the causes to ignorance, bad social conditions, and superstition. Professor J. Salwyn Schapiro puts it succinctly, "Man, according to liberalism, is born ignorant, not wicked."[1] Liberals believe that if people use reason they will be able to solve most problems. They contend that institutions that demand obedience to authority because of reverence for tradition, revelation, or faith—rather than reliance on reason—are, consequently, threats to social progress.

Specifically in this connection, wars come about because of the misunderstanding that results from the inadequate use of reason, and liberals try to maximize the channels of communication to avoid that misunderstanding. Crime happens not because people are bad, but rather because of miserable social conditions. Crime will be eliminated when people prosper

---

[1] J. Salwyn Schapiro, *Liberalism: Its Meaning and History* (Princeton, N.J.: D. Van Nostrand, 1958), p. 12.

and achieve a stake in society, according to liberal premises.

Progress

Liberals have an optimistic belief in progress. They argue that by expanding knowledge and perfecting reason, and by improving economic conditions, mankind will advance. People ought to turn away from superstition based on religious doctrine or rote patriotism. Eliminate the old attitudes and replace them with the new, and progress will ensue, the liberals say.

Equality

Classical liberals believe in equality of opportunity. In the nineteenth century the belief in equality did not extend to universal suffrage. Liberals contended that democracy was dangerous and, consequently, favored property restrictions on voting. Classical liberals argue, however, that conditions promoting equality of opportunity should be encouraged.

Universalism

Classical liberals believe that liberal values are relevant everywhere in the world. They talk about "the rights of man" or "human rights" rather than the rights of Englishmen or Frenchmen. These rights are universal, and liberals should support them everywhere in the world.

Government

Liberalism was founded on the premise that the protection of the individual against arbitrary government restriction is paramount. Thomas Paine, a pamphleteer of the American Revolution, expressed in his *Common Sense* the liberal hostility toward government: "Society in every state is a blessing, but government,

even in its best state, is but a necessary evil."[2]

Economic Freedom

Classical liberals support *laissez-faire* (see Chapter 5). In the seventeenth century, they were reacting against the privileges of mercantilism with its monopolies granted to strengthen the state. Classical liberals believe that economic freedom and political freedom are both essential in any free society.

Contemporary liberals continue to accept the principal tenets of classical liberalism on most matters other than economics. The basic political philosophy supporting individual liberty remains the same, but the means to achieve that liberty in the economic sector has changed.

Contemporary liberals accept the necessity of the powerful state to regulate business and to establish the welfare state. In this context, they have adapted to changed economic and social conditions. As the character of capitalism has been transformed, with large corporations undermining the small competitive companies of the early nineteenth century, so, too, has liberal philosophy changed. Now liberals support the state to maintain competition in the face of monopoly and to ensure that consumers are not harmed by unfettered capitalism.

Contemporary liberals, moreover, favor the growth of social programs to eliminate the evils produced by a complex industrial society. Now liberals believe that there are *government* solutions to social problems. If people are ill housed, liberals contend that government should provide housing. If people cannot find jobs, then government should employ them. If peo-

---

[2] Thomas Paine, *The Political Works of Thomas Paine* (New York: Worthington, n.d.), p. 7. *Common Sense* was first published in 1776.

ple are ignorant, then public schools should educate them. Government can solve these and other problems, such as crime, the urban crisis, inadequate health care, and malnutrition. As Professor Charles Frankel notes, "To put it starkly, but I think exactly, liberalism invented the idea that there are such things as 'social problems.' "[3] Whether or not contemporary liberals invented social problems, they continue to believe that with the proper application of reason and money, social problems can be solved. This emphasis on government solutions to problems, however, distinguishes contemporary liberals from their classical forebears.

CONSERVATISM

If *liberalism* lends itself to a variety of meanings, so, too, does *conservatism.* A liberal might define a conservative as "someone who believes nothing should ever be done for the first time."[4] Conservatives could correctly note, however, that they have often initiated policies. It was the British conservative Benjamin Disraeli who extended the vote to large segments of the British working class in 1867, and the American conservative Richard Nixon who led the United States in improving relations with the People's Republic of China.

Conservative has been used to mean "reactionary," "cautious," "gradualist," "moderate," and "slow." As a political philosophy, conservatism originated in the latter part of the eighteenth century, although its roots go back to Plato in an-

cient Greece. The British philosopher and politician Edmund Burke is unquestionably the founder of conservatism, although he never used the term. Much of his and early conservatism was a response to the French Revolution. Writing in *Reflections on the Revolution in France* (1790), Burke expressed horror about the premises underlying that revolution. He predicted accurately the political instability and dictatorship that were to arise out of the more moderate phase of the revolution.

The classical conservatism of Burke and others included a variety of beliefs. It was impossible in Burke's time, as it is today, to define precisely the conservative philosophy or program. It is best to look at **conservatism** as a set of general principles. In essence, these conservative principles include: order and stability must be maintained; human beings are by nature wicked; it is essential to rely on experience rather than reason; gradual change is desirable; liberty is more important than equality; diversity rather than universalism should be promoted; and government is a necessary institution.

Order and Stability

Conservatives believe that without order and stability there can be no liberty or civilization. Order and stability are maintained to the extent that authority is respected. Traditional authority based on religion, birth, and patriotism, consequently, must be protected. Those who undermine authority endanger the well-being of civilization.

Wickedness of Man

Unlike the liberals who believe that human beings are by nature good, conservatives derive their philosophy from a different analysis of the human condition. Some conservatives attribute human wickedness to Original Sin, although other

---

[3] Charles Frankel, *The Case for Modern Man* (New York: Harper and Brothers, 1956), p. 33.

[4] As disparagingly cited by Robert Schuettinger in his anthology, *The Conservative Tradition in European Thought* (New York: G. P. Putnam's Sons, 1970), p. 11.

conservatives do not rely on a religious formulation. Many find admirable the writings of Thomas Hobbes, the seventeenth-century English writer who portrayed a society without government as chaotic and bestial. Unless restraints are imposed on human beings through laws and religious practices, conservatives argue, the evil nature of human beings will express itself through war, conquest, violence, and rapacity.

Experience

Conservatives prefer to rely on experience over reason. This does not mean that conservatives are irrational. Rather, they prefer to use reason to counter a belief that reason can solve all problems. Conservatives are intellectually and temperamentally opposed to any grandiose scheme, such as a blueprint for revolutionary change, since they are pessimistic about the perfectability of man. They are skeptical about the usefulness of social programs to quickly change the character of society.

Gradual Change

Those conservatives who are against all changes involving new ideas and programs are correctly labeled **reactionaries.** Most conservatives, however, do not want to return to some golden age. They favor moderate changes and the formation of policy based on the observation of how well these moderate changes work out. Edmund Burke, for example, supported the American colonists against Great Britain in their quest for securing the "rights of Englishmen" in the New World. He saw in the American Revolution an acceptance of free institutions that he could cherish—unlike the French Revolution, which challenged all established institutions.

Liberty

Conservatives are opposed to equality, viewing it as a danger to liberty. Traditionally, they have supported government based on nobility of birth. Initially, they opposed the capitalists who sought power on the basis of wealth. They also resisted the egalitarianism implicit in democracy, perceiving democracy to be a danger to the established order.

Diversity

Conservatives revere diversity rather than uniformity. The same laws that worked well in England could not be transported to every other country, according to them. Separate development of different nations and different races is desirable because the experience of different peoples is never the same.

Government

Traditionally, conservatives were not hostile to government. Conservatives received privileges from government and sought to retain those privileges. They opposed the liberal critics who wanted to deny them these privileges. Besides, government was essential to maintain order and stability, according to the conservative view.

In the twentieth century conservatism has changed. The traditional principles of conservatism—its beliefs in order and stability, wickedness of man, experience, gradualism, liberty, and diversity—remain. Contemporary conservatives, however, are more like classical liberals in their economic ideas than like traditional conservatives. Modern conservatives tend to reject or be skeptical about the welfare state and government management of the economy.

The fact that modern conservatives support at least a respect for free enterprise is one essential modification of conservatism. Another change is the growth since the late 1960s of a philosophy called **neoconservatism** or **New Conservatism.** Neoconservatism is an American political philosophy that maintains the temperament of conservatism, supports the existence of capitalism and a mixed economy, and is critical of some elements of the welfare state.

The major figures of neoconservatism are former liberals who have modified but not rejected all the tenets of liberalism. They are, consequently, critical of programs that they perceive as harmful to the groups they are intended to benefit. Some neoconservatives argue, for example, that many welfare programs encourage people not to work; that attempts to promote racial and sexual equality in the professions through affirmative action programs are wrong; and that busing to promote racial integration actually encourages segregation. Among the leaders of this school of thought are Irving Kristol, Nathan Glazer, and Jeane J. Kirkpatrick.

Perhaps in response to the emergence of neoconservatism, a new movement— neoliberalism—has appeared in America in the 1980s. **Neoliberalism** is a political philosophy that accepts modern liberal values, such as a belief in civil liberties, civil rights, and equality of opportunity. It attempts to provide what it considers to be a more pragmatic or realistic approach to current issues than that offered by most liberals since the New Deal programs of President Franklin D. Roosevelt. In this regard neoliberals assert that they are concerned with economic growth more than with redistribution of income; that they favor over national planning and regulation an industrial policy in which government, business, and labor cooperate closely; and that they support a stronger national defense rather than a weaker one. Charles Peters, the editor of *Washington Monthly,* is perhaps the fore-

most neoliberal. It was he who coined the term *neoliberalism.*[5]

Liberalism and conservatism, then, are best described today in terms of disposition rather than in terms of a fixed ideology or program. It is often the case that a particular person accepts part, but not all, of the agenda of an ideology— whether it be liberal or conservative. A person may hold liberal views on economic issues and conservative views on social issues, for example. In the past few decades American liberalism and conservatism have included both economic and social dimensions. Such a development has created major strategic problems for both the Democratic and Republican parties.

Although differing in temperament, both liberals and conservatives in the twentieth century share a commitment to constitutional government. Both liberals and conservatives, moreover, accept political democracy in stark contrast to the advocates of the political philosophy of fascism.

FASCISM

Like *communism,* the words *fascism* and *fascist* have been used in imprecise ways to describe many kinds of behavior. In the past two decades, for example, the term *fascist* has been used to refer to a geneticist engaged in scientific research relating race to I.Q. scores, American intervention in the Vietnam War, and even to anyone who voted for Ronald Reagan in the presidential elections of 1980 and 1984. In this century, moreover, *fascism* has been applied to capitalists, socialists, soldiers, the police, churches, and even to the Boy Scouts.

---

[5] For a description of neoliberalism, see Randall Rothenberg, *The Neoliberals: Creating the New American Politics* (New York: Simon and Schuster, 1984).

A term with such varied uses can have no analytical utility. To get at a better understanding of the meaning of *fascism*, it is essential to look at the historical roots of this ideology. Fascism as an ideology is a twentieth-century phenomenon. It originated in Italy with the *fasci d'azione rivoluzionaria* of 1914–15 and the *fasci di combattimento* of 1919. The early *fasci* (or political groups organized for limited purposes) were formed in World War I to end Italian neutrality and make Italy join the war. Although he had practically nothing to do with setting the goals of these organizations, Benito Mussolini, whose intellectual heritage was socialist, became the dominant figure in Italian fascism. *Fascism* appeared in popular usage in 1919 with the emergence of Mussolini as a major political figure.

The term *fascism* is derived from the Latin word *fasces,* which means "bundle." In ancient Rome a bundle of rods bound around an ax was the symbol of authority.

Although Italy was a pioneer of fascism, other regimes became associated with this ideology. Spain under Francisco Franco and Portugal under Antonio Salazar are two notable examples. In more recent times the military regime of General Augusto Pinochet in Chile is regarded by some as fascist. Many people have described the political system of **National Socialism** (or **nazism**) under Adolf Hitler in Germany as a prime example of fascism, but some scholars see significant differences between Mussolini's fascism and Hitler's nazism. To be sure, all of these regimes are correctly identified as dictatorships, but there are so many differences among them that scholars cannot agree on a universal definition.[6]

---

[6] See Renzo de Felice, *Fascism: An Informal Introduction to Its Theory and Practice,* an interview with Michael A. Ledeen (New Brunswick, N.J.: Transaction Books, 1976), pp. 72, 89; Noël O'Sullivan, *Fascism* (London: J. M. Dent and Sons, 1983), pp. 4-5.

In spite of the different kinds of regimes that are regarded as fascist, we may distinguish some of the most salient features of **fascism** found in most systems so classified. These are: supremacy of the state over the individual, intense nationalism, antiliberal democracy, militarism and terrorism, rule by a dictator, and anticommunism.

State

A central feature of fascism is a belief in the state as more important than the individual. Fascism, consequently, is a political ideology that is antiliberal in its most fundamental tenet. Liberals believe that the function of the state is to serve the interests of individuals. For fascists, individuals must serve the state.

The state, consequently, is totalitarian (see Chapter 3). It plays a role in every aspect of society. Its economy is centrally directed. In Italy—in theory if not in practice—the central direction of the economy was expressed by Mussolini's concept of the **corporate state,** in which business and labor would work in cooperation with the supreme state acting as arbiter. Such a notion was in sharp contrast to the view of Marxists, with their emphasis on class struggle. Under fascism class cooperation under state dominance is the primary theme. The state, too, purports to control other institutions of society, such as schools, libraries, and social organizations. Leaders of these organizations accept the views of the dictator.

Nationalism

In contrast to socialism in which class solidarity is supposed to transcend national barriers, fascism reveres nationalism. The nation is sometimes equated with a people or a race. All nation-states encourage and promote patriotic respect for national symbols, such as the flag, independence day, and the national anthem.

Fascism, however, requires more than the mere patriotism that every nation promotes, for fascists make intense demands on people to support national symbols above everything else.

Antiliberalism

Fascism is antiliberal not only in its conception of the state but also in its criticism of institutions such as parliamentary government and civil liberties. Fascists reject the notion of constitutionalism with its constraints on power. They regard opposition parties as unnecessary and indeed dangerous to the strength of the all-embracing state. Fascist states are one-party states with no opposition tolerated. Individuals are denied the basic liberal freedoms of religion, speech, assembly, and the press.

Militarism and Terror

Fascism reveres strength both in foreign policy and on the domestic front. Mussolini's invasion of Ethiopia in 1935 was the beginning of Italian fascist militarism. As Mussolini put it, "The program of Fascist foreign policy can be given in one word: expansionism."[7] Hitler's rearmament efforts in violation of the Versailles Treaty restrictions were another reflection of militarism and expansionism.

In fascist Italy and Germany, symbols of terrorism created fear at home. Opposition political leaders were arrested, and some were assassinated. Meetings of dissidents were broken up, and the independent news media were suppressed. Secret police were charged with the responsibility of maintaining fascist supremacy.

---

[7] As quoted in A. James Gregor, *The Ideology of Fascism: The Rationale of Totalitarianism* (New York: Free Press, 1969), p. 162.

Dictator

Fascism requires a supreme leader (in Italy, *Il Duce*), who imposes his imprint on the political system. Sometimes the leader is seen as head of the fascist political party and sometimes he is superior to it. In Nazi Germany, for example, soldiers had to take a personal oath to Adolf Hitler (the *Führer*, or leader) rather than to a constitutional government, as is the case in a liberal democracy. The fascist dictator's role is celebrated in paintings, photographs, and sculptures prominently displayed throughout the country. The dictator in a fascist regime is depicted as endowed with creative genius and is said to be always correct and capable of miraculous feats of leadership and heroism.

Anticommunism

Fascism historically has been anticommunist. Although Mussolini began his life as a socialist, he had rejected socialism by 1914. He and Hitler were strongly anticommunist, although such a belief does not, in fact, mean that communism and fascism have no similarities. For many supporters of Hitler and Mussolini, however, fascism was seen as a worthy opponent of communism (and of democratic socialism, too). Fascism is often portrayed in Marxist sources, consequently, as nothing more than a counterrevolutionary ideology designed to keep entrenched bourgeois forces in power. Many scholars, however, question this evaluation of fascism. They contend, in contrast, that fascism and communism spring from similar historical sources and are kindred totalitarian systems.

While the six components of fascism are generally found in most fascist systems, German fascism, or National Socialism, had an additional feature of *racism* that distinguished it from other fascist systems. Early in his career Hitler became an ardent anti-Semite. In his book, *Mein Kampf* (My Struggle), written in 1924, he argued that the Nordic Aryan race was the superior race because of its culture-giving qualities. He advocated a policy of racial supremacy of the Aryans over all other races, or civilization would end. The German nation was the highest expression of Aryanism, he contended. He attacked the Jews as being responsible for the evils that had befallen the world. He called for persecution of the Slavs and their domination by Germans. He maintained that German blood must remain pure, "uncontaminated" by "inferior" races.

Unlike Hitler, Mussolini was not at first a racist. When he used the term *race* he generally meant it as a synonym for "people" or "nation" rather than in a biological sense. It was not until the late 1930s,

when Italy moved closer to allying with Nazi Germany, that Mussolini began supporting anti-Semitic causes. Under the Nazis, Jews were denied citizenship rights. Books written by Jewish authors were burned. Eventually, Jews in Germany and in German-occupied countries had their property confiscated. The extermination camp and the gas chamber ultimately liquidated six million Jewish people for the offense of being Jewish.

Racism, then, may be viewed as a component of fascism, if nazism is regarded as the prototype of fascism. As a consequence, critics of the South African system of **apartheid** (or separateness), in which strict racial separation laws have been enforced by the white minority over the black majority, often describe South Africa as fascist.

ISSUES

The following issues consider ideologies in different ways. The first debate deals with moral concerns in foreign policy. Many, if not most, conservatives would argue that the United States should avoid making human rights an objective of foreign policy. Many, if not most, liberals would challenge that view. The second debate concerns the character of American society by considering whether America could properly be labeled fascist.

10/YES   SHOULD THE UNITED STATES AVOID MAKING HUMAN RIGHTS AN OBJECTIVE OF FOREIGN POLICY?

Political atrocities in the world—such as the planned extermination of the European Jews by Adolf Hitler, the destruction of millions of peasants by Joseph Stalin, the massacre of the Cambodian people by the communist leader Pol Pot, and the persecutions inflicted on the Ugandan people by Idi Amin—have called the world's attention to horrors that civilized people hoped could not exist. Compassionate human beings can only condemn such depraved acts. Given the fact of such horrors, states have had to respond to them—whether by deeds, words, or even silence. For the United

States, as with most liberal societies, the question arises as to whether the promotion of human rights is a legitimate objective of foreign policy.

We argue that although dreadful evils do occur in countries around the world, the United States should not regard the pursuit of human rights as a legitimate objective of its foreign policy. Five points substantiate our case: (1) there is no agreement about a definition of human rights; (2) the United States has no right to interfere in the internal affairs of other nations; (3) a human rights policy can only hurt our security goals; (4) a human rights policy is counterproductive; (5) a human rights policy is hypocritical for the United States to pursue.

Definition. The phrase *human rights* means different things to different people (see Chapter 7). In classical times, civilizations did not consider that the individual has rights apart from his or her community. The Western world is mostly responsible for the idea that human rights are individual civil liberties that states are created to protect.

As we will see in Chapter 7, however, not everyone in the West accepts the primacy of political rights. Marxists and communists contend that economic rights are essential to any rendering of a definition of human rights. A Marxist interpretation of political rights is that they are part of the superstructure (see Chapter 5). Liberal societies, according to this perception, provide merely the illusion of rights and not the reality, since in modern capitalist economies, the capitalists are really in control anyway. Until capitalism is abolished, consequently, there can be no civil rights, according to this Marxist view.

Although liberalism and Marxism derive from a Western tradition, they are not in agreement about individual rights. The lack of agreement is even more noticeable when the liberal view of rights is contrasted with the political beliefs of African and Asian governments, many of which are steeped in traditions in conflict with the notion of human rights. Given such ambiguity about the definition and desirability of human rights, the United States cannot realistically pursue a human rights policy.

Interference. To be sure, governments have done horrible things to their people. The world, however, is organized into sovereign states. The term *sovereignty* means supreme power and authority. If states can determine what standards must be applied in other countries, the principle of sovereignty will be undermined.

The principle of sovereignty is widely accepted. Article 2, Section 7, of the Charter of the United Nations, for example, asserts that nothing in the Charter will authorize the United Nations "to intervene in matters which are essentially within the domestic jurisdiction of any state." The right to take action to protect a state's sovereignty has a long history that

an activist human rights policy would destroy.

If the United States could interfere in the internal affairs of other countries, then it, too, could legitimately be the object of intervention from its enemies. The effect of the right to intervene when applied universally would be to undermine the basis of world order.

Security. In a multistate system, national security is paramount. In a world without a world government, states must make alliances and enter into agreements with other states that may have abhorrent political systems. If the United States is to survive as a state with its institutions intact, it must act as other states—with security as the primary objective. States that violate human rights may possess a strategic position or scarce resources that the United States needs for its security. The United States cannot assure its security if it requires its allies to pass morality tests.

We may take as examples to prove our point the cases of Spain under the fascist General Francisco Franco, and the People's Republic of China under Mao Zedong. At the conclusion of World War II, the United States and its Western democratic allies feared the military strength of the Soviet army. Although Spain was governed by a dictator, it was anticommunist. Protected in part by a natural frontier, the Pyrenees Mountains, Spain offered a relatively safe location in which to build American bases. Those bases could be used for defense against the Soviet forces invading across Western Europe. Given the Soviet danger, the United States supported the Franco government in spite of its dictatorial character. Security requirements were primary.

Security, too, was a factor involved in American support of the People's Republic of China under Mao Zedong in the 1970s. Between 1949, when the Chinese communists seized control of Mainland China from the Nationalist Chinese government, and the early 1970s, when the Nixon administration sought better relations with the communist Chinese government, the United States and China had been bitter foes. Although a communist country, the People's Republic of China had been engaged in a fierce ideological and political struggle with the Soviet Union by the early 1970s. Border clashes between the two communist countries flared from time to time, and many Soviet divisions were sent to the Chinese frontier. To the extent that Soviet troops were diverted from Europe to meet the Chinese threat, the United States and its North Atlantic Treaty Organization (NATO) allies were made more secure. Had the United States refused to promote good relations with the People's Republic because of China's extensive violations of human rights, American security interests would have been harmed.

States have no friends; they have only interests. The cases of United States relations with Franco and Mao Zedong support the view that the United States must pursue its security interests regardless of how foreign governments treat their own people. By encouraging the promotion of human rights everywhere, the United States has weakened governments that were friendly to it. Iran is a classic case study. To be sure, the leader of that country—the shah—was a dictator who used his secret police to oppress his own people. The shah, however, was pro-West. When an oil embargo was instituted by Arab countries during the October War of 1973, the shah ordered Iran to continue to supply the West with oil. For more than three decades, the shah was a friend of the United States.

Because President Jimmy Carter emphasized human rights, the forces opposed to the shah were encouraged to rebel. The Ayatollah Khomeini became the symbol of resistance to the shah. Eventually, the shah's regime was toppled. The new government was hostile to the West and particularly to the United States. It sought to humiliate the United States when it took American hostages at the American Embassy in 1979 and called for a holy war against American imperialism. The effect of President Carter's human rights policy was to replace the pro–United States government with an anti–United States government. The security consequences of that political transformation were harmful to the United States.

If an activist human rights foreign policy can harm American security interests with respect to its allies, it may also adversely affect those interests in superpower relationships. The Soviet Union is a country whose domestic policy many Americans find abhorrent. Although the political liberties of Soviet people are constantly violated, the United States has found it essential to improve relations with the Soviet Union and has concluded arms control

agreements with that country. The United States realizes that there will be no victor in a nuclear war with the Soviet Union. The result has been the strengthening of the security of both states. Had the United States required the ending of human rights violations in the Soviet Union as a basis for any negotiations with that country, it would have created distrust; and agreements dealing with arms control would not have been forthcoming. The security of the two superpowers, consequently, would have been imperiled.

Careless rhetoric about human rights, moreover, may lead to revolution in the communist countries. In the 1950s, for example, some people within the administration of Dwight D. Eisenhower talked about "liberating" Eastern European states from communist rule. When, in 1956, the Hungarians rose up against the Soviet Union, the United States did not intervene to assist the Hungarians after all. Thousands of Hungarians were slaughtered by Soviet tanks and troops, and American prestige among the peoples of communist countries declined. The United States had spoken about liberation, Hungarians felt, but when the crucial moment came, the United States did not act. An activist human rights policy by the United States today would encourage more revolutionary spirit, which will only lead to disappointment on the part of the Eastern European peoples under communist rule when the United States does not measure up by deeds to its proud pronouncements.

Counterproductive Results. The United States is not the policeman of the world, as its failure to win the war in Vietnam reveals. The United States does not have total ability to influence political behavior in other countries. All of America's armed might, for example, did not prevent the Ayatollah Khomeini from incarcerating the hostages held at the American Embassy in 1979 and 1980.

The United States, moreover, witnessed the limits of its power when it tried to promote human rights abroad. Quiet diplomacy, as former United States Secretary of State Henry Kissinger pointed out, achieved more benefits than loud pronouncements about human rights. Kissinger's behind-the-scenes diplomacy was able to increase Jewish emigration from the Soviet Union to a record annual level of thirty-five thousand. The figure declined sharply once the Carter human rights policy was initiated.

If changes are to occur in the Soviet Union that will bring about respect for human rights, these changes will have to evolve slowly. Only when the Soviet Union does not feel threatened by others telling it what to do can there be an internal relaxation of tensions. Even before the Carter emphasis on human rights, we can observe that the internal political situation was improving inside the Soviet Union. There was less arbitrary rule under Nikita Khrushchev and Leonid Brezhnev than under Joseph Stalin.

Hypocrisy. A human rights foreign policy would be hypocritical because the United States could not maintain it consistently and because America could not itself live up to the civil liberties standard it professes to the world. Such hypocrisy would undermine America's moral standing in the world.

In the real world of foreign policy, states must finally pursue security rather than moral objectives. When, at the beginning of his term in office, President Carter made a strong point about the absolutist character of human rights, he created expectations that could never be realized. In his record as president he showed a constant retreat from that policy. Since the United States needed the oil and support of Iran, for example, the President continued to supply arms to the shah. American arms were sent to dictatorial South Korea as well. Anx-ious not to upset the arms control and trade ties between the United States and the Soviet Union, President Carter eased off on the human rights rhetoric dealing with internal Soviet matters. The effect of such a manipulation of the human rights issue, consequently, was to subject America to charges of hypocrisy—the selective use of a moral principle to serve American foreign policy goals.

Perhaps a more significant charge of American hypocrisy can be raised when the American blemishes of human rights are put on stage for the world to view. The violations of human rights in the treatment of American blacks, Hispanics, women, and Indians are well known. Police brutality occurs from time to time. Freedom of speech and the press has been violated, particularly during periods of tension in international relations. The activities of federal government officials during the administrations of Presidents Lyndon Johnson and Richard Nixon in infiltrating antiwar protest organizations were major breaches of civil liberties. How can the United States tell other countries how to behave when *it* violates human rights? The answer is that it cannot, lest it be subject to charges of hypocrisy. Americans should clean up their own house before passing judgment elsewhere. They should follow the advice of John Quincy Adams, who commented, "We are the friends of liberty everywhere, but the custodians only of our own."

10/NO SHOULD THE UNITED STATES AVOID MAKING HUMAN RIGHTS AN OBJECTIVE OF FOREIGN POLICY?

Human rights must be a goal of foreign policy. Self-professed realists in international politics display a cynicism in analyzing foreign policy that makes them overlook the realism of moral purpose as an objective of diplomacy. We can show by considering the same points as the *Affirmative* that human rights ought to be a goal of American foreign policy.

Definition. To be sure, the term *human rights* has lent itself to different definitions. Those who have wanted to cloud the issue have pointed to the divergencies in the West about civil liberties and the differences in tra-dition between the West and the non-Western world. Those who revere liberty, however, know that it is political rights, or civil liberties, which are human rights (see Chapter 7). We may have difficulty in accurately delineating the line between individual liberty and the need for public order, but that is a matter for courts to determine. The political freedoms of speech, religion, the press, assembly, fair trial, and the franchise are the rights at issue.

It is certainly true that these rights originated in the West, but they have often been accepted in the non-Western world as well. When Western colonialism controlled the world, the anticolonial critique was based on these Western principles. Many of the twentieth-century Third World leaders were educated in the West. They not only accepted Western aspirations about economic development, but they forced Western leaders to apply their own standards to the way they were treating the colonial peoples. When colonial powers imprisoned nationalist revolutionaries in the Third World, the anti-imperialists denounced these violations of civil liberties. The ideological support of human rights helped to undermine Western imperialism both in the Western imperialist countries and in the colonies and contributed to the rise of self-government for the peoples of Africa and Asia. The *Affirmative,* consequently, is on shaky ground when it says that a Western concept is being imposed on non-Western governments.

One need not necessarily accept this interpretation about the widespread support of the Western idea of human rights to prove its universality. Although the concept of human rights may be a Western value, many of the major violations of these rights are also violations of the religious and philosophical heritage of all peoples. When we consider modern political crimes, such as torture and the persecution of religious and racial minorities, we can see that non-Western traditions have also been hostile to such behavior.

Sociologist Peter L. Berger points out in this connection that Cambodia is a Buddhist country, and Buddhism "has as its highest moral tenet the 'respect for all sentient things.' " The atrocities committed by Pol Pot can be condemned, consequently, in Buddhist terms. Berger also notes that when China under the government of Mao Zedong separated children from their parents in the course of communist experiments, it was violating the entire body of Chinese tradition that holds, among other things, that government should be "human-hearted" and that "filial piety" is one of the highest human goods. Berger cites the ethical basis of Islam, moreover, which commands men to be compassionate.[8] Many of the violations of human rights, then, are condemned by universal standards of justice.

Interference. The record of international relations reveals that human rights have been considered as international in scope. As early as 480 B.C., Gelon, prince of Syracuse, upon defeating Carthage, included in the peace terms a provision requiring the Carthaginians to end their custom of sacrificing their children to Saturn.[9] In the twentieth century states have continued to show that certain problems are truly international in scope. Racism, for example, has been held in this light.

Throughout the post–World War II period, Third World countries particularly have viewed the retention of political power by the white minorities in Rhodesia (now Zimbabwe) and South Africa as a matter of international concern. When white-dominated governments of both those countries denounced the invasion of their sovereignty by outside states, Third World countries pointed to international norms. They correctly did not say that racism was an internal matter.

Human rights now constitute an international norm. Violations of these rights are matters of international concern. Such an international concern has been affirmed in the Charter of the United Nations, the Universal Declaration of Human Rights, and the Helsinki Accords. The U.N. Charter includes in its Preamble a purpose of the organization: "to reaffirm faith in fundamental human rights." Articles 55 and 56 also mention the subject. The Universal Declaration of Human Rights was adopted by the U.N. General Assembly in 1948 without a dissenting vote. The Helsinki Accords of 1975, which had thirty-five signatories, contained "Basket 3" provisions designed to protect and expand human rights. When a norm is given international approval, as in these cases, a country cannot legitimately charge a violation of sovereignty.

Security. In the long run, security will be benefited rather than hurt by a concern with human rights. Concern does not mean preoccupation or fixation. Of course, the United States must reconcile moral with security considerations. It may well be, as the case of Iran in the post–World War II period indicates, that it cannot jeopardize its security and that of its

---

[8] Peter L. Berger, "Are Human Rights Universal?" *Commentary* (September 1977) p. 62.

[9] Walter Laqueur, "The Issue of Human Rights," *Commentary* (May 1977) p. 29.

allies by promoting a vocal and absolute human rights policy. It should, however, do what is within its power to promote human rights abroad. Tactics may vary from public denunciations to quiet, suggestive diplomacy, but its security interests will best be served if it keeps human rights always as a goal. We may take the case of Third World dictatorships and the Soviet Union as examples to prove our point.

Governments cannot endure forever without some popular support. The more countries rely on force at home, the more they suppress rather than eliminate dissent. When governments friendly to the United States suppress dissent and imprison people who openly and peacefully disagree with their governments, then the chances are that dissent will grow. Repressive governments holding **political prisoners** (those people who are put in prison for their political beliefs rather than for illegal actions) tend to imprison people from ever more diverse groups in the political community. Eventually, the political leader becomes isolated from his people, and revolution occurs. American security interests would be served if friendly leaders have broad support for their actions. A number of people argued during the 1980s that Ferdinand Marcos, as president of the Philippines, was responsible for the growing communist insurgency in that country although he was an anticommunist. Marcos had engaged in repressive policies against his own people. Many who worked to topple him from power hoped that the democratic government of Corazon Aquino with its respect for civil liberties would undermine the communist movement.

The Soviet Union also serves as an example of how promoting human rights might be helpful to American security interests. The United States ought to tell the Soviet Union that it is pursuing the expansion of human rights everywhere and that it is going to be free to pursue its goals just as the Soviet Union continues to proclaim its ideological aspirations.

Freedom in the Soviet Union is a vital security interest of the United States. Historian Walter Laqueur notes, for example, that arms control agreements depend upon many sources of information.[10] The Soviet Union and the

United States both possess satellites to monitor compliance with the provisions of the agreements. The Soviets, moreover, rely upon the freedoms in American society as another monitoring device. In the post-Watergate era, as reporters seek to uncover wrongdoing in American government, one can imagine how journalists would rush to publication if they discovered that the United States was cheating on its arms control commitments. If political freedom comes to the Soviet Union, moreover, then America would have the same security benefits that the Soviet Union derives from an open and free America.

Maintaining an ideological human rights offensive against the Soviet Union need not create tensions between the superpowers. During his visit to Moscow in 1988 President Ronald Reagan spoke eloquently on the subject of human rights. He said that the United States supports the freedom of political prisoners and the end of religious persecution in the Soviet Union. At the same time, the trip to Moscow culminated in the adoption of the Intermediate-range Nuclear Forces Treaty that eliminated Soviet and U.S. medium-range nuclear missiles from Europe. Reagan showed that a commitment to human rights need not hurt U.S. security interests.

The United States should, however, not encourage revolution in the Soviet Union or other communist countries. It should make its case with the hope that a freer communist society would help rather than hinder American security.

Counterproductive Results. The record shows that when the United States and its Western allies have promoted human rights, they have been effective in many cases. Of course, *how* effective depends on the political leverage available to the United States. A country such as South Korea is heavily dependent upon the United States for its security. The United States has interceded for dissidents, and some were released from prison under the South Korean dictatorship of General Park Chung Hee.

The Soviet Union has also been pressured successfully. Dissidents such as Anatoly Scharansky may have been released in part because of pressure from outside the Soviet Union. Under Stalin, dissidents were shipped to Siberian prison camps, where many of them died.

---

[10] Ibid., p. 33.

Spotlighting human rights violations can bring results. The record shows that it can be effective—perhaps not in every case, but at least in many.

Hypocrisy. It is certainly true that the United States could be judged hypocritical if it were to pursue an activist and absolutist human rights foreign policy. That accusation, however, would not be valid if its policy were consistent with its security goals. Quiet, behind-the-scenes warnings to a friendly country would be one way to deal with the problem. In those cases in which the United States could be effective, however, it can profess a bolder policy. There is nothing hypocritical about such political behavior.

The case of El Salvador is instructive. A communist insurgency threatened to undermine the political system of that country. Widespread abuses of human rights increasingly alienated the people from their government. The United States asserted its influence to prevent such atrocities as the killing of innocent people by right-wing death squads. It also encouraged free elections in which Jose Napoleon Duarte was elected. Duarte committed himself to social reform and political democracy. Although his government had some failures and Duarte himself was subjected to criticism that he moved too slowly in bringing about social reform, most observers agree that the situation for United States security in El Salvador was better because of Duarte's reforms than would have been the case if someone else who was not committed to human rights had been in power.

Finally, with respect to its own civil liberties,

the United States should indicate that it has faults and it has tried to correct them. It should denounce the communist efforts to equate unrelated political phenomena. In this regard, it should challenge the communist assertion that the persecution of blacks in America, long opposed openly by American political leaders and protest groups, is equivalent to Stalin's slave labor camps, which Soviet political leaders tried to keep secret from the world; that the internment of Japanese-Americans in relocation camps during World War II, which was a temporary wartime measure condemned by American civil libertarians at the time, is on a par with the deportation of the ethnic Chinese into unseaworthy boats by the communist Vietnamese governments, which was a permanent racist effort to remove an entire ethnic minority at a great cost in human life; and that press censorship during wartime, a temporary move monitored by an independent judiciary, is the same as the Soviet government's control of the press, which is a permanent feature of a totalitarian political system.

It is certainly true that the United States should work to make itself ever more vigilant in promoting civil liberties at home. That does not mean, however, that it should be indifferent to such acts as the extermination of Jewish groups by Adolf Hitler, the liquidation of Cambodian people by Pol Pot, the suppression of dissent by Mao Zedong, the terror imposed by Idi Amin, and the racial discrimination of South Africa. To eliminate or limit evils such as these, the United States should pursue an activist human rights policy.

11/YES IS AMERICA A FASCIST SOCIETY?

Many of us like to think of the United States as a democracy. We should recall, however, the comment of the Louisiana demogogue Huey Long, who said that if fascism reaches America, it will come under the slogans of democracy and 100 percent Americanism. If we take a look at some of the central features of fascism—racism, militarism, and dictatorship—we can see that the United States is, indeed, a fascist country. Let us examine the

realities of the American political system to substantiate our case.

Racism. America is a racist society, as the history of black people in America attests. The record begins with the long period of slavery that blacks endured at the very time when the great American documents, the Declaration of Independence and the Constitution, eloquently proclaimed universal principles of freedom and justice. Even after black people were "emancipated," they continued to be denied real equality of opportunity. Blacks were also denied their legal rights through terrorism, such as the acts of the Ku Klux Klan. Other restrictions against their political rights were legal and effectively denied them voting rights. The most important of these were the **poll tax,** which voters had to pay in order to vote; **"grandfather" clauses,** in which black people had to show that their ancestors had voted before Reconstruction in order to vote; and the **white primary,** in which blacks were excluded from voting in primary contests. Moreover, **"Jim Crow" laws** established segregation in education, public accommodations, and transportation.

Even after the so-called civil rights revolution, blacks continue to encounter discrimination. More than one-third of the families living in poverty in the United States are black (three times the rate of whites). Black median income is only 56 percent that of whites; and black unemployment is twice that of whites.[11]

Blacks figure prominently in the rise of a group that social scientists refer to as the underclass. The **underclass** is composed of poor men who have no permanent regular job, women who are dependent upon welfare, street criminals, alcoholics, and drug addicts. Many of the government programs designed to help black people have not significantly helped those in the underclass.

The criminal justice system in America works against blacks. Black people constitute an extraordinarily high proportion of the people in American prisons. David Baldus's study of Georgia from 1973 to 1979 points to racial prejudice in the American criminal justice system. Baldus found that of the twelve hundred Georgia murder sentences imposed during this period, a black who killed a white was 3.7 times as likely to be given the death penalty as a white who killed a white.[12]

Racism is a fact of political life, too. With 12 percent of the population, not one black person is currently a United States Senator. Proposals to change the Constitution to allow two senators to be elected from predominantly black Washington, D.C., failed because the white power structure recognized they will result in the election of two black senators and a black representative.

If one looks at the figures in the professions, moreover, one sees that black professionals are disproportionately represented. The number of black doctors, college professors, and lawyers is still abysmally small and constitutes sheer tokenism. It is true that *some* minority members rise in business and the professions, but generally they are placed in token leadership jobs, such as vice-president of community affairs. One can look at the *Fortune 500* top corporations in vain to find any significant powerful corporate officers who are members of minorities.

It is true that other groups have experienced discrimination and have risen above it. But blacks are different from other groups. Psychologist Thomas F. Pettigrew explains this fact by noting that blacks are "the only group to experience the confluence of race, slavery, and segregation."[13]

American political leaders proclaim that there has been a change in racial relations. Superficially, that may be true since it is rare to hear politicians use racial epithets to attack minority groups. What we have in America today is rather symbolic racism, as programs that are of particular benefit to blacks and other minorities are denounced. Code words, such as welfare, busing, and affirmative action, are used in a derogatory manner. The real targets are minorities.

Militarism. America has always been an expansionistic nation. It started out as thirteen states along the eastern seaboard. By 1900, it had become an empire: It had conquered a continent; waged or threatened war with its immediate neighbors; moved across the Pa-

---

[11] Tony Brown, "Economics: The Final Stage of the Civil Rights Revolution" [Speech delivered on February 20, 1987]. *Vital Speeches of the Day* 53 (April 15, 1987): 401.

[12] Cited in Diana R. Gordon, "Equal Protection, Unequal Justice," in *Minority Report: What Has Happened to Blacks, Hispanics, American Indians, and Other Minorities in the Eighties?* ed. Leslie W. Dunbar (New York: Pantheon, 1984), p. 164.

[13] Thomas F. Pettigrew, "Integration and Pluralism," in *Eliminating Racism: Profiles in Controversy,* ed. Phyllis A. Katz and Dalmas A. Taylor (New York: Plenum Press, 1987), p. 24.

cific to Hawaii and the Philippines; and menaced Caribbean nations.

In this century, America's military forces have been deployed all over the world. Since 1945, American armed forces have fought in such places as Korea, the Dominican Republic, Vietnam, Grenada, and Lebanon. As historian Barbara Tuchman notes, "We have been antimilitarist in thought and sentiment while remarkably combative in character and practice."[14]

Since the end of World War II, the United States has spent more than three trillion dollars on what is euphemistically called "defense." Although it pretends to promote peace, the United States has engaged in major "hot" wars in Korea and Vietnam—wars, incidentally, waged against nonwhite peoples. In addition, it has since the end of World War II supported fascist regimes, such as Chiang Kai-shek's China, Francisco Franco's Spain, Antonio Salazar's Portugal, Raphael Trujillo's Dominican Republic, Fulgencio Batista's Cuba, and the shah's Iran.

Moreover, the United States has become the biggest arms dealer in the world. Because of its desire to maximize profits for its munitions makers, or "merchants of death" as they should properly be called, it exports armaments to the poor Third World countries and encourages them to engage in the arms race. Instead of devoting their wealth to the pursuit of economic development of the world, the developing countries waste their money on military expenditures. It is not unusual to find that American weapons sold or given to one country are used to fight American weapons sold or given to another country. During the Middle East War of 1967, for example, Jordan fought Israel, with each side using American-made weapons.

Ostensibly, the weapons are given to dictators to make them strong enough to defend themselves against foreign attack. In actuality, however, the armaments and military training extended to these forces entrench unpopular governments in power. American military assistance becomes, consequently, an obstacle to democratic rule. Elections are curtailed, freedom of speech thwarted, and peaceful protest prevented with the instruments of coercion and torture supplied by the fascist United States. It is no wonder, then, that when these regimes are toppled—as was the case in Iran and Nicaragua—there is popular hostility against the United States.

Dictatorship. What we have in the United States is what Professor Bertram Gross refers to as "friendly fascism" because it does not appear to be as ruthless as fascism in Mussolini's Italy or Hitler's Germany.[15] Power in America is controlled by the political leaders and some top wealthy people rather than the masses of people. To be sure, one often sees criticisms of the government, but the result of any election is merely to put another faction of the rich and their friendly politicians into power.

The electoral process and the system of laws in the United States prove our points. To run as candidates in political campaigns requires enormous amounts of money. The big corporations subsidize the candidates who favor their own points of view. Candidates who do not reflect the views of the wealthy do not receive these contributions, so that most people do not even know who they are.

The laws that come out of such a dictatorial system reflect the interests of the wealthy. In spite of all the talk about how the defense contractors are making high profits at the expense of the American people, they still operate without restrictions of any specific consequence. Tax laws contain so many loopholes favoring the wealthy that ordinary taxpayers bear the burden of paying a disproportionately high share of their income on taxes.

Tax laws are but one example of the capitalist dictatorship. The government bailouts of Lockheed and Chrysler, the imposition of high tariffs to prevent competition from abroad, and the system of subsidies that help rich American farmers are other illustrations of the capitalist dictatorship. A dictatorship of the capitalists is fascism—as it was in Benito Mussolini's Italy and Adolf Hitler's Germany.

[14] Barbara Tuchman, "The American People and Military Power in an Historical Perspective," Adelphi Paper 173 (London: International Institute for Strategic Studies, 1982), p. 5.

[15] Bertram Gross, "Friendly Fascism: A Model for America," *Social Policy,* 1 (November-December 1970): 44–52.

11 / NO   IS AMERICA A FASCIST SOCIETY?

The notion that the United States is a fascist society is absurd. Some critics like to point to the weaknesses of America and ignore the positive achievements that do not support their case. Let us take a look at the charges of racism, militarism, and dictatorship.

Racism. It is certainly true that the treatment of black people in the United States has been harsh. There is no need to challenge the criticisms of slavery and the repression that followed after slavery was ended. It is important to keep in mind, however, that during the entire period of slavery there was open criticism in the North of the evils of such a system. In the twentieth century, moreover, major steps have been taken to end the centuries of racism, so that the charge that America is a racist society is without merit.

The civil rights revolution from the 1960s to the present witnessed an end to the worst ravages of discrimination. Voting rights are now assured to all, regardless of race. It is certainly true that there are no black United States senators currently in office. That, however, is a misleading fact. Particularly with the franchise extended to southern blacks, blacks have been elected to many different posts: sheriffs, mayors, state legislators, and members of the House of Representatives. From 1968 to 1987 the number of black elected officials in the United States rose six times over, to a total of nearly seven thousand. Black mayors increased in number from 48 to 303.[16] By May 1989 black mayors were in power in some of the major American cities, including Atlanta, Baltimore, Birmingham, Detroit, Los Angeles, New Orleans, Philadelphia, and Washington D.C. Congress has more black members today than at any time since Reconstruction.

Blacks have been appointed to other government positions and serve as judges, ambassadors, and cabinet members. A racist society would not permit members of a minority race into such positions. Even southern white political leaders—themselves raised in a segregationist period—make conscious efforts to appoint black leaders to prominent positions. Former segregationists, such as Strom Thurmond and John Stennis, voted for the extension and strengthening of the Voting Rights Act in 1982.

The economic situation for blacks is improving. Black per capita income in 1988 was about $7,500 which is a 50 percent increase in constant dollars over the 1968 level. In the same period, white per capita income increased by 40 percent.[17] Afro-Americans earn $200 billion in income and spend $180 billion a year on goods and services. According to Tony Brown, the chairman of Buy Freedom (an organization formed to promote economic development among blacks), "This is equivalent to the GNP of Canada or Australia, or the ninth largest nation in the free world."[18]

Blacks have also made major gains in education. The median number of school years completed by blacks rose from nine in 1968 to twelve in 1985. The percentage of blacks twenty-five years or older who finished high school doubled since 1968, from 30 percent to 60 percent. Black educational attainment in high school and college has increased more rapidly than for whites in this time period.[19] In some fields, such as law, teaching, and nursing, the gains have been extraordinary. To be sure, the problem of hard-core unemployment is still with us, but this is a class problem of concern to poor blacks *and* poor whites and requires economic rather than racial solutions.

Militarism. It is wrong to equate a military establishment with militarism. For most of American history, expenditures in military matters were kept low. To a country primarily concerned with its internal development, support of a large military establishment was seen

---

[16] Karl Zinsmeister, "Black Demographics," *Public Opinion* 10 (January/February 1988): 41.

[17] Ibid., p. 42.

[18] Brown, "Economics," p. 402.

[19] Zinsmeister, "Black Demographics," p. 41.

as inimical to economic development and prosperity. Major expenditures in defense in peacetime became a constant feature of American society for the most part only after World War II. With the economic decay caused by the ravages of two world wars, Western Europe could not stand up against the strongest power in Eurasia—the Soviet Union. The United States *had* to devote its resources to military matters lest freedom be extinguished in the noncommunist countries of the world. The extent of defense expenditures has been exaggerated by critics of the United States. Although the administration of Ronald Reagan is identified as a big defense spender, for example, it spent a smaller percentage of both the gross national product and the federal budget on defense than was disbursed in the 1950s. The percentage figures in these categories are estimated by some scholars to be half of their Soviet counterparts.

The wars the United States has waged have not been racist. In the wars in Korea and Vietnam, the United States had the support of many nonwhite countries. The South Korean and South Vietnamese governments were nonwhite, too, so the charge of racism in these wars is ridiculous.

The United States does export armaments to other countries, but these armaments are sent at the request of the governments. Democratic Israel, for example, has been able to maintain its security because of the arms aid provided by the United States. The Western democracies of France, Great Britain, Holland, and West Germany, for example, are stronger because of American military support during the immediate post–World War II years.

It is certainly true that some of the regimes the United States has aided have been dictatorships. A distinction, however, must be made between support of a state for security reasons and support of a government. In the uncertain world of international relations, it is not always possible to have only democratic regimes on one's side. It may be essential to support a dictatorial regime because of the particular value that the state it runs possesses, such as geographical location, military strength, or scarce resources. Often, moreover, these dictatorships are authoritarian and not totalitarian. The South Vietnamese government under Ngo Dinh Diem, for example,

was certainly repressive, but it never deported an entire ethnic minority as the communist Vietnam government did with the Chinese community of Vietnam in 1979. This is not to portray the South Vietnam government as a paragon of virtue. It is, however, to put it in contrast to the more horrible regime that replaced it.

Dictatorship. The concept of the dictatorship of the capitalists is an old Marxist shibboleth that has no basis in fact. The electoral process and the system of laws can prove our point for the United States, as well as for other democracies.

Capitalists do not control the American electoral system, although they certainly influence it. The power of the big contributors in presidential campaigns has been diminished with the Federal Election Campaign Act of 1974, which limits the size of campaign contributions in presidential elections. It is certainly true that capitalists are capable of contributing to other campaigns, but so, too, are other organizations, such as trade unions and professional associations. There are countervailing forces at work, then, to weaken the power of the capitalists.

The laws, moreover, do not prove that a capitalist dictatorship exists in the United States. It is certainly true that there are evils in the tax system. On net, however, capitalists, too, pay taxes. They have resisted the income tax, yet such taxes have been imposed on the national and state level. Legislators, moreover, are often impressed with the plight of the disadvantaged and the poor and serve as eloquent advocates for these weak groups in the councils of government. A peaceful protest movement has been successful in bringing about changes in the American system, not only in changing tax legislation but also in protecting consumers and working men and women. The fact that capitalists rant about government regulations shows that on these issues, at least, the power of capitalists is much diminished. Capitalists have been forced to do things that they did not want to do, such as reduce the level of pollutants their factories eject into the atmosphere; make automobiles more energy efficient; label the contents of their products; and take greater safety measures for their employees. The fact that many laws such as these have been enacted clearly shows the importance of groups opposed to unlimited power of the capitalists and proves that the United States is a free society and not a fascist one.

KEY TERMS

Apartheid
Classical liberalism
Conservatism
Corporate state
Divine right of kings
Fascism
"Grandfather" clauses
"Jim Crow" laws
Legitimate government
Liberalism
National Socialism

Nazism
Neoconservatism
Neoliberalism
New Conservatism
Political ideology
Political prisoners
Poll tax
Reactionaries
Social contract
Underclass
White primary

QUESTIONS

Liberalism, Conservatism, and Fascism

1. What effect does government intervention in the economy and the expansion of the welfare state have on individual freedom?
2. What are the similarities and/or differences between conservatism and fascism?
3. What positions on domestic and foreign policy matters does one have to maintain in order to be labeled a liberal?
4. How is it possible for people who are committed to the same ideology to differ among themselves in supporting particular government policies or laws?
5. What criteria should be used in evaluating whether the United States is a racist society?

Human Rights

1. What would be the consequences to U.S. security interests if the United States treated violations of human rights by its friends in the same manner as it treats violations of human rights by its enemies?
2. What is the relationship between moral purpose and national security in the conduct of foreign policy?
3. What are the conservative values expressed in the *Affirmative's* case on human rights?
4. What are the liberal values expressed in the *Negative's* case on human rights?
5. At what point would liberal values be jeopardized by the United States if it vigorously pursued a human rights foreign policy?

RECOMMENDED READINGS

Liberalism, Conservatism, and Fascism

ARBLASTER, ANTHONY. *The Rise and Decline of Western Liberalism.* New York: Basil Blackwell, 1984. An analysis, criticism, and history of liberalism.

BERLIN, ISAIAH. *Four Essays on Liberty.* New York: Oxford University Press, 1969. A classic work on liberalism.

BROWN, TONY. "Economics: The Final Stage of the Civil Rights Movement" [Speech delivered on February 20, 1987]. *Vital Speeches of the Day.* 53 (April 15, 1987): 400–404. A plea for making economic improvement a priority of the civil rights agenda.

BUGROV, EVGENY, PAVEL IVANOV, ALEXEI NIKOLIN, ANATOLY RASSADIN, and ANATOLY CHAPIS. "The Military-Industrial Complex: Its Aims, Interests and Mechanism." *New Times* (Moscow), no. 48 (December 8, 1986): supplement. A Soviet analysis of the U.S. military-industrial complex.

BURNHAM, JAMES. *Suicide of the West: An Essay on the Meaning and Destiny of Liberalism.* New York: John Day, 1964. An indictment of liberalism.

DE FELICE, RENZO. *Fascism: An Informal Introduction to Its Theory and Practice.* An interview with Michael A. Ledeen. New Brunswick, N.J.: Transaction Books, 1976. A discussion of fascism by a leading scholar of the subject.

DUNBAR, LESLIE W., ed. *Minority Report: What Has Happened to Blacks, Hispanics, American Indians, and Other Minorities in the Eighties?* New York: Pantheon Books, 1984. Essays on the condition of minorities in the 1980s.

GELMAN, DAVID, KAREN SPRINGEN, KAREN BRAILSFORD, and MARK MILLER. "Black and White in America." *Newsweek* 111 (March 7, 1988): 18–21, 23. A survey of blacks in America.

GERBER, WILLIAM. *American Liberalism: Laudable End, Controversial Means.* Rev. ed. Lanham, Md.: University Press of America, 1987. An analysis of liberalism in the United States.

GOTTFRIED, PAUL, and THOMAS FLEMING. *The Conservative Movement.* Boston: Twayne, 1988. A study of American conservatism since the end of World War II.

GREGOR, A. JAMES. *The Ideology of Fascism: The Rationale of Totalitarianism.* New York: Free Press, 1969. A classic introduction to fascism.

———. *Interpretations of Fascism.* Morristown, N.J.: General Learning Press, 1974. A survey of social science efforts to explain the fascist phenomenon.

JENCKS, CHRISTOPHER. "Deadly Neighborhoods." *New Republic* 198 (June 13, 1988): 23–32. An appraisal of the underclass in the United States.

KATZ, PHYLLIS A., and DALMAS A. TAYLOR, eds. *Eliminating Racism: Profiles in Controversy.* New York: Plenum Press, 1987. Essays on racism in the United States.

KIRK, RUSSELL. *The Conservative Mind: From Burke to Eliot.* Rev. ed. Chicago: Henry Regnery, 1960. A study of the political philosophy, religious thought, and literature of conservatives.

KRISTOL, IRVING. *Reflections of a Neoconservative: Looking Back, Looking Ahead.* New York: Basic Books, 1983. Essays by a leading neoconservative.

LENS, SIDNEY. *Permanent War: The Militarization of America.* New York: Schocken Books, 1987. A critique of U.S. foreign policy and the rise of militarism in the United States.

NISBET, ROBERT. *Conservatism: Dream and Reality.* Minneapolis: University of Minnesota Press, 1986. A survey of conservative thought.

ROTHENBERG, RANDALL. *The Neoliberals: Creating the New American Politics.* New York: Simon and Schuster, 1984. A history of neoliberalism.

SCHUETTINGER, ROBERT, ed. *The Conservative Tradition in European Thought.* New York: G.P. Putnam's Sons, 1970. An anthology with an excellent introductory article.

SOWELL, THOMAS. "Black Progress Can't Be Legislated." *Current*, no. 270 (February 1985): 24–27. A critical assessment of the accomplishments attributed to liberal legislation to help blacks.

WILSON, WILLIAM JULIUS. *The Truly Disadvantaged.* Chicago: University of Chicago Press, 1987. A discussion of the social pathologies of innercity life.

ZINSMEISTER, KARL. "Black Demographics." *Public Opinion* 10 (January/February 1988): 41–44. An analysis of the economic and social factors of American blacks.

Human Rights

BERGER, PETER L. "Are Human Rights Universal?" *Commentary* 64 (September 1977): 60–63. Yes, says the author.

DERIAN, PATT. "How to Make Dictators Look Good." *Nation* 240 (February 9, 1985): 1, 146, 148. A critical assessment of the Reagan human rights policy.

HOFFMANN, STANLEY. "Reaching for the Most Difficult: Human Rights as a Foreign Policy Goal." *Daedalus* 112 (Fall 1983): 19–49. A defense of human rights as a goal in foreign policy.

KAGAN, DONALD. "Human Rights, Moralism, and Foreign Policy." *Washington Quarterly* 6 (Winter 1983): 86–95. An argument that human rights and national interest often do not dovetail.

KIRKPATRICK, JEANE. "Dictatorship and Double Standards." *Commentary* 68 (November 1979): 34–45. A controversial article about human rights.

LEFEVER, ERNEST W. "The Trivialization of Human Rights." *Policy Review* 3 (Winter 1978): 11–26. An assessment of human rights policy.

MAECHLING, CHARLES, JR. "Human Rights Dehumanized." *Foreign Policy*, no. 52 (Fall 1983): 118–35. A critique of the Reagan human rights policy.

NOVAK, MICHAEL. *Human Rights and the New Realism: Strategic Thinking in a New Age.* New York: Freedom House, 1986. A case for a moderate use of human rights as an instrument of foreign policy.

ULLMAN, RICHARD. "Both National Security and Human Rights Can Be Served Simultaneously." *Center Magazine* 176 (March/April 1984): 21–29. An eloquent defense of human rights as a foreign policy goal.

VINCENT, R. J., ed. *Foreign Policy and Human Rights: Issues and Responses.* Cambridge, England: Cambridge University Press, 1986. Essays on the relationship between the two concepts.

chapter 5

Capitalism, socialism, and communism

"Capitalism is a system of exploitation of man by man; and communism is the exact opposite," is one of the quips about the two systems sometimes appreciated in communist and noncommunist countries alike. Capitalism and communism have had such vehement supporters and critics that these systems lend themselves to many humorous remarks. The same is true of another system—socialism. Often, however, the humor about these systems is based on misunderstandings of their central features. The misunderstandings arise because of confusion and disagreement about the definitions of these systems, the need to protect the beneficiaries of these systems, and differing assessments about the consequences of each system to society.

We will begin our discussion of this subject by noting that capitalism, socialism, and communism owe much to the development of industrialism throughout the world. Although receiving their im-

petus from economic factors, these ideologies go beyond economics and deal with such matters of political philosophy as the role of government in society, the relationship between citizen and state, and the extent of individual liberty.[1]

WHAT IS CAPITALISM?

In most countries of the world today, capitalism is unpopular. Leaders of communist countries denounce capitalism as being synonymous with exploitation of the masses. Noncommunist Third World representatives equate capitalism with Western colonialism. Even in the West, where modern capitalism originated, cap-

---

[1] Part of the material in this chapter is drawn from the author's *Communism and Democracy: Principles and Practices* (Dubuque, Iowa: Kendall/Hunt, 1971).

italism is criticized daily not only for exploitation and colonialism but for greed, pollution, war, and injustice as well. To be sure, capitalism has its defenders in the business, academic, and political communities in the United States and abroad. In the 1980s, in particular, capitalism has achieved renewed support in many countries.

To sort out rhetoric from fact, it is essential first to describe objectively the features of a capitalist system. We can then examine its historical development and note its many changes. We can study some of the principal critics of capitalism and their prescriptions for remedying its evils—evils both real and imaginary.

The term *capitalism* is an invention of nineteenth-century socialists who were critical of business practices. Some commentators prefer to use the terms *free enterprise, private enterprise,* or *market economy* rather than *capitalism.* In doing so, they wish to distinguish between an ideal system of economic organization and the actual behavior of people who call themselves capitalists but who act in ways that conflict with the ideal system. Recognizing that the distinction between the theory of capitalism and the practice of capitalism is a valid one, we shall use the terms capitalism, **free enterprise,** and **private enterprise** as if they are the same when discussing the theory of capitalism. We shall define **capitalism** as an economic system characterized by private property, competition, a market economy, and freedom of managerial decision.

Economic System

Capitalism is first and foremost an *economic* system. It should not be confused with a *political* system, such as political democracy. Some observers contend that capitalism is an essential prerequisite of democracy since individuals should be free to spend their own money just as they should be free to vote. In spending and in voting, people are expressing their individual preferences, as required of a free society. If, however, we accept the definition of democracy as characterized by, among other things, a feature such as majority rule, then we can conclude that a majority acting through its representatives can support *either* a capitalist economy *or* some other economic system.

Private Property

A second feature of capitalism is private property. In this context property includes not only land but also such components as tools, factories, ships, and stock. In a capitalist system individuals are permitted to acquire as much property as they are legally capable of collecting. There are few restrictions imposed by the state. Heavy taxation, particularly, is viewed as theft—the taking away of private property from someone who possesses it and distributing it to others who do not.

Competition

In a capitalist system competition among many units is an important characteristic. A basic feature of capitalism is that buyers rather than monopolists or government bureaucrats are the best judges of what they want. A system that permits individuals to choose how they spend their money and where they work creates a free society in which the consumer is sovereign in the marketplace. Business people (or *entrepreneurs,* as they are sometimes called) are free to enter the marketplace to satisfy consumer demands. Competition assures that prices remain low. If a product is very much in demand, many entrepreneurs will rush to furnish that item or something similar to it, thus reducing prices. The public will be able to get the best goods at the cheapest prices through this arrangement. As Adam Smith, a Scottish political economist, put it: If each individual seeks to maximize his own self-interest, an "invisible hand" will maximize the economic satisfactions of the entire community.

Market Economy

A market economy, as distinguished from a command economy, is an essential feature of capitalism. A **market economy** is a system in which individuals are free to buy and sell goods and services as they wish with no or few restrictions. A **command economy,** in contrast, is a system in which decisions about production and distribution are centralized in the hands of government or of a few monopolists.

Freedom of Managerial Decision

According to capitalist theory, for society to prosper there must be complete freedom for the entrepreneurs to invest as they deem appropriate. If capitalists invest their savings in things that the public does not want, they lose money and go out of business. A capitalist system, consequently, encourages the most ambitious and innovative individuals to demonstrate their moneymaking talent, and the system rewards those who have proven their ability to satisfy consumers.

Entrepreneurs, then, are free from any government interference in their decision making. They hire and fire workers as they deem fit. They pay whatever wages they choose. If workers are not satisfied with the wages they are earning, then they are free to move elsewhere. Market forces determine if workers are worth more money than they are receiving. Capitalists who choose to discriminate on the basis of race, religion, or gender soon find that they are neglecting the services of a pool of qualified talent, and, consequently, they suffer economically from their prejudices. When talented people from groups experiencing discrimination are selected by a more intelligent entre-

preneur, that entrepreneur's business is more likely to prosper.

Anything that inhibits the entrepreneurs from making decisions based on economic efficiency is detrimental not only to them but to the rest of society as well. Taxes are bad because they curb incentive. Minimum wage laws are harmful because they place restrictions on the freedom of the capitalist. Worker safety laws, legally mandated antidiscrimination policies, and environmental protection rules are all detrimental to society because they impede the freedom of the managers to decide how to direct their companies.

The expression *laissez-faire*, literally "to leave alone," vividly describes managerial freedom. This expression is derived from a French merchant named Le Gendre who, in 1680, suggested to the French government that the best way to promote commerce and industry is for the government to "leave them alone." Today, *laissez-faire* is a synonym for a market economy or free enterprise system.

CAPITALISM AND THE INDUSTRIAL REVOLUTION

The features of capitalism—private property, competition, market economy, and freedom of managerial decision—were described most thoroughly by Adam Smith in his *Inquiry into the Nature and Causes of the Wealth of Nations* (known more commonly by its shortened title, *The Wealth of Nations*), published in 1776. Smith, however, never mentioned the term *capitalism*. In writing his book, which has become the bible of capitalism, Smith denounced the prevailing system of **mercantilism**—an economic system based on the theory that the wealth of a state may be calculated on the basis of the gold, silver, and other precious metals it possesses. Under mercantilism, monopolies, tariffs, and state regulation had become central features. Smith urged that a free economy be established instead of a mercantile system.

Although Adam Smith's concepts became the adopted philosophy of capitalists, the philosophy of capitalism and the practices of capitalism varied over time. It is essential, therefore, to examine the historical development of capitalism.

Capitalism has roots going back to ancient times when individuals owned property and traded for a profit. Trade across continents existed in Greece and Rome, but modern capitalism emerged first in Europe and North America in the late eighteenth century after a long process of development.

Although profit was a feature uniting the old and the new capitalism, what distinguishes the two is that modern capitalism is based on the idea of economic development and growth. That is to say that in ancient capitalism, profit was perceived as being derived at someone's expense: a gain for someone in a static economy is a loss for someone else. In modern capitalism, it is possible to create wealth that will be beneficial to many people rather than to a select few. According to British economist Arthur Shenfield, "Capitalism was the first system in human history in which it became possible to become rich by uplifting the poor."[2]

Modern capitalism coincided with the Industrial Revolution. In fact, capitalism became the first economic system to bring about the Industrial Revolution. In the twentieth century, the state—rather than capitalists—has played a more important role in bringing on the Industrial Revolution in developing countries. Because of the role of capitalism as originator of the Industrial Revolution, we must understand the central features of that revolution.

The **Industrial Revolution** is the name given to the rapid transformation in economic life brought about by the application of science and technology to the production of goods. The Industrial Revolution involved methods of production based on the use of new scientific inventions driven by the steam engine.

The Industrial Revolution started in England and spread elsewhere. Through that revolution, production of goods expanded rapidly. Other major changes appeared: Roads were built, canals were opened, steamship services were begun, and railroad operations increased. New markets and sources of raw materials became available as a result of the demands of an industrial society. Banking and finance played important roles in the new economic order.

The Industrial Revolution did not appear all of a sudden without centuries of slow development in science, technology, philosophy, laws, and business practices. By the nineteenth century, however, it was clear that the processes of industrial development were moving so rapidly that the world would never again be the same. It has been said that the changes in the world brought on by the Industrial Revolution transformed the world more than anything the world had experienced in all of its preindustrial history.

From the point of view of the development of capitalism, three major changes are notable: the growth of cities and urban life, the formation of new classes, and the creation of a new political world.

Cities and Urban Life

The Industrial Revolution was marked by the rapid growth of cities. Urban growth was caused by a rise in population brought on by industrial society and economic inducements. The Industrial Revolution produced a higher standard of

---

[2] Arthur Shenfield, *Myth and Reality in Economic Systems*, no. 4 (Washington, D.C.: Heritage Foundation, 1981), p. 7.

living and better health conditions, which extended life expectancy. People flocked from the countryside to the cities because of economic opportunities and because in many cases economic difficulties drove them from the farms. The new factories in the cities manufactured goods far more efficiently than did individuals at home or in small shops, so there was a rapidly diminishing market for the goods produced outside the factory system.

As millions of people fled to the cities to find work, the quality of life for many people deteriorated. Housing was inadequate, and the cities became marked by slums, poor sanitation, and crime.

Urban life was a misery for many of the factory workers. Conditions in many of the factories were appalling, as often the machinery was dangerous and the working environment was unhealthy. Men, women, and children worked in "sweatshops." There was little that the workers could do to alter these miserable conditions since the laws generally supported the business leaders at the expense of the working class. If workers were injured on the job, for example, their wages were stopped immediately. Children were whipped if they fell asleep at the machines.

Many of the workers were paid low wages, and work was not always available for them. To be sure, there had been poverty in earlier periods of history. What made the poverty of the Industrial Revolution different was its concentration and visibility to the rest of society. Because the suffering was concentrated in urban areas, it could be seen and deplored.

Formation of New Classes

The two classes that emerged in power and influence as a result of the Industrial Revolution were the middle class and the working class. The middle class, or **bourgeoisie** as it is sometimes called, consisted of factory owners, bankers, merchants, and lawyers. Gradually, these men took power from the aristocracy, whose influence was based on land and family ties. The bourgeoisie encouraged laws to be passed that expanded the influence of capitalists in economic development. In many cases these laws hurt the interests of both the aristocrats, whose privileges were based on inheritance, and the factory workers, who were often the victims of rapid economic development.

The political power of the factory workers (or **proletariat,** as they are sometimes called) grew more slowly. In most countries factory workers were initially excluded from certain kinds of political participation, such as voting in elections and organizing trade unions. Labor unions and strikes were illegal in the early stages of the Industrial Revolution. Typical antilabor statutes of the eighteenth century included the Le Chapelier Law in France and the British Combination Acts, which made unions illegal.

As industrialism developed, the number of factory workers increased and the political power of these workers grew stronger. Gradually, in Western democracies, the factory workers received the franchise and were permitted to form trade unions. Collective bargaining and the strike became legal weapons.

A New Political World

As indicated in Chapter 2, the nineteenth century was marked by the unleashing of the forces of nationalism. Although nationalism cannot be explained exclusively in terms of the rise of an industrial system, there is a close affinity. Industrialization meant a mobilization of society into an immense economic effort. It required a cooperative venture on the part of people of diverse religious, ethnic, and social backgrounds for the purpose of economic development. With the building of better transportation and communication systems, there was much more interaction among people residing within a state than had occurred earlier.

Not all countries adapted readily to the aspirations of the new industrial order. At first, the Industrial Revolution was limited to Western Europe and North America. It gradually spread to Eastern Europe. By the twentieth century it had encompassed the world. There is scarcely a country that has not accepted the principles of an industrial society, although the pace and style vary from one to another.

THE CHANGING CHARACTER OF CAPITALISM

In Adam Smith's time, capitalism was quite different from what it is today. When we think of capitalism today, we think of giant corporations—Exxon, General Motors, and IBM—businesses so big that they play major roles in their industries. When Smith thought of capitalism, he perceived many entrepreneurs engaged in small-scale operations. In that context, the owner of a factory was usually also its manager.

Even Smith noted storm signals ahead for a competitive economy, observing that free market economy principles could be violated. "People of the same trade seldom meet together," he wrote, "but the conversation ends in a conspiracy against the public, or in some diversion to raise prices."[3]

During Smith's lifetime, joint stock companies were limited in purpose—created to build a railroad or canal, for example—and were often limited in time as well. In the late nineteenth and twentieth centuries, large corporations began to emerge. In these corporations, as Adolf A. Berle, Jr. and Gardiner C. Means observe, there has been a separation between the owners and the managers—a radical change from early capitalism.[4] In the new capitalism the managers play the dominant role in making decisions for the corporation.

Modern capitalists, moreover, differ from their forebears in that they have often tried to avoid price competition. The biggest corporations attempt to provide "market leadership" in price so that competition focuses on the quality of the product, technological innovation, and service. In this manner, cutthroat competition can be avoided. In general, attempts to break up the giant corporations through antitrust legislation have not been successful. Many entrepreneurs with limited resources have lacked the financial base to compete effectively against the giants.

The big corporations have at various times attempted to form **cartels**—organizations of companies controlling supply and demand of products. They have increasingly sought government support through tariffs, government contracts, and subsidies. When facing economic difficulties, they have not let Adam Smith get in the way of requesting government bailouts, as the cases of Lockheed and Chrysler Corporation in the United States and Rolls-Royce in Britain attest. In some industries, such as armaments, corporations have become so enmeshed with the state as to really lose their "capitalist" identity. Capitalism in practice, then, differs considerably from capitalism in theory.

THE SOCIALIST CHALLENGE

Socialism is the major ideological challenge to capitalism. Like *democracy*, the term *socialism* is ambiguous and lends it-

---

[3] Quoted in Robert L. Heilbroner, *The Worldly Philosophers: The Lives, Times, and Ideas of the Great Economic Thinkers*, 6th ed. (New York: Simon and Schuster, 1986), p. 70.

[4] Adolf A. Berle, Jr. and Gardiner C. Means, *The Modern Corporation and Private Property* (New York: Macmillan, 1933), chap. 5.

self to many definitions. Communists sometimes refer to socialism as being almost synonymous with communism. Some anticommunists use the term *socialism* to distinguish themselves from communists. No universally accepted definition of socialism has been adopted. Although it is possible to go back to antiquity to find early examples of socialistic communities, socialism is better understood as a modern phenomenon—a reaction to the excesses of capitalism.

Although recognizing that no one definition of socialism will satisfy everyone, we will define **socialism** as a system in which the major economic institutions are in public rather than private hands. Generally, in a socialist system, the state acts as a representative of the public and owns and manages the major economic institutions, such as factories, railroads, and farms. Its planning institutions play a central role in the management of the economy, and the welfare state is prominent. In practice, however, there is much variation in the amount of public ownership and the extent of welfare programs even in countries that profess to be socialistic.

Like capitalism, socialism is an *economic* system. It is possible for a country to adopt a socialist economy and still be a democracy, if democracy is defined in political terms. The reverse is also true—that is, it is possible for a country to be a dictatorship and have a socialist economy.

As a response to capitalism, socialism has appeared in many varieties. The early socialists of the nineteenth century were utopian socialists. The most influential of the nineteenth-century socialists were the scientific socialists (or Marxists). We shall deal with these two groups first and emphasize the Marxist critique because of its significance. We can then look at later socialist philosophies, such as democratic socialism and communism.

Utopian Socialists

Utopian socialists believed that capitalism could be reformed by establishing **utopias** (ideal communities). These communities would be based on cooperation. Frequently, utopian socialists favored the building of communities that were self-sufficient. Their leading proponents were Claude Henri de Saint-Simon, Charles Fourier, and Robert Owen.

The utopian socialists failed because they all shared the belief that the capitalists would cooperate in the new schemes. The utopian socialists believed in *voluntary* socialism and had no conception of a class struggle between those who owned the means of production and those who did not. As we shall see, this belief in voluntary socialism placed them in stark contrast to Marx.

Marxists

Of the nineteenth-century critics of capitalism, the Marxists made the most enduring and influential attack. Because of his predominant position in the socialist movement, we shall examine the writings of its founder, Karl Marx, in greater detail than we have done with other critics of capitalism.

Marx's writings consist of books, polemical tracts, and newspaper and scholarly articles. No single work by Marx contains a synthesis of all his ideas. In part, this failure to provide a "bible" for his followers resulted from the activist, revolutionary nature of his work. As a leader of *one* faction within the socialist movement, Marx often directed his attention not against established institutions but rather against other critics of industrial society, such as the utopian socialists. Marx, moreover, stressed different points in arguing against his fellow radicals. Writing over a period of forty years, he was bound to change his mind on various issues and also to sometimes contradict himself. His work, consequently, is filled with many ambiguities and inconsistencies, so that it is possible to find criticisms of Marx in various works written by Marx.

Probably the two best known of all Marx's works are *The Communist Manifesto* (1848) and his unfinished *Das Kapital*, of which the first volume appeared in 1867 and the second and third volumes were published posthumously. During his adult life, Marx wrote constantly, and in addition to *The Communist Manifesto* and *Das Kapital*, these are considered among his principal writings: *German Ideology* (1845–46), *Theses on Feuerbach* (1845), *Poverty of Philosophy* (1847), *Class Struggles in France* (1850), *Eighteenth Brumaire* (1852), *The Critique of Political Economy* (1859), and *Civil War in France* (1870–71).

Cleared of all ambiguities, certain pillars of thought have come to constitute Marxism, the philosophy of Karl Marx. **Marxism** may thus be defined as a theory of human development that purports to explain all history on the basis of immutable economic laws. Marxists claim their analysis is scientific; hence the phrase **scientific socialism** to describe their ideas. These main ideas are: historical materialism, the dialectic, the class struggle, a theory of capitalism, revolution, and the inevitable emergence of the classless society.

Historical Materialism. **Historical materialism** is an explanation of history in terms of the material or economic foundations of society. According to this interpretation of history, the way in which a society uses its resources and produces its goods determines its political and social structure. If the system of production changes, corresponding changes in politics and society will result. Marx referred to the economic foundation of society as the **substructure** and everything else, such as laws, government, religion, culture, and ideology, as the **superstructure.** If the substructure is changed, so, too, will the superstructure change.

The relationship between substructure and superstructure may be seen from two examples concerned with religion and the state. Christians believe that God created man. A Marxist, in contrast, believes that man created God—or rather the *idea* of God—to serve the interests of a ruling class. A Marxist argues that if a ruling class can convince the masses of people that their kingdom is not of this earth and that their rewards are to come in some heavenly kingdom rather than in the material present, the ruling class will be able to more easily exploit the masses by paying them low wages and providing few benefits. Workers would be happy with the knowledge that they will enter the Kingdom of God. The statement by Marx that "religion is the opium of the people"[5] can be understood in this light.

Marxists view the state with as much disdain as they do religion. In this regard, they are in conflict with a classical view of ancient Greeks, such as that held by Aristotle, who described the state as a natural and essential institution of society. Marxists characterize the state as an artificial creation—part of the superstructure. The state is really an instrument of the ruling class and is consequently an evil institution. Ultimately, the state will wither away if exploited classes are liberated. This hostility to the state is a feature of Marxist philosophy that is shared by anarchists, who are opposed to the very existence of any state.

The Dialectic. Marx was influenced by the writings of the German philosopher G.W.F. Hegel. Marx derived his notion of the dialectic from Hegel although he used it in a different way. Hegel viewed history as a continuous unraveling of God's

---

[5] Karl Marx, "Contribution to the Critique of Hegel's Philosophy of Right," 1844, as excerpted in *Essential Writings of Karl Marx,* ed. David Caute (New York: Collier Books, 1967), p. 87.

design for the world. For Hegel, the real world is a reflection of the world of ideas. History unfolds progressively through a process of the dialectic.

By **dialectic,** Hegel meant the clash of opposites in which every idea is opposed by a contrary idea. The main components of the dialectic are thesis, antithesis, and synthesis. First an idea (**thesis**) is presented out of which an opposing idea (**antithesis**) is formed. Out of the struggle between the two comes a third idea (**synthesis**), which takes the best aspects of the thesis and the antithesis. This process is a continuing one and is dynamic, as the synthesis becomes a thesis, which creates a new antithesis resulting in a new synthesis, and so on.

It has often been said that Marx took Hegel's ideas and turned them upside down. For Marx, the ideal world is a reflection of the real world. Historical development unfolds on the basis of the dialectical process, but is keyed to the driving *economic* forces of the times.

According to Marx, history shows several stages of development, which he describes as primitive communal, slave, feudal, capitalist (bourgeois), and socialist. With the exception of the primitive communal, these correspond to control over the means of production by particular classes: slave owners, feudal lords, capitalists, and workers, respectively. In the primitive communal state, there is communal rather than private control over the means of production.

According to Marx, history unfolds progressively from one stage to the next as the economic foundations of society change. When too many obstacles impede movement to the next stage, "contradictions" arise. **Contradictions** are problems that cannot be solved without changing the basic structure of society. Revolution is the process that resolves the contradictions.

For Marx, the dialectic works to move historical development forward. For ex-

ample, **feudalism** (thesis), which was a society based on landed privilege and self-sufficient agricultural units, gradually produced a commercial class of entrepreneurs. These entrepreneurs grew stronger with the development of capitalism (antithesis) and eventually challenged the feudal leaders, resulting in a synthesis marking the triumph of capitalism. Capitalism, however, creates a proletarian class. As we shall see, for Marx the dialectical process terminates with the triumph of the working classes over their exploiters—the capitalists—or with the common ruin of the contending classes.

The Class Struggle. According to Marx, the history of all human society, except for primitive communities, is a history of **class struggle.** Marx never defined *class* explicitly. In general, he used the term to mean how groups are related to the means of production. Two major classes are thus distinguished: those who control the means of production and those who do not. It is the conflict between the "haves" and the "have-nots" that moves history forward.

New classes emerge as the forces of production change. The capitalists as a class are created when they are able to manage the new productive forces of society more efficiently than the feudal lords. The capitalists then create a new class—the proletariat, or workers. The proletariat and the capitalists struggle against each other in the same manner as the middle class and the guild workers earlier fought the feudal lords. Eventually, the workers take control of the means of production when the capitalists become unable to administer the productive forces of society efficiently. This is the dialectic applied to economics.

History, then, becomes the end product of the resolution of contradictions through the class struggle. The final class struggle between the proletariat and the capitalists will end either with the victory of the former and the end of exploitation, or in the common ruin of the contending classes.

Theory of Capitalism. Marxism is both a critique of capitalism and a praise of its virtues. The criticisms dealing with the exploitation of man by man have been noted. Marx, however, extolled the virtues of capitalism also. He admired the capitalists because they were able to produce material benefits in such abundance as to control the worst ravages of nature. In *The Communist Manifesto,* he and Friedrich Engels, his collaborator in many of his writings, observed:

It [the bourgeoisie] has been the first to show what man's activity can bring about. It has accomplished wonders far surpassing Egyptian pyramids, Roman aqueducts, and Gothic cathedrals; it has conducted expeditions that put in the shade all former Exoduses of nations and crusades.[6]

Although Marx approved of the achievements of capitalism and thought of the capitalists as providing a necessary historic mission, he condemned them as exploiters of the proletariat. In his view, capitalism was responsible for the destruction of the family, the workers' alienation from their work, and a declining standard of living for ordinary people. He perceived capitalism, however, as containing within itself the seeds of its own destruction. How this was to occur can best be understood by examining Marx's analysis of capitalism. Marx began with the **labor theory of value,** a theory that he drew from other economists. According to this theory, the value of a commodity is equal to the amount of labor-time necessary for its production.

Marx built upon this theory. He contended that capitalism treated the workers as if they were commodities. The workers receive wages that are just enough to provide for themselves and their families. Unlike all other commodities, labor produces a value greater than its own market value. Marx referred to **surplus value** as the value that labor produces over and above the amount that is necessary to produce an item, and viewed it as exploitation. Profit is derived solely from the surplus value created by the proletariat.

In the quest for more profits, the capitalists find themselves in a competitive situation with other capitalists producing similar goods. They are constantly trying to reduce costs of production by lowering the wages they give their workers and by introducing labor-saving machinery. Less efficient capitalists are driven out of business, and industry becomes concentrated in fewer and fewer companies. Society is polarized into those few who control the means of production and the army of the proletariat thrown out of work by machines. Wages are driven to a point below the subsistence level; many workers are unemployed. When the capitalists are unable to control the forces that they have unleashed, they call upon the state (which, according to Marx, is nothing more than the executive committee of the bourgeoisie) to stop the agitation of the proletariat.

Revolution. At the point in which the crisis is the greatest—when the proletariat is most exploited, when people are out of work, when capitalism and industrialism are most advanced; and when the state is most coercive—a revolution occurs. The revolution is an armed uprising of the proletariat unwilling to tolerate these most wretched conditions. There is nothing the capitalists can do to stop the revolution, since capitalism has created these irresistible forces that will destroy it.

---

[6] Karl Marx and Friedrich Engels, *The Communist Manifesto,* trans. Samuel Moore (Baltimore, Md.: Penguin Books, 1967), p. 83. *The Communist Manifesto* was first published in German in 1848; Samuel Moore's translation was first published in 1888.

It is important to emphasize that Marx attributed to the proletariat and to no other group the historic revolutionary mission. Because of its organization, cohesion, and numbers, it is that class that has the inevitable historical revolutionary role. The proletariat must be the instrument of the revolution because only the proletariat is capable of becoming masters of the productive forces of society.

The **peasants,** those poor farmers who work the land, play no revolutionary role. Marx viewed the peasantry as a reactionary element in society. He condemned both the "idiocy of rural life" and the peasant quest for private property.[7] Marx also criticized the *Lumpenproletariat*— that class of people who cannot find a place in the workers' world (in other words, the unemployable or the "parasite")—as a reactionary force in society.

To provide leadership for the workers, Marx advocated the primacy of the *communists,* a name he gave to his socialist faction to distinguish it as being more radical than others. He indicated, moreover, that there should be some role for intellectuals like himself in helping to educate the proletariat to develop a class consciousness. That class consciousness will arise, however, from economic conditions and not from planned activities of intellectuals.

The Classless Society. It may seem odd that there is scarcely any description in the writings of Marx and Engels as to what is to take the place of the old capitalist system when the revolution occurs. Like many an orthodox religion, the secular religion of Marxism directs its attention to the kingdom of this earth rather than to the Kingdom of God.

Marx did say that the state will wither away. There is no need for a state apparatus since there will be no classes— no group to exploit others. In other words, there will be a **classless society** based on the principle: "From each according to his ability, to each according to his needs." Marx provided no blueprint for socialism. Those writers and political leaders who came after Marx had to guess as best they could about the future of socialism, since they had scarcely any guidance from Marx's writings.

Marx and Engels did acknowledge that there is a short transition stage between the destruction of capitalism and the establishment of the new order. This stage is labeled the **dictatorship of the proletariat.** This dictatorship exists only for the purpose of eliminating the last vestiges of capitalism. Having completed this "mopping up" operation, the state withers away. Community interest rather than exploiter interest then guides human development in the new classless society.

COMMUNISM

The words *communism* and *communist* create certain familiar images, such as the Soviet Union, Joseph Stalin, Fidel Castro, and collectivism. Communism, however, also means different things to different people. In the early part of this century conservative business people viewed trade unionists as communists if they made demands for higher wages and better working conditions. The *communist* label has also been applied to liberals advocating minimum wage laws, hippies rejecting values of established institutions, civil rights advocates engaged in peaceful protest marches, and even doctors who favor fluoridation.

Etymologically, *communism* is derived from **commune,** a small isolated community. Communes go back to ancient times. Throughout the centuries people

---

[7] For a discussion of Marx's views on the peasantry, see David Mitrany, *Marx Against the Peasant: A Study in Social Dogmatism* (New York: Collier Books, 1961).

have joined communes—religious and secular—for varying reasons, and *commune* can be used to describe anything from a monastery of orthodox Christian holy men in prayerful dedication to God to a modern urban shelter dedicated to self-realization.

The use of the term *communism* to signify communal living is now somewhat dated. A more modern use appeared in the nineteenth century when *communism* was sometimes applied to the political philosophy of Karl Marx. As we have seen, Marx himself chose *communist* to mean the most radical of socialist groups. Today, however, many Marxists would chastise anyone who would identify them as communists.

Recognizing the ambiguity of the word **communism,** we will use it to mean a political ideology based on the writings of Karl Marx and the Russian revolutionary V. I. Lenin. The term *communism,* then, is synonymous with **Marxism-Leninism.** We have already described the political philosophy of Marx, so we shall now consider Lenin and those communists who came after him. To understand communism, we must first take a look at some of the central economic and political features of the period leading up to Lenin's rise to power. Later we shall examine changes in the communist world from 1917 when the first communist state was established to the present.

1848–1914: A Period of Prosperity and Reform

The period between 1848 and 1914 in Europe and North America was marked by widespread prosperity, the expansion of the suffrage, the growth of trade unions, the enactment of social reform legislation, the spread of nationalism, and the emergence of imperialism. Such profound changes were bound to have an impact on society.

Marx had predicted severe economic crises with increasing misery for the proletariat—a condition that would lead to revolution. The period between 1848 and 1914 saw, however, widespread prosperity instead of poverty. Rather than experiencing a decline in the standard of living, the workers in advanced industrial countries made gains in real wages.

In many countries, moreover, the franchise was enlarged to include ever greater numbers of people. In Great Britain, for example, the Reform Act of 1832 expanded the franchise to the middle class, and the Reform Act of 1867 gave the vote to part of the working class. By 1884, universal manhood suffrage was almost achieved. By 1928, women, too, were given the vote, and universal suffrage was a reality in Britain.

Not only was the franchise expanded but restrictions against trade unions were abandoned, and the number of workers enrolled in these associations rose. The power of trade unions, consequently, grew. To be sure, throughout this period there were acts of brutality against workers and their unions, but it could not be denied that their power was growing.

Workers and others benefited, too, from more humane state legislation to remedy the evils of uncontrolled capitalism. Child labor laws were passed. Working conditions improved. Germany in particular pioneered in establishing the welfare state based on the notion that the state has a responsibility to guarantee that every citizen is provided educational opportunities, medical care, and social security. The welfare state eventually was adopted by all advanced industrial countries, whatever their political persuasion.

Marx's prediction about the political behavior of the proletariat did not hold true. The workers did develop a class consciousness within their own countries in Europe, but they did not develop a class unity transcending national boundaries. They did not, moreover, achieve a revolutionary consciousness. Workers found that they had a vested interest in maintaining national ties to their state rather than in extending their primary loyalties to a world proletariat.

Another important development in this period was the territorial expansion of Western and other industrial countries into Africa and Asia, a process that was labeled **imperialism** (or colonialism). Great Britain and France led the advanced industrial countries in acquiring enormous overseas territories. The imperialist fever spread to Germany, Italy, the United States, and Japan. Although the motives for expansionism varied, the industrial countries were thus able to secure cheap sources of raw materials for their burgeoning economies.

The Ideological Response to Marx

Prosperity, the franchise, trade unionism, the welfare state, nationalism, and imperialism all became prominent features of the analysis that was being made by the socialists who followed Karl Marx. A central doctrinal problem of socialists was how to explain the events that were occurring in advanced industrial societies. Two principal views were put forward: the evolutionary and the revolutionary. These views, which had their origins in the latter part of the nineteenth century, continue to split the socialist movement to the present day.

Democratic Socialism. The evolutionary view contended that socialism could be achieved through peaceful and gradual change. Its foremost intellectual spokesman was Eduard Bernstein, a German socialist who had served as Engels's secretary. Bernstein argued that socialists should abandon the idea of violent revolution that could be found in Marx and other socialist writers. According to Bernstein, socialists should form parties of

peaceful protest, reform, and democracy.[8] To that end, socialists should continuously wage a protest campaign for improved working conditions, educational opportunity, and political participation. By organizing to vote in free elections, Bernstein contended, the workers could achieve their goals through the ballot box rather than through the turmoil of street barricades. Bernstein's prescription for socialism was to elect public officials responsive to socialist needs. He wrote, "To me that which is generally called the ultimate aim of socialism is nothing, the movement is everything."[9] By this he meant that the final aims of revolution and the creation of a utopian society are meaningless; what really counts is the practical day-to-day improvement of the condition of working people and increased popular participation in political life.

Bernstein also attacked many of the assumptions of Marxist ideology itself. Specifically, he criticized the idea that capitalism was doomed to reduce the standard of living of the proletariat. He questioned the validity of dialectical materialism. Bernstein became the chief proponent of the **revisionists**—those who revised the ideas of Marx. He did more than merely revise Marx's writings, however; he set forth a clearly new philosophy in conflict with Marx.

Although many writers and political leaders in Bernstein's time and thereafter did not support his entire analysis of the direct assault on Marxism, many agreed with the fundamental principle of achieving socialism through evolutionary and peaceful democratic reform. This approach to socialism is known as **social democracy** or **democratic socialism**. On

---

[8] See Eduard Bernstein, *Evolutionary Socialism: A Criticism and Affirmation,* trans. Edith C. Harvey (New York: Schocken Books, 1961).

[9] Ibid., p. 202.

the continent of Europe the social democratic movement developed in response to Marxist writings. Because of their insular positions and their nonideological approach to politics, many British and American writers and political leaders with similar views argued with little or no reference to Marx, although they reached the same conclusions as Bernstein. Social democrats, then, are champions of social reform and the welfare state through political democracy.

Social democrats today are likely to favor programs that provide greater benefits for medical care, housing, public education, and aid for the poor. When in power in capitalistic economies, social democrats have had to reconcile their desire for economic equality with a need to stimulate economic growth by encouraging market forces. Attempts at such a reconciliation have led to differences among social democrats about whether the goal of social reform is being sacrificed in the quest for political success at election time.

Lenin. The evolutionary approach to socialism was challenged by the more radical sections of the socialist movement. The principal critic was a Russian intellectual, Vladimir Ilyich Ulanov, better known as Lenin. As a leading radical political writer and agitator, Lenin has become one of the best-known revolutionaries of any age. In communist countries his portrait is to be seen in offices and homes, on billboards, and in museums. His writings and speeches are quoted endlessly in every field from pure science to the arts. In noncommunist countries he is condemned by some government officials as the creator of a fiendish scheme to destroy the well-being of all nations. In these same noncommunist countries this same Lenin serves as a model to young, romantic radicals of a revolutionary who actually "shook" the world in spite of almost hopeless odds against him.

To understand the man, his ideas, and his policies, it is essential first to look at Russia, the country that he eventually ruled, during the period before World War I. While Western Europe was industrializing its economy and involving more groups in political participation, Russia was slow to change. Economically, it remained dominated by agriculture. Politically, the czar and his close supporters ruled in an authoritarian way over a society consisting mostly of a peasant population.

Economic and political transformation of society was slow in coming. Russian people had difficulty in expressing discontent with the pace of change through legitimate, peaceful expression because of government repression, censorship, and police surveillance. By the end of the nineteenth century, however, certain reforms in the economy were instituted, and Russia embarked on a policy of industrialization. At the time World War I began in 1914, Russia was still a poor country—although an active newcomer to industrialization—with an autocracy ruled by a monarch, Czar Nicholas II.

It was the tragedy of World War I that brought down the czar. Although he played no role in ending czarist rule, Lenin was able to skillfully manipulate popular dissatisfaction with the war, so that his faction—the **Bolsheviks**—eventually came to power in November 1917.

Leninism. Lenin's contributions to political thought must be considered in relationship to Marxism since Lenin contended that he was actually applying Marxism to conditions of Russia in the twentieth century. Critics of Lenin—including even some Marxists—argue, however, that Leninism is in fact anti-Marxist. Debate on the relationship between Lenin and Marx is made even more complicated because, like the works of Marx, the writings and speeches of Lenin are often contradictory. Lenin, consequently, can be and has been quoted to support nationalism and internationalism, coalition government and noncooperation with noncommunist parties, and peace and war. The essence of Leninism, however, deals with Lenin's ideas on the nature of the Communist party, the dictatorship of the proletariat, the skipping of revolutionary stages, the flexibility of tactics, and imperialism.

COMMUNIST PARTY. Marx had offered no analysis of the nature or role of political parties. The revolution was to occur when economic conditions were ripe, according to Marx. Intellectual leaders, moreover, might help educate the working classes, but economic conditions—not the actions of leaders—would produce revolutions.

Lenin developed a concept of a Communist party in stark contrast to Marx. In his view the party should be small, disciplined, and conspiratorial. Lenin argued that since the Russian police under the czar would not permit a dissenting group to openly criticize the government, the party must of necessity be small and conspiratorial. Even after the czarist government was destroyed, however, Lenin continued to maintain a similar view of the Communist party.

Like Bernstein, Lenin believed that workers left to themselves would find that their economic conditions would gradually improve. Unlike Bernstein, Lenin felt that such a situation was harmful to the cause of the revolution. To the extent that the workers achieved a higher standard of living, education, and health care, they would have a vested interest in the perpetuation of the capitalist system. In other words, Lenin perceived that the workers would not develop a proper revolutionary consciousness.

According to Lenin, it is a Communist party composed of dedicated revolutionaries that possesses the proper revolutionary consciousness. Without the party,

it is not possible to achieve communism. The party must be small and disciplined, since its strength comes from its unity and resolve. It is this party that knows what is in the best interests of the masses of people, since the party would not be swayed by false ideologies propounded by the bourgeois publicists. The party would be "the military staff of the proletariat." The basic decision-making principle would be **democratic centralism.** By this Lenin meant that party members could debate issues, but once a decision was made, every party official had to support it. In this way, top party leaders controlled the government. Although while in power Lenin tolerated debate and lost in some party issues, he instituted actions that restricted opposition not only from noncommunists but from Communist party members as well. It was not until actions by his successor, Stalin, however, that any opposition was crushed.

DICTATORSHIP OF THE PROLETARIAT. Marx had written that the dictatorship of the proletariat, coming soon after the proletarian revolution, would last only for a short transitional period. Its function was to rid society of the last vestiges of the old capitalist order. With its work completed, the dictatorship of the proletariat would disappear, and the state would wither away.

Lenin, however, made the dictatorship of the proletariat and the building of a communist state a central element of his theory. Since the communists came to power not, as Marx had predicted, in an advanced industrial society but, rather, in one of the economically weakest industrial powers in Europe, Lenin argued that the dictatorship of the proletariat would last for a long period of time. It would be the instrument for building the new industrial society. Lenin reinterpreted Marx to mean that when Marx said the state would wither away, he was referring to the bourgeois state, but the proletarian state would be required to build socialism. In power, Lenin constructed a communist state commensurate with his view.

THE SKIPPING OF STAGES. As indicated above, Marx had argued that history would move according to the inevitable historic stages. Although he wrote occasional contradictory comments, the thrust of his argument was that socialism would not be achieved unless capitalism had run its course.

Lenin contended, in contrast, that it was possible to skip stages—to move from feudalism to communism without going through the bourgeois stages of economic and political development. The instrument of that transformation would be the Communist party, which would create an industrial order. Leninism, consequently, provides more flexibility than Marxism for leaders to manipulate events in pursuit of communist goals.

FLEXIBILITY OF TACTICS. At first, Lenin believed that he was to be the leader not of a Russian revolution but, rather, of a *world* revolution. It soon became obvious that the world revolution was going to take much longer to come about than Lenin had anticipated. Lenin devised tactics for communist revolutionaries to support, and these tactics were in stark contrast to Marxism.

For Lenin, world communist revolution was the essential goal. Morality consisted of communist victory, and any means used to achieve this objective was acceptable. The task of communists, therefore, was to disrupt legitimate organizations and political parties for their own ends in noncommunist countries.

In 1919, Lenin established the **Third International**[10] (sometimes referred to as

Communist International or **Comintern**) and set forth the policies that caused social democratic parties to withdraw from the organization of a world socialist movement under the dominance of the Soviet Union—the new name of Russia. According to Lenin, socialists everywhere must subvert reform movements in bourgeois countries for the ultimate goal of communist revolution and identify their cause with the Soviet Union. Such a view was in conflict with the political convictions of anyone committed to political democracy and patriotism.

Social democrats and liberals saw their work as bringing about peaceful reform within a democratic framework. When noncommunist, reform-minded individuals joined associations such as trade unions, peace groups, civil rights organizations, or anti-imperialist societies, for example, they engaged in open, peaceful protest activities. Communists, however, were ordered by Lenin to subvert these groups for communist ends as determined by the communist leaders of the Soviet Union.

We may take peace groups as a case in point and use the American effort before World War II as an example. When Adolf Hitler and Joseph Stalin concluded a nonaggression pact in 1939, communists in the United States were ordered to strengthen the peace cause by helping to keep the United States from rearming. When Hitler violated the treaty and attacked the Soviet Union, American communists were told to use their influence to get America to rearm at once. Genuine pacifists continued to urge America to stay out of the war and were now condemned by Soviet-oriented communists.

IMPERIALISM. Drawing on the ideas of British writer J.A. Hobson, Lenin devised a theory of imperialism to help explain

---

[10] The First International was Karl Marx's International Workingmen's Association of 1864–76. The Second International, or Labor and Socialist International, existed before World War I as a loose conglomeration of socialist and labor parties. The Second International was re-created after World War I with a social democratic orientation.

why the revolution did not occur in the advanced industrial societies, as Marx had predicted. According to Lenin, capitalism had moved beyond its industrial stage into a new period dominated by monopoly and finance capital. During this new stage, monopolies and cartels were formed. Capitalists carved up spheres of influence all over the world so that capitalism would survive through acquiring cheap sources of raw materials and new markets.

Lenin argued that the reason why prosperity had been rising in the capitalist societies was that the capitalists and the proletariat in the developed societies were profiting from the colonies. Imperialism was essential to capitalism, moreover, and those countries that could not maintain colonies would be a weak link in the capitalist chain and, consequently, were ripe for revolution.

Leninism, then, is the central core of political views held by a leading communist theoretician. Unlike Marx, however, Lenin was both a theoretician and a political leader of a country. As such, he had to adapt his ideas to the practical needs of his times.

Once in power, Lenin occupied himself with solving concrete problems in domestic and foreign policy. In his first two years, he nationalized industry, confiscated bank and church property, and created a secret police (the Cheka). This period, known as War Communism, was also characterized by a civil war, which the Bolsheviks eventually won. Recognizing the need to improve the economy and to regain power, Lenin adopted a moderate pragmatic program, the **New Economic Policy** (NEP), which allowed for some domestic capitalism to operate and for Western capitalists to invest in the Soviet Union.

At the time of Lenin's death in 1924, the beginnings of a dictatorship were apparent. Freedom of the press was suppressed. The Communist party dominated all the political institutions in the country. Lenin refused to permit any non-Bolshevik group to exercise independent power. Even within the Communist party itself, restrictions were placed on the degree of freedom of party members to organize into factions. The secret police were operating in all sectors of society. The seeds of a full-blown dictatorship were planted. It remained for Lenin's successors to fill in the details.

Stalin. Three years after the death of Lenin, Joseph Stalin rose to undisputed leadership in the Soviet Union. Once regarded as the great leader of an innovative and experimental political system, Stalin today has lost his place of eminence in communist folklore. When he ruled the Soviet Union, he could do no wrong— at least so far as all Soviet history books, magazines, and newspapers were concerned. Since his death in 1953, Stalin has become—even for many communists—a symbol of how a noble revolution can be betrayed by one man obsessed with a "personality cult." Even among those communists who condemn him today, there is a respect for his personal cunning and his accomplishments for the Soviet Union. How much of what the Soviet Union experienced in the period of his rule can be attributed to *Stalin the man* rather than *communism the system* is now, and probably will continue to be, debated by social scientists without ever reaching a definitive answer.

Joseph Stalin, born in 1879 as Joseph Vissarionovich Djugashvili, grew up in Georgia, a region of Russia bordering on the Black Sea. Stalin, unlike Lenin, was not an intellectual; nor did he spend most of his time before the Revolution of 1917 outside Russia. Stalin was a shoemaker's son. He entered a theological seminary on a scholarship. Theological studies did not interest him, and he turned his attention to revolutionary activities. Because of these efforts, he was expelled from the seminary. By 1904, Stalin had joined the Bolsheviks, and in 1912 he became a member of their Central Committee. He was exiled to Siberia in 1913 by the czarist government. He went to Petrograd after the March Revolution in 1917 and became editor of the communist newspaper *Pravda*.

Stalin's skills were primarily administrative and organizational, and such skills made it possible for him to maneuver himself into positions of authority. He was people's commissar for nationalities. He later was the head of the Workers' and Peasants' Inspection, an organization that put the workers and peasants into positions of governmental administration. Stalin served on the Politburo (the small group of party leaders) when it was first set up. In 1922, he became general secretary of the Communist party. Crafty and single-purposed in his desire to come to power, Stalin moved adeptly against his challengers for leadership. By 1927, Stalin had taken command and changed the character of life in the Soviet Union.

Stalinism. The two major ideological innovations of **Stalinism** were: an emphasis on building socialism in one country—the Soviet Union—rather than promoting world revolution; and totalitarianism.

SOCIALISM IN ONE COUNTRY. Under the NEP, the Soviet Union made economic gains, but at the cost of making concessions to free enterprise in the industrial sector and to the peasants in terms of individual farms. Thus many communists saw the NEP as a betrayal of socialism. Between 1928 and 1941, however, the Soviet Union embarked on a new program of economic development to radically alter the social and economic life of that country. The decision was made by Stalin to establish **"Socialism in One Country."** To rapidly industrialize the Soviet Union would be the first goal of the Soviet government, and world revolution would be second to that goal. To achieve Socialism in One Country, drastic changes were brought about in agriculture and in industry.

Because the peasants were not producing enough agricultural products and the economic efficiency of the peasant small holdings was low, Stalin instituted collectivization of agriculture in 1929. **Collectivization** meant that private ownership of land would be replaced by public ownership or control. Stalin wanted to use the savings from agricultural development to finance major industrialization projects.

In less than a year's time, about ten million peasants were taken from their land. Some were arrested; others were exiled. Hundreds of thousands perished, and millions were made destitute. The peasants resisted by destroying cattle and crops. Some of the ravages of the resistance produced consequences to Soviet agriculture from which the Soviet Union has still not recovered. The immediate result of collectivization was to produce a famine, which caused many deaths. As a result of the failure at collectivization, Stalin eased up against the peasants by allowing some private incentive to reappear. By the end of the 1930s, however, nearly all the farms were collectivized.

In addition to agricultural programs, Stalin set out in a major effort to industrialize the Soviet Union. The first of the Five-Year Plans (government goals for the economy) began in 1928. Forced labor was introduced into factories. Consumer goods were kept to a minimum as capital was used to develop heavy industry. Penalties for economic "crimes" were made severe. Jail sentences for workers who came twenty minutes late for work were not uncommon. According to Stalin, the Soviet Union would have to modernize rapidly, lest it be vanquished by its enemies.

Under Stalin, the Soviet Union modernized rapidly. Construction in heavy industry, hydroelectric plants, and transportation facilities helped to strengthen the economy in Stalin's time and served as a base for future economic development. Welfare state benefits were established and educational opportunities created. The advances in economic development took place at a high cost in human freedom, however.

TOTALITARIANISM. The cost in human freedom was a direct consequence of rapid industrialization and the establishment of a dictatorship. Stalin created the first totalitarian state (see Chapter 3). The Soviet Union became a police state, and communism became the all-encompassing ideology. The Communist party dominated Soviet society. Stalin ruled the Communist party by instituting purges of party members. Dedicated communist revolutionaries who had fought against czarist forces were sent to prison camps. The purges extended into all sectors of government and society. Millions perished as a result of these policies.

Under the control of the government, the news media hailed Stalin as a great leader. Pictures and statues of Stalin appeared everywhere, and Stalin experienced no public criticism within the Soviet Union.

Communism after Stalin. Toward the end of World War II, Soviet forces swept over Eastern Europe. When the war was over, communist governments loyal to Stalin were established in most of the areas that Soviet troops had entered. Even before Stalin's death, however, opposition to Soviet domination appeared. In 1948, Yugoslavia successfully asserted its independence from Soviet domination. In 1949, a revolution in China saw the emergence of Mao Zedong and his followers, who were resentful of Soviet practices. Although the rift between the Soviet Union and Communist China did not

appear openly in 1949, it grew wider in the 1960s and 1970s.

After a short period of jockeying for leadership of the Soviet Union following Stalin's death, Nikita Khrushchev came to power by 1956. He engaged in de-Stalinization at home and a policy of "peaceful coexistence" abroad.

DE-STALINIZATION. **De-Stalinization** was a policy of blaming Stalin for the evils that the Soviet Union had experienced. Stalin was denounced in a "secret speech" delivered by Khrushchev at the Twentieth Party Congress in February 1956. Khrushchev criticized Stalin for creating a "cult of personality" and committing atrocities against the Soviet people. Khrushchev instituted a certain amount of liberalization in the Soviet Union and a relaxation of Soviet control of other communist countries.

PEACEFUL COEXISTENCE. The Soviet Union proclaimed a policy of **peaceful coexistence** in which the Soviet Union would seek to engage in peaceful competition with the West and avoid military confrontation. The Soviet Union, however, did engage in some military confrontations during the period of Khrushchev's rule, which ended in 1964. Nevertheless, the professed goal was nonconfrontation with the West. Although there have been periods of confrontation and cooperation from 1964 to the present, **détente** (relaxation of tensions) remains the official Soviet goal in foreign policy. Détente, however, has not meant the elimination of the goal of promoting communism everywhere in the world.

Relations between the Soviet Union and other communist countries, and between the Soviet Union and the communist parties of noncommunist countries, have also changed during the regimes of Khrushchev and his successors. At times, the Soviet Union used military force against its communist allies such as against Hungary in 1956 and Czechoslovakia in 1968.

At other times, however, it was unable or unwilling to influence other communist states. Until 1989, it could not heal the breach between itself and the People's Republic of China. It has also been unable to strengthen or control many of the communist parties of Western Europe.

In the period since the death of Stalin, the communist world has become decentralized. Some communist countries, such as China and Romania, have shown independence from the Soviet Union in the conduct of foreign policy. There is, moreover, variation within communist countries in the degree of political and intellectual freedom and even in the amount of free enterprise permitted. China and Hungary have introduced some features of the market economy in efforts to stimulate economic growth, for example.

The Gorbachev Era. In the years before the death of Leonid Brezhnev, the Soviet Union seemed to be in a state of paralysis. An aging leadership resisted changes in the economic, social, and political system, while the economy showed signs of decay. In this regard, the Soviet Union continued to import wheat from the West since it was unable to produce enough food to feed itself. It lagged behind the West and the Pacific Basin countries, such as Hong Kong, Japan, South Korea, and Taiwan, in economic growth. Although it had made impressive gains in production of oil, steel, and electric power, it did not build the kind of sophisticated economy required by what is known as the communications age, with its reliance on computers and electronics.

The Soviet Union ceased to have an ideological appeal to any appreciable extent in noncommunist countries. At the Twenty-Second Party Congress in 1961, Khrushchev had boasted that the Soviet Union would overtake the United States by 1970 and would build a full communist society by 1980. No Soviet leaders were making similar claims in the 1980s. Non-communist countries turned increasingly to the West as a model for economic development.

Soviet society experienced severe problems in the form of alcoholism, pollution, and corruption. Alone among industrial countries, life expectancy in the Soviet Union actually declined in the 1970s and 1980s.

After the death of Brezhnev in 1983, Yuri Andropov came to power in the Soviet Union. Although he attempted to make some changes in the Soviet economy through a campaign against corruption, he died soon after he assumed leadership. An aging and ill Konstantin Chernenko succeeded him, but he, too, died soon after he took office. In March 1985, Mikhail Gorbachev became the Soviet leader. Fifty-four years old, he represented the younger political generation that came of age after Stalin died. His meetings with leading political figures in the West and his statements and actions symbolized vigor and change. British Prime Minister Margaret Thatcher, who had a reputation as an ardent anticommunist, was impressed with Gorbachev, as were other Western political leaders, academics, and journalists. *Time* magazine made Gorbachev "Man of the Year" for 1987, and public opinion polls in Western Europe indicated that he was more admired there than the president of the United States.

Gorbachev took a number of steps on the economic, cultural, political, and foreign policy fronts. The key concepts he promoted were *perestroika* (restructuring) and *glasnost* (openness). Although each term lacks a universally accepted definition, in general, **perestroika** is an effort to modernize the Soviet economy. **Glasnost** is an effort to make Soviet society less secretive and more open to differing and critical viewpoints.

Gorbachev acted to reform the economy. He sought to decentralize economic decision making. Cooperatives were encouraged, and economic viability was to become a key factor in determining whether a factory would continue in operation.

It was clear that capitalism, as such, was not being introduced into the Soviet economy. Soviet citizens still could not hire labor as a business firm does under capitalism. But a cooperative could be formed, and the cooperative's profits could be distributed to its members. Under "moonlighting" laws put into effect in spring 1987, any Soviet citizen could ask local authorities for permission to start a small business.

In agriculture, collective farms could now sell fruits, vegetables, and potatoes directly to the cities at prices that were between the state prices and higher prices in the free markets in the city, where the products of the private plots were sold.

The Soviet government sought to encourage foreign investment in the Soviet Union through joint ventures in which the Soviet Union would have a 51 percent interest and the foreign holder 49 percent. Not permitted were wholly owned foreign plants.

Gorbachev sought to fight the corruption that had become a feature of Soviet society. He also launched a campaign against alcoholism and greatly increased the price of alcohol. Popular opposition to this program made the Soviet leader ease up on the campaign.

Through the policy of *glasnost,* Gorbachev signaled a change in the tolerance of the Soviet government to criticism of the regime. Newspapers carried stories about government wrongdoing. They even reported stories hitherto ignored by the Soviet press, such as those involving poor quality of medical care, demonstrations and strikes, problems of poverty and vagrancy, and drug abuse. Books that had been banned for decades were now printed, including works by Boris Pasternak, Mikhail Bulgakov, and Vladimir Nabokov. The arts—film, theater, and literature—were opened up to innovators,

whose works were either politically critical of the regime or were of a kind that Communist party officials had previously believed improper for the Soviet people because of their subject matter or avant garde character. The jamming of some foreign broadcasts was suspended. The government began to report accurate negative social trends. It admitted that maps of the cities of the Soviet Union had been deliberately distorted for reasons of security, thus confusing tourists and others who tried to use them.

In the realm of human rights, the Soviet Union released some prominent dissidents from prisons. Andrei Sakharov, a leading dissident who had been exiled to Gorky, was brought back to Moscow. The number of Jews allowed to emigrate from the Soviet Union increased.

Gorbachev took steps to change the formal governing system. He amalgamated the head of state and the general secretary of the Communist party into a single position. The person holding this office would now be elected for a specific term. Gorbachev sought and successfully enacted in 1988 the establishment of a new parliamentary body, a 2,250-member Congress of People's Deputies. It would meet every year to select a smaller full-time legislature, the Supreme Soviet, and also a president, who would serve as the chief executive of the country. The Congress of People's Deputies would be elected, with multiple candidacies, from unions and other functional groups, and also from geographical and ethnic constituencies. These elections, however, would not include competition from parties other than the Communist party.

Recovering from a quiescent foreign policy of aging Soviet leaders, the Soviet Union under Gorbachev took new initiatives. Gorbachev met with President Ronald Reagan in five summit meetings. Soviet troops, fighting in Afghanistan since 1979, were withdrawn, despite the fact that it appeared likely that the communist regime in Afghanistan would thus fall to Afghan guerrillas.

Gorbachev took active steps to conclude arms control agreements with the Soviet Union. He presented proposals to reduce strategic nuclear forces by both the Soviet Union and the United States. He was particularly keen to slow down U.S. efforts in strategic defense. Although he was not successful in either of these efforts, the Soviet Union did conclude the Intermediate-range Nuclear Forces Treaty with the United States, ratified in 1988. Under the treaty, both powers agreed to eliminate intermediate-range nuclear weapons—that is, weapons with a range of between one and five thousand kilometers—from Europe.

That the Soviet Union is in a period of great change is without debate. What remains an open question, however, is the significance of that change, and that subject is explored in the final debate of this chapter.

ISSUES

Marxists and other socialist critics of the nineteenth century agreed that capitalism produced many evils. They condemned what they saw as the worst elements of capitalism: the dismal working conditions, the sense of alienation, the self-serving nature of middle-class values, and the breakup of a sense of community. They differed greatly about the causes and the cure of the new industrial order. They assumed, however, that the world could be made better if capitalism were subjected to constraints.

The establishment of communism in the Soviet Union and other countries has provided a record by which communist ideas and practices may be evaluated and compared to noncommunist systems. The adoption of socialism in noncommunist regimes has also provided data about socialist accomplishments. Three questions that have involved those concerned about capitalism, socialism, and communism are considered here: (1) Is socialism better than capitalism? (2) Has Marxism been vindicated? (3) Will the reforms of the Gorbachev era lead to a Soviet Union characterized by political democracy and a peaceful foreign policy?

12/YES   IS SOCIALISM BETTER THAN CAPITALISM?

The fact that socialism in one form or another has been adopted in most countries of the world is an indication of its popularity compared to the tarnished image of capitalism. If we consider socialism as it is practiced in noncommunist countries, it is clear that socialism is superior to capitalism because it: (1) promotes equality, (2) serves public needs, (3) plans better, (4) respects individual freedom, and (5) strengthens democracy.

Equality.

No one who can honestly call themselves a socialist would not agree that equality is the value basic to any imaginable or feasible socialist society; nor that egalitarian behaviour and example is not a necessary part of building any road to socialism.[11]

These words of political scientist Bernard Crick focus on the essential element in any analysis of society. In a world where material resources are available to improve the condition of humanity, there is no excuse for the wide gaps in income between the rich and the

---

[11] Bernard Crick, *Socialist Values and Time,* Fabian Tract 495 (London: Fabian Society, March 1984), p. 16.

poor. These gaps are a natural consequence of capitalism.

Capitalism works for the wealthy. If a person is a Donald Trump or a T. Boone Pickens, he or she would be hard put to knock the capitalist system. If, however, an individual has not been born wealthy, capitalism is not so great. Supporters of capitalism argue about equality of opportunity. Anyone with initiative can make it in a capitalist system, they contend. In theory, this may be so; but in practice, social conditions contribute to making the rich richer and the poor poorer.

Minority group members growing up in slums do not have equality of opportunity. They attend inferior public schools, where they learn little. In contrast, wealthy youngsters go to private schools and are taught by Ph.D.'s. Slum neighborhoods are unsafe because of crime, whereas wealthy neighborhoods are better protected against crime. Public hospitals do not provide the same quality of medical services as do private hospitals.

What does equality mean in such socially and economically disadvantaged circumstances? How can the slum child show initiative? Initiative depends on self-respect, a quality of character difficult to achieve in a slum setting. Socialism, however, would strive to provide equal opportunity to everyone. Schools would be upgraded, and slums would be rebuilt. Socialized medicine would improve medical care for the poor and serve the interests of the masses rather than satisfy the aspirations of the rich and the bank accounts of the private doctors.

Public Needs. Capitalism assumes that in a society in which everyone pursues his or her selfish interests, the public good will be served. In practice, however, society suffers from such a system. Everyone is encouraged to buy an automobile, for example, so the result is pollution, traffic jams, and billions of dollars spent on highways. Public transportation, consequently, is neglected. Public transportation is far more efficient than private transportation, but the emphasis on the private automobile has resulted in the public's transportation needs being poorly served.

Capitalists pursuing the highest profits engage in other harmful practices. Since cost-effectiveness is their most important consideration, they care little about environmental protection. Strip mining, for example, blights the beautiful countryside because the capitalist is more interested in making a fast buck than in protecting the environment. In pursuing profits, capitalists care not at all about the social consequences of their business decisions, such as unemployment or consumer injury.

Planning. Although big corporations plan for their futures, capitalist systems do not promote coordinated planning that takes into account the global effects of business decisions. Scarce resources, consequently, are not managed properly, as the experience of the West in the energy crisis of the 1970s attests.

Lack of planning, too, has been responsible for the inconsistent pattern of economic development. Inflation, recession, depression, and unemployment are all features of a capitalist economy because there is no central plan to allocate the resources of a capitalist society in a rational manner. Why should people remain unemployed if they are willing to work? Yet capitalist economies experience high levels of unemployment.

Planning makes it easier to cope with the evils of social disruption caused by profit calculations. To a capitalist, business decisions are made on the basis of efficiency. To the people who work in a factory, however, the human consequences of these decisions are important. If capitalists decide to close down or move their companies, the lives and well-being of their workers, families, and communities will be adversely affected. Socialist planning would avoid such difficulties, as human costs are brought into the plan.

Freedom. Supporters of capitalism like to emphasize the freedom offered by the "free enterprise" system. The fact is that the free enterprise system is a myth both because of what capitalism actually has become in our times and because the idea that individual consumers can exercise their free will to determine what is produced in the market—**consumer sovereignty,** as it is called—is inoperable.

Big corporations do not believe in free enterprise anyhow. Price competition is not the central feature of the capitalist economy as it used to be. In practice, the big corporations use government to prevent competition from overseas suppliers through the imposition of tariffs or quotas on various products; engage in lucrative government contracts to produce munitions and to build roads, schools, and hospitals; and in general manipulate government regulatory agencies for their own benefit. Adam Smith would turn over in his grave if he knew the sins being committed in the name of a market economy.

Lee Iacocca is a case in point. As head of the Chrysler Corporation, he demonstrated keen business skills in turning his company from a big loser to a big winner in manufacturing and selling automobiles. A good deal of his talent is derived, however, from his ability to influence government. At a crucial moment in Chrysler's tough times, he was able to obtain a federally guaranteed loan for his corporation. He and his fellow capitalists along with the auto union exerted influence on the government, which resulted in limiting the number of Japanese cars being imported into the United States, thus reducing competition.

The idea of free enterprise, then, is largely a myth in the actual operations of corporations. The notion of consumer sovereignty is also a myth. In capitalist economies billions of dollars are spent on advertising every year. Consumers are fed large doses of propaganda calculated to make them feel that luxury products are really basic necessities. Instead of keeping a good old car, they are encouraged to buy the latest model from Detroit. Capitalists hawk their products through slick advertisements in television, radio, magazines, and newspapers. The effect of this media blitz is to coerce people into wanting products that they really do not need and that very often are harmful to them. Cigarettes may cause cancer, but the tobacco industry encourages smoking. Chocolate candy may damage teeth, but children are enticed to buy it. Consumers who are bombarded with so much propaganda soon become slaves to the advertisers and do not have the freedom of choice that capitalists say they have.[12]

Democracy. Capitalists often say that democracy requires a market economy. Indeed, some even argue that democracy cannot exist without capitalism. They base their case on consumer sovereignty and the experience of nations.

Voting in the marketplace is different from voting in the voting booth. The only way that consumers can exercise their ballots in the market is for them to *buy* ballots. As socialist Henry Pachter observes, unless consumers are equipped with purchasing power, producers will be unable to satisfy their desires. "In other words," he notes, "this 'democracy' is based on unequal suffrage."[13]

Democracy, moreover, requires that people or elected representatives be allowed to make choices about important decisions. Business decisions, however, are often made in private—behind closed doors and beyond public scrutiny. If democracy means anything, it means open discussion of issues, not secrecy. Socialism, writes Andrew Levine, "for better or worse, eliminates systemic restrictions upon the scope of public choice."[14]

If capitalism and democracy go hand in hand, we would expect to see democracy flourishing only where capitalism thrives. Such is not the case. Although the Nazi government directed the German economy for military purposes from the early 1930s to the end of World War II, capitalism was able to exist and produce profits. Capitalism in the past existed in other fascist countries, such as Italy, Spain, Portugal, and Greece. Today, capitalists flourish in some of the prominent dictatorships. It is true that socialism does exist in communist dictatorships, but it exists in various forms in vigorously democratic societies, such as Sweden and Holland. Capitalism and democracy do not go hand in hand.

We can see, then, that socialism serves the public good. Its advantages in promoting equality, serving public needs, planning efficiently, respecting freedom, and strengthening democracy are overwhelming.

---

[12] See John Kenneth Galbraith, *The New Industrial State* (Boston: Houghton Mifflin, 1969), pp. 211–18, 272–73.

[13] Henry Pachter, "Three Economic Models: Capitalism, the Welfare State, and Socialism," in Henry Pachter, *Socialism in History: Essays by Henry Pachter*, ed. Stephen E. Bronner (New York: Columbia University Press, 1984), p. 19. The article was originally published in 1964.

[14] Andrew Levine, *Arguing for Socialism: Theoretical Considerations* (Boston: Routledge and Kegan Paul, 1984), p. 134.

12/NO   IS SOCIALISM BETTER THAN CAPITALISM?

Capitalism is the least romantic conception of a public order that the human mind has ever conceived. It does not celebrate extraordinary heroism in combat, extraordinary sanctity in one's religious life, extraordinary talent in the arts; in short, there is no "transcendental" dimension that is given official recognition and sanction.[15]

These words of political philosopher Irving Kristol, a supporter of capitalism, help to explain the unpopularity of that economic system. It is a pity that capitalism has such a bad press especially when its extraordinary accomplishments and the dismal failure of socialism are considered. The issues of equality, public needs, planning, individual freedom, and democracy must be reviewed in order to see the benefits which capitalism gives to a free society.

Equality. Capitalism works for most people who are willing to show initiative and industriousness. Arguments about poor people in capitalist systems are deceptive. Capitalism has revered equality of opportunity. Under capitalism, millions of people have moved up the economic ladder, rising from poverty to affluence; it is not a case of the rich getting richer and the poor getting poorer.

The slums are a case in point. Immigrants coming to the United States lived in slums. Many rose to positions of eminence in business, the arts, and the professions. Many groups that experienced discrimination, moreover, have achieved prosperity. A rising black middle class is a recent example.

To be sure, there is unemployment in capitalist economies, but some of that unemployment is caused by socialist policies in which government pays people not to work. Even if this point is excluded, however, one cannot judge an entire system by its few failures. There is much that we just do not know about poverty, and any system—capitalist or so-

cialist—would find some of the unemployment problems to be intractable.[16]

Although capitalism does not revere equality, it has been responsible for increasing the standard of living for overwhelming numbers of people it encompasses. The average worker's standard of living in most capitalist economies is high. Under capitalism even people classified as poor often have automobiles, washing machines, and television sets. Henry Ford did not become wealthy building cars for a few wealthy people but rather by providing good, inexpensive automobiles to the masses. The riches produced by capitalism benefit all classes in the sense that a rising tide lifts all boats.

Furthermore, there is no evidence to indicate that socialist economies are more egalitarian. Wage disparities in socialist economies are great. Some observers contend that these disparities are even greater under socialism than under capitalism. The only difference is that the economic benefits go to the elite of government employees rather than to the capitalists.

Public Needs. Capitalism better serves public needs than does socialism. Here, too, it is essential to note that capitalism is not perfect. Capitalists do many harmful things, such as damaging the environment by strip mining and polluting the atmosphere. Laws, however, have been enacted to cope with these evils. It is not necessary to accept socialism as a solution. Pollution exists in socialist countries, too, as often the government does not want to allocate resources away from more short-term productive needs.

Socialists enjoy emphasizing public over private transportation in their war against the automobile. The masses of people, however, prefer the automobile to public transportation. Commuters, for example, will put up with the discomfort of traffic jams and high costs of

---

[15] Irving Kristol, *Two Cheers for Capitalism* (New York: Basic Books, 1978), p. x.

[16] See Edward C. Banfield, *The Unheavenly City Revisited: A Revision of "The Unheavenly City"* (Boston: Little, Brown, 1974).

garages and automobile insurance for the convenience of having a means of transportation that will take them directly between home and work. They enjoy listening to the news on the car radio, chatting with a few friends sharing the ride, and relaxing in an air-conditioned or heated setting. In some urban areas, moreover, people have found there is more physical safety—protection against criminal assault—in the private automobile than in public transport's subways, buses, and stations.[17]

Planning. Socialist planning has been a great failure. In theory and practice, capitalism never professed that its institutions would guarantee that there would be no waste of resources. All it contended was that if capitalist planning was poor, the company responsible for the plan would suffer financially and eventually go out of business.

Under socialism, government does the planning, but government is not very good at it. Government planners do not have the business experience necessary to make good plans. Government, moreover, does not have to abide by a profit-and-loss statement, as does private industry. Socialist economies are notoriously inefficient with their plans.

Socialism, moreover, pretends to solve the problems of unemployment, recession, and depression; but it generally fails. Economic crises do appear in socialist countries. Countries ruled by socialists have at times experienced unemployment, inflation, and high interest rates in part brought on by the enactment of socialist programs.

In many countries socialist failures are well documented. Consequently, there now appears to be a new movement toward capitalism. Third World governments that had taken socialist paths are turning to free market methods after their countries' dismal economic failures. The places in Asia that are thriving economically—Malaysia, Singapore, South Korea, Taiwan, Hong Kong, and Japan—rely extensively on private markets.

Freedom. The history of capitalism and the history of freedom are intertwined. The notion of the private company making decisions apart from the state is a central feature of a pluralist democracy. Under socialism, it is easier to put all the institutions of society under government control and, consequently, destroy human freedom.

Consumers, moreover, are free to choose what they wish, whether to buy or sell, or whether to work for a big corporation or change jobs. The ordinary person is not so easily brainwashed. Corporations cannot brainwash if people are not willing to respond to the messages. Advertising campaigns have often failed to convince people of the excellence of a product. The ordinary person is not stupid and knows better what is in his or her interest than does some state bureaucrat. Freedom requires that the individual choose, and not the state.

It is strange that socialists believe that ordinary people are so easily manipulated by shrewd advertising campaigns of a capitalist economy. If, in fact, people are so easily duped by product advertising, then is it not reasonable to assume that they are as easily duped by political advertising for this or that candidate and party? What, then, does the advantage of democratic socialism offer to the consumer?

Democracy. A capitalist economy strengthens democratic rule. In the words of Michael Novak, "Political democracy is compatible in practice only with a market economy."[18] When people, rather than government, decide how to use their financial resources, they are, in fact, exercising their ballot and are getting from the market exactly what they voted for. When government, through its use of taxation, spends people's money, people are not getting what they vote for.

In a general sense, it is true that voters cast a ballot for a candidate or a party in a democracy. In complex societies, however, the voter casts a ballot for a "package"—that is to say, for a candidate and party who espouse views on many issues. The market, in contrast, allows individuals to zero in on exactly what they want and so strengthens democracy.

We can see, then, that capitalism, for all its faults, is worth retaining. Socialism produces consequences detrimental to society.

---

[17] See B. Bruce-Briggs, *The War against the Automobile* (New York: Dutton, 1975).

[18] Michael Novak, *The Spirit of Democratic Capitalism* (New York: Simon and Schuster, 1982), p. 14.

13/YES

HAS MARXISM BEEN VINDICATED?

If we recognize a certain amount of ambiguity resulting from the great volume of work that Marx produced, we can nonetheless establish that his overriding contributions to the study of society were enormous and were essentially correct. We can argue from the point of view of Marx as moralist, economist, and founder of a new ideology.

Marxism as a statement of moral indignation against the evils of an unjust capitalist system has achieved widespread respect. On every continent, followers of Marx seek to eliminate oppression and to promote human freedom. Marxism, consequently, is not merely an economic theory; it is also a plea for human dignity.

Although Marx directed his moral critique against the capitalists, Marxism has become a faith not only for the oppressed in highly industrialized societies but for the victims of colonialism in the less developed countries of the world as well. Many of the Third World leaders, themselves educated in Western universities, have found in Marxism a moral philosophy that condemns Western imperialism of the nineteenth and twentieth centuries, although Marx himself had little to say about imperialism. What these leaders take from Marxism, however, are moral criticisms of capitalism they can apply to the conditions of the Third World.

In addition to the moral criticisms, Marx made a lasting contribution to economic and social analyses. There is not a discipline of the social sciences that has not been influenced by those analyses. Marx accurately predicted developments in capitalist society, such as the concentration of industry, recurrent crises brought on by periods of boom and bust, the growth of industrial society everywhere in the world, the strengthening of the proletariat, and the emergence of imperialism. His description of the class struggle and his advocacy of reform and revolution were influential for many gains by the proletariat, such as the legalization of trade unions, improved working conditions, and the welfare state. Capitalists feared that unless they made such reforms, Marx's predictions about revolution would be proven correct.

Marx's synthesis of history, philosophy, sociology, and economics is a major intellectual achievement. As David McLellan notes, Marx's nineteenth-century ideas have shaped the way we look at the world. These ideas include our perception of people as social beings rather than as isolated individuals, our understanding of sociology, the role of economic forces in shaping historical development, and the contempt that is shown at the inequalities and injustices of capitalism. "In a sense," McLellan observes, "we are all Marxists now."[19]

It is certainly true that historical events did not unfold exactly as Marx had predicted. It is essential, however, to view Marxism creatively. No doubt if Marx had lived, he would have modified certain views to accord with the changing economic and political environment. Marx's visions of the economic trends of historical development have proved valid, however.

In addition to his economic and social analyses, Marx must be credited with providing a philosophy for a new ideology, which has become accepted by many in communist and noncommunist countries alike. Not only is Marxism the accepted philosophy in communist countries from the Soviet Union to Cuba, but it is also widely cherished in anticommunist countries, such as Sweden and France. The ideology of Marxism, consequently, has served the needs of many political systems.

Marxism has found utility to so many ideologies largely because it is a philosophy committed to human freedom. Marx saw human beings degraded and humiliated as a result of an oppressive economic system. By criticizing capitalism, which was the prominent oppressive economic form of the nineteenth century, Marx sought to liberate the masses of people who had become dehumanized by the industrial machine.

After Marx's death, critics of Marxism sought to find misstatements or wrong predictions of Marx as a way to undermine Marx-

---

[19] David McLellan, *Karl Marx: The Legacy* (London, England: British Broadcasting Corporation, 1983), p. 181.

ism. That kind of critique, however, misses the significance of Marx as a humanist committed to human freedom. It is because of such a commitment that Marxism has been adopted widely in the twentieth century.

13/NO   HAS MARXISM BEEN VINDICATED?

Marxism has so many weaknesses it is surprising that anyone takes it seriously anymore. First, for all his concern with the world of materialism and realism, Marx was a utopian. He believed that the state would wither away and that human conflict would disappear once socialism was established. There is no sign that the state is withering away, however, either in advanced industrial societies ruled by communists or socialists or in the newly developing Third World countries. By paying little attention to what would come after capitalism was destroyed and by believing that human beings would be transformed from selfishness to brotherhood, Marx was too much the impractical idealist.

Second, Marx overemphasized economic factors. It is true that economics is one of the most important factors influencing historical development, but not everything can be explained in economic terms. Countries with similar economic systems have significant variations in the superstructure. Highly industrialized Germany produced the Nazi dictatorship in the 1930s, while highly industrialized America developed the democratic welfare state of the New Deal. Economics does not explain everything. Ideas, leadership, and tradition also play a role in historical development.

Third, Marx's main prediction about revolution coming to the most industrially developed nations was wrong. It occurred first in Russia, one of the least developed European countries. Capitalist countries proved to be far more adaptive to nonrevolutionary change than Marx had imagined. By allowing reforms, such as the franchise, collective bargaining, and the welfare state, those who ruled the industrial countries were able to prevent the revolution that Marx had thought was inevitable.

Fourth, Marx's prediction that the workers would become increasingly impoverished proved to be wrong not only over the long run but also in Marx's lifetime. Prosperity descended on the proletariat as capitalism became increasingly vigorous and mature. Rather than the state acting to maintain prosperity only for the capitalists, moreover, it has extended opportunities for the masses of people to improve health care, increase educational opportunities, and obtain a higher standard of living.

Fifth, perhaps the greatest weakness of Marxism is its ambiguity. Marx tried to be prophet, political leader, and social scientist all at the same time. He was bound to be charged with imprecisions and ambiguities. At times he wrote as if human beings possess free will and at other times as if they are compelled to act by the forces of economic determinism. It is not clear, for example, how much influence the intellectual can have in bringing on a revolution. It is also not clear whether Marx favored political democracy or thought it was mostly a sham. Marxism, then, is too imprecise to be a synonym for *scientific* socialism.

Marxism, then, is fatally flawed. Its vision was utopian; its analysis of political and economic institutions faulty; its predictions wrong; and its meaning imprecise.

14/YES

WILL THE REFORMS OF THE GORBACHEV ERA LEAD TO A SOVIET UNION CHARACTERIZED BY POLITICAL DEMOCRACY AND A PEACEFUL FOREIGN POLICY?

The Soviet Union is now undergoing an important transformation that will change its domestic and foreign policy. Such an assessment can be made because: (1) the changes are far reaching and fundamental; (2) it will not be possible to reverse the changes; (3) the West has a vested interest in making accommodations to ensure that the changes are permanent.

Fundamental Changes. What Gorbachev has brought to the Soviet Union are far-reaching changes of the system. In the economy, efforts at decentralization will require factories to be more concerned with the quality of the goods they produce than they have been. In previous years, a centralized command structure imposed a requirement on quantity rather than quality. Managers struggled to meet their production quotas and had no particular inducement to satisfy market needs based on quality.

Gorbachev has taken the first steps in breaking down the bureaucracy, which has impeded economic development. He has already made changes in personnel, bringing to positions of responsibility leaders who are not bound to the old ways of doing things and are in tune with what he and others have referred to as the "new thinking." This younger and more open-minded generation of leaders has a vested interest in making the system work.

In foreign policy, the changes are so clear that even longtime critics of the Soviet Union have taken note of them. The withdrawal of Soviet forces from Afghanistan is unprecedented; the Soviet Union has never withdrawn from a country with which it was engaged in military operations without military compulsion. When Soviet troops marched into Afghanistan in 1979, anticommunist critics of the Soviet Union saw the move as aggressive. The Soviets would now be in a better position to make trouble in the Persian Gulf and to extend their influence over Iran, the critics contended. But now the Soviets are abandoning an area that had ostensibly given them strategic advantages.

Soviet proposals on arms control have been sincere. The Soviets made major concessions on intermediate-range nuclear forces (INF) out of a genuine commitment to arms control. They even initiated a unilateral nuclear test ban in the hope of getting the West to join in. Soviet efforts at strengthening the United Nations, moreover, demonstrate a Soviet desire to promote peace and stability in the world. To this end, the Soviets paid up their debts to the United Nations.

The reasons for the changes in domestic and foreign policy matters are clear. First, the Soviets realize that they must make changes in order to improve the lot of their people. If present trends continue, then it is possible that most of the Pacific Basin countries, which are energetic and making giant economic leaps, will surpass the Soviet Union in the next few decades.

Second, Gorbachev is committed to cultural freedom in his country for at least two reasons. First, he needs the support of intellectuals in his country, because intellectuals are the source of new ideas. Second, the extraordinary amount of secrecy has hindered economic development. Cultural freedom is essential to a sound economy.

Third, Gorbachev realizes that the Soviet Union has been largely unsuccessful in foreign policy. It is no longer able to dominate communist parties throughout the world. It does not offer a model for revolution around the world. Its Eastern European allies cannot be trusted. The Soviet Union has been subsidizing some of its allies, most notably Poland and Cuba, and the political returns of the subsidies are coming into question. Soviet military advisers were ejected from Egypt in 1973 by Anwar Sadat. The Soviets were heavily hit by the Afghan rebels and suffered many casualties as a result of the war, as well as damage to their reputation among countries of Africa and Asia.

Moscow, moreover, must improve relations with the West because it needs the West to help build up its own economy. Good relations might speed up the flow of Western technology and capital to the Soviet Union and its allies. In that way the Soviet Union might be able to keep up with the United States as a superpower without reducing the standard of living of its people.

Fourth and finally, the Soviets realize that they must cut back in military expenditures if they are to develop economically. Estimates vary as to what percentage of gross national product is devoted to the military in the Soviet Union, but a number of analysts say that this figure is at least double that of the United States. To the extent that the Soviet Union devotes its resources to the military, it cannot focus on the civilian sector. In this regard, it has in the past sacrificed better housing and more consumer goods for the sake of nonproductive items.

Irreversible Reforms. The problems that the Soviet leaders face today are different from the problems that previous Soviet leaders faced. V. I. Lenin was able to introduce reforms in the economy under the NEP, which allowed for some use of private initiative among the peasants. These reforms were ended by Joseph Stalin's policies of collectivization. But the Soviet Union today is quite different from the country it was in the 1920s and 1930s both in terms of its economic requirements and its place in the world. Reforms are desperately needed, and, once set in motion, they will not be reversed.

In the years between the two world wars, the Soviet Union began to build an industrial society. Although many methods can be used to construct such a society, Stalinism shaped the infrastructure of a modern industrial society through the building of hydroelectric plants, factories, and key industries. It can be argued that the Soviet Union could have attained the same or even better results had it relied on less brutal means. Nevertheless, Stalinism was the means employed to lead the Soviet Union into the industrial age.

The achievements of the Soviet Union are impressive. Today it mines more oil than any other country in the world. It outproduces the United States in machine tools, steel, cement, and fertilizers. It provides its people with a higher standard of living than its czarist pre-

decessors. And one of its major achievements is a full-blown welfare state.

Because of its welfare state, Soviet citizens are entitled to jobs. The government furnishes big subsidies for essential items like food, housing, and transportation, so that the cost of those items is relatively low. Health care is free to all.

The command economy that has presided over the industrialization of the Soviet Union is no longer useful in the new communications age. When the Soviet Union industrialized, it was competing mostly with Western countries that were industrializing. Most countries of Africa, Asia, and Latin America were either not moving in the direction of industrialization or were only taking small steps. Today, the countries that were hitherto slow in modernizing, such as South Korea and Taiwan, include the most energetic societies in the world. These countries have in many cases made major gains not only in industrial production but in communications and electronics, as well.

It will be a much more difficult task for the Soviet Union to match or surpass these countries. To come close, Moscow will have to produce the same kinds of conditions for its people that exist in the countries with the greatest economic achievements. Such conditions will require more freedom, access to information, and more openness.

Soviet citizens are aware that they do not possess the consumer goods that are available in noncommunist societies. The black market furnishes items that many people in the advanced industrial societies take for granted, such as clothes, tape decks, and cameras. Most Soviet citizens do not have automobiles, and the service industry is poor or in some areas nonexistent.

Ronald Reagan tells the story of the Soviet woman who called an electrician, requesting that the electrician come to her home to repair faulty wiring. The electrician said, "I will be happy to come over, but I cannot get there until ten years from today."

The woman then asked, "That is okay, but will you come in the morning or the afternoon ten years from today?"

And the electrician replied, "What difference does it make if we are talking about ten years from today?"

"Because ten years from today in the morning, the plumber is coming to repair the faulty pipes."

Improving the Soviet economy will take time—much time. Although Soviet citizens do have the benefits of a welfare state, they suffer the consequences of its excesses. Because everyone is assured of a job, there have been little employee initiative and few rewards for excellence. Gorbachev has taken steps to encourage initiative and has introduced incentives that will have to be expanded. The high subsidies for food and other items have led to consumer shortages, and long lines of shoppers waiting for goods are frequent. Housing, although subsidized, is in short supply. Health care in the Soviet Union does not receive the high priority that it does in noncommunist industrial societies.

The Soviets are experiencing major environmental problems that need attention. In political democracies, environmental groups have used their freedom to organize and campaign for political action to make water and air cleaner, reduce the lead content in automobile exhaust, and require protection against industrial exploitation of the land. Environmentalists in the Soviet Union, however, have not been free to organize and campaign in a similar manner, so that the Soviet Union faces extraordinary difficulties in solving its environmental problems.

The condition of the Soviet economy makes it likely that the Soviet government will have to focus on domestic matters for decades to come. For the government to raise the standard of living for the Soviet people will require massive investments in the economy and greater liberalization of society. Positive results will not be achieved immediately.

Unlike the situation in the 1920s and 1930s, moreover, the Soviet Union is today a global power. The Soviet Union has been overcommitted in its foreign policy. Although the country has built a strong military force, it must, in the decades ahead, focus on its economy rather than on foreign policy adventures.

The withdrawal of Soviet forces from Afghanistan is but the first of a series of steps that Moscow must take to reduce its commitments. We can expect to see efforts by the Soviet Union to diminish conflict in areas known as regional problems. It will likely reduce its efforts to promote trouble between Israel and

Arab countries, and its encouragement of Nicaragua in promoting revolution in Central America.

Moscow will have to intensify its efforts at arms control. It is reasonable to assume that the Soviet Union will enter strategic arms reduction agreements with the United States— if for no other reason than to reduce its expenditures on the military.

Moscow will face increasing problems with its Eastern European communist allies. Some of them—notably Albania, Czechoslovakia, and Romania—are resisting *glasnost* and *perestroika* in their own countries. Others, such as Hungary, are somewhat more amenable to some economic restructuring. Most of them are experiencing economic decay. Moscow recognizes that if it ever uses military force in Eastern Europe, it will undermine its efforts at improving relations with the West, as was the case when it sent troops into Czechoslovakia in 1968 and into Afghanistan in 1979.

Moscow also recognizes that the Soviet system is experiencing a crisis of legitimacy. Communism, which has been used to justify political dictatorship, the crushing of dissent, and military adventures, no longer has the appeal at home and abroad that it had in the 1930s. Soviet leaders must adapt to these changes lest they face chaos at home.

Western Response. The West has a vested interest in helping the Soviet Union succeed. We have seen evidence of that already. Even Ronald Reagan, who during his presidency referred to the Soviet Union as an "evil empire," spoke in warm and friendly terms about his "friend" Mikhail. The West, too, wants to reduce its military expenditures so that it can direct resources toward its economy, social problems, and the environment.

It is in the West's interest to see to it that the Soviet economy improves for at least two reasons. First, to the extent that the Soviet economy expands, the Soviet Union will become a better trading partner. It is quite clear that economic development is not a zero-sum game. After World War II, the United States provided vast economic assistance to Western Europe so that it would recover from the devastation of the war. Although Western Europe developed competitive industries, both the United States and Western Europe benefited from the vigor of Western Europe's economy.

So, too, will it be the case with the Soviets as they build a stronger economy.

Second, once economic and political freedoms are granted to the Soviet people, it will be impossible to put an end to the process of change. The genie will be out of the bottle. People will have expectations that life will be better. Any regime that would attempt to go back to the way things were in the old days would be faced with popular opposition at home. Whatever the long-term intentions of the Soviet leaders, they are generating forces over which they will have little control.

The West, then, must be supportive of the changes that are going on in the Soviet Union. The West must be more forthcoming on arms control. Western countries must respond to Soviet overtures for a reduction of tension on regional and other matters. Above all, the Cold War rhetoric so easily evoked by conservative leaders in the United States must be eliminated. If Gorbachev does not succeed, then the alternative will be the horrors of foreign adventurism and possible war.

14/NO WILL THE REFORMS OF THE GORBACHEV ERA LEAD TO A SOVIET UNION CHARACTERIZED BY POLITICAL DEMOCRACY AND A PEACEFUL FOREIGN POLICY?

It is perhaps a weakness of the West that every Soviet statement promoting change and for peace brings euphoria and a loss of reason. What Samuel Johnson said about a second marriage is equally appropriate to this eager embracing of promises for a new democratic and peaceful communism: It is a triumph of hope over experience.

We will address points raised by the *Affirmative* and argue: (1) the changes going on within the Soviet Union are not far reaching and fundamental; (2) the changes are reversible; (3) the West does not necessarily benefit from the Gorbachev reforms.

Fundamental Changes. The relative youthfulness, vigor, and initiative of Mikhail Gorbachev—particularly when viewed against his elderly, immobile, and unimaginative predecessors—creates an illusion that the new Soviet leader is charting a new course for his country. A closer examination reveals, however, that the changes are not nearly so far reaching as to justify the enthusiasm of some Western observers.

In matters of the economy, many of the changes are nothing new. Lenin permitted peasants to sell their agricultural products in the market. He and, subsequently, Stalin allowed foreign companies to build factories and invest in Soviet economic progress. And in spite of the economic successes sparked by such liberalization, Stalin was still able to re-

verse their course. He introduced collectivation of the farms and ended the program of foreign investment. He also established a police state. The economic reforms, consequently, were reversible; and economic improvement did not lead to political freedoms.

Gorbachev has been given much credit for criticizing his predecessors. But nearly all Soviet leaders have criticized their predecessors (with the principal exception that no leader has criticized Lenin). Most notably, Nikita Khrushchev's de-Stalinization program is a case in point, and Gorbachev, too, has denounced Stalin along with Leonid Brezhnev. But Gorbachev, like Khrushchev, has been careful to criticize the individual communist ruler rather than Marxist-Leninist ideology and the primacy of the Communist party. "We do not abandon the role of the ruling party in the country," Gorbachev said. "On the contrary, we want to reaffirm it."[20]

It is true that there is more "openness" in Soviet society, more freedom to express criticism. But the criticism can be made only in those areas approved tacitly or implicitly by the government. Soviet cultural magazines may be among the freest in the communist world, but they are still directed by the ideological department of the Communist party. Party of-

---

[20] Quoted in Willima R. Doener, "More Than Talk," *Time* 132 (July 11, 1988): 25.

ficials must still approve of editorials and content of magazines and newspapers.

Although some political prisoners have been released from prison, many still languish there. The Western media pay attention to the most famous dissidents who are given freedom, but they often ignore the many who are left behind. Andrei Sakharov has been returned from exile because Gorbachev wants to create an image that the new leadership is responsive to change and engages in new thinking about the nature of communism. But the release of Sakharov is merely a propaganda ploy.

Anti-Semitism has in fact been toned down under Gorbachev, and the number of Jews permitted to emigrate from the Soviet Union has increased. By late 1988, however, the Soviet Union was still allowing fewer Jews to leave the Soviet Union than were allowed during the 1970s, when détente was strong between the United States and the Soviet Union.

Theodore Draper notes that, among the great powers today, it is only in the Soviet Union that "a leader can appear to be a liberator by not subjecting his people to the inhumanity of barbarism of his predecessors." He adds:

If a German chancellor tried to claim credit as a humanitarian for not putting millions of people, including little children, into gas ovens, we should consider him to be a moral monster.[21]

In foreign policy, the changes have been equally cosmetic. Soviet broadcast and newspaper propaganda still tells the world that AIDS was invented at Fort Detrick, Maryland, as a biological warfare weapon and that the Central Intelligence Agency murdered the 918 members of the Jim Jones Temple who committed suicide in Guyana in 1978 to prevent their emigration to the Soviet Union.[22] Moscow, moreover, sends arms to Nicaragua, a Soviet client state, for the purpose of strengthening the leftist regime there and in the hope of spreading communism throughout Central America.

The Soviets withdrew from Afghanistan not because of a fundamental change in Soviet policy, but, rather, because they knew they could not win. In a very real sense, Afghanistan became the Soviet Union's Vietnam—a long war of attrition that tested the resolve of the foreign power. When Gorbachev came to power, he *increased* Soviet military forces in Afghanistan. It was only after the United States supplied the Afghan rebels with Stinger missiles—highly accurate ground-to-air missiles that could bring down helicopters and planes—that the Soviets saw that the game was up and beat a hasty retreat.

The move on arms control is nothing really new. Since the first years of the nuclear age, the Soviets have put forward proposals on arms control, always designed to give the Soviet Union an advantage. In fact, the Intermediate-range Nuclear Forces (INF) Treaty is more beneficial to the Soviet Union than to the West. By removing Soviet and U.S. intermediate-range nuclear forces from Europe, it gives renewed strength to the forces of pacifism in Western Europe, which will increase the calls for further reductions of nuclear forces in Europe. The West needs to have nuclear weapons in Europe to counter the superior conventional forces of the Soviet Union, so the INF Treaty undermines the credibility of the United States in resisting a Soviet attack in Western Europe. Now Western Europe has to guess as to whether the United States will use its intercontinental nuclear weapons against the Soviet Union if Moscow engages in a conventional war in Europe. The Soviets have successfully driven a wedge between the United States and its allies.

By making mostly cosmetic changes in its domestic and foreign policy, the Soviet Union has been able to move closer to achieving its objectives over the long run. What the Soviets want is *peredyshka,* a Russian word meaning "breathing space." They need time to catch up with the West. To get this time, they need capital from Western banks, technical assistance, and improved trade relationships with the rest of the world. Gorbachev, then, is not the architect of fundamental changes in the communist system of government in the Soviet Union. He is, rather, making small changes that will ultimately strengthen the communist system in the Soviet Union and abroad.

[21] Theodore Draper, "Soviet Reformers: From Lenin to Gorbachev," *Dissent* 34 (Summer 1987): 293.

[22] See Natan Sharansky, "As I See Gorbachev," *Commentary* 85 (March, 1988): 32.

Reversible Changes. Since changes in the Soviet Union have not been fundamental, it is clear that they are also reversible. Today, the press is "free" to criticize the predecessors of Gorbachev. If tomorrow, Gorbachev is removed, the press will be "free" to criticize Gorbachev. But such freedom is not real freedom.

We will see real, fundamental, and irreversible changes when the Soviet leaders take concrete measures of a political, rather than an economic, nature. We often forget that many dictatorships in the world have allowed for a wide measure of free enterprise. Fascist Italy under Benito Mussolini in the 1930s and right-wing dictator Augusto Pinochet in Chile in the 1980s are cases in point. But political changes are another matter.

These political changes will at the least require the establishment of true pluralism in the Soviet Union, with the rights of groups to freely form and engage in peaceful political activity, including organizing political parties and participating in political demonstrations. If real change is to be effected in the Soviet Union, the regime will have to give up on the primacy of the Communist party, with its notion that somehow it is endowed with a monopoly of truth and the legitimacy to guide the country and the world. A multiparty system would have to be established, and real, rather than symbolic, elections conducted.

Human rights, as *political* instruments of freedom, will have to be established in a fundamentally different Soviet Union. The basic liberties cherished in political democracies will have to be provided. These liberties would, at the least, have to include freedom of religion, press, speech, and assembly.

The Soviet Union can take a number of steps in foreign policy to convince the world that it wants permanent change. As a big power, it has legitimate security interests. Those interests can be maintained without the Soviet Union's supporting the conditions leading to the suppression of freedom in Eastern Europe. If the Soviets support political freedom in Eastern Europe, that would be a good sign of permanent change. If it made real efforts at reducing regional tensions, that would be another sign.

As far as arms control is concerned, whatever agreements are proposed must be beneficial to all parties concerned. Mere arms reductions do not necessarily strengthen global security if the agreements benefit only one side. More important than arms control agreements is the adoption by Soviet leaders of policies that are consistent with a live-and-let-live philosophy, one that recognizes the right of noncommunist societies to exist in peace.

Western Response. It is an open question whether the West will be better off if Gorbachev succeeds. If, contrary to our contention that the reforms are not fundamental, the reforms do succeed in strengthening the Soviet economy so that the Soviet Union is able to move into the communications age, provide greater consumer goods for its citizens, and construct a more sophisticated technology, then this could possibly be bad for the West. Once economically strong, the Soviet Union could then feel sufficiently confident to return to its ideological commitment to spread communism throughout the world. The Soviets have reversed course before, and they can do so again.

On the other hand, it can be argued that the West will be better off if Gorbachev fails. To the extent that the Soviets cannot come to terms with the economic requirements of a postindustrial society, it will be caught up in *contradictions,* to use a Marxist term, in which its situation worsens. Economic weakness and decay will mean that the Soviets will have fewer resources to devote to the military. The country will be less able to project its power overseas. Ultimately, the problems facing the Soviet Union will become so enormous that it will cease to be a superpower, and peace will be more likely to come to the world— at least to the extent that the Soviet Union is responsible for the conflict that now exists.

Whatever view one takes of these changes, the policy of the United States and other Western countries should continue as it has in the past. Back in 1947, the United States adopted a long-term policy of **containment,** which meant that it would take measures to prevent the Soviet Union from expanding. Soviet difficulties today are a reflection of the triumph of containment.

If the West remains strong and keeps up its defenses, it can cope with either a more economically strong or weak Soviet Union. The Soviet Union's difficulties can be an opportunity and a challenge. As President Reagan said to Secretary Gorbachev, "We trust you; but let's cut the deck anyway."

KEY TERMS

Antithesis
Bolsheviks
Bourgeoisie
Capitalism
Cartels
Class struggle
Classless society
Collectivization
Comintern
Command economy
Commune
Communism
Communist International (Comintern)
Consumer sovereignty
Containment
Contradictions
Democratic centralism
Democratic socialism
De-Stalinization
Détente
Dialectic
Dictatorship of the proletariat
Feudalism
Free enterprise
Glasnost
Historical materialism
Imperialism

Industrial Revolution
Labor theory of value
Laissez-faire
Lumpenproletariat
Market economy
Marxism
Marxism-Leninism
Mercantilism
New Economic Policy
Peaceful coexistence
Peasants
Perestroika
Private enterprise
Proletariat
Revisionists
Scientific socialism
Social democracy
Socialism
"Socialism in One Country"
Stalinism
Substructure
Superstructure
Surplus value
Synthesis
Thesis
Third International
Utopian socialists
Utopias

QUESTIONS

Capitalism, Socialism, and Communism

1. What would be the consequences to American society if the United States adopted a free market economy in the manner of Adam Smith's prescription?

2. Which system—capitalism or socialism—is better suited to solve the problems of Third World countries? What are the reasons for your answer?

3. Which system—capitalism or socialism—produces greater (a) economic development and (b) equality? Why?

4. Take one policy area, such as civil rights, national health, or defense spending, and determine if the Marxist analysis is valid in explaining the developments in that policy area.

5. In view of the changing character of capitalism from the eighteenth to the twentieth centuries, are Adam Smith's prescriptions meaningful?

6. How would you evaluate whether Marxism is democratic?

7. Is Leninism a variation of Marxism, or is it something different? What are the reasons for your answer?

8. What is the relationship between capitalism and democracy?

9. What is the relationship between socialism and democracy?

10. Can conflict among communist countries be reconciled with the philosophy of Marx and Lenin? What are the reasons for your answer?

The Gorbachev Era

1. If the reforms of the Gorbachev era are successful, what would the consequences of ending those reforms be to the Soviet Union?

2. What criteria should be used in evaluating whether the reforms of the Gorbachev era are significant or not in changing the communist system in the Soviet Union?

3. What role does ideology play in Soviet foreign policy today?

4. What alternative policies are there to Gorbachev's reforms? Would these alternatives be better or worse for the Soviet Union?

5. Will the reforms of the Gorbachev era be successful? What are the reasons for your answer?

6. Is it in the interest of the United States and other Western countries for Gorbachev to succeed in reforming the Soviet Union? What are the reasons for your answer?

RECOMMENDED READINGS

Capitalism, Socialism, and Communism

BARRY, DONALD D., and CAROL BARNER-BARRY. *Contemporary Soviet Politics: An Introduction.* 3d ed. Englewood Cliffs, N.J.: Prentice Hall, 1987. An introduction to the contemporary Soviet political system.

BERGER, PETER L. *The Capitalist Revolution: Fifty Propositions about Prosperity, Equality, and Liberty.* New York: Basic Books, 1986. An analysis of capitalism.

BERNSTEIN, EDUARD. *Evolutionary Socialism: A Criticism and Affirmation,* trans. Edith C. Harvey. New York: Schocken Books, 1961. A major social democratic work.

BERNSTEIN, PAUL. "Capitalism's Elusive Constituency." *Business Horizons* 29 (November/December 1986): 2–8. An argument that capitalism, which offers many benefits to society, is in need of a supporting constituency.

BOSWORTH, BARRY P., and ALICE M. RIVLIN, eds. *The Swedish Economy.* Washington, D.C.: Brookings Institution, 1986. A description of the Swedish economy by U.S. analysts.

BRUCAN, SILVIU. *World Socialism at the Crossroads.* New York: Praeger, 1987. An argument that the scientific-technological revolution requires changes in communist practices.

CONQUEST, ROBERT. *The Great Terror: Stalin's Purge of the Thirties.* Rev. ed. New York: Macmillan, 1973. An indictment of Stalinist terror during the 1930s.

CRICK, BERNARD. *Socialism.* Minneapolis: University of Minnesota Press, 1987. A short account of the subject.

CUNNINGHAM, FRANK. *Democratic Theory and Socialism.* Cambridge, England: Cambridge University Press, 1987. An inquiry into the reconciliation of socialism with democracy.

DYE, THOMAS R., and HARMON ZIEGLER. "Socialism and Equality in Cross-National Perspective." *PS: Political Science and Politics* 31 (Winter 1988): 45–56. An argument based on cross-national research that economic equality in a country depends on the level of economic development in that country rather than on the nature of the economic system.

FISCHER, LOUIS. *The Life of Lenin.* New York: Harper and Row, 1964. A standard biography.

FRIEDMAN, MILTON, and ROSE FRIEDMAN. *Free to Choose: A Personal Statement.* New York: Harcourt Brace Jovanovich, 1980. A case for the market economy.

GALBRAITH, JOHN KENNETH, and STANISLAV MENSHIKOV. *Capitalism, Communism and Coexistence.* Boston: Houghton Mifflin, 1988. A U.S. and a Soviet economist discuss economics and foreign policy.

GAY, PETER. *The Dilemma of Democratic Socialism: Eduard Bernstein's Challenge to Marx.*

New York: Collier Books, 1962. An evaluation of Bernstein's revisionism.

GILDER, GEORGE. *Wealth and Poverty.* New York: Basic Books, 1981. A defense of capitalism.

HARRINGTON, MICHAEL. *The Accidental Century.* New York: Macmillan, 1965. A case for democratic socialism as necessary in the twentieth century.

HAYEK, FRIEDRICH. *The Road to Serfdom.* Chicago: University of Chicago Press, 1944. A critique of government planning as a form of dictatorship.

"Is There Virtue in Profit?" *Harper's* 273 (December 1986): 37–47. A discussion among Lewis H. Lapham, Michael Novak, Walter B. Wriston, Robert Lekachman, and Peter Steinfels.

KRISTOL, IRVING. *Two Cheers for Capitalism.* New York: Basic Books, 1978. A defense of capitalism against its critics.

LEVINE, ANDREW. *Arguing for Socialism: Theoretical Considerations.* Boston: Routledge and Kegan Paul, 1984. An investigation of the theoretical standards that should be used in assessing socialism and capitalism.

MACHAN, TIBOR, ed. *The Main Debate: Communism versus Capitalism.* New York: Random House, 1987. A presentation of conflicting views of communism and capitalism.

McCLELLAN, DAVID, ed. *Marxism: Essential Writings.* New York: Oxford University Press, 1988. A selection of Marxist writings from Marx to the present.

McCORD, WILLIAM. *The Springtime of Freedom: The Evolution of Developing Societies.* New York: Oxford University Press, 1965. An argument that dictatorship inhibits economic development.

MEYER, ALFRED G. *Communism.* 4th ed. New York: Random House, 1984. An overview.

NOVAK, MICHAEL. *The Spirit of Democratic Capitalism.* New York: Simon and Schuster, 1982. A defense of a system characterized by a democratic polity, a market economy, and cultural pluralism.

PADOVER, SAUL K. *Karl Marx: An Intimate Biography.* New York: McGraw-Hill, 1978. A study of the intellect and personality of Karl Marx.

SCHMITT, RICHARD. *Introduction to Marx and Engels: A Critical Reconstruction.* Boulder,

Colo.: Westview Press, 1987. An introduction to the subject.

ZWASS, ADAM. *Market, Plan, and State: The Strengths and Weaknesses of the Two World Economic Systems.* Armonck, N.Y.: M. E. Sharpe, 1987. An assessment of market and planned economies.

The Gorbachev Era

BIALER, SEWERYN. "Inside Glasnost." *Atlantic* 261 (February 1988): 64–68, 70–72. The Soviet elite sees Gorbachev's program as the country's last hope for greatness.

BRZEZINSKI, ZBIGNIEW. "The Crisis of Communism: The Paradox of Political Participation." *Washington Quarterly* 10 (Autumn 1987): 167–74. A presentation of the dilemma of communist societies: that they need political participation but political participation undermines the communist system.

BUKOVSKY, VLADIMIR. "Glasnost: Genuine Change or Illusion?" Heritage Lecture 103. Washington, D.C.: Heritage Foundation, 1987. An argument that *Glasnost* is an illusion.

DRAPER, THEODORE. "Soviet Reformers: From Lenin to Gorbachev." *Dissent* 34 (Summer 1987): 287–301. An analysis of Gorbachev's reforms in historical perspective.

DYKER, DAVID A., ed. *The Soviet Union under Gorbachev: Prospects for Reform.* London: Croom, Helm, 1987. Assessments of the Gorbachev reforms.

FULLER, GRAHAM E. "The Case for Optimism." *National Interest*, no. 12 (Summer 1988): 73–82. An argument that *glasnost* and *perestroika* may lead to a more peaceful Soviet foreign policy.

HOUGH, JERRY. *Russia and the West: Gorbachev and the Politics of Reform.* New York: Simon and Schuster, 1988. An assessment.

KENNEDY, PAUL. "What Gorbachev Is up Against." *Atlantic* 259 (June 1987): 29–38, 40–43. An argument that the communist system has brought the Soviet Union into economic decline.

McCAULEY, MARTIN, ed. *The Soviet Union under Gorbachev.* New York: St. Martin's Press,

1987. An assessment of Gorbachev's policies by British scholars.

RODMAN, PETER W. "The Case for Skepticism." *National Interest*, no. 12 (Summer 1988): 83–90. A skeptical assessment of the significance of changes in Soviet foreign policy.

part IV

STATE AND CITIZEN

The politics of a society is shaped by the character of the people who reside within the political community. The attitudes and opinions that people hold influence the decisions that government makes. Part IV deals with the relationships between how citizens think and act and the behavior of the state.

Communities vary in terms of their attitude toward government authority, their willingness to accept change, and their respect for their fellow citizens. Chapter 6 examines the ways in which attitudes and opinions are formed.

How citizens behave politically depends in part upon the freedoms that citizens possess. In some societies individuals and groups are free to articulate their demands to government in an open manner.

In other societies, however, government forbids or severely restricts the amount of political freedom available to individuals and groups. Chapter 7 discusses the rights of citizens against the state.

In most contemporary political systems political parties and elections are prominent features. The role and nature of these parties vary, as does the amount of freedom that individuals have in electoral activities. Chapter 8 deals with these matters.

An instrument for articulating demands of people is the political interest group. Political interest groups engage in diverse activities. The degree of autonomy they possess, moreover, differs among political systems. Chapter 9 describes these groups and their role in politics.

chapter 6

Political culture, political socialization, and public opinion

As Western countries prepared to grant independence to their African and Asian colonies in the 1950s, many supporters of national independence anticipated that the establishment of Western-type institutions, such as parliaments and federal systems, would result in governments that would be both stable and democratic. Within several years, however, the new institutions proved to be short-lived in many countries and were replaced by governments dominated by military or one-party rule. As military coups and civil wars became frequent phenomena in the Third World, it became apparent that neither stable government nor democratic systems would be assured by the implantation of Western institutions in the non-Western world. If political stability and democracy were to be achieved, so many chastened commentators now asserted, attention would have to be directed to the sociological and psychological factors that contribute to popular supports for those objectives rather than to formal political institutions.

The attention to the underlying sociological and psychological aspects of a system is not a new development in political science. Since the 1930s, political scientists have been deeply involved in studying not only the mechanics of government institutions but also the patterns of behavior of individuals and groups in different political systems. Such a perspective was essential for analyzing some of the important political phenomena of our times, such as why there are differences among and within political systems in adapting to economic and social change, in participating in civic affairs, in exercising the right to vote, in embarking on militaristic adventures abroad, and in transferring political loyalties from one leader to another.

To understand matters such as these, political scientists have been concerned with the formation of political attitudes by elites and the mass public. Central to this concern are the subjects of political culture, political socialization, and public opinion.

POLITICAL CULTURE

The term *culture* has been defined as a core of traditional ideas, practices, and technology shared by a people (see Chapter 2). **Political culture,** as defined by political scientists Gabriel A. Almond and G. Bingham Powell, Jr., "is the pattern of individual attitudes and orientations toward politics among the members of a political system."[1] The political culture of a society can be measured through public opinion and attitude surveys.

Political culture varies among political systems. In some political systems, for example, active participation in the political life of the community, such as in voting and in joining private associations established to influence government activity, is regarded as a legitimate and worthy objective. In many traditional societies, however, the masses of people do not play an active role in political life.

Even among countries that are properly called democratic, considerable differences may exist in political culture. In France, for example, the political culture has been marked by sharp ideological differences among its people, whereas Great Britain is characterized by a broad consensus of attitudes about government.

Although variations in political culture often mark the features of different states, they may also appear within a political system itself. Ethnic, racial, and generational groups may develop their unique features and are, consequently, labeled **subcultures.** In the 1960s and 1970s, for

example, much attention was directed to the attitudes of young people in America. Specifically, the phrase **youth culture** was used to distinguish attitudes, values, and way of life that separate young people from the rest of American society.

The orientations that exist in a political culture influence the way in which a political system works. Social scientists have become particularly concerned with the relationships between orientations and such matters as nation building, political participation, law and order, and trust in government.

Nationalism has been a paramount force in the past two centuries (see Chapter 2). Nation building generally requires the transferring of loyalties from regional and parochial units to national ones. The new states of Africa and Asia have been particularly troubled in building a national consciousness from widely disparate ethnic groups.

A political culture that encourages the development of a passive and submissive population is unlikely to produce a political system in which people participate actively in government affairs. Religious traditions that emphasize a feeling of fatalism may have consequences to a political system in that they may lead to a political culture in which people accept almost any kind of government. In contrast, a cultural norm that reveres participation and control over one's destiny may result in active popular participation in political affairs.

Respect for law and order is another cultural norm that has an impact on political life. In a political system like Great Britain's, respect for law and order is part of the historic traditions that have evolved over a period of centuries. In other political systems, such as that in Bolivia, disrespect for law and order has made political stability hard to achieve.

A culture that encourages individual trust among people influences the character of a political system. If, for example,

[1] Gabriel A. Almond and G. Bingham Powell, Jr., *Comparative Politics: A Developmental Approach* (Boston: Little, Brown, 1966), p. 50.

a culture produces elites who develop attitudes of tolerance toward each other, the peaceful transfer of power from one group of elites to another may be easier to accomplish than in a culture distinguished by elite distrust. Both the United States and Great Britain have developed elites that trust each other, while many Latin American countries have not.

POLITICAL SOCIALIZATION

Each society seeks to transmit its culture to its members. The process of doing so is known as **socialization.** In the legal profession, for example, young attorneys are taught how to speak before judges and deal with other attorneys. In education the young student is taught about the proper relationship between students and teachers. In many societies, as feminists point out, women are socialized to a life devoted to family rather than to professional pursuits or to *both* family and professional pursuits.

Political socialization refers to the method in which a culture transmits its political culture to its members. Political socialization is the process of learning about political life, and it is the way in which political cultures are maintained and changed. In this regard people learn to respect or not to respect political authority, to participate or not to participate in political activity, to tolerate or not to tolerate dissenting opinion, and to obey or to defy the law. The study of political socialization is important because it shows how a citizen acquires knowledge, attitudes, beliefs, and opinions about the political system. Such a study, moreover, reveals the way in which individuals not only perceive the political world but also how they behave politically.

Although the phrase *political socializa-*

tion was first used in 1959,[2] interest in how people acquire political attitudes has ancient roots. One of the earliest philosophers to deal with this subject was Plato, whose *Republic* described how education was to be used to train an elite to rule. In modern political systems, moreover, much attention is given to transmitting the community's knowledge and norms of political behavior. Both democracies and dictatorships share an interest in influencing the political attitudes of their people toward the mechanics and objectives of their respective political systems, although modern totalitarian dictatorships rely more upon indoctrination than do democratic systems.

Students of political socialization are concerned primarily about the types of political learning, the means by which political learning is achieved, and the objectives of political learning.

Types of Political Learning

Three types of political learning are distinguished: cognitive socialization, affective socialization, and evaluative socialization. **Cognitive socialization** refers to how knowledge of the basic structures and rules of politics is acquired. How, for example, does an American become aware of the president, the Congress, and the Supreme Court? **Affective socialization** is the process in which an individual develops feelings of approval or rejection of a political leader, government unit, or political system. The way in which an individual's affection is shaped in good or bad terms of the president, the police, or the bureaucracy, for example, is illustrative of affective socialization. **Evaluative socialization** refers to the process through which one acquires the judgments and

---

[2] Herbert H. Hyman, *Political Socialization: A Study in the Psychology of Political Behavior* (Glencoe, Ill.: Free Press, 1959).

opinions about the political system on the basis of some moral criteria. An assessment of how an individual decides whether government policy should be more concerned with national health problems is an example of evaluative socialization.[3] Cognitive socialization supplies the rudimentary underpinnings of popular support, but affective and evaluative socialization tell more about the attitudes of a community toward its political system.

Agents of Socialization

The means by which an individual gains knowledge of the political culture are known as the agents of socialization. These agents include the family, peer groups, the schools, social groups, and the mass media.

Family. Political socialization begins before adolescence. In most societies the family exerts a major influence on the child. In their study of the political beliefs of children in Chicago, social scientists Robert D. Hess and David Easton observed that preadolescent children learn to love and identify with the government, and especially with the president, even before they know what the government does.[4] As children reach adolescence, they become more aware of other elements of government. Studies of children's attitudes toward government in other countries, however, indicate that children often do not show affection for the chief executives.[5]

The crucial point in the child's social, psychological, and political development is the period between nine and thirteen years.[6] A good deal of the cognitive and affective orientations of youth is influenced by the family during that period. Many studies of political behavior reveal, moreover, that the identification an individual has with a political party is heavily influenced by parental attitudes toward parties.

Peer Groups. **Peer groups** refer to face-to-face groups of which an individual is a member. Peer groups include friends, classmates, immediate colleagues at work, and fellow churchgoers. Peer groups may serve to support family attitudes in those cases in which the peer groups are similar in attitudes to the family. Peer groups may, however, socialize individuals away from family values in those instances in which there are considerable differences in socioeconomic orientation. In his study of the attitudes of Bennington College students, psychologist Theodore M. Newcomb discovered, for example, that students reared in conservative backgrounds tended to become much more liberal because of peer group influences at Bennington College.[7]

Schools. In modern societies formal education is an important component of political socialization. Every country uses schools to inculcate the basic values and rules of its political system. Patriotic symbols, such as the flag and national anthem, are glorified in the school years. Political scientists Gabriel A. Almond and Sidney Verba note, moreover, that their five-

[3] For a discussion, see Almond and Powell, *Comparative Politics*, pp. 50–51.

[4] Robert D. Hess and David Easton, "The Child's Changing Image of the President," *Public Opinion Quarterly* 24 (Winter 1960): 632–44.

[5] See David O. Sears, "Political Socialization," in *Micropolitical Theory* ed. Fred I. Greenstein and Nelson W. Polsby, vol. 2 of *Handbook of Political Science* (Reading, Mass.: Addison-Wesley, 1975), pp. 99–100.

[6] Fred I. Greenstein, *Children and Politics*, rev. ed. (New Haven: Yale University Press, 1969), p. 1.

[7] See Theodore M. Newcomb, "Persistence and Regression of Changed Attitudes: Long-Range Studies," in *Socialization to Politics*, ed. Jack Dennis (New York: John Wiley, 1973), pp. 413–24.

nation study (United States, Great Britain, Mexico, Germany, and Italy) revealed that education was an important factor in political participation and knowledge about government.[8]

Education has always been regarded as important by society because of both its real and imagined influence. In the United States, for example, concern with the subject matter taught in schools has sparked controversy in many communities. In her study of public school textbooks in American history, Frances Fitzgerald notes that each generation has attempted to revise American history in its textbook treatment of the past.[9] And so, during the Progressive period of American history, textbooks reflected the dominant Progressive themes of social reform. Today, groups of varying interests—religious, feminist, racial, libertarian—peruse the textbooks that are under consideration by state educational agencies responsible for selecting textbooks in order to make certain that the books do not contain "objectionable" material.

Social Groups. Political attitudes are much influenced by the associations people make through their trade unions and the professional, religious, and social organization to which they belong. A union member's voting behavior often shows the influence of union membership on voting, for example.

Mass Media. The **mass media** refer to printed and electronic forms of communication. Printed sources are primarily newspapers, and electronic media include radio and television. People are influenced by the information they receive. In dictatorships the mass media are controlled by government, which attempts to restrict the factual information reaching the public. In democracy freedom of information is regarded as a prerequisite of a free society. Even in democracies, however, some information is restricted because of considerations of national security, morality, and health.

Television, particularly, has become the most prominent media form, as each individual in advanced industrial societies spends on the average several hours a day before the television screen. Even in developing countries television has become an influence in promoting political viewpoints and inculcating patriotic ideals.

PUBLIC OPINION

To some early theoreticians of representative democracy, the voice of public opinion was seen as expressed through democratically elected representatives. The argument was put forward that elected officials actually represent the views of their constituents. In the twentieth century public opinion has been closely examined by political scientists, sociologists, and journalists, and the model of how representative democracy works has had to adjust to the empirical data about public opinion.

When the journalist Walter Lippmann wrote *Public Opinion* in 1922, he became one of the first to portray the ordinary American citizen as ignorant of the major issues of public policy. Other scholars have noted similar findings in their own studies of public opinion, not only in the United States but also in nearly every other country. One of the most significant findings about public opinion is that the masses of people are ill informed about major political issues. At the height of the Vietnam War, for example, more than 25 percent of the American people could not

[8] Gabriel A. Almond and Sidney Verba, *The Civic Culture: Political Attitudes and Democracy in Five Nations* (Princeton, N.J.: Princeton University Press, 1963), pp. 380–81.

[9] Frances Fitzgerald, *America Revised: History Schoolbooks in the Twentieth Century* (Boston: Little, Brown, 1979).

even identify the North Vietnamese leader Ho Chi Minh in spite of the daily news coverage of the war.

Social scientists are not in agreement about the knowledge that ordinary citizens possess about political issues. Although there is a consensus that the masses of people are not well informed, some scholars assert that the amount of political ignorance has been exaggerated. In their view more people in advanced industrial societies are better informed about politics than ever before. They attribute the greater awareness to the expansion of the mass media—particularly television—which increases access to political information; a higher level of education; and political awareness brought on by a larger role that government plays in society.[10]

Revelations of mass ignorance of issues has led to readaptations of democratic theory to take the new data into account (see Chapter 3). Public opinion is still considered to be an important factor in influencing what government does, but now distinctions are made about the different kinds of publics included in public opinion. Studies dealing with systems that are undemocratic, moreover, indicate that public opinion is an important feature in those systems, too.[11]

To better understand public opinion, it is essential to provide a definition, indicate its significant features, show how it is measured, and describe its influence on the behavior of government. Social scientists differ about each of these aspects, however, although much is now known about them.

[10] See Russell J. Dalton, *Citizen Politics in Western Democracies: Public Opinion and Political Parties in the United States, Great Britain, West Germany, and France* (Chatham, N.J.: Chatham House Publishers, 1988), chap. 2.

[11] See Alex Inkeles, *Public Opinion in Soviet Russia: A Study of Mass Persuasion* (Cambridge, Mass.: Harvard University Press, 1958).

Definition

Distinctions are sometimes made among attitudes, beliefs, and opinions. **Attitudes** are dispositions about ideas, policies, and people. **Beliefs** are fundamental commitments, such as religious or philosophical convictions. **Opinions** are attitudes about specific matters. We shall use the phrase *public opinion* to include attitudes and beliefs, however, since it is often difficult to make hard and fast distinctions.

People have opinions about all kinds of subjects, including political candidates, public policy, movie stars, and baseball teams. **Public opinion,** however, is the attitudes and beliefs that people hold about matters of public concern. Such a definition ordinarily excludes attitudes about movie stars or baseball teams, unless those subjects have become politicized. When an actress, such as Jane Fonda, organizes antinuclear rallies, for example, then public opinion may involve attitudes about movie stars.

Elected officials and group leaders are concerned with what the people are thinking. In democracies elected officials normally wish to be reelected, and gauging public opinion accurately is an essential prerequisite for reelection. If the officials endorse policies that do not have popular support, they may find themselves defeated on election day. Group leaders must organize coalitions, and a knowledge of public opinion allows them to more effectively prepare a campaign to broaden their support.

Even dictatorships are concerned with public opinion, although totalitarian dictatorships often ruthlessly squelch dissent through repressive acts, such as liquidation, imprisonment, or torture. Even totalitarian dictatorships must respond to public opinion in some ways, however, lest they topple from lack of popular support.

Features

In describing the essential features of public opinion it is essential to make two distinctions. Quite simply, one distinction refers to public, and the other to opinion.

In the early writings about public opinion a number of commentators described public opinion as if it were of a single mind. For example, statements were made that the American people were against involvement in a foreign war. More recently, however, distinctions have been made between the mass public and the attentive public. According to political scientist Gabriel A. Almond, the **mass public** consists of most ordinary citizens who have little information about issues but who react in a rather generalized manner to political stimuli. The mass public constitutes the bulk of the population. Public opinion polls have demonstrated that large numbers of people cannot even identify the names of their legislators, let alone understand the intricacies of issues.

The **attentive public** consists of those individuals who are concerned with public issues and makes up only about 15 percent of the population. The number of people who constitute the attentive public can vary, and individuals previously not concerned about issues can become vitally involved in political matters. In other words these people may become members of the attentive public if some issue galvanizes their attention. Many citizens of Harrisburg, Pennsylvania, for example, were not particularly concerned about nuclear energy. But when a nuclear reactor malfunctioned at Harrisburg's Three Mile Island plant, ordinary citizens became intensely involved in nuclear issues. They became sensitized to possible hazards to the health of their families and to the value of their property.

Some students of public opinion have noted that the mass public often gets its cues from the attentive public in order to form opinions. Such a process is known as the **two-step flow of communication.** This concept indicates that the masses of people get their opinion from the group leaders with whom they identify. The media reach these group leaders, who make their interpersonal influence felt on their followers by filtering the information to them.[12] When individuals find support among different group leaders, their opinions become reinforced. When their group leaders differ, the individuals are often subject to cross-pressures (political ideas that conflict) that often lead them to avoid expressing an opinion or becoming involved over some issues of public concern (see Chapter 3).

Criticism has been made of the two-step flow theory. Studies have shown that those people who engage in political discussion tend to discuss political issues with people who have equivalent levels of information and knowledge. Evidence does not support the view that there is a flow of information from the top down to the less politically informed. The politically informed follow the media and talk with other politically informed people. Those who are not politically sophisticated neither watch the news media nor talk about politics.[13]

The distinction among publics, then, has provided useful insights into public opinion. Other features of public opinion, however, focus on opinions rather than publics. Opinions are studies to determine direction, intensity, and stability.

In determining **direction,** public opinion analysts are concerned with whether an individual is for or against a policy or candidate. A simple Yes or No answer can determine direction. A percentage of

[12] See Elihu Katz and Paul F. Lazarsfeld, *Personal Influence: The Part Played by People in the Flow of Mass Communications* (Glencoe, Ill.: Free Press, 1955).

[13] W. Russell Neuman, *The Paradox of Mass Politics: Knowledge and Public Opinion in the American Electorate* (Cambridge, Mass.: Harvard University Press, 1986), p. 147.

approval can be compiled about such matters as: "Is the president doing a good job?" "Should the draft be instituted?" "If an election were held today involving Candidate A and Candidate B, would you vote for Candidate A?"

A simple Yes or No answer does not, however, provide enough information about public opinion. Analysts have, consequently, designed scales of measurement to determine more precisely the political sentiments of individuals. Through such a scale, for example, opinion may be distinguished among those who support different kinds of programs, such as a comprehensive national health plan, a limited national health plan, and a national health plan designed to insure only for catastrophic illnesses.

Direction, however, is not sufficient to measure public opinion since the percentage of respondents favoring one or the other position leaves many aspects of opinion still unknown. How strongly people hold their views—that is, the **intensity** of their opinion—is important. Asked by a pollster whether he or she is for or against nuclear energy, a respondent may have little or no interest in the subject. If the respondents have strong feelings, then they are more likely to participate in political affairs for the purpose of influencing political action.

Opinions may be intensely held at various times, but public opinion analysts are also concerned with the **stability** of opinions. That is to say, are the opinions held over a long period of time? Sometimes during presidential primary contests, for example, public opinion can fluctuate rapidly, and candidates fade from public prominence as rapidly as falling pop stars lose their staying power on the disc charts.

Measurement

The method used to measure public opinion is the public opinion poll. The idea of a poll is to take a sample of the total population to be investigated (or **universe,** as it is called) for the purpose of determining what that universe is thinking. Often, the actual number of people constituting the sample is quite small. In public opinion polls about presidential preferences, for example, about 1,200 people are polled from a universe consisting of more than 100 million people. A margin of error of 2 or 3 percentage points is estimated, based on the size of the sample.

Sampling technique is essential for accuracy. Today, the **probability sample** is used in which each person in the targeted population has an equal chance of being selected. There are different forms of probability sampling. A **simple random sample** takes the entire universe and selects samples such as drawing names out of a hat or numbers out of a computer. A **systematic sample** uses a random procedure to choose the *first* respondent but a skip interval to select the remaining respondents. In this latter form the random sample determines, say, that the fiftieth person is selected from a list, and then every fiftieth person from the remaining list would be chosen. A **stratified sample** breaks down the universe into classifications, such as region, race, or religion, in the same proportion as they exist in the universe, and then respondents from those classifications are selected.[14]

In addition to making certain that the sample is scientifically drawn, pollsters must solve other problems. They must

---

[14] For a discussion, see Jerry L. Yeric and John R. Todd, *Public Opinion: The Visible Politics* (Itasca, Ill.: F. E. Peacock, 1983), chap. 3.

phrase the question in an unbiased manner and must interpret the responses correctly. In this regard pollster Burns W. Roper observes, "The major source of survey error stems from question wording. The smallest error comes from the most often cited source of error, sampling error."[15]

Critics of public opinion polls have questioned both the technical aspects of poll taking and the uses to which polls are put. The technical criticisms include the size of the sample, the way in which questions are phrased, the subjectivity or professionalism of the interviewer, and the validity of the response of the interviewee.

Critics argue that it is impossible to measure the opinions of millions by sampling only 1,200 people. Pollsters argue, however, that the size of the sample is sufficiently large so that with the few percentage point margin of error, an accurate measure of the opinion may be recorded.

Critics argue that the way in which a question is phrased can alter the results of a poll. When a *New York Times*/CBS News poll asked people if they favored an amendment "prohibiting abortions," a majority opposed it. But when asked whether they favored an amendment "protecting the life of the unborn child," some 20 percent of them switched sides.[16]

Critics of polls question the subjectivity and professionalism of the interviewer. Although interviewers are trained to be unbiased, they do not always follow the appropriate guidelines. In some cases, moreover, pollsters may rush respondents because of pressures to meet an unspecified quota.

Pollster supporters defend the scientific quality of their profession. Interviewers trained in polling, or in **survey research** as it is sometimes called, can make certain that the questions are not biased and that their own personal opinions do not affect the outcome of the poll. But pollster critics are not convinced that polling is a science.

Some people who are interviewed respond to questions on subjects about which they know little or nothing simply because they do not wish to reveal their ignorance to a pollster. In this regard one group of researchers conducted a poll in Cincinnati and found that 33 percent of the respondents expressed an opinion on the 1975 Public Affairs Act. This law, however, was fictitious, having been "invented" solely for the survey.[17]

Technical questions aside, some of the most pointed criticisms against polling have been directed toward the political uses to which polls are put. Polling results can become part of the political campaign issues, as candidates search for any issue that will strengthen their support.

Polls are also publicized by candidates to show that they can win, or that they are gaining, or that their opponent is slipping. Moreover, "private" polls, conducted by a candidate's paid pollster, can be leaked to the press if they reveal good news. Such uses of polls bring the accuracy of polls generally into question.

Polls can have an influence on the way people vote. During primaries, some people vote for their second choice because the polls indicate that a vote for the first choice would be wasted. There is evi-

[15] Burns W. Roper, "Are Polls Accurate?" *Annals of the American Academy of Political and Social Sciences* 472 (March 1984): 34.

[16] Brock Brower, "The Power of Polls," *Reader's Digest* 133 (July 1988): 53.

[17] George F. Bishop, Robert W. Oldendick, Alfred J. Tuchfarber, and Stephen E. Bennett, "Pseudo-Opinions on Public Affairs," *Public Opinion Quarterly* 44 (Summer 1980): 198–209.

dence, moreover, that the early release of **exit polls** (polls conducted of people as they leave the voting booth) may result in other people who have not yet voted refraining from voting. In the presidential elections of 1980 and 1984, the voting turnout on the West Coast was less than expected because exit polls on the East Coast, in an earlier time zone, indicated that the presidential contest had already been won by Ronald Reagan. It is believed that this lower voting turnout influenced the outcome of a number of electoral contests for Congress and for state and local offices.

Influence on Government

As indicated above, public opinion is a force in government both in democracies and in dictatorships. In democracies public opinion can be freely expressed. Political leaders who act against public opinion face defeat at the ballot box. Dictatorships that ignore public opinion or attempt to suppress it through terror may discover that their base of support has eroded. They may, however, be cunning enough to make accommodations to some segments of opinion in the community. Even Joseph Stalin and Adolf Hitler had to do that in some instances by establishing scapegoats and by creating a climate of fear.

Although it is difficult to show empirically how public opinion influences government behavior in democracies, accounts of tenure by political leaders after they have left public office reveal how greatly they were guided by public opinion. Some political leaders submit readily to every changing whim of public opinion. Because public opinion is volatile and unstable, some political leaders in a democracy attempt to lead public opinion in the hope that they can bring about a change in popular attitudes. Still other political leaders move fearlessly against public opinion when they feel that it is wrong on a subject. John F. Kennedy's *Profiles in Courage* (1956), describes political leaders who defied public opinion on such matters of conscience.

The attention that political leaders give to polling in democratic societies indicates that the link between opinion and political action is a strong one. The toppling of dictators throughout the world suggests, too, that those who ignore or neglect popular support face the prospect of losing power. Political leaders decide for themselves whether to move with or against public opinion. In democratic governments statesmanship requires both a willingness to lead on the basis of objective needs and a responsiveness to opinion. Polls cannot, however, tell a leader what to do.

ISSUE

Since the invention of the printing press, the mass media have had an important influence by informing people about political ideas and events. At first, newspapers and magazines were the principal media in disseminating information to the masses of people. In the twentieth century, however, the electronic instruments of communication have become the dominant media forms. Television particularly, more than radio, newspapers, or magazines, has come to play a dominant role in presenting news and in shaping public opinion in a unique way in the United States, and controversy surrounds its effect on attitudes.

15/YES

DOES TV NEWS HAVE A UNIQUE IMPACT ON PUBLIC OPINION IN THE UNITED STATES?

The uniqueness of television is derived from three factors: (1) the major political events of the past few decades have been television events; (2) television has intrinsic features that no other channel of communication can duplicate; and (3) the American people have come to depend on television for their news more than on any other of the media.

Politics as Television Events. If events are to have political significance, people must know about them. Since television appeared as a major media form in the 1950s, it has become deeply involved in covering political stories as part of the daily national news broadcasts. To a large extent, television determines what millions of people think of as news. Political campaigns, government wrongdoing, protest movements, civil unrest, acts of war and violence, and diplomatic events have become prominent features of the evening TV news in the past few decades.

The reporters decide which candidates to cover and have even made obscure political figures into major national personalities. Moreover, they make political life difficult for a candidate by asking embarrassing questions or revealing information depicting the candidate in a derogatory manner.

TV reporters decide when and how to report the work of government officials. The animosity between TV journalists and Richard Nixon, for example, helped project the Nixon administration's wrongdoing into national prominence. Watergate became a matter of heightened national concern in part because of the daily TV attention given to the illegal acts of Nixon and some of his associates.

Protest movements, too, are made nationally known through TV coverage. Many activities of the civil rights movement in the 1960s, for example, were television events. TV reporters were able to show vividly how segregationist southern police officials were intimidating supporters of racial integration. Major events of the civil rights movement, such as confrontations in southern cities like Birmingham and Selma, are cases in point. Martin Luther King, Jr., came to be recognized as a national civil rights figure in large part because of TV news coverage.

Civil unrest in the form of urban riots in northern cities in the 1960s was vividly depicted on the television screen. The riots in Newark and Detroit, for example, became fixed in the minds of millions of viewers as they were taking place. The TV coverage of riots seemed to trigger riots in other cities.

Television is, moreover, particularly graphic in showing acts of war and violence. The Vietnam War was reported on television in a way no earlier wars could be covered by other media forms. The video films of the fighting in that seemingly interminable war helped to shape public opinion about the war.

Acts of terrorism, moreover—whether they are conducted in the United States or abroad—influence the attitudes of people about terrorists and the ability of government to deal with them. In fact, some terrorists use television as a way of getting their messages across to large audiences. A notable example occurred in 1985 with the hijacking of a TWA jetliner to Beirut. In that case, interviews with the hijackers were broadcast, unedited, on TV network news stations in an effort to influence U.S. public opinion.

Foreign political leaders are aware of how they can manipulate the American media in general and television in particular. They have granted interviews only to friendly reporters and forced unfriendly journalists to leave the country. Ze'ev Chafets, an Israeli journalist, even contends that the lives of Western journalists are threatened if the reporters give unfavorable accounts of the Palestine Liberation Organization. In his view Israel gets a bad press in the United States precisely because Israel is a democratic society that allows journalists to report freely.[18] Political scientist Guenter Lewy comments along somewhat similar lines about unbalanced coverage of the Vietnam War:

---

[18] Ze'ev Chafets, *Double Vision: How the Press Distorts America's View of the Middle East* (New York: Morrow, 1985).

The Viet Cong were notoriously uncooperative in allowing cameramen to shoot pictures of the disemboweling of village chiefs and other acts of terror, while scenes of South Vietnamese brutality, such as the mistreatment of prisoners, were often seen on American television screens.

Lewy concludes that such reporting biased the coverage of the war against the American side.[19]

Diplomacy, too, has become a television event. Summit conferences of leading international figures are now more devoted to public appearances than to private negotiations. The summit meetings between Soviet leader Mikhail Gorbachev and U.S. President Ronald Reagan were "photo opportunities" in which television played a prominent role.

The events of the past decades, then, cannot be distinguished from the phenomena of the television reporting of them. The opinions that people formed of politics were shaped by the medium of television.

Intrinsic Features of TV. Some commentators note that American TV journalists are more liberal than the public they serve and that they use television to project their biases onto the public. It is not essential to establish the political attitudes of TV journalists, however, to show that television news is a distortion of reality and influences public opinion. TV journalists, like judges, may, however, restrain their own personal biases because of a commitment to a professional ethic.

What makes television news biased are the characteristics of that medium. Television news has some unique features that distinguish it from other channels of communication, most notably newspapers. These features include a heavy emphasis on pictures, greater attention to interpretation of the news, and an unusually large and captive audience.

Although newspapers pioneered in using pictures to illustrate news stories, television news is much more dependent upon film. A television reporter who sat in front of a camera and just read the news would soon lose the interest of an audience. Television's attraction is that it shows vivid pictures of events as they are unfolding, such as an urban rioter looting a store, an American hostage held captive by terrorists, or civilians wounded by military bombardment. In this respect two students of TV contend that it is television's "insatiable appetite for action, indeed for gross action" that may set it apart from the other media.[20] Television thrives on instant and visual attractions in ways that other media forms cannot duplicate, however much they try.

Almost as important as the reliance of television on action is its ability to recreate that action by multiple showings of the same footage. Some of the striking examples of this repetition were the attempted assassination of President Reagan in 1981, the destruction of the Challenger spacecraft in 1986, and the highlights of the Iran-Contra hearings in 1987, which investigated the U.S. secret arms trade with Iran and the illegal U.S. military support of the Contra forces fighting the Marxist government in Nicaragua.

In addition to its reliance on film, television news depends heavily on the journalist to interpret events. Newspaper reporters are trained to leave themselves out of a story and, consequently, to let the facts speak for themselves. Because television relies so heavily on the visual picture and because each TV news story must be compressed into a time span measured in seconds, TV journalists become part of the story. It is they who interpret the pictures that are displayed on the television screen. Television journalists, consequently, often become popular celebrities. It is not surprising, then, that CBS News TV anchorman Walter Cronkite was long regarded as one of the most trustworthy Americans in the polls—a status he continued to hold years after he retired as anchorman.

In describing the news, TV news personalities often create a vision of America that is designed to attract the attention of millions of viewers. According to political scientist Michael J. Robinson, television journalism in the United States in the late 1960s and early 1970s promoted images of distrust in the effectiveness

---

[19] Guenter Lewy, *False Consciousness: An Essay on Mystification* (New Brunswick, N.J.: Transaction Books, 1982), p. 104.

[20] Gary L. Wamsley and Richard A. Pride, "Television Network News: Re-Thinking the Iceberg Problem," *Western Political Quarterly* 25 (September 1972): 439.

of government and a feeling of malaise about the American political system. This vision of America has influenced public opinion and voting behavior, Robinson contends. Were there no television news, he argues, there would be less political malaise in American public opinion.[21]

Finally, the character of the audience for TV news is different. Not only is it larger (as we shall see below), but it is often inadvertent as well. Studies of newspaper readers show that most people who buy newspapers do not do so primarily to read the political news of the day. Instead, they may be interested in sports, theater schedules, or department store sales. They select the information they wish to read. In television news programs, however, the viewers interested in one aspect of the news must sit and watch an entire news program. They cannot, consequently, be selective about what they see. They may want to see the films about a football triumph of their favorite team, but they will have to watch stories about foreign affairs and domestic politics. In that way, they learn more news on television than they do with other media forms.

Before the age of television, many people obtained their information about political matters from intermediary agencies, such as family, friends, group associates, or political parties. Television has displaced to a significant degree these intermediary agencies for many, although certainly not all, people. What is significant here is that people who ordinarily are unconcerned about political matters are exposed to politics through television, and this development has an impact on the political behavior of the masses of people, as we shall see below.[22]

Dependency on TV for News. Studies of the media reveal that in the United States most people depend more upon television for their political information than on any other media form. This marks an important change in the kinds of information about politics that people receive. In the United States most newspapers

have been regional, and people have been likely to read the newspapers of their region. Television news, however, is predominantly national, although there are local and regional news broadcasts, too. These local and regional news programs, however, have smaller audiences. Thus, the same evening news on the networks is seen by people across the country. People who used to rely on newspapers and the radio for their information—with the heavy emphasis on local and regional news—now become concerned with issues of national scope that they would have ignored in the pretelevision past.

Children, in particular, are affected by television. Political scientist Austin Ranney notes that from the time children begin watching television (at the age of three months) until the time they finish high school, they "have spent less than 12,000 hours in front of a teacher and more than 22,000 hours in front of a television set."[23]

The political significance of a national audience that includes millions of inadvertent viewers is that attitudes of millions of people will be heavily influenced by this media form. Their political attitudes toward such matters as the effectiveness of political institutions to deal with social problems, the integrity and honesty of government leaders, and the wisdom of political choices will be interpreted in ways determined by TV journalists. Since so much emphasis is placed on interpretation of the news, then, TV news has come to play an extraordinary role in shaping public opinion.

Critics of television news often direct their attacks on the way newscasters express their opinions even through the kind of political issues they choose to highlight. Selection of issues is often subjective. By featuring topics, such as the risks of nuclear energy, the plight of the homeless, the danger of drug addiction, newscasters play a prominent—and often *the* most prominent—role in **agenda setting**—that is, the selection of topics that the general public thinks important. As political scientist Bernard Cohen notes, "The mass media may not be successful much of the time in telling people what to think, but the media are stun-

[21] Michael J. Robinson, "Public Affairs Television and the Growth of Political Malaise: The Case of 'The Selling of the Pentagon,' " *American Political Science Review* 70 (June 1976): 409–32.

[22] Ibid., p. 426.

[23] Austin Ranney, *Channels of Power: The Impact of Television on American Politics* (New York: Basic Books, 1983), p. 4.

ningly successful in telling their audience what to think about."[24]

Political scientists Shanto Iyengar and Donald R. Kinder studied the effect of television on public opinion and concluded that television news powerfully influences which problems viewers regard as the nation's most serious. They write, "Rising prices, unemployment, energy shortages, arms control—all these (and more) become high priority political issues for the public only if they become high priority news items for the networks." They feel, moreover, that the agenda setting function of television is particularly strong in shaping the judgments of citizens with limited political resources and skills, while those who are partisans, ac-

tivists, and close observers of the political scene are less likely to be influenced in this manner.[25]

Iyengar and Kinder also note that television news has an effect that they call **priming**—the changing of standards that people use to make political evaluations. If television news becomes preoccupied with nuclear annihilation, then many people will judge the president in terms of what he has done to make nuclear war less likely. According to their studies, priming affects the politically involved as effectively as it does the politically withdrawn.[26]

All of these factors have contributed to making television a unique media form in the United States.

---

[24] Bernard Cohen, *The Press and Foreign Policy* (Princeton, N.J.: Princeton University Press, 1963), p. 16.

[25] Shanto Iyengar and Donald R. Kinder, *News That Matters: Television and American Opinion* (Chicago: University of Chicago Press, 1987), pp. 4, 60.

[26] Ibid., pp. 63, 95.

15/NO — DOES TV NEWS HAVE A UNIQUE IMPACT ON PUBLIC OPINION IN THE UNITED STATES?

Television has been blamed for many of the great evils that have fallen on society. Arguments have been put forward that television is responsible for encouraging violent crime, contributing to the decline of reading skills by the nation's youth, and weakening family ties. It is perhaps only a faint remembrance that some early enthusiasts saw television as a means of educating the masses of people through such a vehicle as the television news program. The ordinary person who might not have time to read the newspaper, so it was asserted, would certainly be able to become informed about political matters through watching fifteen or thirty minutes of TV news each day.

The hope that television news could create an enlightened citizenry has given way to the feeling that the masses of people are misinformed, misguided, and heavily influenced by television reporters. We argue that such an assessment of TV news is not accurate and we shall deal with the points raised by the *Affirmative.*

Politics as Television Events. It is certainly true that the major political events of the past few decades, such as political campaigns, protest movements, civil unrest, acts of war and violence, and diplomatic events, have been television events. The fact that television has recorded these events, however, does not mean that they would not have occurred if television had not been invented.

Partisan conflict for political power has long been a prominent feature of democratic politics in the United States. Candidates for public office in the nineteenth century sought campaign success by influencing newspaper journalists, for example, and did not need television to get their message across to the public.

As with electoral contests, the major issues of our time have inherent qualities that influence public opinion. Long before the Watergate affair, there was much popular interest in honest government and the uncovering of wrongdoing in office. The Teapot Dome affair in the administration of Warren Harding received as much public scrutiny in 1923 as did Watergate in 1973–74. Investigations of malfeasance in office sparked many a reform crusade in urban politics before television was invented, moreover.

It was not so much television, but rather popular interest in remedying the evils of the post–World War II period, that was responsible for the intense political activism of so many people. The civil rights protests developed out of the patterns of segregation and disenfranchisement affecting black Americans. Television did not create an issue that traced its injustices back to the period before America achieved its independence from British rule.

Urban riots were not born in the television era either. Riots occurred in ethnically diverse urban areas with the rise in European immigration to the big cities of the United States around the turn of the century. The existence of slums, relative social and economic deprivation, and lack of hope by unemployed youth played a more important role in generating urban riots than did the television portrayals of those riots.

War weariness is not new to America, either. In the Civil War, for example, draft riots swept through some northern states. Antiwar protesters were a feature of the nineteenth and twentieth centuries, and conscientious objectors particularly asserted their pacifist feelings without benefit of network television inducements.

It is wrong to blame television for the political behavior that we condemn. Television news reporting is merely a reflection of our society. If what the mirror reflects is ugly, that is not the fault of the mirror.

Intrinsic Features of TV. Television may possess certain unique features, but these do not result in any special effects on society. As early as Greek antiquity, political theorists like Plato and Aristotle warned about the powers of spellbinding speakers who could move crowds to act in frenzied ways.

More recently, however, other media forms have shown powers of persuasion. The "yellow press" of newspaper magnate William Randolph Hearst in the first quarter of this century is often blamed for creating the same kinds of sensationalism today often attributed to TV. Newspapers have also been blamed for their prejudiced accounts of German atrocities in World War I and their undue influence in promoting American intervention.

Radio, too, has become a convincing means of influencing attitudes and behavior. In 1938, for example, Orson Welles broadcast a radio dramatization of H.G. Wells' *War of the Worlds,* which depicted an invasion of Earth by Martians. So convincing was the dramatization that many people fled from their homes to avoid the "invasion."

Too much attention is given to television's unique characteristics of an emphasis on pictures and news interpretation and its attraction to the inadvertent viewer. These are all qualities that accurately describe television's unusual features, but their significance is overstated.

From the early days of photography, pictures have been used in the dissemination of news. Still pictures of the American Civil War were powerful portrayals of that war. Newsreels shown in movie theaters of fighting scenes in pretelevision era wars, moreover, were equally powerful in affecting people's attitudes about war. What strengthened the protest movement against the war in Vietnam was not the television screen bringing war scenes directly into the living room but rather the growing popular feeling that the United States could not or would not win that war.[27] It is well to remember that Americans had become similarly disenchanted with the Korean War about two years after the United States sent its forces to Korea, and that war was not a television war.

Military analyst Harry G. Summers notes that television news has been unfairly blamed for turning American public opinion against the war in Vietnam. He writes that those who make such a claim repeat the same kinds of misconceptions of the early proponents of air power, who believed that terror bombing of civilian targets would evoke so much horror that immediate surrender would be assured. "We now know," he writes, "that such terror bombing during World War II only strengthened national resolve." In Summers's view the decline in public support of the Vietnam War came about because the American people believed that the sacrifices required by the war were too high in terms of the goals set by

---

[27] See Daniel C. Hallin, "The Media, the War in Vietnam, and Political Support: A Critique of the Thesis of an Oppositional Media," *Journal of Politics* 46 (February 1984): 2–24.

U.S. political leaders. He explains, "By its failure to establish the political object, the government failed to establish the 'value' of the war."[28]

It is certainly true that an emphasis on interpretation is a unique feature of television as a media form. It is clear from the past, however, that radio commentators, such as Walter Winchell, Drew Pearson, and H.V. Kaltenborn in their day, were popular because of their interpretation of the news on national radio programs. Print journalists, moreover, also interpret the news, both in the selection of the subject matter with which they deal and in the prominence they give to a subject. While Fidel Castro was a guerrilla fighter in the Cuban countryside in the 1950s, sympathetic accounts of his activities that were reported by journalist Herbert Matthews of the *New York Times* gave Castro a popular following in the United States. After Castro came to power, however, and established a communist regime, his image became tarnished. A witty commentary of his early period in power suggested that the *Times* might promote its want-ad sales by using a photograph of Fidel Castro with the caption, "I got my job through the *New York Times*."

Finally, it cannot be denied that people watch television news programs and hear information that might otherwise come from other sources, such as friends, interest groups, and political parties. As we shall see, however, these factors are not as important as they might superficially appear to be.

Dependency on TV for News. It is true that most people do depend more on TV for the news than on any other media form. This is not a crucial fact as far as influencing public opinion is concerned, however, because none of the mass media change public opinion easily.

Students of communications have observed that the dominant effect of mass media is reinforcement rather than change of existing beliefs.[29] People are more likely to be influenced by interpersonal relations than by television, no matter how many hours they spend before the television box. Family, friends, and social groups have a greater impact on opinions than do the media. The media ordinarily influence mediators rather than the mass public directly. Students who wish to find out about the ability, knowledge, and fairness of a teacher they do not know would more likely be influenced by the comments of a friendly fellow student than by all the praises heaped by Dan Rather during the evening TV news.

Psychologists and sociologists have observed that belief patterns are influenced by the principle of selectivity. **Selectivity** means that people often choose the information they wish to know. In other words, in forming attitudes and opinions, believing is very often seeing, rather than seeing is believing.

Three different kinds of selectivity have been distinguished: selective exposure, selective perception, and selective retention. **Selective exposure** refers to the fact that people choose to see media presentations that are in accord with their predispositions. If a particular news program is biased in a way that viewers do not approve, the chances are that the viewers will turn to another channel. **Selective perception** means that individuals tend to see what they want to see. People who are strong Democrats, for example, may self-censor news that they find in conflict with their predispositions about Democrats. **Selective retention** means that the kind of information individuals remember is also self-censored, so that the information most favorable to their point of view will be remembered and the rest ignored or forgotten.[30]

Much has been said about the role of television news in agenda setting and in priming. What is often ignored, however, is the role of the governing elite in influencing television coverage of the government's agenda.

The Reagan presidency is a case in point. As president, Ronald Reagan appeared frequently on television. It was Reagan and not the television media who set the national agenda in defense issues, as his television speech in 1983 announcing the Strategic Defense Initiative illustrates. The large number of journalists—broadcast and print—who cover

---

[28] Harry G. Summers, "Western Media and Recent Wars," *Military Review* 66 (May 1986): 12.

[29] Joseph T. Klapper, *The Effects of Mass Communication* (New York: Free Press, 1960), p. 15.

[30] Ibid., pp. 19–25.

regular newsbeats in Washington are dependent upon the government for information. The governing elites are, consequently, able to play a major role in agenda setting and in priming.

Television, then, is limited in its ability to influence opinion. Even journalists who might feel that they want to depict the evils of American institutions cannot be sure that they are achieving their desired effects. Outside the Democratic party national convention in Chicago in 1968, for example, television cameras portrayed scenes of policemen clubbing demonstrators. In spite of TV journalists' criticism of the Chicago police, studies of public opinion revealed that there was overwhelming popular support of the police rather than the demonstrators. The principle of selectivity seemed to apply. Television, then, has not become the ogre that its critics have described.

KEY TERMS

Affective socialization
Agenda setting
Attentive public
Attitudes
Beliefs
Cognitive socialization
Direction (public opinion)
Evaluative socialization
Exit poll
Intensity (public opinion)
Mass media
Mass public
Opinions
Peer groups
Political culture
Political socialization

Priming
Probability sample
Public opinion
Selective exposure
Selective perception
Selective retention
Selectivity
Simple random sample
Socialization
Stability (public opinion)
Stratified sample
Subculture
Survey research
Systematic sample
Two-step flow of communication
Universe
Youth culture

QUESTIONS

Political Culture, Political Socialization, and Public Opinion

1. How do we form our opinions?
2. What are the differences and what are the similarities in political socialization processes in democracies and dictatorships?
3. What kinds of civic education should be part of primary and secondary school programs? What are the reasons for your answer?
4. Should the recitation of the pledge of allegiance be made compulsory in the public elementary and secondary schools? What are the reasons for your answer?
5. Can public opinion be measured scientifically? What are the reasons for your answer?
6. What influence does public opinion have on public policy in democracies and dictatorships? Give examples.

Television News

1. Based on your viewing, is the TV evening news positive or negative in its portrayal of American society and American politics? Describe specific evening news stories to illustrate your argument.

2. What effect does the control over television by a dictatorship have on the opinions of its citizenry?

3. What limits should be imposed on the television news media in covering military and foreign policy matters? What are the reasons for your answer?

4. If a known terrorist were willing to give

an interview on a Western television station, should the station be willing to show the interview directly to viewers? What are the consequences of your answer to (a) freedom of the press, and (b) the likelihood that more terrorist acts will be committed?

5. What role do elected public officials play in manipulating the news that appears on television?

RECOMMENDED READINGS

ALMOND, GABRIEL A., and SIDNEY VERBA. *The Civic Culture: Political Attitudes and Democracy in Five Nations.* Princeton, N.J.: Princeton University Press, 1963. An examination, using survey research, of the political culture of democracy and the social structures and processes that sustain it.

————. eds. *The Civic Culture Revisited.* Boston: Little, Brown, 1980. Essays on *The Civic Culture.*

BARNER-BARRY, CAROL, and ROBERT ROSENWEIN. *Psychological Perspectives on Politics.* Englewood Cliffs, N.J.: Prentice Hall, 1985. An overview of political psychology.

BRADBURN, NORMAN M., and SEYMOUR SUDMAN. *Polls and Surveys: Understanding What They Tell Us.* San Francisco: Jossey-Bass, 1988. A comprehensive nontechnical guide to understanding surveys.

BROWN, ARCHIE, ed. *Political Culture and Communist Studies.* Armonk, N.Y.: M. E. Sharpe, 1984. A collection of essays on the subject.

BUDANSKY, STEPHEN. "The Numbers Racket: How Polls and Statistics Lie." *U.S. News and World Report* 105 (July 11, 1988): 44–47. A popular account of the subject.

CONVERSE, PHILIP E., and MICHAEL W. TRAUGOTT. "Assessing the Accuracy of Polls and Surveys." *Science* 234 (November 28, 1986): 1094–1098. An explanation of why polls on similar topics conducted over the same time period or near the same time period vary.

DAWSON, RICHARD E., and KENNETH PREWITT. *Political Socialization.* Boston: Little, Brown, 1969. An introduction to political socialization.

EXOO, CALVIN E., ed. *Democracy Upside Down: Public Opinion and Cultural Hegemony in the*

United States. New York: Praeger, 1987. A critique that public opinion is molded by the dominant economic interests in the United States.

FARAW, TAWFIC E., and YASUMASA KURODA, eds. *Political Socialization in the Arab States.* Boulder, Colo.: Lynne Rienner, 1987. A collection of essays on the subject.

KELLY, RITA MAE, ed. *Gender and Socialization to Power and Politics.* New York: Haworth Press, 1986. An examination of the political socialization of women.

KINDER, DONALD, and DAVID O. SEARS. "Public Opinion and Political Action." In *Handbook of Social Psychology*, ed. GARDNER LINDZEY and ELLIOT ARONSON. 3d ed. New York: Random House, 1985. 2:659–741. An overview of the scholarship on the subject.

LANGTON, KENNETH P. *Political Socialization.* New York: Oxford University Press, 1969. A cross-cultural study of political socialization.

MCCLOSKY, HERBERT, and JOHN ZALLER. *The American Ethos.* Cambridge, Mass.: Harvard University Press, 1984. A study of the values of the American people today and the significance of those values to American history.

NEUMAN, W. RUSSELL. *The Paradox of Mass Politics: Knowledge and Opinion in the American Electorate.* Cambridge, Mass.: Harvard University Press, 1986. A study of the relationship between an informed citizenry and the effectiveness of the U.S. political system.

Television News

GRABER, DORIS A. *Mass Media and American Politics.* 2d ed. Washington, D.C.: CQ Press, 1984. An examination of the pervasive impact of the media on the American political system.

HALLIN, DANIEL C. "The Media, the War in Vietnam, and Political Support: A Critique of the Thesis of an Oppositional Media." *Journal of Politics* 46 (February 1984): 2–24. An argument that the case of Vietnam does not show that American news media shifted to an oppositional stance during the 1960s.

HOFSTETTER, C. RICHARD. *Bias in the News: Network Television Coverage of the 1972 Election Campaign.* Columbus: Ohio State University Press, 1976. An excellent study of the subject.

HOWELL, CASS D. "War, Television and Public Opinion." *Military Review* 67 (February 1987): 71–79. An argument that TV cameras should be banned from the battlefield.

IYENGAR, SHANTO, and DONALD R. KINDER. *News That Matters: Television and American Opinion.* Chicago: University of Chicago Press, 1987. An argument that TV news influences opinion by helping to set the political agenda and affecting the way in which public officials are judged.

KLAPPER, JOSEPH T. *The Effects of Mass Communication.* New York: Free Press, 1960. An analysis of the social and psychological effects of mass communications.

O'NEILL, MICHAEL J. *Terrorist Spectaculars: Should TV Coverage Be Curbed?* New York: Priority Press, 1986. An assessment of the impact of TV coverage of terrorist acts on terrorism.

RANNEY, AUSTIN. *Channels of Power: The Impact of Television on American Politics.* New York: Basic Books, 1983. A broad analysis of the subject.

ROBINSON, MICHAEL J. "Public Affairs Television and the Growth of Political Malaise: The Case of 'The Selling of the Pentagon.'" *American Political Science Review* 70 (June 1976): 409–32. An argument that television has a fundamental impact on the political behavior of the mass public.

ROBINSON, MICHAEL J., and AUSTIN RANNEY, eds. *The Mass Media in Campaign '84.* Washington, D.C.: American Enterprise Institute for Public Policy Research, 1985. Articles from *Public Opinion* about the 1984 presidential election.

SCHRAM, MARTIN J. "The Impact of Television on the Political Process." In *Renewing the Dream: National Archives Bicentennial '87 Lectures on Contemporary Constitutional Issues,* ed. RALPH S. POLLOCK. Lanham, Md.: University Press of America, 1986. Pp. 117–26. An argument that television influenced the 1984 election, but Reagan manipulated the media.

SUMMERS, HARRY G. "Western Media and Recent Wars." *Military Review* 66 (May 1986): 4–17. An argument that political forces rather than the media influence popular support of a war.

chapter 7

Civil liberties

- An old widow, living alone, is raped and murdered. The police apprehend a young man and accuse him of the crime. The state is unable to prosecute because a judge says that the evidence obtained by the police was seized in violation of the constitutional rights of the defendant.
- A group of college students carries the flag of the Viet Cong parade along Main Street at the same time that hundreds of American soldiers are being killed or wounded in a war in Vietnam, and the police keep pace alongside the marchers to protect them from angry citizens.
- An American Nazi party official announces that his organization will march through Skokie, Illinois, a city with a number of Jewish people who had been incarcerated in concentration camps.

Events such as these have brought frustration and indignation to many American people. To some, they are the expression of a nation gone mad—one that lets criminals go free while innocent people become their victims, protects the nation's enemies rather than its friends, and gives support to one of the most horrendous groups the world has ever known while the survivors of Adolf Hitler's atrocities relive in their minds their macabre concentration camp experiences.

So widespread has been the dissatisfaction with such seemingly irrational official acts that some Americans have questioned the wisdom of relying on a constitutional system that permits such behavior. Specifically, they direct their criticisms at the elaborate protections to all citizens and residents, protections that are known as *rights*. A **right** is a power to which a person has a just claim. In the United States, many individual rights are enumerated in the Constitution and the first ten amendments (known as the Bill of Rights). These rights constitute the fundamental protections of the American people against encroachments by the federal government. Other amendments, statutes, and judicial interpretations have extended many of these rights to include protections against not only the federal government but against state governments and private groups as well.

The notion that individuals have rights that must be protected by government is a principle found not only in the American Constitution but in other constitutions as well. Even countries that violate individual rights have constitutions that profess in principle the rights they are in fact violating. Some private groups, such as the Ku Klux Klan and the American Nazis, which would destroy individual rights if they came to political power, rely on the rights of a free society for their protection.

Rights, then, are both condemned and honored. Rights are important in determining what the proper relationship is between the citizen and the state. To understand different perspectives about rights, it is essential to specify different kinds of rights, describe their historical development, and then look at the justification and criticisms of a political system that reveres rights. An examination of two issues—civil disobedience and capital punishment—will show some of the complexities involved in any discussion of rights.

WHAT ARE RIGHTS?

Rights have been defined as powers to which a person has a just claim. Rights may be further broken down into political rights and economic rights. **Political rights** are defined as those rights that assure an individual freedom of expression, opportunity to participate in the political process, fair treatment in criminal proceedings, and equal treatment under the law. **Economic rights** are those freedoms that allow for material security, such as freedom to get a job, good housing,

adequate education, social security, and welfare (see Chapter 3).

A great deal of ambiguity marks any discussion of rights, since often the term is used in different ways for different purposes. Political rights are frequently said to be composed of civil liberties and civil rights. The phrase **civil liberties** is used to refer to the rights of an individual against the state, freedom of expression, and rights in criminal proceedings. In general usage **civil rights** consist of those rights that assure minority group equality before the law.

Recognizing the definitional difficulties, we shall include civil liberties and civil rights as synonymous with political rights, as defined above. We shall also introduce a new term, **human rights,** which we shall define exclusively as synonymous with political rights. Some writers include economic rights in the definition of human rights. They point to the meaninglessness of political rights to those people who cannot achieve at least the basic minimum of health, housing, and employment. So broad a definition of human rights is, however, beyond the traditional use of the term *rights.* More important, perhaps, is that it permits political leaders who imprison their opponents without legal justification, suppress dissent, oppress minorities, and destroy a free press to argue that they are advocates of human rights merely because they provide the benefits of a welfare state. Adolf Hitler and Joseph Stalin could be included as human rights activists in such an interpretation, although each was responsible for the liquidation of millions of people[1] (see Chapters 3, 4, and 5).

It is important to keep in mind that even if political rights are viewed as the only component of civil liberties, the application of those rights varies among free

---

[1] See Maurice Cranston, *What Are Human Rights?* (New York: Taplinger, 1973), pp. 65–68.

societies. The United States, for example, gives wider latitude to the press to publish confidential government information than does Great Britain. The use of evidence illegally obtained by the police is a basis for dismissing cases against defendants in some free societies and not in others. Many of the political rights described below are drawn from the experience of the United States. We can categorize these rights as freedom of expression, freedom to participate in the political process, fair treatment for criminal suspects, and equal treatment under the law.

Freedom of Expression

Freedom of expression includes freedom of speech, freedom of petition, freedom of assembly, freedom of the press, and freedom of religion.

Freedom of speech refers to the right of an individual to speak in support of any idea, however unpopular it may be. It includes the right to denounce one's government, a political party, a cherished religious institution, and widely held beliefs. It could mean a Republican's right to espouse Republican causes in a predominantly Democratic neighborhood, but extends to the advocacy of controversial ideas, such as nazism and communism in the United States. It protects the scientist whose findings reveal genetic differences in intelligence among different racial groups as much as it does the civil rights activist in a racist district.

Rightly or wrongly, legal limits have been placed on freedom of speech even in democracies. **Slander,** which is the telling of untruths about an individual is a limit on freedom of speech. Other limitations are **obscenity** (the reciting or portraying in the media of acts regarded as lewd), and **blasphemy** (statements that describe a religion in sacrilegious ways).

Free speech has also been limited in cases in which it presents a **"clear and present danger"** to the public. As as-

serted by Supreme Court Justice Oliver Wendell Holmes:

The question in every case is whether the words used are used in such circumstances and are of such a nature as to create a clear and present danger that they will bring about the substantive evils that Congress has a right to prevent. It is a question of proximity and degree.[2]

In this connection courts have upheld restrictions of speech deemed contrary to the national interest in times of war.

Freedom of petition is the right to present written statements that criticize or recommend changes to any public official. In many countries such a petition is regarded as **sedition** (an incitement to resist lawful authority) and is punishable by imprisonment or death.

Freedom of assembly includes the right of people to meet in their homes or other meeting places without interference from government. So long as the meeting is conducted peacefully and is not conspiratorial, the freedom to assemble is supposed to be assured. When in South Africa opponents of the government met in the 1980s to discuss changes in that country's racist policies, their meetings were broken up by the police. When Soviet dissidents meet, moreover, they are often subjected to similar harassment by the Soviet government. Such harassment has declined in the Gorbachev era, although it continues to exist. The South Africa and Soviet examples are both violations of freedom of assembly.

Freedom of assembly means that the police must protect all groups who wish to meet for political purposes, provided their methods are peaceful. Courts have held that government may determine the manner in which such meetings are held, such as time and location. Police, how-

---

[2] *Schenck* v. *United States,* 249 U.S. 47 (1919).

ever, cannot legally deny to one group what they allow another merely because they agree with the one and disagree with the other.

The right of groups to meet peacefully, then, is assured in a free society. In this regard distinctions among dissent, resistance, and civil disobedience often complicate the discussion of those concerned with civil liberties and must be clarified.

Dissent means disagreement. A free society must permit individuals to disagree with prevailing sentiments no matter how absurd their statements. The requirement is made, however, that the disagreement will be peaceful; and so long as it is peaceful, government will protect the dissenters.

Resistance refers to taking illegal acts to undermine legal authority. It means that peaceful protests are ruled out, and acts of violence or terrorism are adopted, such as the assassination of a political leader, the blowing up of an abortion clinic, and the kidnapping of opponents. A political system that permits peaceful dissent has an obligation to prevent resistance. Resisters in a democracy assume that their will is superior to that of the majority as reflected in the laws of the land. The majority has a right to protect the fundamental basis of its rule.

Civil disobedience is an intermediate step between dissent and resistance. It is the taking of a token action in defiance of the law for the purpose of changing the law. People who engage in civil disobedience say, in effect: "We realize that the majority is against us. We feel the law or policy is so bad that we must take this step in violating it in the hope that we shall convince the majority of people to change their minds. We are willing to be punished for our offense."

In the United States the civil rights "sit-ins" were regarded by many as acts of civil disobedience. More recently, demonstrations in front of the South African embassy in Washington, D.C., in which people were arrested for blocking traffic, are further examples. At some university campuses, moreover, students have been arrested for illegally building a shanty-town on campus as a protest against their university's investments in companies doing business in South Africa. Whether or not civil disobedience is justified is a matter that will be debated below.

Freedom of the press assures journalists the right to report the news as they deem fit. In free societies members of the press are given special privileges to protect their sources because of the belief that the people have "a right to know." Freedom of the press is strengthened when journalists are not restricted by **prior restraint**—the requirement that articles or books must be submitted for government approval before they may be published.

Governments have placed some regulations on the media, particularly radio and television. In those two media they have imposed standards for broadcasts regarding the way in which religious or sexual matters are treated, for example.

How much freedom reporters have varies from one free society to another. In the United States, for example, the press has published classified government information when it deemed it in the public interest to do so. In Great Britain, in contrast, an Official Secrets Act prevents government documents from being published in an unauthorized manner. Where the line is drawn for freedom of the press differs from place to place. The underlying assumption of freedom of the press is, however, that only when people have all the information can they be expected to make intelligent judgments about what the government is doing.

Freedom of religion includes the right to practice one's religion without interference from others. It is one of the most recent of civil liberties. In the seventeenth century religious tests were often made a requirement for government service in European countries. Gradually, religious toleration has replaced discrimination.

Today, freedom of religion is a fundamental tenet of those who revere liberty. It means that not only do people have a right to believe in a religion but they have a right not to believe in one as well.

Countries differ as to how separate church and state should be. The United States has the greatest separation, with constitutional restrictions limiting government interference. Other countries do not make such sharp distinctions. Although accepting the principle that people should be free to practice their own religious faith, countries have limited certain religious practices that they have regarded as offensive, for example, human sacrifice, polygamy, and preventing children from being vaccinated.

Freedom to Participate in the Political Process

Civil liberties include those freedoms that permit maximum political participation in the political process. Some of these freedoms are contained in the freedom of expression. The right to assemble peacefully, for example, is essential for a citizenry that has a right to select its political leaders.

Of the freedoms to participate in the political process that are not included in freedom of expression, the most notable are the right to vote, the right to fair elections, and the right to form a loyal opposition.

The right to vote must be assured. Restrictions on the basis of race, religion, belief, property, or sex must be eliminated. The history of the suffrage is the history of the enlargement of the electorate, so that today universal suffrage is the goal of a free society.

Elections must be fair. In countries that revere freedom, ballots must be counted honestly. Campaign workers must be permitted to make their appeals for support without harassment from government.

The right to form a loyal opposition must be assured. When out of power, a political party that abides by democratic rules will not be harassed, or its leaders imprisoned, because of their views. It should be regarded as a loyal opposition.

Freedom in Criminal Proceedings

The rights of protection of an individual when charged with a criminal offense are among the oldest of civil liberties. They go back at least to thirteenth-century England, and probably existed for centuries before that time. Today, rights dealing with criminal offenses include the right of habeas corpus, right of trial by impartial jury, right to counsel, right to grand jury indictment, right to be protected from unreasonable searches and seizures, right to confront accusers, due process of law, no self-incrimination, no ex post facto laws, no cruel and unusual punishment, no excessive bail, and no double jeopardy.

Habeas corpus literally means "to hold the body." In legal terms this means that when a public official, such as a policeman or a warden, holds an individual in custody, that official must go before a judge to explain why that individual is being detained. If the judge decides that the imprisonment or detention is authorized by law, the individual in police custody remains in captivity. If not, the judge sets him or her free. According to legal scholar Zechariah Chafee, Jr., this right is the most important in the Constitution because when imprisonment is possible without explanation or redress, every form of liberty is impaired. "A man in jail," he writes, "cannot go to church or discuss or publish or assemble or enjoy property or go to the polls."[3]

---

[3] Zechariah Chafee, Jr., ed., *Documents on Fundamental Human Rights* (New York: Atheneum, 1963), 2:1.

Right to trial by impartial jury assures the defendant of a fair trial. Juries decide the guilt or innocence of individuals on the basis of the facts of the case, and they are supposed to be impartial. In an era of mass communications that sensationalize major crimes, such as the assassination of a popular political figure, it is sometimes difficult to find a jury that has not prejudged the guilt or innocence of a defendant.

Right to counsel assures a defendant that his or her case will be handled by a qualified attorney. While, theoretically, every person accused of a felony is entitled to be represented by an attorney, the quality of legal service available to the poor is obviously much lower than that available to the rich. In the United States, however, indigent defendants are assured the services of attorneys paid out of public funds.

Right to grand jury indictment provides a defendant an opportunity to have the evidence evaluated. A **grand jury** is a body of people who decide whether there is enough evidence for a trial to be justified. Such a body prevents frivolous charges from becoming court cases.

The denial of unreasonable searches and seizures is another bulwark of human freedom. In a free society, an individual is presumed innocent until proven guilty. Police officials are not legally free to go on "fishing expeditions" merely because they do not like an individual. They must secure a **warrant,** which is authorization by a judge to search or seize an individual or his or her property when there is evidence that an individual has committed a criminal offense. If evidence is seized without such authorization, it often may not be used in the criminal proceedings against the defendant. The result may mean that an individual goes free although he or she committed a crime. Those individuals who consider human rights to be paramount contend that although some guilty people may go free

because of "legal technicalities," treme alternative—a **police state** i the police are free to act without r tion—is worse.

The **right to confront one's accus** assures a defendant that he or she kno who the individuals are who are providing damaging testimony. Often, people are more likely to make accusations in secret than in public, and the right to know one's accusers limits hearsay evidence and gossip from being used against a defendant.

Due process of law, though used in different ways, from the point of view of a defendant's rights means that no person may be denied property or freedom without proper legal justification. Such justification includes the statement of the actual provision of the law that the defendant has allegedly violated. The purpose of due process is to prevent arbitrary harassment of an individual by public authorities.

The government does not have the right to force defendants to testify against themselves. In other words, **self-incrimination** is forbidden unless voluntarily accepted by a defendant. The assumption of a just legal system is that an individual is innocent until proven guilty. This means that the burden of proof is on the prosecution, not the defendant. The state must make its case against an individual and respect his or her right to remain silent. Once a defendant's attorney calls his or her client to the stand, however, the state's attorney may cross-examine that person.

Ex post facto laws are regarded as violations of freedom. An **ex post facto law** is one that subjects people to criminal punishment for acts committed at an earlier time when no such law existed. If in 1995, for example, a federal law were enacted that made the consumption of alcohol illegal, an individual could not be tried for having consumed liquor in 1990.

Defendants are protected, too, by the nature of the punishment. The Consti-

"no cruel and un-
~rts have applied
~ ways. In the
~ maiming, for
nt, which is
~n challenged as
~shment. Countries
~out the legitimacy of
~ity. However applied, the
~ no cruel and unusual punish-
~eans that there must be some re-
~nship between the crime and the degree of punishment.

No excessive bail assures defendants of freedom while their cases are being considered. **Bail** is the posting of money that will be forfeited if a person accused of a crime does not appear for trial. How high bail is set depends on the nature of the case and the character of the defendant. An alleged murderer may be denied bail. A bank teller accused of stealing $2,000, however, may be released with a low bail. Indigent defendants sometimes stay in jail for months while their cases are being considered because they are unable to post bail.

Defendants are assured that they will not face **double jeopardy** —the trying of a person a second time in the same jurisdiction for the same crime after having been found not guilty. Even new evidence cannot compel a defendant ruled innocent by a jury to be tried again in the same jurisdiction for that offense.

Equal Protection of the Law

Equal protection of the law is guaranteed by the Fourteenth Amendment to the U.S. Constitution, but its meaning binds the legal systems of many countries. It means that the law cannot discriminate because of class, race, sex, or religion. Equal protection has been used as a basis for extending civil rights to minority groups, and even to majority groups when they have felt that they were being punished by being a member of a specific group. This right was the basis of racial integration rulings in housing, education, and voting in the United States. It was also the basis of rulings against racial quotas in university admissions, which had been established to promote the education of minorities.

HISTORICAL DEVELOPMENT OF RIGHTS

The idea that individuals have rights apart from the state is for the most part a modern concept stemming from the seventeenth century. In ancient Greece, in contrast, individuals were generally perceived to be a natural part of a political system with no private concerns outside of the state.

Although the prevailing political philosophies from ancient times to the seventeenth century had no concept of private rights, there were exceptions. Citizens in some Greek cities enjoyed freedom of speech and equality before the law. The Stoic philosophers of ancient Greece and Rome, moreover, argued that there are universal natural laws that belong to everyone regardless of what man-made law indicates. These laws, according to the Stoics, were superior to man-made law. Human beings were supposed to be subservient to the natural law, with its notion of a "higher law." In medieval times some philosophers perceived natural law as part of God's law. The principle was asserted that man cannot violate these divine laws.

Not all early assertions of individual rights were derived from philosophical speculation. In England, for example, traditional practices guaranteeing some rights go back to before the thirteenth century. In this respect the English common law, which is judge-made law, revealed customary practices respecting rights, such as trial by jury and habeas corpus. The common law had its origins in the twelfth and thirteenth centuries, when royal judges traveled throughout England for the purpose of establishing what were the cases and customs of the local communities. **Common law** is the law that was "common" to the whole kingdom.

The idea of individual rights draws its modern origins from the social contract theorists of the seventeenth and eighteenth centuries, principally John Locke and Jean-Jacques Rousseau. Although there were great differences of interpretation between these theorists, they both referred to the social contract. This pertains to the notion that men had at some early time consented to form a state and had made a compact establishing a relationship between the government and the people (see Chapter 4).

The philosophical aspirations of individual liberty were enshrined in great documents, such as the English Bill of Rights (1689), the Declaration of Independence (1776), the Constitution of the United States (1787) and its Bill of Rights (1791), and the French Declaration of the Rights of Man and of the Citizen (1789). The rights in these documents were political rights and were adopted in constitutions in the nineteenth and twentieth centuries. In the twentieth century, particularly, rights have received a great prominence and have come to include even economic rights. The Universal Declaration of Human Rights, adopted by the United Nations in 1948 without a single dissent, established a universal acceptance of these rights—at least in principle. Even governments that violate human rights in practice pay lip service to human rights either by denying that they are in fact violating rights or by focusing on economic rather than political rights. In principle more than practice, then, the protection of human rights constitutes a norm of international behavior.[4]

JUSTIFICATION OF RIGHTS

The protection of human rights is based both on philosophical principles of natural law and on the practical benefits that accrue to a society revering human rights.

Natural Law

Philosophers justified human rights as being rooted in **natural law.** In the first century A.D., Cicero, the great Stoic philosopher, was one of the first to contend that universal laws are superior to man-made laws, which must be subservient to them. Later philosophers, like Thomas Aquinas and John Locke, asserted the superiority of higher over man-made, or **positive law.**

Critics of natural rights argue that there is no such thing as "natural rights." They attack the idea that human rights must be defended in terms of a belief in absolute or inalienable rights that exist prior to the establishment of a community. They contend that there is no way to determine objectively what such absolute rights are and that the evaluation of rights must be made in terms of the consequences for society.[5]

Benefits to Society

According to some human rights' advocates, human rights are desirable because they protect individual liberty and because they allow a society to make decisions in a peaceful and rational manner. Many liberals justify their belief in human rights on the basis of their reverence for the dignity of the individual. Each individual, in their view, should be free to participate in political and social life as he or she deems fit. A society is just to the extent that it promotes human rights.

Advocates of human rights point also

---

[4] For a discussion of human rights as a goal of foreign policy, see Issue 10.

[5] See Sidney Hook, *Heresy, Yes—Conspiracy, No* (New York: John Day, 1953), p. 19.

to the many other benefits involving peace and reason that accrue to a polity granting human rights. First, the society protects itself from becoming a police state in which the government cannot be challenged. Without civil rights and civil liberties, the state is free to suppress any opposition to its will, and human freedom is, consequently, destroyed.

Second, a system that reveres human rights allows for a rational mechanism to change laws peacefully. Without rights, the most powerful groups within and outside of government can prevent change through use of force and other means of coercion. Totalitarian dictatorship would be the most extreme result of such a society (see Chapter 3).

Third, a system that assures rights to all who accept the legitimacy of the system provides a vehicle for popular support of government. For government to maintain its legitimacy, it must adapt to changing economic and social conditions. If it suppresses groups demanding changes, a dissident element may be forced to operate outside of the system since its only means of protest is violence.

Fourth and perhaps most important, a system that reveres liberty allows the opportunity for intelligent decision making. The great English liberal John Stuart Mill argued in this connection in *On Liberty* (1859) that a society benefits when people are free to discuss issues openly. The truth,

Mill claimed, is difficult to determine, and only in open discussion and debate can it be known. Oliver Wendell Holmes made a similar observation when he observed, "The test of truth is the power of thought to get itself accepted in the competition of the market."[6]

Critics of this justification of human rights have made many rejoinders. Marxists and communists have argued that political rights are fictional in a capitalist society because there can be no freedom without economic rights. Fascists have denounced rights either because they regard the state as superior to the individual or because they contend that certain racial groups (which they regard as inferior) should not be allowed to participate in the political process. Conservatives, while accepting constitutional principles granting rights, have emphasized the duties imposed on an individual who benefits from rights.

In spite of the criticisms leveled at human rights, today constitutions throughout the world openly proclaim a commitment to them. That rights are, in fact, violated in varying degrees from country to country is a reflection of the scarcity of freedom in the world and not the denial of the norm that is almost universal.

---

[6] *Abrams* v. *United States*, 250 U.S. 616 at 630 (1919).

ISSUES

Even when human rights are accepted as a legitimate objective of society, they are not "self-evident" as the Declaration of Independence asserts. A right sometimes conflicts with another right, for example. Does freedom of the press include the right to tape jury deliberations, or are the rights of defendants in criminal proceedings violated by such an act?

Often, however, the problem of rights is made complex near the point the limits of rights are reached. Justification of civil disobedience is one case of such complexity. A discussion of points raised in debating the justification of civil disobedience shows how difficult it is to set the legitimate limits of rights.

Even when there is agreement that the people who break the law in a democratic society should be punished, there is strong disagreement about how much punishment should be meted out to law breakers. One form of punishment inflicted in many societies is capital punishment. Many states have banned the death penalty for any offense. In some countries, such as South Africa, the Soviet Union, the People's Republic of China, and the United States, the death penalty is legal—although the crime for which a death penalty may result varies from country to country. In the Soviet Union and the People's Republic of China, economic crimes involving the theft of government property can bring a death penalty. In Iran, political crimes can bring a similar punishment. In the United States, however, the death penalty is today reserved for those convicted of the most heinous murders.

16/YES IS CIVIL DISOBEDIENCE JUSTIFIED IN A REPRESENTATIVE DEMOCRACY?

Although laws must be obeyed in a democracy, common sense dictates that there are exceptions to this rule. An individual in a democracy has the option to dissent from the majoritarian point of view. No one who reveres democracy would challenge that point. The individual, however, has no right of resistance, because such behavior challenges the legitimacy of the system. If, however, an individual cannot in conscience accept the decisions of the majority because he or she regards them as unjust, that person may choose to engage in acts of civil disobedience. Democracies must allow for acts of civil disobedience.

Civil disobedience has been defined as the taking of a token action in defiance of the law for the purpose of changing the law. Civil disobedients take the act knowingly, lovingly, and above all peacefully. They are willing to accept punishment, such as fine or imprisonment, because they feel the issue of their concern is of such enormous significance that they are willing to sacrifice their freedom.

Democracies must permit civil disobedience because: (1) human laws are not valid when they violate higher laws of conscience; (2) civil disobedience reveres law; and (3) democracy is ultimately strengthened by accepting the principle of civil disobedience.

Higher Law. The phrase **higher law** refers to a universal law that transcends human law. For some, it has a religious connotation. Thomas Aquinas reflected this religious motivation when he commented, "And if a human law is at variance in any particular with the natural law, it is no longer legal, but rather a corruption of law."[7] Others identify the higher law with natural law, as expounded by John Locke and his philosophical descendants. Still others think of higher law in terms of abstract justice. No matter the source of the concept, what is important is that human law is subject to error or injustice, and there ought to be some legitimate means for an individual to show opposition to that law when it is in conflict with moral principles.

The record shows many instances in which acts of civil disobedience have been justified. Some of the major cases have involved slavery, civil rights, national independence, and war.

When the Fugitive Slave Act of 1850 was passed in the United States, a major issue of conscience faced the opponents of slavery. The law stipulated that fugitive slaves be returned to their owners, even from the free states in the North. Some abolitionists refused to abide by the law. Some even went so far as to promote resistance by organizing an "underground railroad" for the purpose of transporting slaves to Canada. People of conscience could not obey a law duly enacted by an elected legislative body and declared constitutional by its judicial authority.

In the twentieth century, too, civil rights matters affecting black people and women have justified acts of civil disobedience. State and

---

[7] Thomas Aquinas, *Summa Theologica*, Question 95, Article 2, in *Aquinas: Selected Political Writings*, ed. A. P. Entreves, trans. J. G. Dawson (Oxford, England: Basil Blackwell, 1965), p. 129.

local ordinances in the South provided for segregation in public accommodations, such as hotels, transportation facilities, and restaurants. Sparked by leaders like Martin Luther King, Jr., many black people broke the segregation laws by sit-ins at lunch counters, in which they occupied seats in racially restricted facilities and demanded service. White supporters joined southern blacks in "freedom rides" in efforts to integrate buses. King's policy of **direct action** (the taking of nonviolent measures, such as boycotts and sit-ins) was based on the moral necessity of violating unjust laws. Always he acted nonviolently. In Birmingham, Alabama, he willingly went to jail for his act of civil disobedience. King's actions were justified because racial segregation by law is morally reprehensible. Anyone devoted to human freedom in the United States had to oppose the acts of segregation, which treated black Americans as second-class citizens, and support those people—like King and his followers—who experienced imprisonment to end an immoral practice.

Women, too, have been victimized by laws that denied them the right to vote and equal opportunity to participate in the economy. In the United States, for example, the suffragists engaged in acts of civil disobedience, such as chaining themselves to buildings and tying up traffic. How else could they participate in the political process since they were unable to vote in national elections? Ultimately in 1920, the Nineteenth Amendment granted women the suffrage.

Although slavery and civil rights have produced some major examples of civil disobedience, so, too, have independence and peace movements. Mohandas K. Gandhi, the Indian leader, was one of this century's great proponents of civil disobedience. His policy was one of **satyagraha** (literally "firmness in the truth"), which many people (although not Gandhi) equated with passive resistance. He urged his partisans to take peaceful acts, such as marches and boycotts, to win rights for Indians in South Africa and to achieve the independence of India from British colonial rule. Gandhi became famous for his hunger strikes and for other acts of nonviolence. One of his tactics was to have his followers lie down on railroad tracks, thus preventing trains from moving. By taking such peaceful acts of civil disobedience,

Gandhi contributed to the movement—both in India and in Great Britain—for the independence of his country.

Because of his close association with nonviolence, Gandhi became a hero to peace movements around the world. Even before Gandhi, civil disobedience was asserted as an antiwar device. Henry David Thoreau went to prison for his opposition to the war against Mexico in 1848 and for his refusal to pay taxes. In 1849, he wrote the classic work on the subject, *Resistance to Civil Government,* which was republished after his death as *Civil Disobedience* (1866).[8] Thoreau went beyond mere civil disobedience, however, since he was opposed to all government, but he was most associated with civil disobedience in his opposition to war.

More recently, antiwar opponents resorted to acts of civil disobedience during the Vietnam War. Arguing that the United States was engaged in an immoral war, antiwar protesters went beyond dissent and took acts of civil disobedience. Quite rightly, many of them condemned the resisters who entered army draft board offices and ransacked the files or used explosives against government buildings. The truly civilly disobedient did not participate in acts of violence but refused to serve in the armed forces, or withheld part of their income taxes that they believed was devoted to the prosecution of the war, or tied up traffic for the purpose of protesting the war. In their view South Vietnam, an American ally, was a dictatorship, and the only recourse available to them was to act in a civilly disobedient manner.

Reverence for Law. Those who act in a civilly disobedient manner revere legal processes. What they say is that they find a particular act of government to be so horrendous that they regretfully violate the law. It is not easy to take such an action. To burn a

---

[8] According to historian Lewis Perry, "Thoreau actually never spoke of *civil disobedience,* nor did anyone else use the term in print during his lifetime, so far as scholars can discover." Lewis Perry, "Civil Disobedience," in *Encyclopedia of American Political History: Studies of the Principal Movements and Ideas,* ed. Jack P. Greene (New York: Charles Scribner's Sons, 1984), 1:211.

draft card, tie up traffic, chain oneself to a building, and refuse to pay taxes are acts regarded by many citizens as outrageous. To put oneself in a position as an outcast of the community requires a great deal of courage.

Some civil disobedients display a considerable amount of hypocrisy by their actions. They break the law as befits their conscience; but when an outraged mob attacks them, they clamor for protection as required by law.

Civil disobedients accept that criticism as much as they revere the law. What they hope, however, is that the majority will change its mind and come around to a different position. By their actions, they seek to bring public attention to their causes and enlist the majority to change the law. By suffering the loss of freedom and damage to reputation, they hope, eventually, that the law will reflect their judgment. The facts that for the United States racial segregation by law has been eliminated, women have the right to vote, and American participation in the war in Vietnam has ended are a tribute to the acts of civil disobedience that were unpopular at the time they were undertaken. Reverence for law has not been undermined because of acts of civil disobedience.

Democracy. Democracy is strengthened by a tolerance of civil disobedience. For a system to be democratic, it must have broad support among diverse elements of society. The processes of a representative democracy work slowly, and often groups become disenchanted with the slow responsiveness of government. Groups subjected to discrimination or injustice cannot be expected to rely exclusively on constitutional processes that take years to institute remedies.

Faced with moral dilemmas deeply felt by a group, its leaders must have recourse to dissent or disobedience. In the 1960s, for example, black people felt that the processes of change, particularly social and economic change, were moving too slowly to produce tangible benefits. Most of them rejected extremist solutions as not suitable for democracy. Many saw in civil disobedience a remedy that would allow them to accept the legitimacy of the system. In some cases, they peacefully occupied schools to demonstrate that faculty in minority neighborhood schools should be more racially representative of the community. Like the civil rights activists, antiwar protesters acted nonviolently. They felt that the pace of bringing about peace was proceeding too slowly. Every day saw more people, Americans and Asians, maimed or dying in jungle warfare. By committing acts of civil disobedience, activists remained committed to the democratic ideal. Although not sanctified by law, the civil rights and peace activists strengthened democratic institutions because they channeled their energies in directions that a broader segment of the community would ultimately accept—racial justice and peace.

16/NO   IS CIVIL DISOBEDIENCE JUSTIFIED IN A REPRESENTATIVE DEMOCRACY?

"Saints should always be judged guilty until proven innocent," the English political critic George Orwell once wrote in commenting about the saintly Mohandas Gandhi.[9] Orwell's warning should be applied to the many self-appointed saints in the civil disobedience community. Civil disobedience cannot be justified in a representative democracy because: (1) there are no higher laws than the laws that are constitutionally enacted; (2) laws must be respected; and (3) democracy is weakened to the extent that civil disobedient acts are committed.

Higher Law. In a representative democracy there are means whereby laws that the majority come to feel are wrong can be changed. The repeal of the Prohibition Amendment in 1933 is a notable example. So long as such means exist, there is no justification for ap-

---

[9] George Orwell, "Reflections on Gandhi," in *The Collected Essays, Journalism and Letters of George Orwell,* ed. Sonia Orwell and Ian Angus (Harmondsworth, England: Penguin, 1968), 4:523. The essay was originally published in January 1949.

pealing to a "higher law" and disobeying the laws that are duly enacted.

People who justify their actions in terms of the higher law, appeal invariably to conscience as a guide to behavior. It is certainly true that conscience should guide the behavior of states and people. Respect for religious beliefs and philosophical commitments to justice or rights should be encouraged. The problem, however, is that there is no universal agreement about what constitutes principles of justice, rights, and natural law. The very idea that there are such universal principles of natural rights that reason can determine has been properly labeled "nonsense upon stilts" by Jeremy Bentham, an English writer of the late eighteenth and early nineteenth centuries.

Higher law is the justification for illegality by a variety of political partisans. We may well approve of the good intentions of the people who have spoken for the abolition of slavery, the expansion of civil rights, the establishment of national independence, and the promotion of peace; but we should understand that the methods used to attain those desirable goals are all important to liberty and order. It is not enough that the intentions of social critics are noble. We should remember the old saying that the path to hell is paved with good intentions.

Many *opponents* of these lofty principles have also asserted the principle of higher law. Segregationists, who resisted the desegregation rulings of the United States Supreme Court and the civil rights laws of Congress, also violated these laws with appeals to higher law. Even many young Nazis committed illegal acts in the 1920s, contending that the duly elected democratic government in Germany was corrupt and that they would not abide by the policies of such an immoral government. In more recent times some of the people involved in the Watergate affair during the administration of Richard Nixon took illegal acts, such as breaking into offices, wiretapping, and burglarizing, because they felt that they were acting out of conscience against imagined enemies of the United States. If a legitimate democratic government permits individuals to determine for themselves what constitutes the higher law, there can never be a peaceful way to resolve differences of opinion.

The *Affirmative* cites cases of antislavery, civil rights for blacks and women, national independence, and peace as legitimate examples for justifying civil disobedience. We argue that in the first three matters, many of these acts cannot properly be included in their examples of civil disobedience.

A system of slavery is one that excludes a group of people from participating in the political process. In the South, black people were not permitted to vote. Indeed, they were considered to be not human beings, but rather property, which white slaveholders could buy and sell at will. Blacks, moreover, were not permitted the right to engage in open political activity lest they be punished with imprisonment, beatings, and even death. It is wrong to use the civil disobedience application to such a case since civil disobedience is a concept that is by definition a process of a polity allowing legitimate means of political protest; and slaves had no political standing.

A similar case can be made for the sit-ins. Even after slavery was abolished, blacks were prevented from offering candidates in elections and from voting. If blacks had had the power to vote, the segregation laws would not have been on the books, as the later record of legislation attests. We argue that the sit-ins and freedom rides were justified because unless all people—except the young, criminals, and the insane—are assured the right to vote, they are permitted to take extraordinary, though nonviolent, measures. We would include the suffragists in this category.

Another point can be made in connection with the sit-ins and freedom rides. Often many of the people who engaged in these practices believed that the local and state statutes requiring segregation were in violation of First Amendment rights in the Constitution. They were *testing* the constitutionality of segregation by creating incidents requiring judicial deliberation. Testing a law is not an act of civil disobedience in the United States, since in the American judicial system a real case, rather than an advisory opinion, is essential before a court makes a judgment.

Acts of colonial peoples to achieve national independence, moreover, cannot be properly classified as civil disobedience. Gandhi as an Indian leader sought to end British authority over his homeland rather than force the British government to merely change a law.[10]

A clearer case in evaluating civil disobedience can be made for war resisters. Many countries, among them the United States, allow for a right of **conscientious objection** in which an individual may legally refuse to serve in the armed forces because of religious or deeply held philosophical beliefs against all wars. Conscientious objection is not the same as civil disobedience, however. In the Vietnam War, some partisans of civil disobedience did not have the religious or philosophical views against wars generally, but rather objected specifically to the war in Vietnam. These people often committed acts that we would classify as civilly disobedient.

We argue that their actions were both illegal and immoral. They had no right to substitute their judgment for that of the majority, as reflected in the laws. We contend that the historical record supports the assertion by some proponents of United States foreign policy that if South Vietnam went communist, a worse dictatorship would result. The fact that a totalitarian regime in Vietnam has been established under communist rule, complete with the taking of political prisoners, the suppression of religion, and the monolithic control over the media, education, and the economy lends weight in retrospect to the soundness of their views. Even if this contention is not supported, however, the case of the wisdom or justice of American involvement in the Vietnam War was not so clear-cut as to justify acts of civil disobedience.

Reverence for Law. Those who act in a civilly disobedient manner have no respect for law. It is impossible to have a law that authorizes individuals to violate it. Respect for law is essential for any system to function. An effective system of law is possible only when appeals cannot be made to principles outside the legal system.

Civil disobedients determine for themselves what laws to obey and what laws to violate. Without law, there will only be chaos as each individual and group decides unilaterally what is right. "Like law itself," legal scholar Alexander M. Bickel notes, "civil disobedience is habit-forming, and the habit it forms is destructive of the legal order."[11] The victims in such a lawless society will probably be many of the very same people who argue so adamantly for the right of civil disobedience, namely, the advocates of civil rights, social justice, and peace. If one group can decide for itself which laws to obey, so, too, will other groups. A system of law protects all groups in society. Without it, discussion ceases and violence begins.

Democracy. Civil disobedience in a democracy undermines the basis of the democratic order. A democracy by definition allows for many forms of protest activity to win the support of the majority. People are free to picket, publish articles and books supportive of their views, and petition their elected representatives. What civil disobedients do by their acts is to substitute their voice for the majority, and there is no justification for that kind of behavior in a democracy. So long as a democratic system allows for peaceful channels to register protest, civil disobedience cannot be justified.

Totalitarian systems have no ethical constraints in coping with civil disobedients. As George Orwell observes, a Gandhi could engage in passive resistance because the British treated him forbearingly, and his appeals for justice could always command public attention. "It is difficult to see," Orwell writes, "how Gandhi's methods could be applied in a country where opponents of the régime disappear in the middle of the night and are never heard of again."[12] Orwell's point deals with an individual seeking to undermine foreign authority in his country, but it is also insightful in the context of civil disobedience. Democracies are vulnerable to civil disobedients because of their tolerance for heretics and dissenters. Too many acts of civil disobedience, however, and the basis of a democratic order is undermined.

If one group is entitled to substitute its will for that of the majority, then why not others? Before much time has passed, the basic underpinnings of a democracy are eroded, and

[10] See Carl Cohen, *Civil Disobedience: Conscience, Tactics, and the Law* (New York: Columbia University Press, 1971), pp. 46–47.

[11] Alexander M. Bickel, *The Morality of Consent* (New Haven: Yale University Press, 1975), p. 119.

[12] Orwell, "Reflections on Gandhi," p. 529.

the system can collapse by too many appeals of civil disobedience. If democracy is to be maintained, then all who disagree with the prevailing laws or policies must use the legit-imate means of redress, lest they discover that they lose both the specific goal they seek and their fundamental freedoms.

17/YES SHOULD CAPITAL PUNISHMENT BE ABOLISHED?

The uncivilized practice of capital punishment should be outlawed. Capital punishment is bad because: (1) it does not serve as a deterrent to killings; (2) it signifies a disrespect for life; (3) it makes a mockery of the law; (4) it is cruel and unusual punishment; and (5) it cannot bring back to life innocent people who were unjustly put to death.

Deterrence. Supporters of capital punishment have been moved to frenzy by gruesome stories of murders and other violent acts. They have incorrectly concluded that the safety of their families, their friends, and themselves would be more assured if the death penalty were imposed on the most violent criminals.

Although popular revulsion at murders is understandable, there is no conclusive evidence to indicate that capital punishment serves as a deterrent to murder. In the United States, for example, some states have permitted capital punishment and others have not. An examination of the homicide rate in different states does not reveal that capital punishment is linked to a lower homicide rate. States that have reinstituted the death penalty have not experienced a decline in the murder rate. Many of the social science studies dealing with the subject suggest that the death penalty does not lower a homicide rate. At best, the evidence is inconclusive.

It is important to keep in mind that many kinds of homicides will clearly not be prevented when capital punishment is legal. Crimes of passion are a case in point. People who have severe psychological problems caused by brutalizing formative experiences, moreover, will not be deterred from murdering because they may be incapable of making rational decisions to thwart their violent impulses. The kind of person like Stephen T. Judy, who murdered a woman and then drowned her three children, is obviously a deranged human being. Anyone who would commit a crime like that has to be deranged. A death penalty on the law books would not serve as a deterrent to the Stephen T. Judys of the world.

If, as the advocates of capital punishment contend, capital punishment serves as a deterrent, then they should favor maximizing publicity generated by capital punishment through such spectacles as public hangings in city parks or electric-chair executions live and in color on national television. In that way, most people would be made more aware of what the consequences are to murder. In fact, death penalty advocates do not call for such a display of perverse taste.

Although proponents of the death penalty say that capital punishment saves lives, there is some evidence to indicate that capital punishment may cause homicides. In this regard psychologists have noted that there are some people who wish to take their own lives but are afraid to commit suicide. By causing murders, these people will feel assured that someone else—government—will execute them by punishing them with the death penalty.[13] However rare such people are in society, they constitute a refutation of the view asserted by the supporters of capital punishment about the life-saving feature of capital punishment.

To be sure, the imposition of the ultimate sanction on a murderer ensures that *that* murderer will take no more lives. Few released murderers kill again in any event. One major study of eight American states, including California, New York, Ohio, and Connecticut, found that only half of 1 percent of murderers paroled

---

[13] Statement of Hugo Adam Bedau, professor of philosophy at Tufts University, in U.S. Congress, Senate, Committee on the Judiciary, *Capital Punishment,* Hearings, 97th Congress, 1st Sess., 1981, p. 521.

or serving time were ever guilty of another homicide.[14]

Disrespect for Life. The act of taking a life through the imposition of the death penalty makes the point to society that life is of no value. Some years ago opponents of the death penalty in Canada put it aptly when they said, "Why do we kill people who kill people in order to teach that killing people is wrong?"[15]

There are sanctions other than the death penalty that should be imposed against violent criminals. Society should send a message to criminals and would-be criminals that they will be punished. As important as sending a message to the violator of the law, however, is a message that society sends itself. That message should be: Life is important, and we should not take another life when one already has been taken.

Disrespect for the Law. Supporters of the death penalty cite the need for the ultimate sanction in order to uphold law and order. In the way that the death penalty is actually implemented, however, an irreverence and disrespect for the law are revealed. The imposition of capital punishment is arbitrary and capricious, and is often the result of racial or economic discrimination.

In most countries that have the death penalty, but in the United States in particular, being put to death for a specific offense is not universally mandated by the law. Some states in the American federal system have the death penalty for a particular offense, and other states do not. Some juries and judges are more severe than others, moreover. A legal system in a free society purports to be unbiased and impartial. Yet the application of the death penalty to one person instead of another is often an arbitrary decision.

Capital punishment is also disrespectful of law because the principal losers in the system are the poor and members of minority groups. Rarely is someone in the middle or upper classes executed for a capital offense. Often these people can obtain excellent lawyers who can plea bargain their cases. In **plea bargaining,** a defendant admits guilt to a lesser charge than the prosecuting attorney prepares to bring so as to avoid a more severe punishment.

In the United States, moreover, minority group members are disproportionately represented on Death Row. Writer Mary Meehan notes that of the 1,058 prisoners on death row on August 20, 1982, 42 percent were black, although black people constitute about 12 percent of the American population.[16] The evidence indicates that a black offender who kills a white person is more likely to get the death penalty than a black person who kills a black person or a white person who kills a black person.[17] There is much wrong with a system that is so arbitrary and capricious as to victimize one important segment of the population merely because of race or economic condition.

Cruel and Unusual Punishment. Inflicting the punishment of death upon law breakers is a practice with roots in ancient times. In the past some methods of death have been particularly depraved, such as boiling people alive, dismembering them bit by bit, drawing and quartering, and impaling.

The standards of universal decency have changed. Many civilized people now believe it is not humane to kill anyone—even under the sanction of law—by hanging, the guillotine, electric chair, gas, or even lethal injection. Amnesty International has justly called for the abolition of the death penalty. Nearly every Western democratic nation has banned this practice except the United States.

Standards of punishment are not immutable. In earlier centuries the death penalty was inflicted for all kinds of offenses, and particularly for any form of murder. About two centuries ago, distinctions were drawn between first- and second-degree murder on the basis of the callousness of the act. Subsequent ef-

[14] Judith Murciano, "Death Penalty—No!" *New York Times* (New York edition), August 14, 1982, p. 23.

[15] Quoted by Henry Schwarzchild in U.S. Congress, House, Committee on the Judiciary, Subcommittee on Criminal Justice, *Federal Criminal Law Revision,* Hearings, 97th Congress, 1st and 2d Sess., 1981 and 1982, pt. 2, p. 1181.

[16] Mary Meehan, "The Death Penalty in the United States: Ten Reasons to Oppose It," *America,* 147 (November 20, 1982): p. 311.

[17] Bedau, statement in *Capital Punishment,* p. 203.

forts have been made to further delineate different degrees of punishment for different kinds of crimes. Among these include distinctions between intentional and unintentional murders, and planned and unpremeditated killings. The psychological condition of the person who commits a harsh crime has been a mitigating factor in sentencing, moreover.

It would seem, then, that capital punishment should be abolished in those nations that revere civil liberties and civil rights. To say that capital punishment should be abolished does not mean to say that criminals who commit vicious crimes should go unpunished. A life sentence in a penal institution is a horrible sentence for anyone to experience. It is sometimes said that being in some prisons is worse than a sentence of death because of the prisoner's loss of freedom and, in some cases, lack of personal safety.

A purpose of punishment is to inflict suffering and deprivation of liberty on law breakers. Prisons safeguard the community from law breakers, and they provide sufficient retribution to those who commit horrible crimes on other members of the community.

Legal Mistakes. The possibility of making mistakes about a person accused of committing a horrible crime is another argument for abolishing the death sentence. Who can say if some of the more than one thousand condemned people on Death Row in the United States are in fact innocent? No system of criminal justice is perfect. In the past innocent people have been unjustly sent to prison for crimes that they did not commit. When people are in prison, they can still be set free if evidence emerges of their innocence. Once they are put to death, however, the truth will not benefit them at all.

The death penalty is barbaric, then. It does not deter criminals from committing violent crimes, and it does not strengthen respect for life and law. It allows for no corrections of mistakes in the criminal justice system, and it should, consequently, be abolished.

17/NO SHOULD CAPITAL PUNISHMENT BE ABOLISHED?

Let those who want to abolish capital punishment hear the horror stories of people whose loved ones have been murdered, maimed, or crippled and perhaps even their sensitivity will be touched for the victim rather than the perpetrator of uncivilized behavior. Only then will they be likely to see the merits of capital punishment.

Capital punishment is a necessary form of punishment in a civilized society because: (1) it serves as a deterrent to killings; (2) it signifies a respect for life; (3) it affirms the principle of the rule of law; (4) it is a fitting punishment for certain kinds of crimes; and (5) it is for the most part likely to hurt the guilty rather than the innocent.

Deterrence. It is difficult to prove that capital punishment prevents people from killing. Clearly, some murderers will not be deterred by capital punishment. Some of these would include people who commit crimes of passion or insane acts. The law recognizes distinctions in the different kinds of murders that are committed, although, to be sure, the victims are dead no matter what the mental state of assailant. Many murders are committed, however, because the killers feel that they can get away with their crimes.

In the United States, for example, only three out of one hundred felonies ever lead to imprisonment. In New York, as conservative writer Ernest van den Haag points out, "Such offenses as car theft, minor muggings, and minor burglaries have been *de facto* decriminalized."[18] This is to say that people are hardly ever punished for committing those offenses. In many respects crime pays when there is no effective punishment.

Although the evidence is sketchy, it is reasonable to assume that there is a relationship between the kind of punishment meted out

---

[18] Ernest van den Haag, "Thinking about Crime Again," *Commentary* 76 (December 1983): 74.

and an offense. With the stringent enforcement of laws against drunken drivers, people are probably less likely to drive under the influence of alcohol. In the People's Republic of China, where there has been a publicized swift implementation of capital punishment against violent criminals, people who live in previously crime-ridden neighborhoods note how safe it is to walk through their neighborhoods—even at night.

Some social scientists have provided evidence that capital punishment serves as a deterrent, although there is much controversy on this point. Isaac Erlich, an econometrician at the University of Chicago, argues that capital punishment prevents more murders than do prison sentences. Admittedly, it is impossible to speak scientifically on the subject since, as political scientist James Q. Wilson notes: "To study behavior that does not occur is all but impossible."[19]

Many criminals act in a rational manner. They are not likely to commit crimes in locations where the police are out in high numbers. They make cost-benefit analyses based on an evaluation of risk to gains. If they feel that they can get away with murder, they will murder. A system that provides prompt and effective implementation of the death penalty would, consequently, be calculated into their cost-benefit assessments. If crime pays, there is no practical deterrent to people lacking moral values. If crime is punished, the immoral people will more likely be deterred.

In the United States, there has been an increase in the number of murders at the same time that there has been a decrease in the number of people legally executed for committing capital offenses. In 1950, 82 convicted felons were executed, many of whom were convicted for homicide. During the same year, 7,020 homicides were reported. In 1960, the number of legal executions dropped to 56, and the number of criminal homicides rose to 9,140. In the 1960s, there was a steady increase in the number of homicides, with 14,590 reported in 1969. In 1980, there were 22,958

criminal homicides and only a few executions.[20]

Reverence for Life. Critics of capital punishment berate proponents of this form of punishment because it shows a disrespect for life. That is not the case. Capital punishment signifies a reverence for life.

In Western societies more people are killed than are punished in violent crimes. In the United States a real bloodbath takes place every year, with more than 20,000 homicides. The media report the daily toll: A six-year-old child abducted, tortured, and dismembered; a housewife raped and brutalized; an elderly retiree robbed and hammered to death; a skid-row derelict beaten to death. So common has murder become in the United States that reports of multiple killings are no longer considered to be important news items and wind up in the middle of a newspaper or at the end of a newscast—just more incidents in the life of a big city.

Writer Karl Spence aptly notes, "If a foreign power did to American citizens just one-tenth of what our own criminals do to us every year, we would surely be at war."[21] Let us then fight fire with fire and show our respect for life by punishing the perpetrator of violent crime in a manner befitting the crime.

Opponents of the death penalty like to point to the horrors of the death penalty—how the criminal suffered during the execution by electric chair or through lethal injection. What they ignore, however, are the lurid descriptions of the innocent victims of the assailants who commit murders and rapes. Even from their graves, the victims cry out for justice.

Respect for the Law. Capital punishment demonstrates a reverence for law. In free societies law constitutes what a society regards as permissible or impermissible. A purpose of law is to permit people to abide by rules peacefully without resorting to violent means. In this sense law is essential in a civilized society.

[19] James Q. Wilson, "Thinking about Crime," *Atlantic Monthly* 252 (September 1983): 76.

[20] These figures are drawn from a statement by Norman Darwick, executive director of the International Association of Chiefs of Police, in *Capital Punishment*, pp. 116–17.

[21] Karl Spence, "Crime and Punishment," *National Review* 35 (September 16, 1983): 1144.

Most basic to a system of law is that human life is to be protected. Legal systems that do not at the minimum guarantee that principle will lose a sense of authority and legitimacy, which is essential to the stability of any political community.

Punishment should reflect the outrage of a community when illegal acts are committed beyond the pale of civilized behavior. The Nuremberg trials that were held after World War II to bring Nazi leaders to justice for their violations of international law were an apt demonstration of the outrage of the world community over Nazi acts. So, too, does capital punishment reflect the outrage of communities for extremely vicious crimes. Preserving the life of vicious criminals is too great a price to pay when the sanctity of the law is in jeopardy.

Nor is it relevant that members of minorities are disproportionately represented on Death Row. Statistics may be misleading in matters of the death penalty. Former Supreme Court Justice Lewis Powell has pointed out that, according to one study, only 4 percent of black homicide defendants got the death penalty, as opposed to 7 percent of white defendants. Conservative writer William F. Buckley, Jr., comments from Powell's observation, "So, a case can be made that capital punishment discriminates against whites."[22]

Moreover, whatever disparity exists along racial lines in this matter is irrelevant to the debate at issue. As psychologist David Lester notes:

This is not an argument against the death penalty. It is an argument against discrimination. For example, discrimination in public transport or housing or restaurants did not lead to the elimination of buses, houses, or restaurants. It lead to efforts to eliminate the discrimination.[23]

Fitting Punishment. Capital punishment is an appropriate punishment for the people who commit crimes that are so gruesome as to warrant the most supreme penalty that society can inflict. It is not true that the death penalty is "cruel and unusual" punishment.

The death penalty is an ancient form of punishment. The men who forbid "cruel and unusual punishments" in the Eighth Amendment of the Constitution did not mean to exclude capital punishment. What they had in mind was that certain methods of inflicting the death penalty, such as burning, drawing and quartering, and impaling, be eliminated. Criminals were put to death before and after the Bill of Rights was adopted, and it is clear that the Framers supported the principle of the death penalty. It is true that the Supreme Court in *Furman* v. *Georgia* outlawed the death penalty under certain conditions in 1972, but that was only because of the wording of the death penalty statutes in certain states. In *Gregg* v. *Georgia* the Court in 1976 upheld the principle of the death penalty for certain kinds of punishment.

To be sure, because we support the death penalty does not mean that it should be applied in all cases. We do not justify the death penalty for economic crimes, as is the practice of many communist countries. Nor do we justify the death penalty for offenses that are accidental, unpremeditated, or committed as a result of mental disorders. But the death penalty should be applied for certain criminal offenses so horrible as to require that supreme penalty.

When society puts a killer to death, it is paying him or her back in kind for the atrocity that that individual has committed. It is retribution pure and simple. Retribution must be paid in kind for the offense committed. By not instituting this kind of penalty, the people who abide by the law are being punished. That betrayal of people who obey the law is a travesty to any just legal system.

Legal Mistakes. To eliminate capital punishment because of the possibility of mistakes is not a justification for doing away with the death penalty. If a mistake is the criterion, then we ought to wipe all penalties off the books because of the possibility of mistakes.

It is, of course, true that there always exists the possibility of mistakes. In Western democratic systems, however, that danger is remote. Cases involving capital punishment are subject to review at different levels of the courts. In the United States the trying of the case and the cumbersome appeals process result in a delay of several years before all legal methods are exhausted.

It should also be recognized that there is

---

[22] William F. Buckley, Jr., "The Bench and the Chair," *National Review* 39 (May 22, 1987): 15.

[23] David Lester, *The Death Penalty: Issues and Answers* (Springfield, Ill.: Charles C. Thomas, 1987), p. 61.

much more professionalism in law enforcement than used to be the case. Police departments often demand that their police officials have academic credentials that are relevant to the work they are doing. Law enforcement agencies, consequently, are more likely than ever before to be composed of expert criminologists, medical technicians, and intelligent police officers, so that the risk of punishing the innocent person by mistake is not likely.

Capital punishment, then, should not be abolished. It helps deter certain kinds of crime; it saves lives; it upholds the law; it is the appropriate punishment for certain kinds of offenses; and it is more likely to be applied carefully than ever before.

KEY TERMS

Bail
Blasphemy
Capital punishment
Civil disobedience
Civil liberties
Civil rights
"Clear and present danger"
Common law
Conscientious objection
Direct action
Dissent
Double jeopardy
Due process of law
Economic rights
Equal protection of the law
Ex post facto law
Freedom of assembly
Freedom of petition
Freedom of religion
Freedom of speech
Freedom of the press

Grand jury
Habeas corpus
Higher law
Human rights
Natural law
Obscenity
Plea bargaining
Police state
Political rights
Positive law
Prior restraint
Resistance
Right
Right to confront cne's accusers
Right to counsel
Right to trial by impartial jury
Satyagraha
Sedition
Self-incrimination
Slander
Warrant

QUESTIONS

Civil Liberties and Civil Rights

1. Are human rights meaningful if defined exclusively in political terms? Why?
2. Should a suspect go free merely because a police officer committed a technical violation of the law in securing evidence? Why?
3. What role should government play in regulating pornography? Why?
4. How would you reconcile freedom of the press with the rights of accused in criminal proceedings?
5. What affect do constitutional rights protecting persons accused of committing a crime have on crime?
6. What is the meaning of equality in civil rights?
7. What criteria should be used in determining whether a particular group in a country is the subject of discrimination? Why do you select these criteria?

Civil Disobedience

1. Is resistance ever justified? Why?
2. Is there a higher law that takes precedence over human law? Explain.

3. What effect does civil disobedience have on strengthening a respect for law?

4. What effect do acts of civil disobedience have on popular support for the views that civil disobedients favor?

5. Should a democracy tolerate civil disobedience? Why?

Capital Punishment

1. What criteria should be used in determining whether capital punishment constitutes "cruel and unusual punishment"?

2. What effect would evidence indicating that capital punishment is inflicted disproportionately on minority and poor members of society have on your opinion of the issue? What are the reasons for your answer?

3. What is the relationship between capital punishment and crime deterrence?

4. What kinds of crimes should warrant a sentence of capital punishment? What are the reasons for your answer?

5. What methods should be used in carrying out the death penalty? Are these methods humane? Does it matter whether they are humane or not? Why?

RECOMMENDED READINGS

Civil Liberties and Civil Rights

ABRAM, MORRIS B. "What Constitutes a Civil Right?" *New York Times Magazine*, June 10, 1984, pp. 52–54, 58, 60, 62, 64, 66. An analysis of the meaning of civil rights.

BENEDICT, MICHAEL LES. *Civil Rights and Civil Liberties.* Washington, D.C.: American Historical Association, 1987. A survey of civil rights and civil liberties in the United States.

BICKEL, ALEXANDER M. *The Morality of Consent.* New Haven: Yale University Press, 1975. An argument that the morality of consent to law is essential to a free and civilized society.

BRANDT, IRVING. *The Bill of Rights: Its Origin and Meaning.* Indianapolis: Bobbs-Merrill, 1965. The story of the Bill of Rights.

CRANSTON, MAURICE. *What Are Human Rights?* New York: Taplinger, 1973. Clarification by a political philosopher of the assumptions underlying human rights.

DORSEN, NORMAN, ed. *Our Endangered Rights: The ACLU Report on Civil Liberties Today.* New York: Pantheon, 1984. A perspective of the American Civil Liberties Union.

HOOK, SIDNEY. *Heresy, Yes—Conspiracy, No.* New York: John Day, 1953. An argument that the liberal has a commitment to protect heresies (unpopular ideas) but not conspiracies that would destroy fundamental liberties.

LEVINE, HERBERT M., and JEAN EDWARD SMITH, eds. *Civil Liberties and Civil Rights Debated.* Englewood Cliffs, N.J.: Prentice Hall, 1988. A collection of debates on civil liberties and civil rights.

NEW YORK NATIONAL URBAN LEAGUE. *The State of Black America 1987.* New York: New York National Urban League, 1987. An assessment of conditions for black Americans in 1987.

RUTLAND, ROBERT ALLEN. *The Bill of Rights, 1776–1791.* Chapel Hill, N.C.: University of North Carolina Press, 1955. An examination of how the English common law, colonial charters and legislative enactments, and a variety of events in colonial times contributed to the rationale for a Bill of Rights.

SOWELL, THOMAS. *Civil Rights: Rhetoric or Reality?* New York: Morrow, 1984. An analysis of contemporary civil rights in the United States.

WILLIAMS, JUAN. "Closed Doors: Benign Racism in America." *New Republic* 195 (November 10, 1986): 22, 24, 25. An argument that racism is a powerful force in the United States.

Civil Disobedience

BAY, CHRISTIAN, "Civil Disobedience." *International Encyclopedia of the Social Sciences* (1968), 2:473–87. A survey of civil disobedience.

COHEN, CARL. *Civil Disobedience: Conscience, Tactics, and the Law.* New York: Columbia University Press, 1971. A general theory of civil disobedience.

FISCHER, LOUIS. *The Life of Mahatma Gandhi.* New York: Harper, 1950. A biography of a leading advocate of passive resistance.

FORTAS, ABE. *Concerning Dissent and Civil Disobedience.* New York: World Publishing Co., 1968. An essay by the former Supreme Court justice about civil disobedience.

HOOK, SIDNEY. "Neither Blind Obedience Nor Uncivil Disobedience." *New York Times Magazine,* June 5, 1966, pp. 52–53, 122, 124, 126, 128. A discussion of the limits of civil disobedience.

"On Civil Disobedience, 1967." *New York Times Magazine,* November 26, 1967, pp. 27–29, 122, 124, 126, and 128–32. A symposium dealing with the limits of civil disobedience including articles by William F. Buckley, Jr., Noam Chomsky, John Cogley, John Dollard, James T. Farrell, Lewis S. Feuer, Paul Goodman, Sidney Hook, Herbert S. Kelman, Irving Kristol, Dwight Macdonald, Richard Rovere, and Bayard Rustin.

ORWELL, GEORGE. "Reflections on Gandhi." In *The Collected Essays, Journalism and Letters of George Orwell,* ed. Sonia Orwell and Ian Angus. Harmondsworth, England: Penguin, 1968. 4:523–31. An important essay on Gandhi.

PERRY, LEWIS. "Civil Disobedience." In *Encyclopedia of American Political History: Studies of the Principal Movements and Ideas,* ed. Jack P. Greene. New York: Charles Scribner's Sons, 1984. 1:210–17. A survey of civil disobedience.

WICKER, TOM. "Moralism's Limits." *New York Times,* February 8, 1985, p. A31. A contention that abortion clinic bombers are not acting in a civilly disobedient manner.

Capital Punishment

AMNESTY INTERNATIONAL. *United States of America: The Death Penalty.* London: Amnesty International Publications, 1987. An analysis and critique of the death penalty in the United States.

BEDAU, HUGO ADAM. *Death Is Different: Studies in the Morality, Law, and Politics of Capital Punishment.* Boston: Northeastern University Press, 1987. A critique of capital punishment.

BERGER, RAOUL. *Death Penalties: The Supreme Court's Obstacle Course.* Cambridge, Mass.: Harvard University Press, 1982. An analysis of how the Supreme Court has dealt with capital punishment.

BERNS, WALTER. *For Capital Punishment: Crime and the Morality of the Death Penalty.* New York: Basic Books, 1979. A case for the death penalty.

BLACK, CHARLES L., JR. *Capital Punishment: The Inevitability of Caprice and Mistake.* 2d ed. New York: Norton, 1981. A case against the death penalty.

KOCH, EDWARD I. "Death and Justice." *New Republic* 192 (April 15, 1985): 12–15. A case for capital punishment.

LESTER, DAVID. *The Death Penalty: Issues and Answers.* Springfield, Ill.: Charles C. Thomas, 1987. An analysis of capital punishment in terms of social science research on the subject.

U.S. CONGRESS, HOUSE OF REPRESENTATIVES. *Capital Punishment.* Hearings before the Subcommittee on Criminal Justice of the Committee on the Judiciary, 99th Congress, 1st and 2d Sess., 1985 and 1986. Hearings to reinstate the federal death penalty.

WHITE, WELSH S. *The Death Penalty in the Eighties: An Examination of the Modern System of Capital Punishment.* Ann Arbor: University of Michigan Press, 1987. A legal analysis of the death penalty in the United States.

ZIMRING, FRANKLIN E., and GORDON HAWKINS. *Capital Punishment and the American Agenda.* New York: Cambridge University Press, 1986. A critique of capital punishment.

chapter 8

Political parties and elections

When in the summer of 1988, delegates of the Democratic party assembled in a national convention and nominated Michael Dukakis for president, and delegates of the Republican party selected George Bush as their standard bearer, they were acting out an important role in a democratic system: the choosing of candidates by political parties to compete in meaningful electoral contests for the right to run the government. In democratic countries, members of legislative and top executive offices are subject to some form of electoral competition, whether directly or indirectly chosen by the people, and political parties often play an important part in deciding who will occupy those positions.

Although the term *political party* in the United States is often associated first with Democrats and Republicans, it is used as a label for many different kinds of associations. Parties are found in dictatorships, too. In Adolf Hitler's Germany the

Nazi (National Socialist) party and in Joseph Stalin's Soviet Union the Communist party monopolized party rule. Critics labeled those parties as totalitarian (see Chapter 3). Political parties, moreover, are a feature of some developing states in Africa and other Third World countries and are different from either the totalitarian parties or the competitive parties found in many Western countries.

Although many studies have been made of political parties, students of the subject differ considerably in defining them. We will define a **political party** in its democratic context as an organization formed to contest elections by selecting candidates to run under its own party label. Since political parties in democracies are diverse in composition, objectives, and relationships to government, we recognize that such a definition does not adequately describe all democratic political parties. It certainly does not define political parties in undemocratic countries, where elections are a sham.

To understand political parties, we shall examine first the origin of political parties, the functions they perform in political systems, party systems, and the debate over the possible decline of political parties. We shall then study the different kinds of electoral systems in which competitive parties operate in democratic systems before concluding with an evaluation of two prominent electoral methods that influence the character of political parties.

ORIGIN OF POLITICAL PARTIES

If the term *political party* lacks precision in definition today, it is in part due to the varied organizations called political parties over the centuries. The term *political party* was used to describe groups of nobles and their followers in ancient times. From then until the seventeenth century, it connoted "faction" or "interest."[1] With the development of parliamentary bodies in eighteenth-century England, groups of leaders acting collectively in Parliament were sometimes called "parties." Parties in the modern sense are a development of the nineteenth century and arose from the need to mobilize the electorate, which was being made increasingly more numerous by the expansion of suffrage. Because the United States was the first country to grant the suffrage broadly, it became the first to have modern political parties. Some scholars date the formation of parties to 1800, when Jeffersonian Republicans achieved electoral success over the ruling Federalists, but others trace it to the 1830s, when white manhood suffrage became wide-

---

[1] See Austin Ranney, "The Concept of 'Party,' " in *Political Research and Political Theory*, ed. Oliver Garceau (Cambridge, Mass.: Harvard University Press, 1968), p. 145.

spread. In Great Britain, modern parties were propelled by the Reform Acts of 1832 and 1867, which expanded the suffrage. It was in the 1860s, however, that the British electorate became big enough for parties to engage in organizational activities. Many Western European nations, moreover, developed parties in about the middle of the nineteenth century. Modern political parties, then, originated in a democratic context: namely, the need to organize voters in competitive elections.

FUNCTIONS OF PARTIES

Political parties developed in the Western democracies, but they have become a feature of most political systems in the twentieth century. Although the functions of political parties vary among and within political systems, some of their more essential functions may be highlighted. These are aggregating interests, formulating programs, nominating candidates to contest elections, running government, and strengthening ties between the government and the people.

Aggregating Interests

An important function that some political parties perform is to bring together a variety of interest groups under a single organization. Such a process is known as **interest aggregation.** Particularly in countries that have two major political parties, such as the United States and Great Britain, each party consists of followers from a wide spectrum of economic, social, racial, and ethnic groups. It is usually the case that the differences separating the parties are not as great in two-party systems as they are in multiparty systems, such as exist in some Western European democracies. In developing countries, parties are often devices for uniting populations into a national identity, transcending local, tribal, or regional loyalties.

Political parties are not the only organizations that aggregate interests. Government agencies and interest groups themselves perform a similar function. In Western democracies, however, parties have often served an important role in uniting different interests. A key distinction between interest groups and political parties, in fact, is that generally the political parties play a greater role in interest aggregation.

Formulating Programs

Political parties prepare programs for consideration by the public. Parties serve to organize opinion that is often otherwise unclear and undirected, so that voters can make rational judgments about policies and candidates. The **party platform,** which is a statement of party objectives and promises, reveals to the people what the party stands for. The platform itself results from the reconciliation of conflicts and the assertion of common principles by the different segments of the party. Without such reconciliation, party splits become likely.

Party programs and platforms are important features of what is called **party government.** This is a system (usually consisting of two parties) in which each party presents a clear program for government action. In such a structure, the electorate decides on the party and its platform in periodic electoral contests. The victorious party then assumes control of government and puts its program into action. The British party system is often the model used by advocates of party government (see Chapter 11).

Nominating Candidates

The recruitment of political leaders is one of the most prominent party functions. Selection processes vary consider-

ably. In Israel, for example, a small group of party leaders determines who will be the party's designees in an election. In other countries, the nominating system may be highly decentralized. In the United States, **primary elections,** in which ordinary members of a political party decide who will be the party's candidate in an election, constitute one method of selecting candidates. Sometimes only people who have preregistered for a political party may vote in that primary, and such a contest is known as a **closed primary.** When any registered voter can vote in any party's primary, it is known as an **open primary.** Other methods of selection in the United States involve district conventions, state conventions, and state committees. To choose a candidate for the presidency, a national convention is called every four years in which the delegates selected on a state-wide basis designate a party nominee. Much variation in the selection process prevails in different countries, but the recruitment of candidates is an important feature of political parties in both democratic and undemocratic political systems.

Running the Government

Parties nominate candidates and contest elections for the purpose of controlling government. The term of office for controlling the government varies from country to country. In democratic systems electoral contests are the recognized manner of transferring power from one group of leaders to another. In some democratic countries the elected officials in the executive branch can bring into office thousands of political appointees to help run the vast bureaucracy. In other systems, however, the number of political appointees is kept small (see Chapter 12). The relationship between the political party members in a legislature and the extra-parliamentary party organizations varies among many political systems as well.

Government and the People

Political parties often serve as an important link between government and people because of the character of the electoral process and the legitimizing functions of elections. During periods of elections, masses of people become mobilized to engage in political activity to a greater extent than at other times. They listen to debates about policy issues, and they consider candidates expressing their views. Such activity educates voters about politics.

By engaging in electoral contests directed by political parties in a democracy, ordinary citizens tend to accept the rules underlying the democratic system as well as the electoral outcomes. Political parties, then, constitute the legitimizing function of government in those instances in which the masses of people accept the way in which political leaders are selected to run the government.

By focusing on these functions of political parties, some writers define a political party as an organization that aggregates interests, formulates programs, nominates candidates to contest elections, runs a government, and serves as a link to diverse groups in a polity. A difficulty arises because many parties do not fulfill these functions. Some parties, for example, are organized along narrow ideological lines and do not attempt to aggregate interests. Still other parties have no concern in running a government but act as a kind of interest group to attract national attention. In developing countries, moreover, political parties play a greater role in modernization and economic development than they do in developed countries.

PARTY SYSTEMS

A **party system** is the pattern of party relationships that exists within a political unit. Party systems are often compared in terms of their number, objectives, strength, structure, and sources of support.

Number

In the past, party systems used to be described in terms of whether they were one-party, two-party, or multiparty systems. Many writers today, however, regard such a distinction as inadequate in describing political systems because the patterns of parties are much too diverse within each category.

One-party Systems. Some scholars contend that the notion of a *one-party system* is a contradiction in terms. A party is derived from "a part," they argue, and more than one party is required to make up a party system. Other scholars note, however, that the expression *one-party system* has empirical utility. They distinguish different kinds of one-party systems, moreover, and we shall consider these variations here. One-party systems include not only totalitarian parties in dictatorships but also dominant parties in democracies. The party systems of some developing countries, moreover, may be considered in the one-party category.

The one-party totalitarian system characterized Germany under Hitler and the Soviet Union under Stalin. Both the Nazi party and the Communist party constituted an elite group concerned with the transformation of society. Totalitarian parties seek to promote their political control over all sectors of society, and ideological considerations play an important role in their behavior (see Chapter 3).

A **dominant political party system** is one in which, although parties are free to compete in electoral contests, one party wins elections and rules all the time. Southern states in the United States, for example, used to be dominated by the Democratic party. The dominance has been challenged by the Republicans with some success—particularly in presidential contests—in the past few decades. In some countries outside the United States, such as Mexico and Singapore, one party wins all the time. In 1988, however, the dominant party in Mexico declined in voting strength, and it is an open question whether the Mexican party system is undergoing systemic change.

One-party rule has also appeared in some of the developing countries. In Tanzania and Kenya, for example, the one-party systems are not the same as the totalitarian model. They consist of different social, economic, and ideological segments of the countries, and competition within the party is greater than in communist systems. An all-embracing ideology is not a feature of such a one-party system, moreover. The justification for that kind of system is often that the needs of economic development and political integration for a new country require a measure of unity that only the one-party system can generate.

Two-party Systems. Two-party systems are found in the United States and Great Britain and also in most countries settled in part by British emigrants. A two-party system is one in which two major political parties are the principal contenders for power, and there is alternation of office between them at periodic intervals. The Democratic party and the Republican party in the United States, and the Labour party and the Conservative party in Great Britain, are the major parties in those countries.

Although the British and American examples are often used to illustrate two-party systems, both systems generally have more than two parties. In the United States, third parties, such as the Progressive party of Henry Wallace in 1948 and the American Independent party of George Wallace in 1968, appear periodically. In Great Britain, minor parties have played an important role since the nine-teenth century. Such parties as the Liberal Unionists, the Irish Nationalists, the early Labour party, and the Liberal party and Social Democratic party today are cases in point.

Minor parties have played important roles in both Great Britain and the United States. They have served as parties of economic protest, and their rising strength has influenced one or both of the major political parties to alter their party programs. When minor parties have formed by seceding from major parties, they have influenced the prospects for electoral success of the major parties. Minor parties also bring new issues to the attention of the nation. In Great Britain, minor party support of the larger major party has been a prerequisite for forming a government in many instances.

Multiparty Systems. Multiparty systems, consisting by definition of more than two parties, are found in many countries, most notably in Western European states. In the Scandinavian countries, Belgium, Holland, and Italy, for example, no one party is strong enough to win control of parliament. Instead, after an election is conducted, a government is set up, composed of different political parties. In other words, the cabinet contains members from a coalition of parties.

No Parties. Although most countries of the world possess political parties, some countries have none. Traditional monarchical systems existing mostly in the Middle East and parts of Asia, for example, have no parties and rule on the basis of traditional ethnic ties. Saudi Arabia and Jordan are cases in point. Military regimes, which are found mostly in developing countries, also often rule without political parties. On occasion, the military rule is replaced by party rule when the military finds it essential to broaden its base of support.

Objectives

Political parties vary in terms of their goals. The terms *doctrinaire* and *broker* are used to contrast two parties with different kinds of objectives. A **doctrinaire party** is one which is concerned with promoting an ideological objective. In that sense, communist and socialist parties at their inception were doctrinaire parties, since they were devoted to establishing a political system based on strict adherence to communist and socialist ideologies, respectively. A **broker party,** in contrast, is one that mediates among diverse interest groups and avoids narrow ideological goals. Broker parties are said to be pragmatic, since they are willing to make adjustments to include ever larger numbers of voters. The Democratic and Republican parties in the United States are both broker parties, as are most socialist parties in Western Europe today.

Other classifications are also used, and a complete list of categories would be long. Among the most important, however, is the **revolutionary party,** which seeks to undermine the existing political system. Political parties formed in Third World areas at the time of colonial rule were often revolutionary as they sought to rid their country of colonial authority.

Strength

The strength of political parties varies. In dictatorships the strength of an illegal political party may be based on its elite character, conspiratorial activities, and unity. The Communist party in czarist Russia is a case in point. In democracies, however, strength is usually measured in terms of both the votes a party receives in an election and the number of seats it is able to win in the legislature. A major party usually can count on winning some districts nearly all the time. These are safe districts. Other districts, however, often swing from one party to another.

As we shall see, the percentage of votes that a party receives is often not directly transferred to a proportionate share of legislative seats. In Great Britain, for example, the Alliance (of Liberals and Social Democrats) won 25.4 percent of the vote in the general election of 1983 but obtained only 3.5 percent of the parliamentary seats.

Structure

Parties vary in terms of relationships between the few party members who rule the party, or party elite, and the masses of party members; between parliamentary and extraparliamentary organizations; and between national and regional party units.

In **cadre parties** a small group of *notables,* to use sociologist Max Weber's term, dominates party decisions, such as securing nominations and dispensing **patronage** (jobs given to political favorites). In the early development of political parties in the United States and Great Britain, for example, cadre parties played an important role. The Communist party of the Soviet Union is a modern cadre party.

Mass parties are those in which large numbers of the electorate are members of the party, which is usually led by a small group of professional leaders. The mass party is organized nationally into branches, with power ultimately at the national headquarters. The mass party has a program and provides a method for members to state policy preferences, select leaders, choose candidates for public office, and participate generally in the political process. The mass party arose from the expansion of the suffrage and political participation—features that have evolved most notably since the middle of the nineteenth century. European socialist parties are examples of mass parties in which millions of dues-paying members are organized.

The relationship between the parliamentary party and the extraparliamentary party differs among political systems. In Great Britain, for example, the parliamentary party has often resisted the demands of the party conference—the organization of the party outside of Parliament. Other political systems show a much stronger influence of the extraparliamentary party on the parliamentary party.

Parties differ, too, on the relationship between the national party organization and the regional party organizations. In the United States, political parties are largely decentralized. The power to nominate legislative candidates is often determined by a decision among party members at the state or local level. In other parties, such as the communist parties in Western democracies, power is more centralized at the national headquarters. There are noncommunist parties, too, that are more powerful at the center than in the regions of the country.

Sources of Support

Political parties vary in the kinds of membership they contain, their socioeconomic composition, and their sources of finance. In some systems the party may deliberately be kept small. The Communist party of the Soviet Union began as an illegal party that had to operate in a secret manner. It has retained its elite status, although it is much larger today than it was in its formative period. Becoming a member of the Communist party is a far more meaningful event in a communist country than is registering as a Democrat or Republican in the United States. In the latter case, party membership is even difficult to determine, since often it consists of registering for a party at election and not engaging in any other political activity except voting in the general election.

Members of a political party can be distinguished in several ways. One method is to distinguish among **voters,** who merely cast their ballots for a party's candidate; **supporters,** who give some time to getting the party's candidates elected; **activists,** who devote a considerable amount of their time and energy to party affairs; and the elite, who rule.

Another way to consider party support is by examining the party's social composition. Some parties are composed of broad segments of society. Both the Democratic party and the Republican party in the United States, for example, consist of people from broadly based economic classes, ethnic groups, and social organizations. Other parties may consist of a more narrow element of society.

The social composition of a party is often influenced by the way a person becomes a party member. In some systems, becoming a party member consists of making an individual choice to do so. In others, an individual automatically becomes a member of a party merely by being a member of a particular group. When the Labour party was formed in Great Britain, for example, there was a close association between the party and the trade unions. Part of that association consisted of financing campaigns of Labour party candidates for Parliament. Today, an individual trade union member can **contract out** (that is to say, make a formal refusal to contribute to a political party), however, but most members do not. In effect, then, the Labour party consists of many trade union members. Still, many of the members are free to vote for another political party and often do so.

Financial support varies among parties. In some countries the government provides money to candidates to run for office. In many democratic countries, however, money is raised from private sources. Laws regulating the amount of contributions and the manner of making donations influence the amount of money that a particular party can raise.

DECLINE OF PARTIES?

In Western democracies political parties have been declining in power in the twentieth century, although the extent of the decline is in dispute. The decline may be seen by examining some of the principal functions that parties are supposed to perform.

The role of the party in interest aggregation has diminished, as evidence in different countries attests. In describing the civil rights movement of the 1960s in the United States, the efforts of the British government to gain entry into the European Community, and the upheaval in France in 1968, political scientist Anthony King concludes, "To the extent that political integration and mobilization took place, they occurred in structures largely set apart from the parties."[2] In more recent times the antiwar movement and the environmental protection campaigns were formed by institutions outside of the parties, too.

Parties in democracies no longer set forth meaningful programs; nor do they initiate discussion of major issues. Often, party platforms consist of vague generalities, carefully crafted to avoid offending a significant segment of the electorate. Issues are put forward by other actors in the political process, such as interest groups, individual politicians, the media, civil servants, and academics.

The selection of candidates in some Western democracies is no longer dominated by party organizations. In the United States many candidates emphasize their "independence" from parties. Primaries have weakened the party's ability to select candidates. Candidates seeking public office secure their own independent sources of finance through political action committees and voluntary contributions by citizens. The media, particularly television, have allowed candidates to appeal to voters directly rather than through the parties.

The rise of the civil service has diminished the ability of the political party to run the government. The number of posts of an appointive nature make up a smaller percentage of government employees than was the case in the nineteenth century. The party, consequently, has lost much of its patronage opportunities.

The decline of parties is not only a feature of Western democracies. In newly independent African countries, the power of political parties has eroded. In Third World countries generally, political parties have often been the victims of revolutionary movements or military coups.[3]

Some writers argue that the decline of political parties in democracies is bad for the future of democracy. In their view the rise of the political party and the rise of democracy go hand in hand. Without political parties to perform their traditional functions, these writers contend, other organizations, such as the media and single-interest groups, will do so. Such a development will lead to a loss of accountability in government and an erosion of national unity, they conclude.

Other writers take issue with this evaluation. As societies become more complex, they say, interests become diverse and differentiated. Parties in such a modern setting do not wither away, but they must share functions that they used to perform with other associations, according to this viewpoint.

Recent scholarship challenges the view of the decline of political parties. The argument put forward is that political parties are not declining but rather are in a transitional period. Some writers of this viewpoint assert that some national party

[2] Anthony King, "Political Parties in Western Democracies: Some Sceptical Reflections," *Polity* 2 (Winter 1969): 117–18.

[3] Richard L. McCormick, ed., introd. to his *Political Parties and the Modern State* (New Brunswick, N.J.: Rutgers University Press, 1984), p. 12.

organizations have adopted new functions to meet the needs of the contemporary political environment. In the United States, for example, national party organizations are playing an active part in getting candidates to run for national, state, and local offices. They are providing candidates with campaign services, including training sessions, survey data, and media assistance. Some political action committees, moreover, are taking cues from the political parties in deciding where to dispense campaign contributions.[4] Party bureaucracies are larger than in the past, and more than two of three citizens continue to think of themselves as Democrats or Republicans. Many people still make their voting decisions based on party considerations, moreover.

Another example of party resurgence is found in France. In 1980, French political parties were stronger than they had been at any time since the immediate postwar years. According to political scientist Frank L. Wilson, the French political parties adopted new political approaches and strategies; public confidence in political parties was restored; party organizations were more active than they had been before 1980; they became a significant part of the political process; and parties fulfilled more capably their linkage to the people.[5]

Political parties are for the most part a development of the nineteenth century. It is an open question whether the political party is in a permanent state of decline or whether it is going through a period of transition.

---

[4] For a discussion, see Peter Hain, *Proportional Misrepresentation: The Case against PR in Britain* (Aldershot, England: Wildwood House, 1986), pp. 590–91.

[5] Frank L. Wilson, "When Parties Refuse to Fail: The Case of France," in *When Parties Fail: Emerging Alternative Organizations*, ed. Kay Lawson and Peter H. Merkl, (Princeton, N.J.: Princeton University Press, 1988), p. 506.

ELECTORAL SYSTEMS

Political parties in democracies devote most of their attention to contesting elections. Their prospects of electoral success depend in part on the electoral methods used that are sanctioned by law. These methods are rarely neutral in the sense that they are created for an objective registering of popular will through the ballot box. Rather, they are shaped by diverse historical traditions and social and political forces. We shall consider here some of the principal electoral systems of representation to show how the structure of electoral contests can affect voting outcomes.

Among the principal electoral methods are those based on territorial, functional, and proportional representation.

Territorial Representation

One of the most important electoral rules governs the size of the **constituency,** or electoral unit. In only a few countries is an entire country considered as the single unit for selecting legislative members. As indicated above, Israel is one case in point. In most countries, however, the unit for designating candidates is the electoral district.

The population and the shape of a district depend upon many factors. Sometimes the shape of a district is determined by constitutional features, such as in the federal system in the United States (see Chapter 10). Districts, however, may be unequally represented. In England, for example, a system of **rotten boroughs** existed from the sixteenth through the eighteenth centuries in which a member of Parliament could be elected by only a small number of people, while another member would have a constituency of millions. The situation of voting districts being unequal in population is known as **malapportionment.**

The shape of a district is a matter of

concern to all elected public officials. A variation in the district boundaries that would reduce or enlarge the size of a group—whether economic, racial, or ethnic—can have a decisive impact on the prospects of a candidate from that district. The drawing of district lines to secure a political advantage is known as a **gerrymander,** named after Governor Elbridge Gerry of Massachusetts, who introduced the practice in the United States in 1812. As a result of redistricting, Gerry's party secured twenty-nine state senators with 50,164 votes, while the opposition party obtained only eleven members with 51,766 votes. The practice of gerrymandering continues in the United States, although the Supreme Court has restricted its use in certain extreme cases.

The apportionment of voting districts and the drawing of district lines influence the prospects of success for different political parties and candidates. Another influence is the number of officials selected from each voting unit. In Great Britain and the United States, the single-member district is the method used for selecting legislators. In a single-member district, only one person is chosen for an office from that district.

The method used for selecting legislators in the British House of Commons and the American House of Representatives is the **plurality system,** or **first-past-the-post system.** Whoever gets the largest number of votes is the winner. It is possible in a three-way contest for the winning candidate to receive less than a majority if more than half the votes are split among the losing candidates. In some countries, and even in some primary elections in the United States, a **majority system** is required, in which a candidate must win more than 50 percent of the votes. In that event the two candidates receiving the largest number of votes face each other in a second election, or **run-off,** to determine who the victor will be.

The president of France is elected in this manner.

Although the principal method of legislative elections in the United States and Great Britain consists of voting within the single-member constituency, many countries and some localities vote for more than one candidate in a constituency. In such **multiple-member districts,** a voter is permitted to cast a ballot for more than one person. In a municipal contest in which five members of a city council are to be selected, for example, a voter may vote for five candidates.

Functional Representation

Representation based on territorial considerations is not the only electoral method; some systems employ functional representation, that is, representation by economic or social groups. Such a method is both ancient and modern. In ancient times representation was based on class and status. In medieval England the great estates were represented in Parliament. As early as the thirteenth century, representatives of the clergy, the nobility, and the burgesses constituted the Parliament.

Functional representation has also been used in the twentieth century. In fascist Italy, for example, a corporate state was established in which the legislature was composed of groups from different economic and social segments of society. The legislature in fascist Italy did not have the power of a legislature in a democratic society, but the corporate character of representation constituted a form of representation that, the fascist leaders believed, would lend legitimacy to their government.

Proportional Representation

More common as an electoral system is the system of **proportional representation** (PR). PR is a system in which candidates of political parties are elected in proportion to their voting support. This is the dominant system in Western countries and has also been used in many American cities. There are hundreds of variations in the PR system. The two most prominent, however, are the list system and the Hare system.

In the simple form of the **list system,** each political party nominates as many candidates as there are seats to be filled in that constituency. National list systems operate in Guyana, Israel, and Turkey. Israel is perhaps the best example of a country that has adopted the list system. In the Israeli parliament, called the Knesset, there are 120 seats. Each party nominates 120 candidates. Each party determines for itself who is ranked from first to 120th position. The voter has no choice of individual candidates but votes for a party. When all the votes are counted, each party receives the percentage of parliamentary seats equal to the percentage of votes that it has secured at the polls. Usually, in countries that have adopted the list system, no single political party obtains a majority of the vote. A **coalition government** (an alliance of parties that generally constitutes a majority) is formed. In a coalition government, most often the cabinet is composed of members from each of the elements of the coalition, but this does not have to be the case. Sometimes, some minor parties are more concerned with having particular policies adopted than with staffing cabinet positions.

In the **Hare system** the voter ranks his or her choices of candidates as first, second, third, and so on. When a candidate achieves a quota of votes set on the basis of law or calculated from a formula of seats in that constituency, that candidate is elected. Then the candidate's surplus votes are given to the candidate to whom his or her supporters gave their second preference. If enough candidates still have not reached the quota, the weakest candidates are eliminated, and the second preferences of the voters who cast their ballots for them are counted until the victorious candidates have been elected. The idea of the system is to transfer votes until the number of seats is filled.

Since there are hundreds of different PR systems, it is often difficult to make generalizations about such systems. In a number of countries with the PR system a party must have a minimum percentage of the total vote to be accorded any seats in the legislature. In only a few PR countries do voters cast their ballots in a system in which the country forms one large multimember electoral district. Most PR nations have a number of multimember electoral districts with each district electing a particular number of representatives through PR. In the Norwegian Storting each of 19 districts elects from 11 to 13 representatives according to the population to fill that 155-seat legislative body.

One unusual electoral form is that of the Federal Republic of Germany, which has a **"topping-up" system.** Half of the members of the Bundestag are chosen from individual constituencies on the first-past-the-post basis. The rest are selected from political parties participating in the election, so that the overall balance in the Bundestag constitutes the national distribution of the party vote.

ISSUE

Particular electoral systems have their supporters and critics. For more than a century one of the more debated electoral issues is the relative merits of the majority or the plurality system and the proportional system of representation—a subject that is debated below.

18/YES

ARE MAJORITY OR PLURALITY SYSTEMS BETTER THAN PROPORTIONAL SYSTEMS OF REPRESENTATION?

Although proportional representation has its partisans in every democratic country, it is not nearly as good a system as majority and plurality systems. The case for the first-past-the-post system rests on: (1) the two-party system it encourages; (2) the democratic processes it strengthens; and (3) the political stability it enhances.

Party Systems. The first-past-the-post system encourages the formation of two-party systems. The experience of Great Britain and the United States, each possessing two major parties, confirms that fact. The voter in a system of two parties who seriously considers casting his or her ballot for a third party is often deterred from doing so by a realization that the vote will be "wasted"—that is, it will have no direct impact on deciding which of the candidates of the two major parties will win.

Although there are only two parties, the voters are presented with a real choice. Since each party offers an alternative candidate and an alternative program, the voter knows in advance that if his or her party wins, the victorious candidates will run the government. The voter also knows in advance what the policy of government is supposed to be. This is particularly true for the British system, but is also true for the American system in those instances when the executive and legislative branches are controlled by the same party (see Chapter 11). Of course, the government need not implement the program it professes, but then it can be held accountable for its omissions in the next general election. Often, party pledges are kept. Political scientist Gerald M. Pomper concludes from his analysis of 1,400 platform pledges over a period of twenty years (1944–64) that in the United States the political parties do pay attention to their platforms and do enact a good deal of their platforms into law.[6]

---

[6] Gerald A. Pomper, *Elections in America: Control and Influence in Democratic Politics* (New York: Dodd, Mead, 1971), p. 178.

A PR system, in contrast, promotes a multiparty system. The voter does not even know before the election is conducted what the composition of the government will be if his or her party does well in gathering votes because no single party in a multiparty system is likely to achieve a clear-cut victory. A voter, moreover, cannot know what a coalition government (composed of cabinet members from different political parties) will do. The existence of the coalition government, then, means that the voter has decided very little as far as policy is concerned.

Democracy. Democracy is strengthened from the first-past-the-post system in many ways. Because the system encourages the electoral competition of two big parties, each party must seek the support of a broad spectrum of social, economic, and cultural groups in order to achieve electoral success. In the United States, for example, both the Democratic party and the Republican party have some support in all segments of American society.

Under a two-party system, the majority, in effect, constitutes a collection of many minorities. Since the margin of difference between the two parties is frequently under 5 percent, it is essential that neither party slight minority groups. To do so would mean a loss of electoral support. Party leaders are so concerned about minority support that it is not uncommon for the top candidates in statewide elections to come from different social backgrounds.

Advocates of PR argue that PR offers more opportunities than first-past-the-post systems for women and minority members to be elected to legislative posts. What they often fail to note, however, is the variation in the percentage of women or minority members in the legislative systems using the same PR electoral processes. Peter Hain concludes from his study of countries with similar list systems that Finland has four times greater a representation of women than Israel.[7] Wilma Rule asserts that in party list systems in twenty-three democracies in 1980–82, women's parliamentary representation varied from a high of 28 percent in Sweden to a low of 4 percent in Greece.[8] In Hain's view, political culture, the strength of feminist ideas and social attitudes, as well as economic circumstances all play their part, and the exact role of the electoral system is not obvious.[9] Some of the same factors affect minority-group representation, as well. So it is wrong to hold electoral forms exclusively responsible for the amount of female and minority representation in the legislature.

Democracy, too, benefits from the diversity of views that are reflected within the two parties in the legislature. In this regard, proponents of PR have an inaccurate conception of what a legislature is supposed to be. They regard a legislature as a place that represents the electorate in some sort of mirror image. In fact, however, all that is essential is that the legislature should reflect popular sentiment *in some general way*. The historical record reveals much evidence of this proposition from British and American experience. Catholic emancipation in Britain was approved by Parliament at a time when no Catholics were members of Parliament. Women were granted the suffrage in the United States, moreover, at a time when few women held elective posts. What was essential in each case was that the legislators advocating such positions were freely able to convince their colleagues of the wisdom of changing policy.

PR systems hurt democracy by often giving undue influence to small parties. Israel is a case in point. Because of the nearly equal strength of the Labor party and the Likud party, the balance of power has often been held by small religious parties that have been able to impose their orthodox religious views on what is primarily a secular society.

Finally, PR supporters argue that first-past-the-post systems are undemocratic because they produce electoral distortions favoring one or another party. PR districts can be and have been drawn to favor one or another political party, as is also the case in plurality systems. If electoral rules can be manipulated in both systems, it makes neither system more virtuous as far as democracy is concerned.

Stability. First-past-the-post systems are likely to produce more stable political systems, as the British and American experience attests. Political parties must appeal to broad segments of the electorate and avoid becoming parties of the extreme ends of the political spectrum if they are to win elections. The major parties, consequently, reach toward the center of the political spectrum. They adopt somewhat similar programs lest they lose sizable segments of support. Such a practice encourages moderation in policy. Minor political parties that cater to extremist views cannot secure enough electoral support to become serious challengers to government power, and so the first-past-the-post system aids stability.

In contrast, PR encourages sharp divisiveness in government and society. All the political party must do to gain a foothold in the legislature is to gather a small percentage of the vote. The system of PR that existed in the Weimar Republic after World War I allowed the Nazi party to gain some seats in the German legislature, the Reichstag. Both the Nazi party and the Communist party were aided by PR. Extremist groups with limited support prefer PR because it allows them a certain measure of legitimacy through legislative representation. Political parties committed to destroying democracy should not be permitted to gain a foothold in parliamentary government—a prospect made likely by PR.

Not only do political systems become unstable because of the strength given to extremist groups through PR, but the very essence of a multiparty system—namely, coalition government—is inherently unstable. One can cite many examples, the most prominent of which was the Fourth Republic in France. France went through twenty-six governments in fourteen years. The average government lasted less than six months, and such instability in government made it difficult for France to provide coherent rule. Italy since World War II has also suffered from political instability

---

[7] Hain, *Proportional Misrepresentation*, p. 69.

[8] Wilma Rule, "Electoral Systems, Contextual Factors and Women's Opportunity for Election to Parliament in Twenty-three Democracies," *Western Political Quarterly* 40 (September 1987): 483.

[9] Hain, *Proportional Misrepresentation*, p. 69.

caused by small parties withdrawing from the coalition constituting the government. That demonstration of weak government has had its impact on society, as the random and reck-

less acts of terrorist groups in Italy attest. First-past-the-post systems, in contrast, give a government time to rule, which is a measure for stability.

18/NO   ARE MAJORITY OR PLURALITY SYSTEMS BETTER THAN PROPORTIONAL SYSTEMS OF REPRESENTATION?

Proportional representation is the major electoral system of the continental European democracies. PR is better than first-past-the-post systems because it: (1) encourages a multiparty system; (2) is more democratic; and (3) is more stable.

Party Systems. Most students of political parties agree that the existence of PR encourages a multiparty system. They differ, however, about whether or not this is a good thing. We contend that two parties are too few to reflect the interests of mass democracies, with their differing economic, social, and ethnic elements. In addition, we argue that multipartism offers as much responsible government as does bipartism.

Advocates of a two-party system praise a model of party government that bears no resemblance to the real world. First, the British experience reveals that one-party majority rule is the exception rather than the rule. Political scientist Harry Eckstein notes in this respect that "in the 77 years between 1885 and 1962, the era of modern parties and elections, Britain has had only 43 years of straightforward one-party majority rule."[10] British governments, then, ruled as a result of one or more small parties supporting a big one.

Second, the notion that in first-past-the-post systems party platforms and politicians' promises are meaningful is questionable because the platforms and pledges are often ambiguous and often violated. In the electoral campaign of 1932, for example, Franklin Roosevelt promised that if he were elected, he would balance the budget. Jimmy Carter promised in 1976, moreover, that he would

reduce defense spending. Neither Roosevelt nor Carter lived up to his promise, and they were not unique as politicians in two-party systems either.

One further point needs to be noted about the relationship between electoral systems and the number of parties. The assertion that simple majority voting leads to a two-party system with alternation in power is valid in some cases, such as Great Britain and the United States. It is not true in others, such as Belgium before 1894, Sweden before 1911, Denmark before 1920, and contemporary Canada.[11] With such different results in the number of parties, it is difficult to even generalize about the first-past-the-post system.

Democracy. Proportional representation serves the interests of democracy in many ways. The individual voter can be assured that he or she will not have to cast a ballot for a candidate he or she does not like. In proportional systems, there will be many, narrowly defined parties, so a voter can feel confident that his or her interests are being represented by at least one of them.

Minorities, too, benefit from such a system. Minorities, who felt that they would be better protected by such a system, were an important influence in bringing about PR in the period before World War I. Countries containing ethnically diverse groups were the first to adopt PR: Denmark in 1885, the Swiss cantons in 1891, Belgium in 1899, Moravia in 1905, and Finland in 1906.[12]

PR would aid minorities and women in another way. Minority members and women are

[10] Harry Eckstein, "Parties, Political: Party Systems," *International Encyclopaedia of the Social Sciences* (1968), 11:440.

[11] Ibid., p. 448.

[12] Stein Rokkan, "Elections: Electoral Systems," *International Encyclopaedia of the Social Sciences* (1968), 5:12.

more likely to hold parliamentary seats in PR systems than in first-past-the-post systems. In Great Britain, for example, there has been no black or Asian MP since the 1920s, yet blacks and Asians constitute about 4 percent of the total British population. Although women constitute more than half the population of Great Britain, they have never won even 5 percent of the seats in the House of Commons. In this regard a party will often feel that it should include minority members on a list system to show that its appeal extends to all sectors of the constituency. In the first-past-the-post system, in contrast, the party would be more likely to feel that the selection of a minority member may offend many voters and, consequently, cost the party votes.[13] Political scientist Wilma Rule concludes from her study of twenty-three democracies that the party list system of PR provides the most political opportunity for women.[14]

A democracy, moreover, requires that a legislature represent its people. Representation means that the legislature should be a mirror image of the society. PR assures the proper form of representation as befits a democracy.

Democracy is further strengthened by avoiding the electoral manipulations of a plurality system. Such manipulations can lead to major distortions of voters' preferences. In the 1983 general election in Great Britain, the Liberal/Social Democratic Party Alliance won 25.4 percent of the popular vote, but gained only 3.5 percent of the seats in the House of Commons.

First-past-the-post systems are usually based on territorial districting. Gerrymandering is often used by the party in power to redraw district lines for an electoral advantage. Historically, too, districts under plurality systems have not been composed of an equal number of people, thus giving an advantage to one of the major parties. PR can do away with many of the partisan advantages that in effect diminish the influence of many voters.

It is important to keep in mind that majority rule—an essential component of democracy—is often the exception in two-party systems. In Great Britain, for example, the ruling government has rarely won a majority of the votes. It usually has a plurality, which means that more than half of the people preferred some other parties. PR would be more democratic in that a coalition would be formed based on the political preferences of the majority.

Stability. Proportional representation produces stable political systems. "Multipartism" need not be synonymous with "instability." The Scandinavian countries, for example, have experienced a great degree of political stability through coalition governments. If the British and American systems are stable, it is because of the social harmony that exists among the people and the mutual trust the people have for their two major parties, and not because of the particular electoral system they employ.

Opponents of PR like to point to the experience of France in the Fourth Republic and to Germany in the Weimar Republic. Those examples are not valid because they ignore the underlying social, economic, and political forces that operated in both those societies. France experimented with eight different kinds of electoral systems in the past century, yet each system produced a multiparty structure. No system was adequate to prevent the sharp cleavages of French society from producing political instability. Given the nature of post–World War I problems faced by the Weimar government, moreover, even a different electoral system would not have been able to resist the Nazi onslaught. It is essential to recall that in 1932, a majority of the German people voted for political parties (such as the Nazi and the Communist) that were committed to the destruction of democracy. A two-party system could not have stemmed that tide. Political scientist Enid Lakeman notes that under the almost exact same electoral system in Weimar Germany, Czechoslovakia in the period between the world wars produced the most stable and successful democracy in Eastern Europe.[15]

[13] Vernon Bogdanor, *What Is Proportional Representation? A Guide to the Issues* (Oxford, England: Martin Robertson, 1984), pp. 113–15. See also Enid Lakeman, *Power to Elect: The Case for PR* (London: Heinemann, 1982), pp. 134–38.

[14] Rule, "Electoral Systems, Contextual Factors and Women's Opportunity for Election to Parliament," pp. 477–98.

[15] Enid Lakeman, *How Democracies Vote: A Study*

Stability in the political system is further aided by the character of coalition governments brought on by PR. An election in a multiparty system does not produce a brand new government. Ordinarily, it produces at most a shift of a few seats and cabinet posts to reflect changing popular sentiment. Continuity, consequently, is preserved. In the winner-take-all situation that arises from plurality systems, an entirely new government can bring about major policy shifts that may be a source of political instability.

In the four post–World War II decades since the adoption of the Italian Constitution of 1948,

Italian parliamentary regimes lasted an average of ten months. *But* there was much stability, as many party leaders attained office, lost office, and returned to office. As Joseph LaPalombara observes, "Since the war, five men—Christian Democrats Alcide de Gasperi, Amintore Fanfani, Aldo Moro, Mariano Rumor, and Giulio Andreotti—have served as prime minister five or more times. That they headed, all told, 29 different governments is almost irrelevant."[16]

PR systems, then, are superior to first-past-the-post systems.

---

of Electoral Systems, 4th ed. (London: Faber and Faber, 1974), p. 212.

[16] Joseph LaPalombara, "Partitocrazia," *Wilson Quarterly* 12 (Spring 1988): 104.

KEY TERMS

Activists
Broker party
Cadre party
Closed primary
Coalition government
Constituency
Contract out
Doctrinaire party
Dominant political party system
First-past-the-post system
Gerrymander
Hare system
Interest aggregation
List system
Majority system
Malapportionment

Mass parties
Multiple-member district
Open primary
Party government
Party platform
Party system
Patronage
Plurality system
Political party
Primary elections
Proportional representation (PR)
Revolutionary party
Rotten boroughs
Run-off
Supporters (political parties)
"Topping-up" system
Voters

QUESTIONS

1. If in fact political parties in Western democracies are declining, is this a desirable trend? What are the reasons for your answer?

2. What are the strengths and weaknesses of a two-party over a multiparty system?

3. What do elections decide?

4. What is the value of party platforms?

5. If the United States were to adopt a system of proportional representation, what would be its consequences to the American political system?

RECOMMENDED READINGS

BIBBY, JOHN F. *Politics, Parties, and Elections in America.* Chicago: Nelson-Hall, 1987. An assessment of the U.S. party system.

BOGDANOR, VERNON. *What Is Proportional Representation? A Guide to the Issues.* Oxford, England: Martin Robertson, 1984. A case for PR in Great Britain.

DELURY, GEORGE E., ed. *World Encyclopedia of Political Systems and Parties.* 2d ed. New York: Facts on File, 1987. A useful reference.

DUVERGER, MAURICE. *Political Parties: Their Organization and Activity in the Modern State,* trans. Barbara and Robert North. 2d ed. London: Methuen and Co., 1962. A classic study of political parties.

ECKSTEIN, HARRY. "Parties, Political: Party Systems." *International Encyclopedia of the Social Sciences* (1968), 11:436–53. An overview of party systems.

ELLIS, TOM, ROSALEEN HUGHES, and PHILIP WHITEHEAD. *Electoral Reform.* Fabian Tract 483. London: Fabian Society, 1982. A debate on PR.

EPSTEIN, LEON D. *Political Parties in the Western Democracies.* 2d ed. New Brunswick, N.J.: Transaction Books, 1979. An analysis of political parties.

HAIN, PETER. *Proportional Misrepresentation: The Case against PR in Britain.* Aldershot, England: Wildwood House, 1986. A case against PR.

HERMENS, FERDINAND A. *Democracy or Anarchy? A Study of Proportional Representation.* Notre Dame, Ind.: University of Notre Dame, 1941. A classic critique of PR.

HERTZBERG, HENDRIK. "Let's Get Representative." *New Republic* 196 (June 29, 1987): 15–18. A case for the adoption of a modified Hare system of electing Congress.

HOAG, CLARENCE GILBERT, and GEORGE HARVEY, JR. *Proportional Representation.* New York: Macmillan, 1926. A major work in defense of PR.

INGLE, STEPHEN. *The British Party System.* Oxford, England: Basil Blackwell, 1987. An account of British political parties within the context of the functions they are generally supposed to fulfill.

KATZ, RICHARD S., ed. *Party Governments: European and American Experiences.* Berlin, F.R.G.: Walter de Gruyter, 1987. Essays on party government in eight countries.

KING, ANTHONY. "Political Parties in Western Democracies: Some Sceptical Reflections." *Polity* 2 (Winter 1969): 111–41. A questioning of the role attributed to political parties in Western democracies.

LAKEMAN, ENID. *Power to Elect: The Case for Proportional Representation.* London: Heinemann, 1982. A case for the single-transferable vote system.

LAWSON, KAY, and PETER H. MERKL, eds. *When Parties Fail: Emerging Alternative Organizations.* Princeton, N.J.: Princeton University Press, 1988. A collection of essays on the subject.

RAE, DOUGLAS W. *The Political Consequences of Electoral Laws.* New Haven: Yale University Press, 1967. A major study of electoral systems.

ROKKAN, STEIN. "Elections: Electoral Systems." *International Encyclopaedia of the Social Sciences* (1968), 5:6–19. An overview of the subject.

SARTORI, GIOVANNI. *Parties and Party Systems: A Framework for Analysis.* Vol. 1. Cambridge, England: Cambridge University Press, 1976. A general theory of party-based politics.

SCHLESINGER, JOSEPH A. "Parties, Political: Party Units." *International Encyclopaedia of the Social Sciences* (1968), 11:428–36. An overview of the subject.

WARE, ALAN. *Citizens, Parties and the State: A Reappraisal.* Princeton, N.J.: Princeton University Press, 1987. An analysis of the role of parties in the advancement of democracy.

chapter 9

Interest groups

- Thousands of antiabortion activists assemble on the Mall to demonstrate in favor of the Human Life Amendment.
- A computer bank prepares to process messages to members of the National Rifle Association (NRA). The messages will alert NRA members to a gun control bill being considered by Congress.
- A representative from Common Cause appears before a congressional committee and asks the members to approve legislation that would provide for government financing of congressional elections.

Scenes such as these are representative of a form of political participation common in Washington, D.C., and in other cities of the country where political decisions are made. These are the kinds of actions that interest groups take. An **interest group** may be defined as an association of individuals who have common goals and who interact to achieve those goals. An interest group is sometimes called a **voluntary association** or a **pressure group,**[1] and the people who represent the interest group in its dealings with government officials are known as **lobbyists.**[2]

Interest groups in one form or another have been in existence for centuries. They have, however, become stronger and more varied with the rise of both a complex

---

[1] Some writers object to the phrase *pressure group* because of its sinister connotations and often because the work of political interest groups does not consist of applying pressure but rather of making a case for a particular point of view.

[2] According to one view, the term *lobbyist* had its origin in 1829 when *lobby-agent* was used to refer to those who sought special privileges at the Capitol in Albany, New York. Journalists shortened the word to *lobbyist.* See Karl Schriftgiesser, *The Lobbyists: The Art and Business of Influencing Lawmakers* (Boston: Little, Brown, 1951), p. 5. Another view traces the term *lobby* to mid-seventeenth century England, when *lobby agents* approached members of Parliament for special favors. *The Washington Lobby,* 2d ed. (Washington, D.C.: Congressional Quarterly, 1974), preface.

industrial society and big government. It is in the United States that interest groups have emerged in greatest abundance and variety. It is in the United States, too, that the study of interest groups has received the most prominent attention from political scientists, although the literature being written by political scientists about interest groups in other Western democracies, communist systems, and developing countries is growing.

Because of the prominence of the American experience, most of the discussion that follows will deal with different groups in the United States. An examination of the different kinds of interest groups, why they were formed, and how they work in the United States will be made before a consideration of interest groups in other countries is undertaken.

VARIETIES OF INTEREST GROUPS

Interest groups may be classified in many ways. We may distinguish between multiple-issue groups that are organizations with diverse objectives, such as trade unions, and **single-issue groups.** In the latter case, the group is formed to deal with only one issue, such as abortion, gun control, and disarmament. Here it is important to note that many interest groups have been created to promote a variety of objectives. These groups include economic, professional, civil rights, public interest, religious, and government associations.

Economic groups consist largely of business, union, and farm associations. Business associations include such large organizations as the Chamber of Commerce and the National Association of Manufacturers; trade associations, such as the American Petroleum Institute and the American Bankers Association; and individual corporations, such as Exxon and General Dynamics.

Business groups may seek a variety of goals. They may be interested in keeping to a minimum the general level of government spending because of its potential inflationary impact on the economy. They may be concerned about specific areas of policy, such as tariffs and import quotas. They may favor government regulation to reduce the level of competition, or they may oppose government regulation because they find it meddlesome and costly. They may seek government subsidies or government contracts.

Unions have their own agenda. They have sought government protection to organize workers into trade unions. When it serves their purposes, they support industries in their quest for government assistance, as the case of the bailout of Chrysler through a federal government guaranteed loan in 1979 attests. They may also favor the enactment of rules requiring government agencies to purchase only from those firms who employ trade union members. They may seek broad objectives, such as welfare legislation, because they perceive that the principal beneficiaries will be their own members.

Farm groups are deeply involved in influencing government. Vast government subsidies have been given to some farmers in order to make certain that they are assured a basic minimum income for their efforts. Farmers have received many other benefits from the government, including weather information, grants for agricultural research, and low-interest loans. In 1988, many American farmers experienced hard times because of a particularly heavy drought that destroyed crops. Facing bankruptcy, these farmers requested financial assistance, which was granted by Congress.

Professional groups seek to influence government. The American Medical Association (AMA) wants government regulations assuring that only qualified physicians can practice medicine. When malpractice insurance rates skyrocketed in the 1980s, the AMA turned to government to help deal with the problem. The national and regional bar associations are concerned with matters of interest to the legal profession, such as qualifications for practicing law and appointments to the courts. University professors have organizations that are concerned not only with educational matters but with employment conditions, such as salaries and tenure, as well.

Civil rights organizations are active participants in the political process. The National Association for the Advancement of Colored People (NAACP) and the National Organization for Women (NOW) are cases in point. Such organizations devote their efforts to eliminating the barriers to equality brought on by discrimination based on race and gender.

For the most part, economic, professional, and civil rights associations are formed to achieve direct benefits for their members. In the 1970s, another type of group emerged in influence—the **public interest group** (PIG). This group may be defined as an association concerned with the improvement of the economic, social, and political environment without any immediate direct tangible gain to its members. Consumer and environmental groups fall into this category. So, too, does an organization like the American Civil Liberties Union (ACLU), which is primarily concerned with the protection of civil liberties and civil rights.

Religious groups have been particularly active in the United States in the 1980s. Their concerns are not only spiritual. Issues of moral and practical interest have occupied their attention, such as abortion, pornography, prayer in schools, and tuition tax credits.

Government has interest groups, too. Lobbies from state governments and some municipalities have offices in Washington, D.C. They attempt to influence policy makers in the federal government on programs beneficial to them, such as mass transit and education. Departments and agencies of the federal government make their case before executive and legislative officials in such matters as defense and welfare. The Department of Defense, for example, pleads with appropriate congressional committees not to cut what it deems to be vital weapons systems.

Interest groups vary because people have different incentives for joining groups. As Peter Clark and James Q. Wilson observe, these incentives may be classified as material, solidary, or purposive. **Material incentives** are primarily economic, such as wages and salaries. **Solidary incentives** are intangible rewards derived from belonging to an organization, such as a fraternity or a club, and include such rewards as congeniality and the status resulting from membership. **Purposive incentives** arise from advancing a particular cause or ideology and include goals that do not benefit the members in any direct or tangible way, such as the beautification of the countryside or the elimination of government inefficiency.[3]

WHY HAVE INTEREST GROUPS GROWN?

Interest groups have a long history in the United States. Even before the Constitution was adopted, differences arose between debtors and creditors, commercial and landed classes, and people who lived in coastal or outlying regions. The struggle over the adoption of the Constitution reflects some of the conflicts among these groups.

Various explanations have been put

---

[3] See Peter Clark and James Q. Wilson, "Incentive Systems: A Theory of Organizations," *Administrative Science Quarterly* 6 (September 1961): 129–66; James Q. Wilson, *Political Organizations* (New York: Basic Books, 1973), pp. 30–51.

forward to explain the growth of interest groups. The most prominent reasons include economic development, increased heterogeneity, social disruption, the rise of government, the constitutional system, and political culture.

As the United States moved from an agrarian to an industrial society, the division of labor became more complex. Economic differentiation resulted in new economic associations, many of which were concerned with rather specialized interests. And so, for example, specialized trade associations have been created representing such interests as the semiconductor industry and the magazine industry. An advanced industrial society, moreover, made it possible to form national organizations relying on modern means of communication and transportation, linking members with a central organization.

The opportunities presented by a burgeoning economy in the United States produced a vast influx of immigrants from many countries. America has been called the "melting pot" because it has sought to bring together so many people of different ethnic, racial, and religious backgrounds. Such diversity encouraged the formation of groups.

Groups do not arise spontaneously merely because of their economic and social specialization. As political scientists Allan J. Cigler and Burdett A. Loomis note, "Farmers and a landed interest existed long before farm organizations first appeared; laborers and craftsmen were on the job prior to the formation of unions."[4] In this regard, periods of economic and social disturbance sparked group formation. Unions grew powerful as a response to the Great Depression of the 1930s, and civil rights organizations proliferated

as the demand for racial equality became more widely asserted.

Because government has grown so dramatically in the twentieth century, groups have been formed in an effort to influence government decisions. Government regulation of business in such matters as the formation of monopolies, the protection of trade unions, the requirement of safety standards for workers, the inspection of products for safety and health hazards, and the imposition of antidiscrimination standards in hiring has sparked the growth of business associations.

Economic groups are not the only associations to form in response to government growth. As government has involved itself in so many different policy areas, such as racial discrimination, women's rights, environmental protection, consumer safeguards, commercial advertising, and human rights abroad, organizations have been formed to promote these causes.

Government itself has been responsible for the formation of some groups. It has sometimes mandated the establishment of advisory boards consisting of economic, professional, or community representation. It has often enacted legislation requiring some kinds of citizen participation.

The constitutional system provides a reason for the establishment and development of groups. The Constitution allows for First Amendment rights of speech and association—a prerequisite for the uninhibited formation of groups. The separation of powers between the executive, legislative, and judicial branches of government and the division of power between the national and state governments offer groups an opportunity to influence government at many different points in the political process. The relative weakness of political parties in the United States also provides interest groups with opportunities to influence policy.

American political culture has been conducive to group growth. Alexis de

4 Allan J. Cigler and Burdett A. Loomis, "Introduction: The Changing Nature of Interest Group Politics," in *Interest Group Politics*, ed. Allan J. Cigler and Burdett A. Loomis, 2d ed. (Washington, D.C.: CQ Press, 1986), p. 7.

Tocqueville noted in *Democracy in America* (1835) that Americans had a tendency to join groups. He attributed this inclination to a desire for individuality and personal achievement. The tendency for Americans to join groups remains a constant in contemporary America.[5]

WHAT DO POLITICAL INTEREST GROUPS DO?

Interest groups seek to obtain economic, social, or ideological goals. To achieve their aims, they often use similar techniques, including shaping public opinion, making alliances with other groups, working directly to influence government decisions, and supporting candidates in electoral contests.

The success of a group in achieving its objectives depends considerably upon its ability to equate its own interests with the public interest. If it is successful, it has legitimized its claims on society. Issue 19 focuses on the concept of the public interest. For the moment, however, the **public interest** is defined as the interest of all, or the common good.

To influence public opinion, interest groups rely on a variety of techniques. They take advertisements in national magazines and in other media outlets, such as radio and television. Military contractors publicize weapons for national security, for example. Some political interest groups organize peaceful protest marches, such as the March on Washington in 1963, to dramatize widespread support of civil rights activities. Other political interest groups may, however, engage in

violent acts, such as those pursued by extremist groups like the Ku Klux Klan from the end of the Civil War until the 1960s, or by the Weathermen in the 1970s.

Not all attempts to influence public opinion are successful, of course. Publicity campaigns by one group are often challenged by similar campaigns by opposing groups. For example, after the early attempts by advocates of the Equal Rights Amendment succeeded in getting about half of the state legislatures to ratify the amendment within the first year after congressional approval, an opposition formed that was able to slow down and ultimately defeat ratification of that amendment.

Groups not only attempt to influence public opinion but also try to influence the president, the legislature, the judiciary, and political parties. At the national level, groups may urge the president to propose legislation favorable to them or to veto hostile bills. They may request that advisory boards composed of interest group leaders or representatives be consulted before an administrative decision is made.

Because legislative committees play such an important role in the American political system, interest groups concern themselves with the work of committees dealing with policy areas that involve them. Farm groups, consequently, seek to influence the agriculture committees of the House and the Senate. Defense contractors focus their attention on the armed services committees. In some cases, an interest group makes an alliance with a relevant congressional committee and executive agency concerned about a policy area of mutual interest to each. This kind of alliance is known as the **iron triangle,** in which decisions are made in a policy area of mutual concern by a rather self-contained political community.

Groups seek to influence the judiciary, too. They may bring cases before the court in the hope of striking down a law or in interpreting existing law in a dif-

---

[5] Some of the most dramatic evidence showing faith in group participation in the United States is presented in Gabriel A. Almond and Sidney Verba, *The Civic Culture: Political Attitudes and Democracy in Five Nations.* Princeton, N.J.: Princeton University Press, 1963.

ferent way. The NAACP has been active in bringing cases involving racial discrimination before the courts, for example. Some writers suggest that this avenue is used by groups that are unlikely to prevail in Congress, the executive branch, and public opinion.

An interest group may work within political parties. It may try to have its views adopted by the platform committee of the major parties at their national conventions. It may give its support to particular candidates who are friendly to their views. Walter Mondale was endorsed by the AFL-CIO even before the first Democratic primary was conducted in 1984. Union support for his candidacy helped him win the Democratic nomination for the presidency in that year.

Although interest groups may try to influence political parties in the United States, they act differently from political parties in the American political system. An interest group is generally concerned with achieving some specific objective for its members. The principal function of a political party in the United States is, however, to take public office by winning elections. Political parties, consequently, must be more broadly based than interest groups if they are to win votes from the many segments of the electorate. Interest groups are, of course, concerned with influencing political parties by supporting candidates favorable to their objectives, but this is merely a tactic to achieve their aims rather than a design to constitute a government.[6] Although there is a clear difference between interest groups and political parties in the United States, the two associations are more closely tied in Western European political systems. In such systems, a party may solely represent an interest group.

Since interest groups generally have a

stake in the outcome of elections, they often contribute money in electoral contests. In the United States interest groups have formed **political action committees** (PACs) specifically to provide financial support to candidates for public office. These PACs are keen observers of the political behavior of elected public officials in public policy areas of concern to the committees.

PACs "grade" political candidates. A high grade on labor union matters is likely to result in campaign contributions from trade unions. Similarly, business, environmental, and medical PACs are likely to support their "friends." Since candidates need money to conduct campaigns, they are solicitous of PAC endorsements and financial support.

INTEREST GROUPS IN OTHER COUNTRIES

Interest groups are not a unique American phenomenon, and how they organize and behave politically varies from political system to political system. The American political system, with its fragmentation of power among legislative, executive, and judicial branches, and between the national government and the states, furnishes a battleground for interest groups that is quite different from the British political system, for example. British interest groups pay more attention to the executive than to the legislature and, consequently, usually present their cases to cabinet ministers and ministry officials rather than to an ordinary member of Parliament. Unlike the American congressional committees, British parliamentary committees play a very limited role in legislation. British pressure groups, therefore, do not spend their time with these committees.

How political interest groups behave differs in other countries, as well. In Canada and France lobbyists give their attention to the cabinet and bureaucracy rather than to the legislature. The locus of power

---

[6] See Harmon Ziegler and G. Wayne Peak, *Interest Groups in American Society*, 2d ed. (Englewood Cliffs, N.J.: Prentice Hall, 1972), p. 2.

varies from political system to political system. In this context the maxim of Professor Samuel H. Beer is valid: "Where the power is, there the pressure will be."

As indicated above, the relationship between pressure groups and political parties also varies from country to country. Although some groups are associated more with one political party, in the United States most groups tend to be nonpartisan. Some contribute money to both major political parties. American political parties are composed of so many elements that, as one observer has suggested, "they must compromise group interests rather than clearly speak for them."[7] In continental Europe, in contrast, the tendency is for a close association between pressure group and political party, especially in multiparty systems.

Up until this point, our discussion has centered on interest groups in democracies. Because democracies are open societies, the activities of political interest groups are often known and publicly reported. Dictatorships, in contrast, are closed societies, so that much of interest group behavior is unknown or relatively secret. Until recently, scholars tended to ignore interest groups in dictatorships, particularly totalitarian ones. Power was generally portrayed as centralized in dictatorships, with no evidence of the existence of autonomous interest groups. Two prominent scholars of totalitarianism recognize some independent sources of power, such as the churches and the technicians, but refer to them as "islands of separateness."[8]

With the passing of Adolf Hitler and Joseph Stalin and an easing of the harshness of the Cold War, in which Soviet-American relations were marked by confrontation politics, scholars have now concerned themselves with interest group behavior in the Soviet Union.[9] Some of them find that interests are put forward in the Soviet Union to the Communist party leadership and that the clusters of individuals who share common attitudes resemble in many instances the standard definition of an interest group. They note a key exception is that interest groups form differently in the Soviet Union than they do in such Western countries as the United States and Great Britain. Professor H. Gordon Skilling contends that interest groups are not formally organized, but "are more often loose groupings of like-minded or like-interested persons."[10] He and others point to groups such as judges, the secret police, churches, scientists, and the army as clearly identifiable in the Soviet Union and other communist countries. The fact that they are consulted and influence government behavior indicates that some sort of interest group approach may be useful in studying communist political systems. Professor Franklyn Griffiths cites several factors contributing to the rise of interest groups in the Soviet Union: the increased complexity of the economy, internal division in Communist party leadership, withdrawal of terror as a ready instrument of leadership control, and the relative improvement in the international situation of the Soviet Union.[11]

Although many political scientists agree that interest groups exist in dictatorships—even in totalitarian ones—they also

---

[7] Lester W. Milbrath, *The Washington Lobbyists* (Chicago: Rand McNally, 1963), p. 200.

[8] Carl J. Friedrich and Zbigniew K. Brzezinski, *Totalitarian Dictatorship and Autocracy*, 2d ed. rev. by Carl J. Friedrich (New York: Praeger, 1965), chap. 6.

[9] See H. Gordon Skilling and Franklyn Griffiths, eds., *Interest Groups in Soviet Politics* (Princeton, N.J.: Princeton University Press, 1971); H. Gordon Skilling, "Interest Groups and Communist Politics Revisited," *World Politics* 36 (October 1983): 1–27.

[10] H. Gordon Skilling, "Groups in Soviet Politics: Some Hypotheses," in *Interest Groups in Soviet Politics*, p. 29.

[11] Franklyn Griffiths, "A Tendency Analysis of Soviet Policy Making," in ibid., pp. 373–75.

assert that public officials in a democracy are far more vulnerable to interest group pressure than are their counterparts in a dictatorship. Unlike democratic political leaders, dictators can refuse to listen to

"lobbyists."[12] Dictators may also dominate private associations by insisting that group leaders show loyalty to the dictator.

_____

[12] Milbrath, *Washington Lobbyists*, p. 12.

ISSUE

Political leaders frequently blame the "special interests," such as oil companies, armaments manufacturers, or labor unions, for the evils of high prices, war, and inflation. These same leaders call for the pursuit of the public interest. Such clamor gives rise to an important issue of the role of interest groups in society.

19/YES   ARE POLITICAL INTEREST GROUPS DETRIMENTAL TO THE PUBLIC INTEREST?

As in the first section of this chapter, we shall focus our attention on the American experience. We can see, consequently, that political interest groups are harmful to good government. Our case is based on three arguments: (1) interest group power is strongest among the most privileged few in American society; (2) because of interest groups, government officials must respond to narrow interests in opposition to the public interest; and (3) interest groups are inherently undemocratic.

Privileged Few. Interest groups are powerful because they possess resources that allow them to form, lobby, and obtain their objectives. These resources include first and foremost money. Without money, a group cannot even organize, communicate with its members, hire researchers to watch government policies in a particular area, retain the services of high-priced lobbyists, and get its message across to the public.

Realtors, automobile manufacturers, liquor interests, medical doctors, and the oil industry have no difficulty in organizing and articulating interests before appropriate government officials. People of lower economic classes are less likely to participate in politics than are people with higher incomes. Government responds to pressure. The old adage that the wheel that squeaks the loudest gets the grease is applicable to the political process.

When the powerful are faced with economic difficulties, they are strong and rich enough to influence government. The Chrysler Corporation was on the verge of bankruptcy but received government-guaranteed loans that allowed it to stay solvent. Poor farmers facing bankruptcy because of declining agricultural prices and land values do not have the necessary clout to prevent foreclosure of their farms because they are unable to pay their debt. "Street people" exist because they do not have the political talent and financial resources to get government to do for them what it was willing to do for Chrysler—keep it off the street.

Narrow Interests and the Public Interest. The number and variety of interest groups in America have already been described. What has not been stressed, however, is that each of these groups is concerned with its own well-being at the expense of the public interest. Just as the Scottish economist Adam Smith was wrong when he posited a society in which each individual pursuing his own selfish interests would lead to the good of all, so, too, do modern interest group partisans err when they support political interest groups along similar lines.

We can take an issue like inflation as a case in point to see how selfish interests harm the public good. A factor that contributes to inflation is the level of government expenditures and the prices that consumers must pay for goods. The growth of government expenditures has come about largely as a result of pressure group activity. Farm groups have demanded price supports to assure a "fair price" for their agricultural products. The effect of government price supports to farmers was not only to make life better for the farmers, but also to raise the price of farm products for consumers. Business groups asked for government contracts to build such items as federal highways for transportation and military hardware for defense, both of which raised public costs. Environmental groups played their role in contributing to public expenditures by asking for government support to clean up dump sites and purify waterways.

Expenditures such as these contributed in the 1970s to inflationary pressures on the economy—pressures that drove up interest rates, weakened the value of the dollar on foreign exchange markets, increased unemployment, and moved the country into an era of double-digit inflation.

Besides asking for government funds, interest groups sought other objectives that also contributed to inflation. When environmental organizations demanded that gasoline emissions from automobiles be reduced, government responded by mandating auto-emission standards at specified intervals, becoming more stringent over time. The effect of such legislation was to drive up the price of automobiles. When business groups used their influence to have the government establish tariffs to prevent lower-priced goods from competing with American products, they, too, were promoting inflation. When unions insisted that American ships (rather than low-bid foreign carriers) transport American wheat to foreign countries in government foreign-aid programs, that action, too, drove up prices.

The point is not that the goals of a particular private interest group are necessarily harmful. There is much support for many of the actions mentioned on behalf of American business, the poor, and those many people helped from

environmental protection statutes. Rather, the effect of each group pursuing its own selfish interests is to contribute to inflationary pressures that are detrimental to all. Inflation has a deleterious effect on most groups in American society: business, labor, the poor, and environmentalists, for example. Since government is unable to treat the entire problem but must respond to the different constituencies, the public interest is not served. Political leaders are unable to stand up to powerful interest groups and must, consequently, work against the public good.

The evils of interest groups have long been noted. Jean-Jacques Rousseau argued in *The Social Contract* (1762) that the sum of private interests may work against the common good. James Madison criticized factional interests as "adverse to the rights of other citizens or to the permanent and aggregate interests of the community."[13] Walter Lippmann echoed these voices by favoring the public interest, which he defined as "what men would choose if they saw clearly, thought rationally, acted disinterestedly and benevolently."[14]

Critics of the concept of the public interest contend that it is impossible to define. It may be true that the public interest has no *analytical* utility in that it cannot be defined precisely or its influence evaluated properly. It does, however, possess an *ethical* meaning by which actions of individuals, groups, and government officials may be judged.[15] In its ethical sense, the concept may have merit in describing what policy should be according to a moral standard. The phrase *public interest,* then, may be viewed as "a spur to conscience and to deliberation"[16] and is a reminder that the interest of all is not equal to the sum of the interests of each group.

---

[13] James Madison, *Federalist,* no. 10, in Alexander Hamilton, James Madison, and John Jay, *The Federalist Papers,* ed. Clinton Rossiter (New York: New American Library, 1961), p. 78.

[14] Walter Lippmann, *Essays in the Public Philosophy* (Boston: Little, Brown, 1955), p. 42.

[15] See C. W. Cassinelli, "The Public Interest in Political Ethics," in *The Public Interest,* ed. Carl J. Friedrich (New York: Atherton Press, 1962), p. 45.

[16] J. Roland Pennock, "The One and the Many: A Note on the Concept," in ibid., p. 182.

Democracy and Interest Groups. If the strengthening of democracy is a desired goal, then political interest groups may be viewed as weakening that goal. We can support this assertion in three ways: (1) the groups themselves are run in an oligarchic way; (2) the groups are not responsible to the electorate in the same manner as are elected public officials; and (3) the emergence of special interest groups has resulted in a weakening of political parties.

Interest groups, like any large organizations, are run in an oligarchic manner in which only a few rule. Sociologist Robert Michels refers to this development as the **iron law of oligarchy,** in which there are only a few who rule—rather than the masses—in large organizations.[17] Adolf A. Berle, Jr. and Gardiner C. Means describe an example of this phenomenon in the corporate world. They conclude that the managers of corporations are the rulers of those corporations in contrast to the stockholders, who do not participate actively in corporate affairs.[18]

It does not matter whether the organization is a corporation, a trade union, or a professional association. The masses of members do not participate actively in the running of the group. Even public interest groups are ruled in an oligarchic manner. Jeffrey M. Berry, a leading scholar on public interest groups, observes that the staff of these organizations expend significant resources for communicat-

ing to the public interest group members, "but only a minority of the organizations give their members formal opportunities to communicate back." Berry adds that most of these groups do not even go through the "pretense of structuring their organization in a democratic mold so they would at least have the appearance of being open to constituency influence."[19] If public interest groups that are committed to strengthening and extending democracy do not have an adequate mechanism for popular control, then little more can be expected from other associations.

Interest groups undermine democracy in another way. These voluntary associations are not accountable to the public. Public officials deliberate in the open. Their activities and policies are investigated by government agencies, the Congress, and the media. In contrast, private interest groups conduct much of their work in secret. In some cases, they even withhold the lists of their members from government authorities. If government attempts to impose controls on private associations, it subjects itself to the criticism of destroying a free society.

Finally, the rise of interest groups in America has developed as political parties have weakened. What is needed in America to strengthen democracy are strong political parties. The electorate must have an opportunity at election time to choose between different programs offered by competing parties. Interest groups contribute to the fragmentation of the American political process by weakening political parties and so diminishing the significance of the electoral process.

---

[17] Robert Michels, *Political Parties: A Sociological Study of the Oligarchical Tendencies of Modern Democracy* (New York: Free Press, 1962), p. 15. The book was first published in 1911.

[18] Adolf A. Berle, Jr. and Gardiner C. Means, *The Modern Corporation and Private Property* (New York: Macmillan, 1933), chap. 5.

[19] Jeffrey M. Berry, *Lobbying for the People: The Political Behavior of Public Interest Groups* (Princeton, N.J.: Princeton University Press, 1977), p. 210.

19/NO   ARE POLITICAL INTEREST GROUPS DETRIMENTAL TO THE PUBLIC INTEREST?

Political interest groups have too often been described in derogatory terms, such as *pressure boys, influence peddlers,* or *special interests.* An unbiased analysis of their role in

a democratic political system reveals that they are essential to a free society, and that they perform important functions in the political process. Our case is based on three arguments:

(1) interest groups provide representation for all groups, not just the privileged few; (2) to the extent that there is such an identifiable object as the public interest, it is best served through the free play of interest groups seeking to achieve their objectives; and (3) political interest groups are essential for democracy regardless of their internal character.

Representation. American history shows many examples of disadvantaged individuals improving their condition as a result of the formation of interest groups. Poor farmers facing threats from monopolists and the railroads organized groups and successfully fought these powerful interests through government legislation. Labor unions emerged in response to oppressive and arbitrary actions by capitalists to exploit the working class.

If the system is rigged so that only the privileged few benefit, then how can our adversaries account for the major programs of social reform enacted after vigorous opposition by the privileged in American society? Such social reform legislation includes Social Security, worker's compensation, Medicare, minimum wages, welfare assistance to the poor, and government aid to education.

Many of the disadvantaged in American society have surrogates for them who organize interest groups, known as public interest groups. It is they who lobby before government officials on such matters as health care, nutrition, environmental protection, and legal defense. Such organizations do not have the financial resources of their adversaries, but money is not the only component of influence—knowledge and status are important, too. The American Civil Liberties Union, Public Citizen, and Common Cause have had influence in getting government to reflect the interests of the less privileged in society.

Interest Groups and the Public Interest. Many social scientists are skeptical about using the phrase *public interest* or similar concepts such as *national interest* or *public good.* Historian Charles A. Beard studied how the phrase *national interest* has been used in American history and found a close relationship between the claims of special interests

and the definition of the public interest.[20] Political scientist Glendon Schubert concludes much the same in his study of the public interest.[21]

The phrase *public interest* is used by all political interest groups to justify their demands on society. When business groups seek high profits, they argue that it is in the public interest. They support their case by contending that higher profits mean more investment for management, jobs for employees, and dividends for stockholders. When labor unions demand more benefits, or environmentalists ask for greater controls against pollution, or teachers seek better working conditions, or defense contractors urge more government expenditures for national security, they justify their claims by referring to the public interest or to the good of all. There is scarcely any issue that everyone agrees is consistent with the public interest—outside of survival. Even war, which is often supposed to symbolize national unity, finds pacifists and war resisters in opposition.[22]

If anything, the public interest, then, may best be understood not in terms of some identifiable policy prescription but rather as the *process* by which political interest groups are free to compete within the context of democratic procedures, or "rules of the game" as they are sometimes called. Unless a philosopher-king furnishes a universally accepted grand design of a program covering all aspects of life, then what government does is best justified by free group interplay.

Viewed in this light, we can see that political interest groups serve three vital functions in the political process: advice, acquiescence, and approval.[23] Even big government with its large

---

[20] Charles A. Beard and G. H. E. Smith, *The Idea of the National Interest* (New York: Macmillan, 1934).

[21] Glendon Schubert, *The Public Interest: A Critique of the Theory of a Political Concept* (Glencoe, Ill.: Free Press, 1960).

[22] Ziegler and Peak, *Interest Groups in American Society,* p. 21.

[23] For a discussion, see Robert J. Lieber, "Interest Groups and Political Integration: British Entry into Europe," in *Pressure Groups in Britain: A Reader,* ed. Richard Kimber and J. J. Richardson (London: Dent, 1974), p. 28; S. E. Finer, *Anonymous Empire: A Study of the Lobby in Great Britain,* 2d ed. revised

and specialized bureaucracy needs to gather information and advice from interest groups. Any effort to evaluate why a particular type of aircraft crashed requires investigators to question representatives of the airlines and the airframe manufacturers. If government is to have a health program, it must get information about health problems from the medical associations.

Government needs interest groups to acquiesce in programs, moreover. In a free society laws are often obeyed because people feel that the laws are just, not only because of fear of the penalty for violating the laws. If political interest groups are consulted rather than ignored in the framing or administration of the laws, their members are more likely to accept the outcome.

In addition to advice and acquiescence, interest groups are needed for the approval of government decisions. A government that passes laws without taking into account the groups involved may find itself having to cope with strikes, slowdowns, or even sabotage. The police, for example, can show their disapproval of a mayor's action by ticketing violators of the most minor traffic offense for the purpose of creating popular dissatisfaction with the mayor.

We can well imagine the difficulty that government would face in governing without the help of interest groups. The "public interest" would not be served well without these groups actively working in the political arena.

Democracy and Interest Groups. Interest groups are essential to a democracy because they are evidence of a free society, and they are subject to effective political controls. We can argue the case of freedom although we accept the *Affirmative's* contention that there is little democracy *within* interest groups in the sense of mass participation in elections and the overall working of the organization.[24]

The right of groups to form freely is a prerequisite of a free society. In the United States, the legal right is assured by the First Amendment to the Constitution, which forbids Congress from making any law abridging free-dom of speech, press, peaceable assembly, and the right to petition the government for redress of grievances. The courts have properly been hesitant to restrict the right of groups to form so long as they abide by the "rules of the game."

There is another way in which freedom is protected by interest groups. The notion that voluntary associations are legitimate—that is, that any number of individuals displeased with the policies of government may form groups to bring about change—is inherently hostile to the totalitarian ideal. Totalitarianism assumes a uniformity of purpose, an integration of society under some ideology. To the extent that groups are permitted in totalitarian societies, they must be "harmonized" with that ideology, unless in practice they are so powerful as to defy control. In totalitarian systems, interest group leaders are appointed by or controlled by the ruling party. One of the first actions of totalitarian leaders upon coming to power is to destroy the autonomy of interest groups. For example, when the Bolsheviks came to power in Russia in 1917, they sought to make the Russian Orthodox church subservient to the communist regime.

A free polity assumes a distinction between state and society. The practice that groups may arise when necessary and act to change government policy serves as an impediment to totalitarian rule.

We can also argue that interest groups are subjected to a variety of constraints that limit their power. Because of these constraints, groups must act according to democratic practices. There are laws that make it a crime for individuals and groups to bribe public officials to achieve their objectives. To be sure, these rules are violated, but often the violators are subjected to criminal punishment.

In addition to the constraints imposed by law, interest groups are limited by other interest groups and by political parties and elections. Business must confront labor. Environment groups must face business associations. Conflicts such as these give policy makers some discretion in making policy.

Other institutions, such as political parties, must work to aggregate the many interests that are asserted in the political arena, thus limiting the power of any single interest group. Elections continue to make a difference in the outcome of public policies. The interest group beneficiaries in the administration of Ronald

and enlarged (London: Pall Mall Press, 1966), pp. 30–31.

[24] Grant McConnell, *Private Power and American Democracy* (New York: Knopf, 1967), pp. 122–23.

Reagan were different in many cases from the beneficiaries under Jimmy Carter. Interests representing the military, business, and social conservatives were more likely to see their goals realized under Reagan than under Carter. Even with declining political parties, as the presidential election contests of 1980, 1984, and 1988 indicate, elections continue to have significance in an interest-group state. Democracy in America continues to remain strong, consequently.

Although James Madison warned about the dangers of factions, he recognized that factions are inherent in the "nature of man." He realized that factions could not and should not be eliminated. He hoped that the system of American government with its dispersion of power would prevent any one interest or group of interests from controlling American society. The past two centuries have shown Madison to be right.

KEY TERMS

Interest group
Iron law of oligarchy
Iron triangle
Lobbyists
Material incentives
Political action committees
Pressure group

Public interest
Public interest group
Purposive incentives
Single-issue groups
Solidary incentives
Voluntary association

QUESTIONS

1. How would you compare interest groups in democracies with interest groups in dictatorships?
2. How do political interest groups differ from political parties?
3. Do public interest groups serve the public interest? What are the reasons for your answer?

4. What restrictions should be placed on interest groups in a democracy?
5. If there is a public interest, how would you describe it in policy terms?
6. In a democratic society in which interest groups are important, what types of interests are most likely to be unrepresented? What, if anything, can be done to guard against this?

RECOMMENDED READINGS

BERGER, SUZANNE, ed. *Organizing Interests in Western Europe: Pluralism, Corporatism, and the Transformation of Politics.* Cambridge, England: Cambridge University Press, 1981. An analysis of interest groups in Western Europe.

BERRY, JEFFREY M. *Lobbying for the People: The Political Behavior of Public Interest Groups.* Princeton, N.J.: Princeton University Press, 1977. A scholarly account of public interest groups.

CIGLER, ALLAN J., and BURDETT A. LOOMIS, eds. *Interest Group Politics.* 2d ed. Washington, D.C.: CQ Press, 1986. Essays on group politics in the United States.

COCHRAN, CLARKE E. "Political Science and 'The Public Interest.'" *Journal of Politics* 36 (May 1974): 327–55. An evaluation of contemporary theories dealing with the concept of the public interest.

CONGRESSIONAL QUARTERLY, INC. *The Washington Lobbyists.* 5th ed. Washington, D.C.:

CQ Press, 1987. A study of how lobbies operate in Washington.

COXALL, W. N. *Parties and Pressure Groups.* 2d ed. London: Longman, 1986. A study of parties and pressure groups in Britain in the context of their roles in the political system.

ETZIONI, AMITAI. *Capital Corruption: The New Attack on American Democracy.* San Diego, Calif.: Harcourt Brace Jovanovich, 1984. A critique of political action committees.

FALKENHEIM, VICTOR C., ed. *Citizens and Groups in Contemporary China.* Ann Arbor: Center for Chinese Studies, University of Michigan, 1987. Studies of interest groups in China.

FRIEDRICH, CARL J., ed. *The Public Interest.* New York: Atherton Press, 1962. A collection of essays on the public interest.

JORDAN, A. G., and J. J. RICHARDSON. *Government and Pressure Groups in Britain.* Oxford, England: Clarendon Press, 1987. A study of British interest groups.

KEOCHANEK, STANLEY A. *Interest Groups and Development: Business and Politics in Pakistan.* New Delhi, India: Oxford University Press, 1983. A study of modern business associations in Pakistan and their role in the political system.

LIPPMANN, WALTER. *Essays in the Public Philosophy.* Boston: Little, Brown, 1955. An argument that mass democracies have weakened the executive and have exerted influence contrary to the public interest.

MALVERN, PAUL. *Persuaders: Influence Peddling, Lobbying and Political Corruption in Canada.* Toronto: Methuen, 1985. A critical look at Canadian interest groups.

MCCANN, MICHAEL W. *Taking Reform Seriously: Perspectives on Public Interest Liberalism.* Ithaca, N.Y.: Cornell University Press, 1986. An analysis of recent public interest groups.

ODOM, WILLIAM E. "A Dissenting View on the Group Approach to Soviet Politics." *World Politics* 28 (July 1976): 542–67. An argument against the view that interest groups play a role in Soviet politics.

OLSON, MANCUR. *The Rise and Decline of Nations: Economic Growth, Stagflation, and Social Rigidities.* New Haven: Yale University Press, 1982. An explanation of the decline of states in terms of the rise of interest groups.

PERTSCHUK, MICHAEL. *Giant Killers.* New York: W. W. Norton, 1986. An insider's account of public interest lobbying.

RASKIN, MARCUS G. *The Common Good: Its Politics, Policies and Philosophy.* New York: Routledge and Kegan Paul, 1987. A plea for a social reconstruction to preserve the common good.

SCHLOZMAN, KAY LEHMAN, and JOHN T. TIERNEY. *Organized Interests and American Democracy.* New York: Harper and Row, 1986. An evaluation of the role of organized interests in the United States that relies on an analysis of Washington lobbies and other data.

SCHUBERT, GLENDON. *The Public Interest: A Critique of the Theory of a Political Concept.* Glencoe, Ill.: Free Press, 1960. A critique of the concept of the public interest in theories of political behavior.

SKILLING, H. GORDON. "Interest Groups and Communist Politics Revisited." *World Politics* 36 (October 1983): 1–27. An evaluation of the literature on Soviet interest groups.

SKILLING H. GORDON, and FRANKLYN GRIFFITHS, eds. *Interest Groups in Soviet Politics.* Princeton, N.J.: Princeton University Press, 1971. A major work in evaluating the role of interest groups in the Soviet Union.

U.S. CONGRESS, SENATE. *Congress and Pressure Groups: Lobbying in a Modern Democracy.* Committee Print S. Prt. 99–161. Report prepared for the Subcommittee on Intergovernmental Relations of the Committee on Governmental Affairs, 99th Congress, 2d Sess., June 1986. An examination of the role of interest groups and lobbyists in shaping U.S. public policy.

WILSON, FRANK L. *Interest-Group Politics in France.* Cambridge, England: Cambridge University Press, 1987. A study of interest groups in France.

part V

GOVERNMENT INSTITUTIONS

Politics involves the making of public choices. Government is the agency of making those choices (see Chapter 1). How the machinery of government is organized affects the policies of government and the responsiveness of government to different groups and individuals. A government that is structured so that power is fragmented, for example, may make economic and social change difficult to achieve.

For years, as a case in point, the cumbersome process of enacting laws in the United States delayed the realization of civil rights of black Americans. Dilatory tactics of southern legislators in Congress and southern governors in the states impeded change and prevented black people from participating equally in the political process.

How government is organized, then, has an important bearing on political life. The next three chapters deal with some of the major government institutions, how government structure has an impact on public policy, and the character of political systems. First, the relationship between central and regional institutions of government is considered in Chapter 10. Then, Chapter 11 describes the three principal institutions of government: legislatures, executives, and judiciary. Chapter 12 deals with the role of the bureaucracy.

chapter 10

Federalism

In every political system government must have some way to relate its central governing units to smaller territorial divisions of the state. What that relationship is may have an impact on individual freedom, economic and social development, and political stability. Two principal institutional forms that have different links between central and regional governments are federal and unitary systems.

Of the eight largest countries in the world, seven—Argentina, Australia, Brazil, Canada, India, the Soviet Union, and the United States—are organized on a federal basis. Other federal countries are found on every continent and include Austria, Czechoslovakia, the Federal Republic of Germany, Malaysia, Mexico, Nigeria, Switzerland, Venezuela, and Yugoslavia. According to one estimate, nearly 40 percent of the world's population now lives within political systems that are formally federal, while another third lives in

political systems that utilize federal arrangements in some way.[1]

As a concept, the term *federalism* has attained a widespread respectability, not nearly as much as the term *democracy*, but nonetheless significant. Like democracy, federalism is difficult to define. It is derived from the Latin word *foedus*, which means "contract," or "alliance," or "covenant." Throughout past centuries, however, *federal* has been used as a synonym for such words as *national, league,* or *decentralized.* Even in *The Federalist*, a collection of essays by three supporters of the ratification of the U.S. Constitution—John Jay, James Madison, and Alexander Hamilton—the term is used in different connotations.

---

[1] Daniel J. Elazar, "Introduction: Why Federalism?" in *Federalism and Political Integration,* ed. Daniel J. Elazar (Lanham, Md.: University Press of America, 1984), p. 3.

If the past is cloudy about federalism, the present is even more so. Countries with varying political systems are today characterized as federal. From 1922 until the present the Soviet Union has been officially classified as a **federation**—that is, a federal system. The United States, which has a political system quite different from the Soviet Union, is also a federation.

Political scientists, moreover, are as much in disagreement about what constitutes a federal system as are government leaders and the general public. Some observers refer to federal and its related terms even to describe private associations, such as the American Federation of Teachers (AFT) in the United States.

One useful standard definition of **federalism,** however, is a political system organized on a territorial basis in which sovereignty is divided between two units—a central government (sometimes referred to as the national government or the federal government) and regional governments (sometimes known as states, provinces, cantons, republics, or *Länder*)—and in which an individual is a citizen of both. Generally speaking, in a federal system the regional units are fixed and can be changed only with their consent.

Examples of a federal system are plentiful. The United States is composed of fifty states. Canada has ten provinces. The Soviet Union includes fifteen republics. Each, however, has a central government, and the relationship between the central government and its federal units varies considerably from case to case in spite of their federal status.

A federal system may be more clearly understood if compared to two alternative systems of organizing government territorially: a confederation and a unitary system. A **confederation** is a loose association of regional units in which sovereign power is retained by the regional units rather than residing in the central government. The central government has no direct jurisdiction over individuals, consequently. Prior to the adoption of the Constitution, for example, the United States was governed as a confederation. Its constitutional authority was in fact named the Articles of Confederation. In that system states retained sovereignty, and the constitution could be amended only with the unanimous consent of the states. To a considerable extent, the United Nations may be classified as a confederation today, since power and sovereignty are retained by the countries that make up its membership rather than residing in the international organization itself.

In a **unitary system** sovereign power is retained in the central government and regional units are changed at will. All governmental authority is exercised directly over the citizens by the central government, except in those areas of responsibility delegated to regional or local authorities. In unitary systems, the territorial subdivisions are not permanently fixed. In 1974, for example, the British government reorganized the regional governing units, merging some, eliminating others, and enlarging or reducing districts as it deemed appropriate. Such an act is forbidden in the American Constitution as far as states are concerned, and the boundary lines of the states remain intact.[2]

Most of the countries of the world have unitary systems. Unitary governments, moreover, include a variety of political systems, among which are democratic, authoritarian, imperial, and totalitarian forms. In addition to France and Great Britain, countries that have unitary systems are Nicaragua, Zimbabwe, Japan, the

---

[2] One exception is West Virginia. That state was created out of the Commonwealth of Virginia as a Civil War measure and has continued to retain its separate identity.

People's Republic of China, Poland, and many others.

Terms such as *federalism* and *unitary systems* may be difficult to distinguish because all governments have some links with regional units. A unitary system may, in fact, grant power to regional units so that those units have more power than even states or similar political entities possess in federal systems. Some writers contend that whether a unitary system gives power to a regional unit by legislation or whether a central government must share power with a regional unit, both are examples of decentralization—the allocation of power from higher to lower units.

Daniel J. Elazar, a leading scholar on federalism, and others challenge this contention. They point to the major distinction of a federal system: namely, that there is an agreement to share power between central and regional units. In a decentralized system the central authorities may decide to take that power back from a regional unit. In a federal system the central government is impeded from taking power back because of constitutional arrangements. In that sense a federal system is noncentralized rather than decentralized.[3]

FEDERAL SYSTEMS: CHARACTERISTICS

Because of the variety of federal systems extant in the world, it is difficult to use the term *federalism* in a precise manner. Varieties of federal systems are described below. In general, federal systems are characterized by a division of powers, a written constitution, constitutional interpretation, and agreement to share responsibility.

Division of Powers

In any federal system power is divided between a central government and regional governments. In the United States federalism has been perceived to be a system in which certain areas of public policy are dealt with by the national government and others by the states. The national government plays a preponderant role in foreign policy, defense, and interstate commerce. The states have primary responsibility in education, civil and criminal law, police power, and public order. This traditional view has been described in the United States as the doctrine of **dual federalism**—a system in which each sphere, the national and state, has rather distinct powers. According to political scientist David C. Nice, "Dual federalism is a fairly accurate portrayal of the early years of our governmental system, although perhaps not totally accurate."[4] Within the past two centuries, however, the role of the central government has grown with respect to the states, and many of the powers of the national and state governments now overlap and are shared. All that the principle of federalism requires is that there be a division of powers and some guarantee of the autonomy of each government in its own sphere.[5]

Written Constitution

The American federal system, like most federal systems, has a written constitution that sets forth the basic powers of both the central government and the states. To be sure, constitutional development depends not only on the specific state-

---

[3] Daniel J. Elazar, "The Role of Federalism in Political Integration," in *Federalism and Political Integration*, p. 14.

[4] David C. Nice, *Federalism: The Politics of Intergovernmental Relations* (New York: St. Martin's Press, 1987), p. 5.

[5] William H. Riker, *Federalism: Origin, Operation, Significance* (Boston: Little, Brown, 1964), p. 11.

ments of the Constitution but also on statutory laws, judicial interpretation, custom, and political practice; but the fact that there is a written constitution helps to solidify the federal character of the system.

The constitutional stipulations about federalism vary from country to country. The U.S. Constitution specifies the powers belonging to the federal government. The Tenth Amendment provides that those powers not delegated to the central government are reserved to the states or to the people. The Canadian Constitution, in contrast, specifies the powers of the provincial governments, and the residual powers belonging to the national government. A written constitution of a federal system asserts that each governing unit is given permanent recognition.

Constitutional Interpretation

Because in constitutional theory and practice conflicts arise between regional governments and the central government, some institution is essential to act as an umpire. In the United States the Supreme Court has this function. Similar courts exist in other countries.

At certain times the Supreme Court has decided in favor of the national government and at other times in favor of the states. Relying in part upon the national **supremacy clause** of the Constitution that declares that the Constitution, national laws, and treaties "shall be the supreme law of the land," the U.S. Supreme Court has struck down as invalid many state statutes that were in conflict with that clause. In the early period of the American republic, critics of national government supremacy asserted that the states have a right to nullify a national law in conflict with the Constitution. The defeat of the South in the American Civil War settled the matter in favor of the national government.

Agreement to Share Responsibility

Federalism is more than just a legal compact to divide powers. It represents an agreement to share responsibility for governing between national and regional leaders. The U.S. Constitution, for example, offers formal legal devices in which this kind of cooperation is essential, such as in the amendment process (requiring action at the national and state government levels) and in the method of selecting senators by state legislatures (changed to popular election by the Seventeenth Amendment in 1913). The sharing has also become part of the developing historical process as national and state governments work together, often in a cooperative way, to make laws. Matching grants, in which the central government and state governments jointly fund programs in such areas as transportation, health, and education, serve as one example. Many federal government programs, moreover, are administered by state governments.

Political scientist Morton Grodzins points out that most people think of federalism in the United States as a three-layer cake, with national on top, state in the middle, and local at the bottom. A better way to describe the federal government-state government relationship, he argues, is by seeing it as a "marble-cake" pattern, in which the political and legal relationships are so mixed as to make it difficult to clearly distinguish between the responsibility of state and national governments. Thus, any place one "cuts into" the cake, one finds a mixture of powers.[6] Similar sharing occurs in the politics of other federal systems. Such a pattern has been described as **cooperative federalism.**

---

[6] Morton Grodzins, *The American System: A New View of Government in the United States,* ed. Daniel J. Elazar (Chicago: Rand McNally, 1966), pp. 7–10.

FEDERAL SYSTEMS: HISTORICAL EVOLUTION

Federalism is generally regarded as an American invention. Ancient writers did not discuss this concept. Some political scientists date the precursors of federalism back to the ancient Jews, but the early attempts at federalism were more alliances and leagues than true federal systems in the modern sense. In the thirteenth century B.C. the Israelites sought to maintain national unity by linking their several tribes. Ancient Greek city-states established leagues, mostly for purposes of defense. The Achaean League (280–146 B.C.) was one of its notable examples. These, however, were more like confederations than federal systems. So, too, were the leagues of medieval commercial towns in Central Europe, which were established for purposes of military defense. In 1291, the Swiss cantons organized a confederation to promote security. That confederation has gone through many changes and ultimately became, in the nineteenth century, a federation (although it retained the title of Swiss Confederation). Scholars differ about whether or not the Netherlands of the sixteenth century could be called a federal system, although clearly it was not federal in the same sense as the American political system established in Philadelphia in 1787.

The U.S. Constitution was a landmark in the development of federalism. Before the American Revolutionary War broke out, each of the thirteen North American colonies was individually linked to Great Britain. The war for independence required a greater degree of unity, and, consequently, the revolutionary Continental Congress served as an instrument of unity. Members of Congress, however, served as delegates of their states rather than as national legislators.

The weakness of the confederation became apparent in the postwar period. Amendments to its constitution required unanimous agreement by the states. Important legislative matters required the consent of at least nine of the thirteen states. The Articles of Confederation provided for a weak executive and did not establish a federal judiciary. In the important area of national defense, the Confederation Congress was dependent upon the contributions of the states.

The convention called at Philadelphia to revise the Articles of Confederation led to the writing of the Constitution with federal features. This federal form of government, as political scientist Carl J. Friedrich notes, was a "novel, unprecedented concept."[7]

The American practice of federalism influenced other countries concerned with promoting unity while at the same time allowing for some regional autonomy. Canada particularly shows a strong influence from the American system. Its Constitution, which was framed in the British Parliament in 1867, is the eighth oldest of a federal nature. Paradoxically, Great Britain, which has a unitary system, served as one of the principal forces of federalism in the world by encouraging federal systems in its former colonies. In 1901, consequently, Australia was established as a federal system. In 1947, moreover, both India and Pakistan were created as independent countries with federal systems. Other former British colonies to become federal systems were Malaya (later Malaysia), Nigeria, and Cameroon. One notable failure was the British West Indian Federation, which had sought in 1958 to unite within one legal framework the ten British island colonies in the Caribbean. That federation lasted for only four years before it broke up.

The American model also influenced many Latin American countries in the

---

[7] Carl J. Friedrich, *Trends of Federalism in Theory and Practice* (New York: Praeger, 1968), p. 17.

nineteenth century. Argentina, Brazil, Mexico, and Venezuela continue to be federal systems at least in name. Many Latin American federal systems are more nominal than real, however.

In the mid-nineteenth century Switzerland adopted a federal constitution. Today, the Swiss federal system, comprising different ethnic groups, flourishes. About 70 percent of Swiss people speak German, 19 percent speak French, and less than 10 percent speak Italian. The indigenous language, Romansch, is spoken by only a small minority. In the post–World War II period many nations composed of diverse ethnic groups followed the Swiss model in the hope of providing unity amid diversity.

The Constitution of the German Empire of 1871–1918 is sometimes described as federal. Some scholars contend, however, that the overwhelming influence of one of its constituent units—namely, Prussia—was so great as to make Germany a poor example of a federal system.[8] The Austro-Hungarian Constitution of 1867—the Dual Monarchy, or *Ausgleich*— is sometimes cited as an example of a federal system. Under this structure Austria was centralized under German domination and Hungary centralized under Magyar authority. None of the other nationalities in Austria-Hungary, however, had representation. In effect, Austria-Hungary was not really a federal system.

Federal systems have become popular in the post–World War II period. Several countries in Africa and Asia have looked upon the federal system as a mechanism to allow for modernization while at the same time preserving diverse ethnic identities. Federal crises, in which secessionist movements emerged, have revealed, however, that the political form of federalism is not necessarily a sufficiently strong

unifying element. The case of the Biafran civil war in Nigeria in the late 1960s is perhaps the major example of the failure of a federal system. Even in an old established federal system like Canada, the secessionist movement by the French-speaking province of Quebec had significant strength in the 1970s.

The federal idea also has been prominent in the building of international institutions since the end of World War II. The hope has been expressed of using federalism to tie nations into some larger association. The European Community is one illustration. Another example, but one that failed, is the East African Community, linking Kenya, Uganda, and Tanzania. The United Nations may be viewed at least as a confederation. The World Federalists Association (formerly the United World Federalists) supports the idea that the federal principle could be used to unite the nations of the world into a global community in the manner that the thirteen American states became one nation with the establishment of the U.S. Constitution.

FEDERALISM: VARIETY

The character of federal systems varies widely. In fact, federalism is but one form of dividing power along territorial lines. In this respect a unitary system that allows for considerable power to be exercised on a regional or local basis may have more in common with, say, the United States federal system than it does with other unitary countries. Similarly, countries that have federal constitutions may in fact have unitary governments in spite of the federal label.

Federal systems, consequently, vary in terms of the division of powers, the underlying social composition of the federal units, and the degree to which federalism may be sharing nominal rather than real power.

---

[8] Kenneth C. Wheare, *Federal Government*, 4th ed. (New York: Oxford University Press, 1963), p. 50.

Division of Powers

As indicated above, the formal constitutional provisions of federal systems vary. The constitutions of Canada and Australia enumerate powers of the regional governments and reserve power to the central government. In India, in contrast, the powers of both governments are enumerated. How much should belong to the regional units and how much to the central government? That is a question that has been answered in different ways at different times.

In the early part of American history advocates of states' rights argued for at least coordinate state powers. Thomas Jefferson and John C. Calhoun became spokesmen for this point of view. In contrast, John Marshall and Andrew Jackson became leading proponents of national supremacy. The federal government–state government conflicts continue to the present day. Generally, the conflicts are muted in an age of cooperative federalism.

Power can be divided in other ways. In the American and Canadian pattern the major issue has involved the exercise of all components of power—legislative, executive, judicial, and administrative in policy areas—although the sharing of power has become prominent in the twentieth century. In West Germany and Switzerland, however, administrative power is largely in the hands of regional units. Even in these countries, some functions, such as foreign affairs and defense, are handled at the national level.[9]

Social Composition

The districts that separate one regional unit from another may or may not be composed of a fairly homogeneous population. In Canada, the province of Quebec is predominantly French-Canadian. In Switzerland, the cantonal divisions are based principally on ethnic configurations. Switzerland was the first modern federation organized on the need to build on indigenous ethnic and linguistic differences. The federal republics of Yugoslavia are also organized on ethnic lines. India and Nigeria have even reorganized their federal boundary lines to take into account new ethnic demands.

In the United States, however, the "melting pot" ideal, the historic origin of states based on colonial rather than ethnic considerations, and the mobile character of the American people have all contributed to the heterogeneous composition of most states. Certainly, ethnic communities have at times been centered in particular states, such as Chinese in California, Irish in Massachusetts, and Jews in New York; however, no entire state has become as distinct ethnically as, say, Quebec is in Canada.

Nominal or Real?

Scholars of federalism differ about the proper application of the word *federal* to specific countries. Political scientist Kenneth C. Wheare views the United States, Australia, and Switzerland as the best examples of federal systems. Wheare includes Canada with the qualification that the Canadian Constitution is "quasi-federal."[10] He and others, however, perceive the Soviet federal system as a sham. Critics of the Soviet federal system contend that the Soviet Constitution may in fact provide for a federal system, but principal components of such a system—such as an

---

[9] For a comparison of West German and American federal systems, see S. Kenneth Howard, "Similarities and Differences: A Glimpse at How Federalism Is Practiced in West Germany and in the United States," *Planning and Administration* (The Hague) 11 (Autumn 1984):34–42.

[10] Wheare, *Federal Government,* p. 20.

independent judiciary and a real independent regional power as a check upon the authority of the central governing unit (in this case dominated by the central Communist party)—are lacking. The critics' views would be in accord with Marxist theory, which looks at federalism as a temporary expedient in some cases until a unitary communist system can be imposed.[11]

Because of the variation of systems, it might be best to view federalism as a continuum rather than as something precise and fixed. Professor William H. Riker suggests that the range of possibilities between regional and national governments in a federal system may best be described in such a manner. Riker sets as a minimum condition that "the ruler(s) of the federation can make decisions in only one narrowly restricted category of action without obtaining the approval of the rulers of the constituent units." The maximum condition, according to Riker, is that "the ruler(s) of the federation can make decisions without consulting the rulers of the member governments in all but one narrowly restricted category of action."[12]

FEDERALISM: MOTIVATING FACTORS

In the past century an increasing number of countries have adopted federal systems, sometimes by choice of national leaders and at other times under the influence of foreign powers. Federalism arises as a result of a political decision by the ruling elites to establish such a system. Several factors other than political ones have contributed to the establishment of federal states, and these may be best classified as military, economic, historical, ideological, social, and opportunistic.

Military

Professor William H. Riker asserts that federalism "is a bargain between prospective leaders and officials of constituent governments for the purpose of aggregating territory." According to Riker, the parties are predisposed to accept this bargain by "the expansion condition" and "the military condition." By *expansion condition*, Riker means that the politicians want territorial control either to meet an external military or diplomatic threat or to prepare for military or diplomatic aggression and aggrandizement. By *military condition*, Riker refers to the willingness of politicians to give up some of their independence because of the external military threat or opportunity.[13]

The American experience of the eighteenth century is a prime example of military and diplomatic factors playing a role in producing a federal system. Another example is Canada, since some of the Canadian provinces felt compelled to join the Canadian union in 1867 out of fear of an encroaching neighbor from the south.

Economic

Interdependent economies and the expectation of economic benefits contribute to a working federal relationship. The economic difficulties existing in the period immediately after the American Revolutionary War encouraged a federal system that would bring about a healthier economy. The fact that economic factors did not link the units of the short-lived. West Indian Federation in the post–World War II period was a cause of its demise. Lack of economic integration also played a role in the Biafran secessionist movement against the Nigerian federation in

---

[11] For a Soviet view of federalism in theory and practice, see Victor Shevtsov, *The State and Nations in the USSR* (Moscow: Progress Publishers, 1982).

[12] Riker, *Federalism: Origin, Operation, Significance*, pp. 5–6.

[13] Ibid., pp. 12–13.

the 1960s, and in the secession of East Pakistan from Pakistan in 1971.

Historical

A long period of close association among territorial entities is often a contributory factor in enabling federalism to take hold. British colonial rule over the thirteen American colonies for more than a century before the Revolutionary War established a common legal system and a basis for unity. The association of the thirteen states during that war helped to promote a sense of unity. Australia and Canada also had a history of existing territorial units out of which a federal system could be constructed.

Ideological

For federalism to work, there must be a commitment on the part of the leaders of the federation to make it work. Such has been the case with federal countries like the United States and Australia. One scholar, analyzing why four federations in the Third World failed in the post–World War II period, concluded that in all four federations a commitment to the "primary political ideal of federation itself" was lacking.[14]

Social

A federal system can work only if the people who constitute it can get along with each other. In the 1930s there had been talk that an independent federal India could be established. India would, consequently, be composed of many ethnic and religious groups. By 1940, the Muslims, constituting a minority of the Indian subcontinent, rejected a federal solution for India and sought an independent Muslim country, which in 1947 became Pakistan. In cases in which subnational feeling is so strong, federalism will not work. In the United States of the eighteenth century a feeling of such divisive subnationalism did not characterize the individual thirteen states, and a federal arrangement, consequently, became practical.

The Swiss experience is somewhat similar to that of the Americans. When the Swiss federation was established in 1848, the different nationalities of the country already had a long period of alliance or confederation. In the words of Kenneth C. Wheare, "They had come to think of themselves not only as German or French or Italian but also as Swiss."[15]

Opportunistic

As indicated above, many observers contend that the federalism of the Soviet Union is a sham because power is centralized in the ruling Communist party. Federalism is an un-Marxist idea. Neither Karl Marx and Friedrich Engels nor V.I. Lenin favored the federal form of government. Lenin adopted federalism in the hope that the many nationalities would look at communist rule in the Soviet Union as a vehicle of national self-determination rather than side with anticommunist or nationalist forces. He assured the nationalities, moreover, that their republics had the right of secession. That right continues to exist in the Soviet Union although it has never been exercised.[16]

---

[14] Thomas M. Franck, "Why Federations Fail," in *Why Federations Fail: An Inquiry into the Requisites for Successful Federalism*, ed. Thomas M. Frank (New York: New York University Press, 1968), pp. 196–97. For a discussion of the reasons why federations fail and succeed, see Daniel J. Elazar, *Exploring Federalism* (Tuscaloosa, Ala.: University of Alabama Press, 1987), pp. 240–48.

[15] Kenneth C. Wheare, "Federalism and the Making of Nations," in *Federalism: Mature and Emergent*, ed. Arthur W. MacMahon (Garden City, N.Y.: Doubleday, 1955), p. 34.

[16] Ivo D. Duchacek, *Comparative Federalism: The Territorial Dimension of Politics* (New York: Holt, Rinehart and Winston, 1970), pp. 137–38.

Soviet federalism allows for cultural and linguistic heterogeneity within a political system dominated by the centralized rule of the Communist party.[17]

[17] Alexander Shtromas, "The Building of a Multi-National Soviet 'Socialist Federalism': Success and Failures," *Canadian Review of Studies in Nationalism* (Prince Edward Island) 13 (Spring 1986): 79–97.

None of these motivating factors guarantee that a federal system must evolve. The national principle may be more powerful than the federal principle in some cases, and secessionist movements may emerge. Nor is it essential to have all of these factors present before a federal system is constituted. Over the past few centuries, however, these factors have played a role in building federalism in most cases.

ISSUE

The federal system has a modern history of two centuries. Federalism is sometimes seen as a problem and at other times a solution to achieving political order and individual liberty. The debate below considers the pros and cons of federalism.

20/YES IS FEDERALISM BENEFICIAL TO SOCIETY?

The widespread adoption of federalism throughout the world suggests that this institutional device serves a broad range of purposes. Among the most significant benefits of federalism are that it: (1) promotes freedom, (2) helps solve economic and social problems, and (3) strengthens the ability of government to cope with political problems of change and stability.

Freedom. The need to reconcile individual liberty with public order is a central concern of many political thinkers. In the past few centuries the historical record shows that federalism is well suited to encourage human freedom. Central to this view is the notion that individual freedom is strengthened when government power is fragmented. As British political observer James Bryce notes, "Federalism prevents the rise of a despotic central government, absorbing other powers, and menacing the private liberties of the citizen."[18]

In fact, Bryce's fear of despotic central government echoes the views of early supporters of federalism. The Framers of the U.S. Constitution, for example, hailed the establishment of federalism (along with the separation of powers) because they feared a strong, centralized, and despotic government.

A totalitarian system is centralized, and all elements of society are subordinated to the ruling government. A free society is hostile to such a system. A basic element of federalism—division of powers—is inherently opposed to the totalitarian ideal. Nelson Rockefeller, who served as governor of New York State, asserted this point when he noted that the federal idea "is a pluralistic idea. It gives scope to many energies, many beliefs, many initiatives."[19]

Federalism can protect individual liberty even against the attempts of the majority to constrain it. Professor William S. Livingston notes,

[18] James Bryce, *The American Commonwealth*, rev. ed. (New York: Macmillan, 1931), 1:351.

[19] Nelson A. Rockefeller, *The Future of Federalism* (Cambridge, Mass.: Harvard University Press, 1962), p. 9.

"By its very nature federalism is anti-majoritarian."[20] When majorities become tyrannical, they may destroy or weaken liberty. Federalism serves, consequently, as a bulwark of freedom. As forces of centralization in economic and social areas of life become stronger, the regional units can serve as a counter to uniform rule imposed by the central government. If the central government attempts to establish more and more rules over areas of policy previously outside government activity, such as who should be hired for a job, who should be admitted to a university graduate program, who should have access to an individual's private financial information, or what kinds of products can appear on the open market, then the states may serve as bastions of freedom in opposition to the encroachments of "the new despotism," even when the despots are the majority.

In this regard most federal systems have constitutional checks so that mere majorities may be prevented from acting capriciously. In the United States constitutional amendments, requiring ratification by three-fourths of the state legislatures or by special ratifying conventions in three-fourths of the states, serve as one example of a check on national majorities. In Switzerland constitutional amendments must receive a majority not only of total popular votes in a referendum but also a majority approval of the cantons. The power of less populated cantons, consequently, is made disproportionately strong. Such amendment procedures as exist in the United States and Switzerland, therefore, serve as a bulwark of freedom because they protect against the "tyranny of the majority," to use the expression of French political philosopher Alexis de Tocqueville.

Federalism offers real opportunities for protecting individual liberty. If the national government adopts laws, policies, and rulings that impede individual liberty, individuals and groups adversely affected can turn to state institutions for help. In the past many American conservatives championed the cause of states' rights to protect property rights over human rights. American liberals have now begun to see that

states' rights may serve their cause, too.

This may be seen particularly in matters pertaining to the Supreme Court. During the years when the Supreme Court was led by Earl Warren, liberals looked to the Supreme Court to protect political liberties because the Court was making historic liberal decisions. In the conservative Court led by Warren's successor, Warren Burger, liberals could not expect the same kind of rulings. Many liberals, consequently, directed their energies to state courts. Some decisions of the state courts—notably California, Alaska, and Hawaii—have been most supportive of civil liberties.

Economic and Social Problems. The portrait of federalism as a reactionary force in society is inconsistent with the economic and social development of federal states. In practice, federalism has not been made obsolete by modern economic development, nor has it impeded social reform.

It is certainly true that the economies of countries have transcended regional boundaries, but federalism has adapted to changing economic needs. Federal systems, for example, have not let the giant corporations rule at the expense of the rest of society. With the approval of many states, the central government has adopted national institutions to cope with economic development. In the United States a Federal Reserve Board monitors interest rates and influences the money supply.

State boundary lines, moreover, have not inhibited creative patterns of relationships that transcend the state boundary lines. The Tennessee Valley Authority, for example, is a regional enterprise concerned with treating the Tennessee Valley region as an economic and developmental unit. The Port of New York Authority, which was organized to develop not only the New York metropolitan areas but also sections of New Jersey that are really part of the New York port area, is yet another example of creative federalism.[21]

Federalism, then, has not become antiquated because of a changing economy. Nor has it served to inhibit social reform. In the United States the states have not only pioneered in legislation of social reform, such

---

[20] William S. Livingston, *Federalism and Constitutional Change* (Oxford, England: Clarendon Press, 1956), p. 310.

[21] Since 1972 the agency has been known as the Port Authority of New York and New Jersey.

as child labor and workmen's compensation laws, but have also demonstrated that they are willing to raise the money for welfare programs. Much of state revenues is devoted to the welfare sector—particularly education, welfare assistance to the poor, health, and housing.

Former Canadian Prime Minister Pierre Trudeau contends that federalism is consistent with socialism, which, to some observers at least, is synonymous with social reform. Coming from French-speaking Quebec province, he strongly opposed the movement toward Quebec secessionism. He argued even before he was prime minister that federalism should be "welcomed as a valuable tool which permits dynamic parties to plant socialist governments in certain provinces, from which the seed of radicalism can slowly spread."[22] For Trudeau, each province of Canada is not at the same stage of social development, and federalism could allow for change at the proper time. The fact that the states in the American union responded to social reform programs at different times supports Trudeau's assessment and, consequently, demonstrates the vitality of federalism in our time.

Political Problems. Federalism is ideally suited to cope with political problems of change and stability. James Bryce was one among many writers who saw the political benefits of the federal principle. Two major points he made in this connection are: (1) federalism allows for experimentation on a limited scale before a new program is adopted nationally; and (2) federalism minimizes the risks involved in any political system.

With respect to experimentation, states have been in the forefront of the movement toward social reform. As Bryce asserts, "Federalism enables a people to try experiments in legislation and administration which would not be safely tried in a large centralized country."[23]

Many examples illustrate this point. About a half century before American women were given the right to vote in national elections in 1920, the state of Wyoming became the first state to enact women's suffrage. Before the Twenty-sixth Amendment reduced the voting age to eighteen, Georgia had allowed eighteen-year-olds to vote. In the United States, government inspection of factories appeared first in Massachusetts in 1879, old age pensions originated in Alaska in 1915 even before it was a separate state, child labor legislation started in Massachusetts as early as 1842, and unemployment insurance began in Wisconsin in 1932.[24] Many of the New Deal programs, moreover, had their experimental origins in the period in which Franklin D. Roosevelt was governor of New York. Many lessons were learned from these state programs, which helped to improve legislation when finally enacted on the national level. Bryce observes that a state finds it easier than the central government to make laws and correct mistakes. A state also finds it profitable to observe the outcome of laws of an experimental nature.[25]

In addition to the benefits of experimentation, federalism minimizes risks in the governance of a large and diverse nation. Bryce compares federalism to a ship built with watertight compartments: "When a leak is sprung in one compartment, the cargo stored there may be damaged, but the other compartments remain dry and keep the ship afloat." So, too, does federalism prevent social discord from "tainting the nation at large."[26]

If the United States had a unitary system, many of the policies currently decided on the state and local level would become national issues. Educational matters would, consequently, be decided in Washington rather than in the states. Some of the more volatile issues, such as which textbooks should be used in the schools, could easily become national points of contention, dividing religious and ethnic groups. These issues could, consequently, cause serious discord on a national level in a way they do not on a state level. By taking the pressure off Washington, conflict may occur at the state level and act in the way described by Bryce to keep the ship afloat.

---
[22] Pierre Elliott Trudeau, *Federalism and the French Canadians,* introd. John T. Saywell (New York: St. Martin's Press, 1968), p. 127.

[23] Bryce, *American Commonwealth,* 1:353.

---
[24] Rockefeller, *Future of Federalism,* p. 16.

[25] Bryce, *American Commonwealth,* 1:353.

[26] Ibid.

20/NO   IS FEDERALISM BENEFICIAL TO SOCIETY?

The arguments for federalism on the grounds of freedom, economic and social change, and political consequences are without foundation. Closer evaluation of federalism reveals that these goals are better attained in unitary systems.

Freedom. The notion that federalism is essential to freedom is based on two false assumptions: (1) that federalism promotes weak government, and weak government leads to freedom; and (2) that the central government is more dangerous to liberty than are regional units.

Those who support the first assertion, that weak government promotes freedom, ignore the lessons of history. The British system of government with its unitary structure has a better record on the protection of civil liberties than does the federal United States. Latin American countries that adopted federal systems in the nineteenth and twentieth centuries succumbed in many cases to dictatorships rather than serving as protectors of freedom. The federal system of pre-Hitler Weimar Germany, moreover, did not function as a bulwark of freedom. Instead, Hitler was able to use one of the states—Bavaria—to gain a foothold for nazism in Germany. V. I. Lenin's acceptance of federalism in the Soviet Union was tactical and did not promote freedom in his time and certainly not in the days of his successor, Joseph Stalin.

The second false assumption is that the central government is more dangerous to liberty than are the regional units. In the words of one political scientist, "Sin is no monopoly of the center and virtue no monopoly of the localities."[27] Long after a national majority sought to remove the barriers of racial discrimination and segregation in the United States, it was frustrated because of the acts of regional majorities in the states. For years, segregationists who oppressed black people

were the principal beneficiaries of federalism. Were it not for the acts of the national government in protecting blacks to obtain their rights to vote and to participate in a racially integrated America, freedom would have been thwarted.

Federalism may, in fact, have protected some minorities in Canada, most notably the French Canadians. In the past, however, it has been of little benefit to the Chinese in British Columbia, Hutterites in Alberta, or Jehovah's Witnesses in Quebec. When these groups were unpopular, the provincial governments were more supportive of hostile sentiments directed against them than was the central government in Ottawa. "Had Canada been a unitary state," writes political scientist Garth Stevenson, "these groups might have benefited."[28]

Regional units have often impeded liberty in other matters through censorship of books and films, through the banning of peaceful protest meetings, and through the denial of academic freedom. Professor Franz L. Neumann is correct when he comments that "the federal system may have speeded up inroads into the civil liberties of the United States rather than have protected them."[29]

One additional point about human freedom should be made. Those who argue that federalism promotes freedom because regional governments and the central government check each other often assume that each will restrain the other's authority in public policy areas. In fact, however, the pattern in federations, such as exist in the United States, Canada, Australia, and Switzerland, is such that *both* the central and regional authorities are expanding their power. The liberty of ordinary citizens is the victim of increased government authority.

The record of the many areas of encroachment is generally known. States have enlarged

---

[27] Leslie Lipson, *The Great Issues of Politics: An Introduction to Politics*, 4th ed. (Englewood Cliffs, N.J.: Prentice Hall, 1970), p. 319.

[28] Garth Stevenson, *Unfulfilled Union: Canadian Federalism and National Unity*, rev. ed. (Toronto: Gage, 1982), p. 17.

[29] Franz L. Neumann, "Federalism and Freedom: A Critique," in *Federalism: Mature and Emergent*, p. 48.

their taxing power. Regulation at the state level has brought with it an army of state bureaucrats inspecting labor codes, building regulations, banks, hospitals, schools, businesses, and even private clubs. The argument that federalism will protect freedom is false in view of the expansion of government power at both the state and national levels.

Economic and Social Problems. At a less complex period in the economic and social development of nations, the federal ideal was useful in coping with the major problems of society. In the age of capitalism weak government allowed for creative energy of entrepreneurs to utilize their skills for industrial development. Even Karl Marx approved of the resourcefulness of the capitalists (although not of the social chaos they produced) who went everywhere in the world in quest of profits.

In the twentieth century, however, federalism is more than irrelevant; it is an obstacle to economic and social progress. Let us look first at economic considerations.

The economic problems of the world have become more complex than in earlier centuries. As the preindustrial era has given way to industrial and postindustrial times, the arbitrary boundary lines that were used to set up regional political entities in federal systems have ceased to have any practical economic significance. In the United States, for example, the Tennessee Valley is located in several states, and it is impossible to solve developmental problems in that area without transcending the state boundaries. Similarly, as a national economy has expanded, so, too, has the need for a *national* transportation system. If each state or province engages in planning exclusively along regional boundary lines, then the needs of a modern economy will not be served.

In this context British socialist Harold J. Laski is one of the foremost critics of federalism, and his views reflect a classical criticism based on economic considerations. According to Laski, federalism is "a luxury" in modern industrial society. Laski criticizes its weaknesses: It is insufficiently positive in character; it does not allow for rapid enough action; it inhibits the emergence of necessary standards of uniformity; it requires too many compro-

mises that waste time; and it is reactionary.[30]

Laski's criticism, written in 1939, remains valid today. How can federalism cope with an organization like General Motors, with its many divisions scattered not only throughout the United States but overseas as well, and with its revenues in excess of those of most governments of the world? It can be seen that federalism cannot deal effectively with the problems of a complex capitalism, such as unemployment and economic growth. Only a unitary system with a strong central government can handle giant industry.

The very character of the economy has brought with it many changes. In advanced economies, markets have become national—even global. Communication and transportation systems span continents. Even the labor force is no longer regional. Fifty individual states in the United States or ten provinces in Canada are not structured to solve the needs of such economies.

In addition to being obsolete in dealing with economic matters, federalism inhibits the search for solutions to the major social problems afflicting modern societies. The welfare state—with its demand for greater government involvement in health, education, and housing—has been adopted in nearly every country in the world. Regional institutions are incapable of coping with the clamor for an ever-greater capacity and will to impose sufficient taxes to finance the welfare state.

In matters of economic and social reform, the national government in the United States has made notable achievements through legislation such as the Clayton Antitrust Act of 1914, the La Follette Seamen's Act of 1915, the Civilian Conservation Corps Act of 1933, the National Labor Relations Act of 1935, the Social Security Act of 1935, and the Fair Labor Standards Act of 1938. As historian Henry Steele Commager notes, "These laws did more to establish social justice than the whole corpus of state labor legislation since the Civil War."[31]

Environmental problems, too, have required

---

[30] Harold J. Laski, "The Obsolescence of Federalism," *New Republic* 98 (May 3, 1939): 367.

[31] Henry Steele Commager, "Tocqueville's Mistake," *Harper's*, 269 (August 1984): 73.

national solutions. The Mississippi River runs through several states, and problems of pollution require national rather than state action in keeping that body of water clean. Corporations manufacturing insecticides, moreover, are national in scope, and only the resources of the government in Washington are sufficiently strong to regulate the chemical industry and its far-ranging empire. The awareness of the need for a strong central government is seen everywhere. In the Federal Republic of Germany, the Constitution has been altered to give the central government more powers to legislate and supervise ecological matters. We can see, then, the irrelevance of federalism.

Political Problems. Federalism generates political problems, most notably problems of centralization, experimentation, and accountability. Federalism has not served as a barrier to centralized government either in dictatorships or in democracies. In the Soviet Union, the federal system established by Lenin remains federal in name only, since power is in the hands of the ruling Communist party. Even in democracies, the power of the central governments has grown with respect to regional governments in nearly every federal system. Policy previously thought to be within the exclusive jurisdiction of the regional governments, such as education and transportation, has now become strongly influenced by the center.

In the United States the central government has threatened to use its power to withhold funds from states that do not comply with equal opportunity employment laws in order to force adherence to national standards on the hiring of women and minority group members. State control over transportation policy, moreover, has been influenced in a somewhat similar manner. When some state legislatures in the United States sought to increase a nationally imposed automobile speed limit of 55 miles per hour, national transportation authorities threatened to cut off highway funds, the loss of which would be a severe blow to highway construction. The state legislatures, consequently, backed away from their intended confrontation with the central government in the interest of economics and retained the 55-mph speed limit. They hoped, however, that Congress would enact legislation allowing

them to raise the speed limit, which it ultimately did in 1987 for rural areas.

What is true for centralization in the United States is true for nearly all federal systems. Even the Confederacy of the southern states, which went to war in 1861 on the issue of states' rights, centralized powers in the Confederate central government at the expense of the states. Federalism scholar S. Rufus Davis insightfully describes the emergence of the central government in federal systems "as leader, financier, director, promoter, coordinator, guide, stimulator, pacifier, aggressor, pace-setter, equalizer; the most prestigious, the most influential, the political superior and most effective manipulator of all the parts, singly or collectively."[32]

The increased powers of the center can be seen in many ways. The status of national figures is generally higher than that of regional leaders. Media attention is directed more to national than to regional matters. In free societies, more people vote in national than in regional elections. The irresistible move toward centralization is clear in nearly every political system.

Supporters of federalism, moreover, make too much of a claim for the role of experimentation and risk limitation in federal systems to meet the needs of diversity in large and complex societies. The advantages of experimentation and risk limitation are not exclusive to federal systems. Unitary systems allow for diversity, too. In Great Britain, for example, a long tradition of local self-government allows for initiative and variation by local authorities. The powers given to a Northern Ireland parliament between 1920 and 1972 also served to decentralize power to allow for regional decision making. Special provisions in Parliament for Scottish and Welsh affairs also allow recognition of the different "nations" that constitute the United Kingdom.

Since unitary systems can support diversity and autonomy, the merits of federalism in this regard are not noteworthy. The crucial point for diversity, as William H. Riker observes, has much to do with whether or not local officials are elected by or are in some other way re-

---

[32] S. Rufus Davis, *The Federal Principle: A Journey through Time in Quest of Meaning* (Berkeley: University of California Press, 1978), p. 148.

sponsive to local citizens. Federalism, consequently, hardly makes any difference in the way people are governed.[33]

Finally, federalism poses problems of accountability in a democracy. The American federal system offers an example. In an era of cooperative federalism, where the relationships among national, state, and local institutions are so complex, it is often difficult to hold accountable public officials at different levels.

Today, national and state governments play important roles in education, health, safety in the workplace, public welfare assistance, and environmental protection. The ordinary citizen cannot know whom to hold accountable for government actions. Democracy requires accountability so that citizens can make rational judgments at election time. With power fragmented in a federal system, however, an important support of democratic rule is undermined.

Too much has been made of federalism. In sum, federalism has been a threat to freedom, inhibited economic development and social reform, and created unnecessary political problems.

---

[33] William H. Riker, "Six Books in Search of a Subject, or Does Federalism Exist and Does It Matter?" *Comparative Politics* 2 (October 1969): 139, 145.

KEY TERMS

Confederation

Cooperative federalism

Dual federalism

Federalism

Federation

Supremacy clause

Unitary system

QUESTIONS

1. Which is closer to the people: the regional governments or the national government? What are the reasons for your answer?

2. If the United States had adopted a unitary system of government in 1787, how would its history have been different?

3. Can a dictatorship have a federal system? What are the reasons for your answer?

4. What effect does federalism have on economic development?

5. Is federalism a stepping stone to world peace? Why?

6. Would a federal solution help in solving problems posed by ethnic and religious differences, such as in Northern Ireland, Israel, and Lebanon? Why?

RECOMMENDED READINGS

AMLUND, CURTIS ARTHUR. *Federalism in the Southern Confederacy.* Washington, D.C.: Public Affairs Press, 1966. An argument that during the course of the American Civil War, the Confederate government resembled the federal system of the Union.

BERGER, RAOUL. *Federalism: The Founders' Design.* Norman, Okla.: University of Okla-

homa Press, 1987. An examination of the Founding Fathers' intent by a legal scholar.

BOWMAN, ANN O'M., and RICHARD C. KEARNEY. *The Resurgence of the States.* Englewood Cliffs, N.J.: Prentice Hall, 1986. An argument that the states are responsive, responsible, and progressive political actors in this scheme of U.S. federalism and intergovernmental relations.

BRYCE, JAMES. *The American Commonwealth.* Rev. ed. New York: Macmillan, 1931. Vol. 1. An analysis of federalism in the United States.

BURGESS, MICHAEL, ed. *Federalism and Federation in Western Europe.* London: Croom Helm, 1986. A study of European federations.

COMMAGER, HENRY STEELE. "Tocqueville's Mistake," *Harper's* 269 (August 1984): 70–74. A defense of a strong central government.

DAS, HARI HARA, and SANJUKTA MOHAPATRA. *Centre-State Relations in India: A Study of Sub-National Aspirations.* New Delhi, India: Ashish Publishing House, 1986. An analysis of federalism in India.

DAVIS, S. RUFUS. *The Federal Principle: A Journey through Time in Quest of Meaning.* Berkeley: University of California Press, 1978. A historical treatment of federalism with an evaluation of its etymological, theoretical, and empirical merits.

ELAZAR, DANIEL J. *Exploring Federalism.* Tuscaloosa, Ala.: University of Alabama Press, 1987. A comprehensive analysis of federalism.

———, ed. *Federalism and Political Integration.* Lanham, Md.: University Press of America, 1984. Articles on the role of federalism in political integration throughout the world.

LASKI, HAROLD J. "The Obsolescence of Federalism." *New Republic* 98 (May 3, 1939): 367–69. A critique of federalism.

LIVINGSTON, WILLIAM S. *Federalism and Constitutional Change.* Oxford, England: Clarendon Press, 1956. A study of the process in which the diversified elements that compose a federal state integrate and compromise their differences.

MADDOX, GRAHAM. *Australian Democracy: In Theory and Practice.* Melbourne, Australia: Longman Cheshire, 1985. Chapters 4 and 5 discuss federalism in Australia.

MATHESON, SCOTT M., with JAMES EDWIN KEE. *Out of Balance.* Salt Lake City: Gibbs M. Smith, 1986. A description of the role of the states in the United States by the governor of Utah.

MORLEY, FELIX. *Freedom and Federalism.* Chicago: Henry Regnery, 1959. An assessment of the impact of centralized government on individual liberty.

NICE, DAVID C. *Federalism: The Politics of Intergovernmental Relations.* New York: St. Martin's Press, 1987. An explanation of the various relationships among the national, state, and local governments in the United States and the issues that both reflect and give rise to those relationships.

PIRZADA, SHAZIAE. "Federalism in the USSR: The Central Asian Context." *Strategic Studies* (Islamabad) 10 (Winter 1987): 67–94. An assessment of federalism in the Soviet Union with particular attention to the Central Asian republics.

RIKER, WILLIAM H. *Federalism: Origin, Operation, Significance.* Boston: Little, Brown, 1964. A major work on federalism.

———. "Six Books in Search of a Subject, or Does Federalism Exist and Does It Matter?" *Comparative Politics* 2 (October 1969): 135–46. The author answers, "Hardly at all."

SHAFRUDDIN, B. H. *The Federal Factor in the Government and Politics of Peninsula Malaysia.* New York: Oxford University Press, 1987. A study of federalism in Peninsula Malaysia.

SHTROMAS, ALEXANDER. "The Building of a Multi-National Soviet 'Socialist Federalism': Success and Failures." *Canadian Review of Studies in Nationalism* (Prince Edward Island) 13 (Spring 1986): 79–97. An analysis of the strengths and weaknesses of the Soviet Union's effort to deal with nationalities through federalism.

SMITH, B. C. *Decentralization: The Territorial Dimension of the State.* London: Allen and Unwin, 1985. A study of the political choices made when decentralization occurs.

VERNEY, DOUGLAS V. *Three Civilizations, Two Cultures, One State: Canada's Political Traditions.* Durham, N.C.: Duke University Press, 1986. A study of the evolution of the Canadian political system.

WHEARE, KENNETH C. *Federal Government.* 4th ed. New York: Oxford University Press, 1963. A classic work surveying federal systems in Australia, Canada, Switzerland, and the United States.

chapter 11

Parliamentary and presidential systems

With the principal exceptions of anarchists and libertarians, most people today accept the inevitability of the state—and particularly government—in any modern complex society. Even Adam Smith, the advocate of a *laissez-faire* philosophy, regarded government to be essential in satisfying at least the minimum needs of national security and police protection. Modern liberals, socialists, and communists clearly accept the existence of government, although they differ about what it should do.

Given the widespread acceptance of government, one problem has been how it should be organized. Those who hold the view that government can be a force for good, which can promote economic prosperity, maintain national security, and provide the benefits of the welfare state, have tended to support a centralized institutional device capable of allowing government leaders to achieve those goals easily. The political systems of Great Britain and the Soviet Union, although differing enormously, are similar in at least one respect: They are both organized to allow for centralized governmental control.

Not everyone, however, is certain that government should be organized in a centralized manner. Even among those who accept the necessity of government, there are many who fear that a government in which power is too centralized can be both dangerous to individual liberty and responsible for policies that are either poorly conceived or unnecessary.

The American political system was founded on the principle that government is dangerous to individual liberty. Based on the theories of the French philosopher Baron de Montesquieu, it adopted an institutional structure in which power was divided not only at the national level among different units of government but also at the regional level between national and regional governments.[1]

Since Montesquieu's formulations in the eighteenth century, many writers have used his classifications of government into legislative, executive, and judicial power to describe the organization of government. In this categorization, legislative power is the making of laws, executive is the implementation of laws, and judicial is the interpretation of laws, or the determination of whether or not acts of governments or individuals are in compliance with the laws.

Since the eighteenth century, distinctions have been made between legislative, executive, and judicial *functions* and the formal *institutions* of government that were set up ostensibly to pursue those functions. Although in theory, legislatures carry out legislative functions; executives, executive functions; and the judiciary, judicial functions; often each of these institutions performs not only its traditional functions but also roles normally attributed to the other branches of government. As we shall see, for example, when in the United States the judicial branch—the U.S. Supreme Court—declares a statute duly enacted by Congress to be unconstitutional, it is in fact performing a legislative function. Because of the ways in which institutions have developed, some scholars use terms other than *legislative, executive,* and *judicial* to describe functions of government. They prefer, for example, to speak of *rule-making, rule-application,* and *rule-adjudication,*[2] terms that allow them to classify government functions and institutions in a more intelligible manner. We shall use the traditional classification of executive, legislative, and judicial, however, since these provide a more familiar basis of understanding government organization.

LEGISLATURES

Legislatures are representative assemblies that enact laws. Not all legislatures are powerful institutions in law making; some are mere showcase institutions without any actual power in public policy. As we shall see, legislatures perform functions other than law making.

Legislatures are known by different names in different countries. In the United States the legislature is known as Congress; in Great Britain, it is Parliament. Senate, Diet, Assembly, Supreme Soviet, and Knesset are also used in different countries to signify legislative bodies.

Organization

Legislatures are either **unicameral** (one chamber) as in Finland, Sweden, and Norway; or **bicameral** (two chambers), as in the United States, Great Britain, and West Germany. In bicameral legislatures, the first, or lower, chamber consists of popularly elected representatives. The second, or upper, chamber often consists of representatives who may be chosen by popular vote or selected on the basis of other considerations, such as geography, birth, or economic classification. United States senators are elected by direct popular vote, but until 1913 they were chosen by the state legislatures. The British House of Lords has been constituted primarily on the basis of inherited rank. Fascist Italy organized its legislature according to economic classifications.

Legislatures are generally too large to conduct the vast amount of government business before all their members. They carry on legislative tasks through committees, consequently. In some countries **standing committees** serve as permanent

---

[1] The division of powers between national and regional governments is discussed in Chapter 10.

[2] See particularly Gabriel A. Almond and G. Bingham Powell, Jr., *Comparative Politics: A Developmental Approach* (Boston: Little, Brown, 1966), chap. 6.

committees that handle specialized matters for the term of the legislature. In this connection an appropriations committee investigates matters involving government spending, and a foreign affairs committee considers legislation pertaining to international relations, for example. These committees can play an important role in the political process. In other countries standing committees are not differentiated according to function and consider any measure sent to them from the point of view of technical legal correctness. Still another form of committee is the **select committee,** which is a temporary committee that handles one problem and then disbands. **Joint committees** are found in bicameral systems and include members from each chamber. A **conference committee** is a committee composed of legislators from different legislative chambers, which adjusts differences on a particular bill.

The committee system is one manner in which a legislature is organized. Still another is by political party (see Chapter 8). In some legislatures party organization is strong, which means that the party members in the legislature generally vote along party lines on important issues. A political party may be strong enough to prevent legislators from securing renomination for election on their party labels if they vote against legislation proposed by their parties, and such discipline helps party unity. In other legislative systems parties are weak, and the legislators are dependent upon their home constituencies rather than on the central party organization for their renomination on the party labels. Great Britain is an example of a strong and centralized party system. The United States is an example of a weak and decentralized party system. In some countries, such as Italy and France throughout most of their modern history, moreover, the legislature is composed of many party groupings. Great Britain and

the United States, in contrast, each have two dominant parties.

Origins

Legislative institutions existed in ancient Greece and Rome. They evolved gradually in the medieval period out of the advisers to the monarch. Great Britain, the Mother of Parliaments, experienced the gradual development of representative legislatures. As early as the thirteenth century the king relied on representatives from the different estates—nobility, the church, and the burgesses (townsmen)—to provide advice and to furnish money. For the most part European legislatures slowly grew in power at the expense of the ruling monarch. At first, legislative chambers were organized and dominated by the landed aristocracy, but gradually their power was diminished by representatives chosen first by the middle classes and later by all elements of society.

Functions

Because the power of legislatures differs greatly throughout the world, it is difficult to generalize about them. Historically, however, the major functions of legislatures have been to make laws, to tax and spend money, to debate issues, to oversee administration, to legitimize the rules that a government proclaims, and to recruit political leaders of government and socialize political elites. Some legislatures are powerful and perform all or most of these functions; some are weak and perform a few of these functions; and others are mere window dressing and perform none of these functions.

Legislation. Legislatures today as in the past deal with **legislation**—laws that are binding on the community. In the nineteenth century legislatures played a forceful role in introducing proposals for legislative action (**bills**). In many countries today bills are prepared in the executive branch of government, although they may be formally introduced in the legislature.

Taxes. A major function of legislatures is to authorize the raising of taxes and the appropriation of money. Most laws are not self-implementing but need government agencies to carry them out. Consequently, if a legislature decides to destroy a government program, it can reduce or deny appropriations to it. Historically, the principle that parliamentary approval is essential in order for the executive to tax goes back to the Magna Carta (1215).

Debate. One important role of legislatures is to serve as a forum where issues are debated publicly. According to the liberal English philosopher John Stuart Mill, Parliament is "at once the nation's Committee of Grievances and its Congress of Opinions" through which every segment of society and every eminent individual it contains can argue a point of view.[3] In Great Britain the principle that public debate is essential in a free society is a fundamental component of the political system. It is institutionalized through the establishment of the loyal opposition in which the minority in Parliament is recognized as having the duty to oppose the government without fear that its opposition will be regarded as subversion. One of the major advances of a free society was the creation of a **loyal opposition** —a group of minority-party members whose criticism of the government was regarded as legitimate rather than as an act of treason.

Administration. Legislators play a role in overseeing the administration of gov-

ernment. They may conduct formal investigations of the behavior of particular government agencies to make certain that these agencies are carrying out the laws in the manner prescribed by the legislature. For example, a special congressional committee was formed in 1987 to investigate the actions of officials during the administration of Ronald Reagan who sold arms to Iran in exchange for the release of U.S. hostages held captive in Beirut and used profits from the sales to finance guerrilla forces (or Contras, as they are called) fighting against the Marxist government in Nicaragua.

In Great Britain the **Question Hour** is the formal device by which cabinet members are asked questions directly by members of Parliament about any matter pertaining to the conduct of government. The ability of a cabinet member to respond intelligently and forcefully to the questions contributes to the reputation of the member within his or her party.

To oversee government agencies some legislators have designated an **ombudsman**—an official whose job is to make certain that government officials apply the law and regulations as legislatively prescribed. The ombudsman conducts investigations of public officials when complaints are made by citizens. Although originated in Sweden, the office of ombudsman has been established in other countries, including Norway, Denmark, and Israel.

Legitimization. A major function of a legislature is to legitimize the rules of a society. Legislatures are regarded as institutions that in some manner represent the people of a political system. John Stuart Mill commented on the legitimizing function in observing that when Parliament allows all diverse points of view to be expressed, those whose opinion is overruled shall "feel satisfied that it is heard, and set aside not by a mere act of will, but for what are thought superior

---

[3] John Stuart Mill, *Representative Government*, in his *Utilitarianism, Liberty and Representative Government* (New York: Dutton, 1951), p. 321. The book was originally published in 1861.

reasons, and commend themselves as such to the representatives of the majority of the nation."[4]

As mentioned above, some legislatures may in reality have no power and serve as mere showcases. The fact that many dictatorships establish powerless legislatures with representatives from different regions, classes, religions, and racial groupings reveals the legitimizing role of legislative institutions that nearly every government attempts to secure.[5]

Political Recruitment and Socialization of Political Elites. Legislatures serve to recruit leaders for membership in the political elite of the nation and to socialize them into the political system. In some political systems executives frequently consult with legislators and make concessions to them in order to get support.

Legislators, moreover, have been a source of candidates for executive office. Such is the case in the United States today, but it has also been true for Chile and the Philippines in the past. John F. Kennedy and Lyndon Johnson served as senators and established national reputations for their work in the Senate before they became president. Chile's last three freely elected presidents—Salvador Allende, Eduardo Frei, and Jorge Alessandri—were senators before they became president. In the Philippines every president except three has risen to that position from the senate.[6]

In addition to recruiting new members into the political elite, legislatures play a role in socializing the political elite. Legislatures often become a place where members acquire shared political values

and institutional attachments. When such attachments are strong, legislators manage conflict through government bargaining so as to prevent or minimize violence in the nation. The effect of such cooperative efforts is to strengthen political stability. Not all legislators, however, develop such shared values, and legislatures may become institutions in which conflict is heightened.

Other. Legislatures may act as courts and try officials for misconduct in office. In the United States, for example, the House of Representatives has the responsibility for **impeachment,** which is an indictment of high officials for malfeasance in office; and the Senate actually tries the official if he or she is impeached. In some systems, moreover, legislatures appoint the chief executive. How extensive and diverse are the powers of the legislature depend on tradition and political relationships underlying different political systems.

EXECUTIVES

The executive branch of government consists of an individual or small group. It, too, is known by different names in different countries. In the United States the executive is known as the president. In other countries the titles include king, prime minister, premier, president, chancellor, and even emperor.

Organization

A major distinction in the organization of executives is between chief of state and head of government. A **chief of state** is usually a figurehead or ceremonial leader—someone who symbolizes the nation. Usually, this person exercises no major political power, although on occasions he or she may play some role. In Great Britain, Holland, and Sweden, the king or queen is the chief of state. In other

---

[4] Ibid.

[5] For a study of the relationship between legislatures and political stability, see William Mishler and Anne Hildreth, "Legislatures and Political Stability: An Exploratory Analysis," *Journal of Politics* 46 (February 1984): 25–29.

[6] Michael L. Mezey, *Comparative Legislatures* (Durham, N.C.: Duke University Press, 1979), p. 226.

countries, such as the Federal Republic of Germany, India, and Israel, the chief of state is known as the president.

The **head of government** is the political leader of the nation who conducts the actual management of government. In parliamentary systems (see below), the political leader is known generally as either prime minister, premier, or chancellor. In the United States the president is both the head of government and the chief of state.

The executive branch of government refers often to the top leaders of the government. In parliamentary systems the executive consists primarily of the prime minister and cabinet. The **cabinet** is a group of top ministers who direct the departments of government.[7] To speak of "The Government" in Great Britain, for example, means the prime minister, cabinet, and other ministers. British cabinet members are in both the executive and the legislative branches since they continue to serve as members of Parliament. In many countries the executive branch includes not only the cabinet of the head of government but others on his or her staff who are close advisers although they do not direct departments of government.

Different methods are used to select chief executives. The chief of state is sometimes chosen through inheritance, as in Great Britain, Holland, and Sweden; or through the direct election by the people, as in France.

Functions

The principal functions of the executive are to serve as a symbolic national leader, to formulate policy, to enforce the law, and to direct the administration of

the law. Executives, however, perform other functions, which, as is the case with legislatures, vary among political systems.

Ceremonial. The executive is regarded as the ceremonial leader of all the people. When the executive makes speeches on national holidays or travels on state visits to other countries, he or she is the symbol of the diverse groupings that constitute the state. Because most democratic countries have chiefs of state who are primarily figureheads and who are generally out of the range of partisan criticism, the chiefs of state can perform their ceremonial functions more easily than can the leader of a country who combines in his or her person the titles of head of government and chief of state.

Policy Making. The executive's powers are not merely ceremonial. Policy making is one of the most important executive tasks. Executives play important roles in foreign policy, national security, and in the presentation of legislation generally.

As chief diplomat, the head of government is charged with the responsibility for conducting a foreign policy designed to serve national interests abroad. The head of government is expected, moreover, to provide a military establishment commensurate with those interests.

Chief executives have expanded greatly their role in legislation. Proposals for new laws may be introduced formally in the legislature by elected legislators, but often they are drafted by the head of government, cabinet, and staff officials. The heads of government in many countries, moreover, can influence the prospects for success of a bill in granting or withholding their support.

Law Enforcement and Administration. Chief executives, too, enforce the law through supervision of the bureaucracy—the executive agencies of the government (see Chapter 12). As the bureaucracies of countries throughout the

---

[7] The term *cabinet* comes from the seventeenth-century use of the word in France, meaning a small, private apartment, or "closet," in which the king met privately with his close advisers.

world continue to grow, the chief executives continue to be held accountable for the actions of the many and varied government agencies. It is the heads of government who often appoint the top layer of political officials supervising the agencies of government. It is the heads of government, moreover, who are held responsible for acts of misconduct that go on under their formal supervision.

Other. Executives serve other functions besides formulating policy and directing administration. They play roles in judicial matters by nominating judges for positions in the courts. They may issue pardons to those convicted of crimes. They also serve as party leaders.

JUDICIARY

The judiciary is that branch of government concerned with the administration of justice. In democratic political systems the independence of the judiciary is regarded as an essential prerequisite of a free society.

Organization

In many countries there is a hierarchy by which courts are structured. Lower courts—**courts of original jurisdiction**—hear cases when first presented. An **appellate court** hears cases on appeal from the lower courts. The highest courts deal with the most important judicial questions. The Supreme Court is the highest court in the United States and hears cases on appeal, but it is also authorized to have original jurisdiction in certain kinds of cases, such as those to which a state is a party.

In some systems special courts exist to deal with such matters as tariffs, taxes, and juveniles. Often, however, the rulings of these courts may be appealed to higher courts.

Justices are selected in different ways. They are often appointed by the executive with the approval of the legislature. In the United States, for example, a federal judge is nominated by the president and confirmed by the Senate. In some countries judges are elected directly by the people, as in Switzerland and in some states of the United States.

The term of the judges varies. In some cases judges sit for life and can be removed only for misconduct in office. Some judges, however, are appointed for fixed terms. Still others must run in elections at specified intervals.

In general in democratic societies, even in systems that do not operate under the separation of powers principle, the independence of judges is assured. The suppression of a judiciary is often regarded as a step toward dictatorship. Efforts to influence judges on specific cases from outside the courtroom are regarded as either illegal or violations of judicial propriety.

Functions

The principal functions of the judiciary include the interpretation of the law, the application of the law to concrete cases, the settlement of disputes among individuals, and, in some political systems, the determination of the constitutionality of the law.

Courts interpret laws, for not every law is clear on particular details. Some laws, moreover, may conflict with other laws, and the courts must determine which have validity in particular cases.

Courts apply the law to concrete cases. Conflicts arise among different segments of the government and between government and individuals, and the courts determine the outcome of these cases based on their interpretation of the law.

Courts perform a role in settling disputes among individuals. Private contractual obligations, for example, are often brought before a court when one of the parties feels that the provisions of the contract are not being carried out by the other party.

In some countries, such as the United States, Australia, and Canada, the court has special powers of judicial review, which is the power of a court to declare unconstitutional any act of the executive or legislative branches of the government (see Chapter 3).

PARLIAMENTARY AND PRESIDENTIAL SYSTEMS

Two principal forms of government in democratic societies are the parliamentary and the presidential systems of government. Great Britain is the leading example of a parliamentary system, and the United States is the major representative of the presidential (sometimes called the congressional system). Other countries have some similarities with each of these systems, although their different traditions and political forces have brought about significant variations from the British and American models in terms of the number of major political parties, the method of electing legislators, and the relationship between the central and regional governments.

Great Britain

The main features of the British parliamentary system are: the supremacy of Parliament; the fusion of the executive and legislative branches; the existence of party government; and the heavy reliance on traditional practices rather than a written constitution.

Supremacy of Parliament. The British Parliament may pass any law, on any subject, and the law of Parliament is the supreme law of the land. A British Parliament can, if it so chooses, suppress civil liberties or suspend elections without fear that its acts are unconstitutional. No court can declare an act of Parliament to be null and void since the power of judicial review simply does not exist in Great Britain.

Fusion of Executive and Legislative Branches. The legislature in Britain consists of the House of Lords and the House of Commons. In the twentieth century the power of the House of Lords has been reduced to a minimal level. The House of Commons is the central legislative unit and consists of 650 members. The House of Lords contains more than 1,150 members, whose tenure in office is variously based on hereditary privilege, appointment for life, and religious or judicial leadership. The executive branch of government consists of the monarch, whose role is mostly that of a figurehead, and the prime minister and cabinet, who are the political leaders of the country. Each cabinet member heads a ministry that directs the government bureaucracy. The prime minister and cabinet are not separately elected but rather are members of the House of Commons and remain in office until such time as an election is called and their party is defeated or they lose a vote of confidence. (When a member of Parliament resigns or dies, a **by-election,** or special election, is held in the member's constituency.) A **vote of confidence** is approval of a government's major proposals. In the event that the government loses such a vote, the prime minister must go to the monarch, who by tradition accepts the call for a general election. Under such a fusion of power, a paralysis of government brought on by conflict between the executive and the legislature cannot occur.

The British cabinet is said to abide by the principle of **collective responsibility,** by which all members of the cabinet are held accountable for the acts of any single cabinet member. If a cabinet member cannot support the decisions of the government, then he or she is expected to resign.

Cabinet members are people who usually have had extensive experience in parliamentary affairs. They have usually risen from the ranks after proving themselves in different government positions. The prime minister is the head of the cabinet and a person who has widespread support in his or her own party. The prime minister must keep that support or risk being replaced without a general election but merely by a decision of his or her own party in Parliament to choose another person from the party to head the government.

Party Government. The British parliamentary system of government is characterized by strong party government. Two major parties, Conservative and Labour, dominate the legislature. At times, however, minor parties can hold votes that are necessary for a party with the largest number of legislators to rule. In Great Britain party leaders enforce discipline among their members. Although members of a party are free to debate issues, in most cases they vote the way that their party decides on major issues. There are cases, however, in which a free vote is permitted. Party members can vote their conscience in a **free vote.** On these matters, a vote of confidence is not at issue.

Members of Parliament vote as their party determines. If they vote against the party that constitutes the government, then they increase the prospects that the government will not receive its vote of confidence and all the members of the Parliament will have to "stand" for election. The central party organization can deny renomination to any of its recalcitrant members, and the evidence indicates that a member of Parliament once denied the party label has difficulty being re-elected.

British members of Parliament are expected to support their political parties. They are not, moreover, required to come from the constituencies that elect them to office.

Tradition. The British system of government is not based on a written constitution in the manner of the U.S. Constitution. Instead, the British constitution is said to be made up of some major documents, such as Magna Carta, the English Bill of Rights, and the Reform Act of 1832, and traditions that have evolved over the centuries. One of these traditions is that elections are called by the prime minister when he or she deems the time is right. A maximum "term" of five years is permitted, but the prime minister may call an election before that. In 1974, for example, Labour Prime Minister Harold Wilson called an election only several months after the British people had voted his party into office. He hoped to increase the size of the Labour majority in the House of Commons and succeeded in doing just that. This power to choose an election date is one that maximizes the prospects of reelection by the party controlling the government.

By tradition, also, the minority party is regarded as the loyal opposition. A **shadow cabinet** of opposition minority party members sits opposite the government cabinet members in the House of Commons, ready to challenge the government and replace it should the government lose a vote of confidence and the subsequent election.

Theoretically, the British system of government could be regarded as tailor-made for a future dictator, since the British system would assure a majority party the right to outlaw the minority party, destroy the free press, and imprison critics of the government. The fact that the system of government is not used in this way reflects the tradition of reverence for dissent that is part of the British political culture.

Other Parliamentary Systems

The British parliamentary system is regarded as one model of a parliamentary system, and a stable one at that. A strong two-party system and the fusion of executive and legislative branches have assured that government can rule and be responsible. Other parliamentary systems are not so stable, however.

France has had many different types of government in the past two centuries. It has experienced republics, monarchies, and empires. Frequent changes have established a revolutionary tradition in French politics.

The political instability of France has been pronounced in this century. The Fourth Republic (1946–58) was a particularly unstable parliamentary system characterized by a multiparty rather than two-party system. The people who formed a government, consequently, had to assemble a coalition of disparate elements to win a vote of confidence. Government tenure was brief in such a system, as the support of one or more parties was frequently withdrawn. Between November 1945 and September 1958, France had six national elections and twenty-five different governments. It was because of such instability in government and the continuous crises that resulted that a different system was established in the Fifth Republic under Charles de Gaulle in 1958. The new Constitution retained only some of the elements of the parliamentary system. A president is not separately and directly elected by the people. Unlike the situation for British ministers, the French ministers are prohibited from being members of the National Assembly.

The political systems of Western European governments are parliamentary. They are also multiparty in which no single party gathers enough electoral support to constitute a majority. After the election results are in, a coalition government—composed of elements of two or more parties—is formed.

United States

The political system of the United States is the principal example of the presidential system of government. The main features of the American political system at the national level are: separation of powers and checks and balances; decentralization of political parties; a written constitution; and judicial review.

Separation of Powers and Checks and Balances. Unlike the British parliamentary system, the American form of national government is based on separate spheres of power. The creation of distinct branches of government—Congress, the president, and the Supreme Court—is the product of a philosophy of **separation of powers** with its assumption that concentrated power is dangerous to liberty. In the words of James Madison, a strong supporter of the Constitution, "The accumulation of all powers legislative, executive, and judiciary in the same hands . . . may justly be pronounced the very definition of tyranny."[8]

The Congress has primary legislative power, the president primary executive power, and the Supreme Court primary judicial power. A system of checks and balances in which each branch of government has some powers of the other two encourages the fragmentation of power. Because of checks and balances, Congress has some executive power (such as the power of the Senate to confirm appointments by the president) and some

---

[8] James Madison, *Federalist*, no. 47, in Alexander Hamilton, James Madison, and John Jay, *The Federalist Papers*, ed. Clinton Rossiter (New York: New American Library, 1961), p. 301.

judicial power (such as the power to create new courts and to enlarge the size of the Supreme Court membership). The president has legislative power (such as the power to veto bills passed by Congress) and judicial power (such as the power to nominate justices to the court). The court has legislative power (such as the power to declare a statute unconstitutional) and executive power (such as the power to administer court rulings). By establishing a system of checks and balances, the Framers deliberately made government cumbersome.

The president is at the center of the system. Originally, the president was supposed to be elected by the Electoral College, a group chosen by the state legislatures, insulated from popular control. In practice today, however, the Electoral College generally reflects the popular vote. The president and cabinet are constitutionally prevented from holding simultaneously both their executive offices and seats in Congress. Unlike the British system, the president may never have even served in the legislature but rather may have moved up from another position, such as military officer, governor, or even private citizen.

The president is elected for a fixed four-year term. With the exception of Richard Nixon, no president has resigned his office. The president's cabinet consists of men and women whom he appoints with the consent of the Senate.

Congress includes the House of Representatives and the Senate. The House consists of 435 members. The number of House seats from each state depends upon population. By tradition, the representatives are chosen from **single-member districts,** in which only one member is elected from each district. Also by tradition, House members reside in the constituencies that elect them. Members of the House must face election every two years. The work of the House of Representatives is done mostly by committees, with leadership of those committees based on seniority and party considerations. At times, however, the seniority principle has fallen when the rank-and-file members of the majority party on the committee so decide. Party leadership plays a role in the organization of the House, but the party does not have the unity that exists in the British House of Commons. The House has real power to deal with all bills and has the special power of originating revenue bills.

The Senate is composed of two members from each state. Senators are elected for six-year terms, but only one-third of them are elected every two years. Originally senators were chosen by the state legislatures but since 1913 by direct election of the people. The Senate's work, too, is conducted mostly in committees along the lines of seniority and party influence that characterize the House committees. Unlike the upper chamber in Britain, the Senate has real power to deal with all bills. A bill does not become a law until it has the approval of both the House and the Senate. In addition, the Senate has special powers of "advice and consent" to confirm presidential appointments and to approve treaties. Senators reside in the constituencies that elect them.

The Supreme Court of the United States stands at the apex of the nation's court system. Today it consists of nine members, although originally in 1789 it contained only five justices. Supreme Court justices receive their office by presidential appointment with confirmation by the Senate. They retain their office for life and can be dismissed only by impeachment by the House of Representatives and conviction by the Senate. As mentioned above, the Supreme Court has the power of judicial review. The Supreme Court, moreover, must deal with real cases and does not give advisory opinions.

Decentralization of Parties. Party organization is decentralized in the American political system. The national party organization cannot discipline legislators as their British counterparts may do. A representative secures the nomination for Congress from a regional constituency. If he or she fails to get support from that constituency, then the person will not secure the nomination of the party.

Party organization in the legislature is at its strongest at the time that each chamber is organized. By custom, the committee assignments for each chamber are determined by party designation. By tradition, the chairman of the committee is the member of the majority party on the committee with the longest seniority on the committee. Also by tradition, the minority party has representation on each committee.

Because of the decentralization of political parties and the separate election of president and Congress, party government does not exist in the United States. It is even possible to have a president of one political party, and both the House and Senate of another. Such was the case in the presidential administrations of Richard Nixon and Gerald Ford, and is the case in the George Bush administration. Republican president Ronald Reagan faced a Republican Senate and a Democratic House in his first term, and a Democratic Senate and House in his second term. Unlike the British system, moreover, the president does not have to confront a vote of confidence. Proposals that his administration puts forward may be voted down without any consequence to the continuation of the president in office until the fixed four-year term has ended.

Written Constitution. The American political system is governed by a written constitution. The Constitution embodies the fundamental principles and political structure underlying the political system.

Since the first ten amendments were ratified in 1791, only sixteen amendments have become the law of the land.

The Constitution provides specific government requirements that have lasted for two centuries, such as the fixed term of office for president and Congress and the system of federalism. It has been flexible enough, however, to allow for change either through amendment, statute, custom, or judicial interpretation.

Judicial Review. The question of whether the Framers intended that the court should have the power of judicial review is still debated among students of the Constitution. Since John Marshall formally asserted this right in *Marbury* v. *Madison* in 1803, the court has played an important role in the legislative process. It is clear that the Framers intended that the Supreme Court should have the power to declare state laws unconstitutional, however. The court has often exercised that power against state laws that were in conflict with legislation of the national government.

TRENDS IN EXECUTIVE-LEGISLATIVE RELATIONSHIPS

Governments throughout the world vary in terms of the relationships among executive, legislatures, and the judiciary. Regardless of the variation, however, it is clear that a trend in the direction of the expansion of the power of executives at the expense of legislatures characterizes most political systems.

In dictatorships power is centralized, and dictators sometimes govern without even the fig leaf of legislatures to legitimize their claims to rule. In other dictatorships, however, legislatures are created but exercise either no or greatly limited power.

Democracies, too, have shown a growth in executive power and a decline in the legislature's power with respect to the executive. The reasons are varied: the requirements of foreign policy, the growth of domestic government programs, the inability of legislatures to act swiftly, and the important role of the media.

Considerations of foreign policy have played a prominent role in the growth of executive power. Particularly in the twentieth century—the age of intercontinental ballistic missiles and jet aircraft—the necessity of taking swift action has enhanced the power of the executive. Wars, too, have played their part, as often legislatures are willing to delegate powers to the chief executive in times of national peril.

Domestic government programs have also worked to increase the power of the chief executive. In the nineteenth century much of the work of the legislature could be handled within a short period of time each year. With the appearance of the welfare state and the regulatory state in the twentieth century, however, even diligent legislators have found it difficult to keep up with complicated details about such diverse subjects as education, health, transportation, and employment. Legislators, consequently, often delegate much of their authority to the bureaucracy that is administered by the executive branch of government.

The sheer variety and complexity of legislative committees and interests make the legislature a cumbersome instrument of action. In many democratic systems, before a bill becomes a law it must go through a long process of "touching bases" with interest groups and legislative power brokers. The chief executive, consequently, is in a much better position to present unified programs and take decisive action.

Finally, the media have focused public awareness on chief executives. The president of the United States, for example, commands the attention of newspapers, magazines, and television. Television particularly has brought the presidential personality to the attention of American citizens nearly every day. What is true of the American president is also true of chief executives in other countries.

Although the power of legislatures has diminished in democracies, it is clear that legislative institutions remain effective in influencing the course of legislation and the course of the political process itself. As the experience of Richard Nixon in the Watergate proceedings—with their revelations about presidential misconduct—and the experience of Ronald Reagan in the Iran-Contra affair indicate legislatures are capable of checking chief executives when their power exceeds constitutional bounds.

ISSUE

The American presidential and the British parliamentary systems of government constitute two of the oldest democracies in the world. Each has survived wars and depressions. Each, moreover, has its champions arguing the virtues of the one or the other. When the subject of institutional reform arises in the United States, it often centers on the question of whether the United States should learn from British experience.

21/YES

SHOULD THE UNITED STATES ADOPT THE BRITISH PARLIAMENTARY SYSTEM OF GOVERNMENT?

Throughout this century many writers, including such notables as political scientist and president Woodrow Wilson and journalist Walter Lippmann, have called for major structural changes in the American political system so that it will more closely resemble British parliamentary government. We concur with this position and contend that the American system should be restructured so as to allow for the designation of two separate officials: a chief of state who would be a ceremonial leader and a prime minister who would be a member of the legislative body. We would also eliminate the system of federalism and put government power completely into the hands of a newly formed Congress. That Congress would be unicameral and would select the prime minister and cabinet. The American prime minister would have much the same powers that his or her British counterpart possesses today. A strong centralized two-party system would assure party discipline, and the loss of a vote of confidence in Congress would bring on a general election. The American prime minister could be dismissed by his or her party without the necessity of going through a general election. The prime minister's cabinet would be composed of members of Congress. Each cabinet member would be in charge of an executive department. The Supreme Court would no longer have its power of judicial review, although it could interpret the law as enacted by Congress.

Such structural changes are essential in the American political system. With such alterations, the system would achieve the following advantages: (1) government would become more accountable and democratic; (2) government would become more efficient; and (3) traditional powers, presently assumed by the executive, would be restored to the legislature. We would then have a government that would be streamlined enough to carry us through to the twenty-first century.

Accountability and Democracy. Representative democracy has been defined in Chapter 3 as a system of government in which elected public officials represent the people. Advocates of democracy differ as to the particular character of the representative. Some view the representative as a **delegate** —a person who must represent the interests of his or her constituency whether or not he or she agrees with those interests. Others view the representative as a **trustee** —a person who votes on the basis of conscience in legislative considerations for those principles in which he or she believes. Either theory, however, implies that representatives must in some way be accountable to the people who elect them.

If a Labour Government is in power in Great Britain, then Labour is held accountable for what happens to the society. If the inflation rates rise rapidly or foreign policy setbacks are experienced, then it is Labour's fault. Accountability is clear in a system in which legislative and executive power are fused.

In the United States, however, power and authority are dispersed. "The splitting of sovereignty into many parts amounts to there being no sovereign," the nineteenth-century British writer Walter Bagehot observed.[9] Particularly in situations in which the president belongs to one party and the Congress to another, responsibility is claimed only for good news and not for bad. When Republican Gerald Ford was president, he blamed the Democratic Congress for inflation because of its spending policies. It was difficult for voters to hold elected public officials accountable in such a diffused system. Democracy requires accountability, and parliamentary reforms in the American political process along British lines would provide for that accountability.

Efficiency. The American political system of government is a highly inefficient way to rule. The U.S. Constitution was created in the late eighteenth century at a time when the population of the United States totaled only about three million people who lived mostly in eastern coastal states. At that time, the American economy was dominated by agriculture. More-

---

[9] Walter Bagehot, *The English Constitution*, 2d ed. (London: Oxford University Press, 1952), p. 201. The study was originally published in 1867.

over, the United States was a country on the periphery of power politics dominated by the big European powers.

The Constitution of 1787 created an inefficient government because government was regarded by many eighteenth-century Americans as a necessary evil. Today, strong government is necessary but not possible, given the constitutional constraints imposed by a document written for the needs of two centuries ago. "The separation of powers between the legislative and executive branches, whatever its merits in 1793," writes Washington attorney Lloyd Cutler, "has become a structure that almost guarantees stalemate today."[10]

Today, the United States needs a structure that can provide positive government to meet the needs of a modern industrial society. The rapidly changing global economic situation makes necessary decisive action that only a unified government can provide. The position of the United States as a superpower, moreover, requires the country to speak with one voice rather than having the executive trying to move in one direction and the legislature trying to get the executive to move in another. A parliamentary system based on the British model, then, would allow for the positive and efficient government that our system currently lacks.

Efficiency in government would be helped by putting people with long experience in government into positions of responsibility. To become a minister requires many years of working one's way up through party ranks and developing a wellspring of knowledge about government. By the time an individual becomes a prime minister in Britain, he or she has learned how to get things done in government.

The separate election of president and Congress, in contrast, means that an individual can come to the presidency with little or no experience in dealing with the Congress. Walter Bagehot commented in 1867 about the low quality of executive talent recruited to the presidency. He regarded this situation as caused by the separation of powers. He did indicate that Lincoln was an able president, but noted aptly that "success in a lottery is no argument for lotteries."[11] In more modern times individuals attaining the presidency from outside the legislative branch have had to "learn on the job" while the country was being impaired by the president's inexperience.

The parliamentary system, moreover, would assure that the most talented members of Congress would retain their seats and not be ejected from the legislature because of electoral defeat. Good people could be given **safe seats** from which members of their party are nearly always elected so as to assure their making a continuing contribution to the government. The country benefits when it retains legislators of talent as active participants in the political process.

Legislative Assertion. In 1885 Woodrow Wilson published a study of the American system of government entitled *Congressional Government,* which reflected where power resided at that time. In the twentieth century, however, the executive branch of government has come to play a more prominent role in government decision making.

The examples are varied and include foreign policy, national security, and domestic matters. In foreign policy executive agreements—which require merely the approval of the president—have increasingly been used instead of treaties requiring Senate approval. In national security matters, moreover, the president has used his powers as commander-in-chief to involve the country in acts of war. The Constitution specifically indicates that Congress shall have the power to declare war, but American involvement in Korea in the 1950s and in Vietnam in the 1960s and 1970s did not come about by formal declarations of war. American casualties in both those wars were high, and the mere fact that war was not declared did not alter the high price the country paid for executive action. Domestic matters, too, have experienced executive encroachment, as presidents have authorized government snooping, wiretapping, and surveillance of private individuals without congressional authority. Executives also have expanded their powers in the management of the economy, determining at times such matters as price and wage controls and import-export restrictions.

---

[10] Lloyd Cutler, "To Form a Government," *Foreign Affairs* 59 (Fall 1980): 127.

[11] Bagehot, *English Constitution,* p. 28.

The high point of executive power came during the Watergate affair, when power became wrongdoing. For a period of more than a year, President Richard Nixon and his top aides struggled to ward off investigations by Congress and the courts. The conduct of government was slowed down by the struggle. Ultimately, Richard Nixon resigned. No American president had been previously thrown out of office before his term expired, and none had previously resigned. The fixed period of four years made it impossible to remove the president without a grave constitutional crisis.

Had the United States been governed by a parliamentary system, it would not have had to go through such an agonizing experience. In 1940, Prime Minister Neville Chamberlain was replaced by Winston Churchill when Chamberlain's policy of appeasement against Adolf Hitler became discredited. In 1956, moreover, Anthony Eden resigned over the failure of his policy on the Suez Canal, and he was replaced by Harold Macmillan. Both Churchill and Macmillan came to power without a con-

stitutional crisis and without a general election. It would have been possible, and much more sensible, to remove Richard Nixon in the same way that Chamberlain and Eden were removed had the United States been governed by a parliamentary system.

The same parliamentary system would be desirable even if a president has not been guilty of wrongdoing. When Herbert Hoover was elected president in 1928, he was a popular figure. The Great Depression beginning in 1929, however, diminished his popularity. In spite of the extended period of economic devastation, Hoover remained in the White House until 1933, when Franklin D. Roosevelt came to power and promised the American people a "New Deal" to get the country out of its economic slump.

As the nation moves toward the twenty-first century, it must streamline its government to meet the even more complex challenges ahead. A parliamentary system would allow for government to be accountable, efficient, and responsive to popular demands.

21 / NO SHOULD THE UNITED STATES ADOPT THE BRITISH PARLIAMENTARY SYSTEM OF GOVERNMENT?

The argument that the United States would have better government if it adopted the British parliamentary system should be dismissed after a close examination is made of both the current British political system and the American political system. We shall leave aside for argument's sake the practical contention that such a reshuffling of powers and institutions would not be possible to implement in the United States. Even Walter Bagehot contended that the parliamentary system worked best in a limited area with uniform standards of wealth and education. He felt that it could not work for the entire American political system.

Let us take the *Affirmative*'s points of accountability and democracy, efficiency, and legislative assertion to justify our case.

Accountability and Democracy. It is true that power is fragmented in the American political system. It is false, however, that government is not held accountable because of the system of separation of powers. In Great Britain the

voter has little choice but to cast a ballot for a particular candidate with a party designation. In the United States, by contrast, the voter can hold a variety of public officials accountable for their actions since the voter casts a ballot separately for a representative, a senator, and the president. As political scientist Don K. Price notes, the presidential system provides the voters with a "double-check on their government" through their president and other elected officials. Price adds that however poorly the president and Congress are carrying out their responsibilities, the voters "are not kept from exercising their controls by a system of mutual deference that results from the fear of disturbing each other's [president and Congress] tenure of office."[12]

The American system of separation of pow-

_____

[12] Don K. Price, "The Parliamentary and Presidential Systems," *Public Administration Review* 3 (Autumn 1943): 327.

ers is in fact more accountable than the British parliamentary system, as the evidence reveals. Because of the separation of powers, the system assures an independent legislature capable of challenging the actions of the executive. The legislature may subpoena civil servants to disclose executive actions in the American system, a practice denied in the British political system. There is much more disclosure about what government is doing in the American political system than in the British. This feature is explained in part by the fact that the laws of press freedom allow more discretion to American journalists than to their British counterparts. Another important reason for the disclosure of so much information, however, is that legislators do not have to fear that their careers will be ruined if they either vote against or organize opposition to the president, who is also a member of their political party. A people who are able to have access to vast amounts of information are in a far better position to hold government accountable for its acts, as befits a democracy.

Efficiency. The American political system is far more efficient than its detractors would have us believe. Although the Constitution is nearly two centuries old, it has been a document that has not put the political system into a cast-iron mold. Not only have amendments changed the Constitution to meet the needs of the times, but custom, political practices, statutes, and judicial interpretation have all contributed to the continuing success of the political system.

Even with an "antiquated" Constitution, the nation has been able to adapt to its foreign policy, national security, and domestic needs. In foreign affairs the small power of the eighteenth century has become the superpower of the twentieth century, with its orientation moving from an isolationist to an internationalist perspective. In national security matters, moreover, the country has been able to maintain its institutions and way of life in spite of threats from enemies abroad. In domestic matters the separation of powers did not prevent the growth of the welfare state, the regulation of big industry, and the protection of the environment.

The key to the success is that although the system of checks and balances may seem, on paper at least, to thwart action by government,

it does not prevent patterns of cooperation between the executive and legislative branches of government. Such cooperation may be seen in foreign policy. The Senate has approved nearly a thousand treaties and turned down about twenty, and only five in the twentieth century. "In general," writes political scientist James Q. Wilson, "the Senate tends to go along."[13]

Often we pay attention to the major conflicts between the branches in such highly dramatic cases as the defeat of the Versailles Treaty by the United States Senate in 1919, the confrontation of President Franklin D. Roosevelt and Congress over the size of the Supreme Court, and the congressional and executive conflicts in the Watergate affair; but these cases are the exceptions rather than the rule of government. In point of fact, cooperation often characterizes the relationships of the two branches of government; if it did not, then it would be impossible for American government to function.

There is no clear case to indicate that a parliamentary system would be more or less efficient to meet the problems of the day. British governments, too, have not always coped well with their problems, as the lack of preparation for World War II and the inflationary spiral of the 1970s testify. More than mere government structure accounts for efficiency in government.

There is no assurance, moreover, that if the United States were to try to adopt a British-type parliamentary system to replace the current presidential system it would retain a two-party system. The experience of France under the Fourth Republic shows that a multiparty parliamentary system may be highly unstable and inefficient. It is wrong to tinker with the Constitution when we do not know what greater problems might result.

Efficiency in government depends, too, upon the quality of the personnel in government. The evidence does not indicate that American presidents have been unqualified to rule. Men such as Thomas Jefferson, Abraham Lincoln, Theodore Roosevelt, Woodrow Wilson, and Franklin D. Roosevelt were outstanding chief

---

[13] James Q. Wilson, "Does the Separation of Powers Still Work?" *Public Interest,* no. 86 (Winter 1987): 48.

executives. Though assuming the office of president from outside the ranks of the legislature, moreover, they did not lack political experience. Wilson and both Roosevelts, for example, were state governors, and their activities at the state level provided them with sound executive experience.

The American system, moreover, allows for clearer political direction of the bureaucracy than does the British system. When a new president is elected, he brings to the administration not only cabinet secretaries but thousands of undersecretaries and other executives. Often, these are people with great experience outside government who inject fresh ideas into government so it operates more effectively. In the realm of defense, for example, Elihu Root was regarded as a superior secretary of war, and James Forrestal an outstanding secretary of defense, although these men came to their positions from law and banking, respectively. Cabinet members, moreover, can be selected on the basis of their administrative competence, which may be tested outside of government, rather than from their skill at debate, a characteristic emphasized in the parliamentary system.

In the matter of personnel many able legislators are reelected for several terms in Congress under the current decentralized system of primaries and elections. Even if an able legislator is defeated in an election, however, that person may continue to have an influence on policy. At times, defeated legislators may be given cabinet positions or be taken into the administration as advisers to the president. The defeated legislators can run again for election. Their influence would be strong, moreover, if they merely concerned themselves with events and wrote occasional articles and books about subjects of national importance. Defeated candidates do not have to become "nonpersons" in the manner of out-of-favor political figures in totalitarian dictatorships.

Legislative Assertion. It is certainly true that legislative power has declined with respect to executive power. Congress, however, has expanded its power with respect to the entire system. In years past Congress met annually for only a few months. Now its work is so vast that it is usually in session for most of the year. As government operations have ex-

panded, so, too, has the scope of congressional activities. The enlargement of the congressional staff, moreover, has given legislators the opportunity to oversee executive actions.

Although legislative power has declined with respect to the executive throughout the world, there is no evidence to indicate that the parliamentary system is any more successful in reversing the trend toward executive dominance. When Woodrow Wilson wrote *Congressional Government,* moreover, he was critical of the undue influence of Congress on legislation and felt that a parliamentary system would strengthen the president. In fact, the British parliamentary system has experienced an increasing amount of centralized control. Some British commentators have argued that the British prime minister's power has become comparable to that of the American president. In this regard the British prime minister has the authority to make appointments to office, conclude treaties, and declare war—all without securing parliamentary consent. Geoffrey Smith observes that one dissatisfaction of British legislators is that "Parliament is thought to be merely a rubber stamp for the decisions of government."[14]

The British parliamentary system encourages a more quiescent legislature and a strong executive. When a political party is in power, the leaders of the party enforce discipline so its members do not vote against the government and thus throw the entire legislature into general elections. The legislator votes the way the party dictates as determined by the executive if he or she is the prime minister and of the same party. The point, however, should not be overstated, since party leaders take into consideration the interests of the different elements of their party. Nonetheless, the party's ability to discipline recalcitrant members of Parliament is a deterrent to "rocking the boat."

In fact, the no-confidence vote has for the most part lost any real effectiveness as an instrument of legislative control of the exec-

---

[14] Geoffrey Smith, "Parliamentary Change in Britain," in *The Role of the Legislature in Western Democracies,* Norman J. Ornstein, ed. (Washington, D.C.: American Enterprise Institute for Public Policy Research, 1981), p. 37.

utive. Not since 1885 has a government commanding a majority by one party in the House of Commons been overthrown by a no-confidence vote. Governments have been toppled through no-confidence votes since then, but in those cases the government did not have majority control and needed the support of members of Parliament from other parties.

The Question Hour, moreover, is another overstated institution of check on the executive. As political scientist James L. Sundquist notes, "One of the first things learned by a rising politician in a democracy is how to artfully avoid giving information he does not want to give."[15] The Question Hour may test the oratorical abilities of government leaders, but it is not really as significant for revealing information as its advocates pretend.

The American system of separation of powers has allowed for legislative assertion when the executive has exceeded his authority. The decade of the 1970s witnessed such legislative activity. A War Powers Act limited the power of the chief executive in the conduct of foreign policy. The Freedom of Information Act assured many Americans unprecedented access to government documents. Scholars have even relied on such previously classified documents to publish devastating indictments of executive actions.[16] Other laws of the 1970s included limitations on campaign expenditures for presidential campaigns and congressional reforms of the budgetary process. The increasing role of Congress in budgetary matters is, in fact, one of the most significant post-Watergate reforms. The entire Watergate story with its televised hearings and forced disclosures of private, taped presidential conversations in the Oval Office of the White House was revealed to the public. Watergate showed that the existing system works to deal with executive usurpation of constitutional authority. The congressional investigation of the Iran-Contra affair, moreover, again demonstrated the power of Congress to hold the president to account for illegal administration activities.

A fixed system of holding office may seem to have some drawbacks, as the cases of Herbert Hoover and Richard Nixon attest. There is, however, another side to the story. A president who is assured of the post for four years is more encouraged to take strong action and disregard the clamor from Congress. Historian Arthur Schlesinger, Jr., observes that John Adams resisted congressional agitation for war with France during his administration as president, and President Harry Truman fought the explosion of congressional wrath when he fired General Douglas MacArthur as supreme allied commander of United States forces in Korea. "Yet in retrospect," Schlesinger notes, "these two doughty Presidents never had finer hours."[17]

The case for the adoption of a parliamentary system has not been proven. It is well to heed the words of John Kennedy, who said in another context, "If it is not necessary to change, it is necessary not to change." It is, consequently, not necessary to change a system that has worked for two centuries.

---

[15] James L. Sundquist, "Parliamentary Government and Ours," *New Republic* 171 (October 26, 1974): 14.

[16] For example, see William Shawcross, *Sideshow: Kissinger, Nixon and the Destruction of Cambodia* (New York: Simon and Schuster, 1979).

---

[17] Arthur Schlesinger, Jr., "Parliamentary Government," *New Republic* 171 (August 31, 1974): 14.

KEY TERMS

Appellate court
Bicameral legislatures
Bills
By-election
Cabinet
Chief of state
Collective responsibility

Conference committee
Courts of original jurisdiction
Delegate theory
Free vote
Head of government
Impeachment
Joint committees

Legislation
Loyal opposition
Ombudsman
Question Hour
Safe seats
Select committee
Separation of powers

Shadow cabinet
Single-member district
Standing committees
Trustee theory
Unicameral legislatures
Vote of confidence

QUESTIONS

Parliamentary and Presidential Systems

1. What effect does judicial review have on democratic processes?
2. What effect does the decline of legislative power and the strengthening of executive power have in democracies?
3. Is it possible today to strengthen legislatures in democracies? If so, how? If not, why not?
4. To what extent does political culture rather than government structure affect political stability? What are the reasons for your answer?
5. What are the advantages and disadvantages of a fixed term of office for the head of government?

American Parliament

1. If a "Watergate" had happened in Great Britain, would the British parliament have handled the situation differently from the way it was handled by the U.S. Congress? What are the reasons for your answer?
2. What are the obstacles in the Constitution that prevent the United States from adopting a parliamentary system of government?
3. Which system—parliamentary or presidential—is likely to have a stronger legislature? Why?
4. How has the calibre of leaders of American presidents compared to that of British prime ministers?
5. Had the U.S. Constitution of 1787 established a parliamentary system, what difference would that have made to the course of American history? What are the reasons for your answer?

RECOMMENDED READINGS

Parliamentary and Presidential Systems

ARTER, DAVID. *The Nordic Parliaments: A Comparative Analysis.* New York: St. Martin's Press, 1984. A study of the Danish, Finnish, Icelandic, Norwegian, and Swedish legislatures.

BARILLEAUX, RYAN J. *The Post-Modern Presidency: The Office after Ronald Reagan.* New York: Praeger, 1988. A contention that the office of the presidency under Ronald Reagan and his successors is fundamentally different from that of its predecessors.

BLONDEL, JEAN. *The Organization of Govern-ments: A Comparative Analysis of Governmental Structures.* Beverly Hills, Calif.: Sage, 1982. A study of the main characteristics of government in the world.

CUNLIFFE, MARCUS. *The Presidency.* 3d ed. Boston: Houghton Mifflin, 1987. A chronological and thematic view of the U.S. presidency.

CURTIS, MICHAEL, ed. *Introduction to Comparative Government.* New York: Harper and Row, 1985. A survey.

HAMILTON, ALEXANDER, JAMES MADISON, and JOHN JAY. *The Federalist Papers,* ed. Clinton Rossiter. New York: New American Library, 1961. Papers, originally published in 1788 to gain support for the ratification of the Constitution, that remain a classic work on government.

HENNESSY, PETER. *Cabinet.* Oxford, England: Basil Blackwell, 1986. A study of contemporary British cabinet government.

LEVINE, MYRON A. "Is a Presidential System for Everyone? Some Reflections on the Dutch Rejection of an American-Style Presidency." *Presidential Studies Quarterly* 18 (Spring 1988): 277–81. An argument that a U.S.-style presidency for the Netherlands would intensify conflicts in Dutch society.

MACRIDIS, ROY C., ed. *Modern Political Systems: Europe.* 6th ed. Englewood Cliffs, N.J.: Prentice Hall, 1987. Studies of the European political system.

MEZEY, MICHAEL L. *Comparative Legislatures.* Durham, N.C.: Duke University Press, 1979. A comparative analysis of legislatures.

MISHLER, WILLIAM, and ANNE HILDRETH. "Legislatures and Political Stability: An Exploratory Analysis." *Journal of Politics* 46 (February 1984): 25–59. An argument that genuinely effective and responsive legislatures enhance the stability of democratic regimes, but token legislatures in authoritarian regimes have little impact on stability and may even exacerbate political disorder and violence.

NORTON, PHILIP. *The British Polity.* New York: Longman, 1984. An overview of the British political system.

ORNSTEIN, NORMAN J., ed. *The Role of the Legislature in Western Democracies.* Washington, D.C.: American Enterprise Institute for Public Policy Research, 1981. Papers and discussion on legislatures by scholars and legislators.

ROSE, RICHARD. "Presidents and Prime Ministers." *Society* 25 (March/April 1988): 61–67. A comparison of the offices of British prime minister, U.S. president, and French president.

American Parliament

BAGEHOT, WALTER. *The English Constitution.* 2d ed. London: Oxford University Press, 1952. A classic work on British government originally published in 1867.

BONAFEDE, DOM. "Reform of U.S. System of Government Is on the Minds and Agendas of Many." *National Journal* 17 (June 29, 1985): 1521–24. A description of efforts to bring about structural reform in the American political system.

CUTLER, LLOYD. "To Form a Government." *Foreign Affairs* 59 (Fall 1980): 126–43. A criticism of the separation of powers and a plea that the United States move to more of a parliamentary system.

GOLDWIN, ROBERT A., and ART KAUFMAN, eds. *Separation of Powers—Does It Still Work?* Washington, D.C.: American Enterprise Institute for Public Policy Research, 1986. Essays on the subject.

LIVINGSTON, WILLIAM E. "Britain and America: The Institutionalization of Accountability." *Journal of Politics* 38 (November 1976): 879–94. An argument against the establishment of a parliamentary system of government in the United States.

PRICE, DON K. "The Parliamentary and Presidential Systems." *Public Administration Review* 3 (Autumn 1943): 317–34. A case that the United States should not adopt a parliamentary system.

ROBINSON, DONALD L. "Adjustments Are Needed in the System of Checks and Balances." *Polity* 19 (Summer 1987): 660–66. A call for changes in the U.S. constitutional system.

———, ed. *Reforming American Government: The Bicentennial Papers of the Committee on the Constitutional System.* Boulder, Colo.: Westview Press, 1985. A reprint of many articles and book excerpts dealing with constitutional reform in the United States.

SCARROW, HOWARD A. "Parliamentary and Presidential Government Compared." *Current History* 66 (June 1974): 264–67, 272. An evaluation of the pros and cons of each system.

SCHLESINGER, ARTHUR, JR. "Parliamentary Government." *New Republic* (August 31, 1974): 13–15. A case against the adoption of a parliamentary system in the United States.

SUNDQUIST, JAMES, L. *Constitutional Reform and Effective Government.* Washington, D.C.: Brookings Institution, 1986. An analysis of the weaknesses of the U.S. constitutional system and a plea for reform.

U.S. CONGRESS, JOINT ECONOMIC COMMITTEE. *Political Economy and Constitutional Reform.* Hearings, 97th Congress, 2d Sess., 1982. Testimony and reprinted articles on structural reforms in the American political system, with attention to the parliamentary system of government.

WILSON, JAMES Q. "Does the Separation of Powers Still Work?" *Public Interest,* no. 86 (Winter 1987): 36–52. The author says Yes.

chapter 12

Bureaucracy

The contest for the presidency between George Bush and Michael Dukakis in 1988 was marked by a general support of the role of the federal government in society. Although differing about specific policies, both the Republican and Democratic party standard bearers indicated that the federal government had an important and positive role to play in such areas as aiding farmers, helping the elderly, strengthening education, and building the economy.

Such a favorable view of government, however, marked a shift in campaign oratory from some earlier presidential campaigns, when candidates were often hostile to government. When he ran for the presidency against Jimmy Carter in 1980, Ronald Reagan seized on big government as a campaign issue. The federal government bureaucracy had reached into too many spheres of our lives, he argued. He echoed the views of many political leaders, scholars, journalists, and ordinary cit-

izens by charging that government—in addition to being too big—is inefficient, incompetent, and intrusive. In fact, he once quipped, "I've always felt that the nine most terrifying words in the English language are: 'I'm from the government and I'm here to help.' "[1] Reagan was not hitting a novel electoral theme. In 1976, Jimmy Carter campaigned using similar antibureaucratic rhetoric.

Concern with big government is not unique to the United States. Nearly every country in the world—regardless of whether it is democratic or dictatorial—has experienced an increase in the number of people who staff government and an expansion in the functions of government. Because of its size and scope, there is little doubt that bureaucracy plays a prominent role in public policy and in

---

[1] Quoted in Karl Frieden, "Public Needs and Private Wants," *Dissent* 34 (Summer 1987): 317.

influencing the character of political systems. To evaluate the power and role of the bureaucracy in one political system—a democracy—it is first essential to examine the central features of a bureaucracy. We shall then study what it does, why it has grown, how it is organized, and how it is composed.

WHAT IS BUREAUCRACY?

The term *bureaucracy,* like the terms *democracy* and *socialism,* lacks a definition that is universally accepted. *Bureaucracy* is sometimes used in a disparaging manner to mean bumbling, unimaginative, rigid, and inefficient government administrators. Many social scientists, however, describe bureaucracy in a neutral way to mean a specific form of social organization involved in administrative efforts, and it is this latter meaning that will be applied in this chapter. Specifically, we shall use the term **bureaucracy** to mean a government agency, established in departments, agencies, and bureaus, that carries out government activities according to fixed rules.

The first person to study bureaucracy in a systematic fashion was the German social scientist Max Weber. In his book *Wirtschaft und Gesellschaft* (Economy and Society), published in 1922, Weber described an ideal-type bureaucracy as one characterized by:

1. officials organized in fixed jurisdictional areas,

2. a hierarchical arrangement of offices (organized in a pyramidlike structure with each lower office under the control of a higher one),

3. written documents ("the files") that contain the rules to be applied in every case,

4. full-time employment by experts in administration,

5. impersonality in applying rules uniformly.[2]

Weber's use of an ideal type was not a description of how bureaucracy actually works. It was, rather, a model highlighting features that would allow for a systematic study of comparative social organizations. In Weber's view, bureaucratic organization was the most efficient form of social organization the world had experienced. The West, according to Weber, had a compulsive cultural drive to rationalize social and economic processes. By *rationalize,* Weber meant to have the ability to control the material and social world in terms of cause-and-effect relationships rather than through religious or mystical explanations.

Weber described bureaucracy as the central feature of modern society. His analysis of bureaucracy included not only government organization but also the administration of large private organizations. Since Weber, social scientists have concerned themselves with further analyses of the management of large organizations at both the government and private organizational levels.

In many respects large private organizations and government organizations have similarities. If the government's United States Postal Service and private corporation's United Parcel Service are taken as examples, it can be seen that the basic work of these two organizations is the same. Parcels must be sent to a depot; rates must be set based on such factors as weight, size, and destination; a distribution center must sort the parcels by destination; and freight vehicles must transport the parcels to their ultimate receivers. A hierarchy of offices of each organization indicates the responsibility of each official in those organizations.

[2] Max Weber, "Bureaucracy," in *From Max Weber: Essays in Sociology,* ed. H.H. Gerth and C. Wright Mills (New York: Oxford University Press, 1946), pp. 196–98.

Although administration has similar characteristics in the public and private sectors, as the example of the transportation of parcels indicates, the differences are vast. First, government organizations pursue a wider range of activities than do private organizations. Second, the kinds of services that government undertakes, such as police protection, education, and welfare, cannot generally be measured in terms of profit-and-loss figures of the private association. Third, government agencies are often required to achieve more goals than comparable private organizations. A private corporation, for example, may seek the most efficient means to secure profits; whereas a comparable government organization may be required to make decisions based not only on efficiency but on "fairness," justice, and external political factors. Fourth, public employees are generally more secure in their jobs and their promotion steps are more stable than employees in the private sector. Fifth and last, since government agencies are held to more public scrutiny and accountability, they must be able to document every administrative act; hence, public agencies pay more attention to the rules, necessitating enormous paperwork and red tape. These differences do not apply in each case, and exceptions are widespread. In general, these differences distinguish the public from the private sector.

WHAT THE BUREAUCRACY DOES

The bureaucracy plays an active role in the political process of most nations, and it engages in many activities. Among its most important efforts are the implementation of laws, preparation of proposed legislation, regulation of the economy, licensing in economic and professional matters, and the providing of welfare services.

Implementation of Laws

Government agencies are established and conduct their activities on the basis of specific legislative authorization. In the justification of its actions, government officials indicate that they are involved in the **administration,** or carrying out, of the law. The distinction between what they do and the legal authorization of their acts was first made in a systematic manner by Woodrow Wilson in 1887 and Frank Goodnow in 1900.[3] For them, politics in a democracy reflected the political values expressed through public opinion, political parties, and interest groups. Elected public officials, they argued, should be concerned with responding to these political forces. In their view, administrators were supposed to be politically neutral, acting only to implement the policies of duly elected officials.

To some extent, the politics-administration distinction is valid. The legislature enacts a law and appropriates money for specific purposes, such as tax collection and coal mine inspection, and the government agencies involved use those funds as directed. Most government agencies do what is mandated to them by constitutional authorities lest they be called to account for avoiding their legal responsibilities.

Many students of government, however, challenge the politics-administration model, calling attention to the prominent role that bureaucracy plays in the political process. Studies of government agencies show that agencies are not merely value-free administrative organizations but are, rather, active participants in all areas of policy.

In fact, some social scientists contend

---

[3] Woodrow Wilson, "The Study of Administration," *Political Science Quarterly* 2 (June 1887): 197–222; Frank Goodnow, *Politics and Administration* (New York: Crowell-Collier and Macmillan, 1900).

that bureaucracies actually legislate. They argue that legislation is often drafted in a vague or general manner, and it is left to the government agencies and bureaus to interpret the legislative mandate as best they can. Agencies may use this discretion to act in an aggressive or passive way depending upon such factors as whether or not the agencies support the legislation and whether or not the legislation diminishes the power of the bureaucratic organization. In the United States, for example, civil rights agencies in the administrations of Presidents Richard Nixon, Gerald Ford, and Jimmy Carter were accused by conservatives of applying the civil rights laws in ways in which Congress did not intend. Specifically, they condemned executive actions in affirmative action and in busing. In the administration of Ronald Reagan, in contrast, civil rights agencies were accused by liberals of failing to implement civil rights laws or of moving too slowly in combating racial and gender discrimination.

The power of the bureaucracy is enhanced not only by the imprecision and incompleteness of legislation but also by the expertise and the time that government agencies possess, permitting bureaucrats to direct policy as they deem fit. Elected public officials, in contrast, often lack this technical information and the necessary time to pursue investigations of government agencies to force them to act in accordance with legislative direction. In effect, then, the bureaucracy legislates.

Preparation of Legislation

Because of its expertise, the bureaucracy plays a role in the preparation of legislation. Although bills are formally introduced by legislative members, they are, in fact, drafted by government agencies most concerned with their content. Members of the bureaucracy are often called to give their views openly or privately about the proposed legislation before legislative bodies.

Differences exist in democratic systems about how open a role the bureaucracy plays in legislation. In the United States the civil servants actually appear before congressional committees when directed to do so. In Great Britain legislative committees are generally not important in shaping legislation, and the influence of the professional bureaucracy is exerted primarily through the ministry and the executive branch.

Regulation

Government agencies play a regulatory role in political systems. They regulate some industries by such methods as determining rate structures and defining the character of competition. In the United States, for example. the regulatory commissions, such as the Federal Communications Commission and the Securities and Exchange Commission, regulate activities of the communications and securities industries, respectively. Other countries have similar agencies that deal with these and other matters. Some countries even nationalize the kinds of industries that are private but regulated in the United States.

Licensing

One form of regulation is licensing, and agencies use their powers of licensing to influence the behavior of private organizations. Licensing may occur on a national scale or on a local or regional one. Licensing to fly aircraft along specified routes is an example of a national license activity. A license may be given locally for permission to sell alcoholic beverages or to dispense prescription medicines. Doctors, lawyers, and dentists are required to have licenses to practice so as to assure standards of professional competence by these specialists.

Welfare Services

Many government services today are in the welfare sector. In principle, teachers in public institutions are part of the welfare bureaucracy. So, too, are welfare workers who look after the poor and the sick. Today, the welfare sector has expanded to include the arts, so music, theater, and dance programs receive government funds to help them survive. Social security, unemployment compensation, veterans' benefits, and public medical care assistance have all generated vast bureaucracies that have contributed to the growth of government personnel and expenditures.

THE GROWTH OF GOVERNMENT

Early historical documents disclose that bureaucracy has roots going back to ancient Egypt and China. Whenever large projects require the recruitment of many people possessing different skills, bureaucracy is necessary to plan the project, organize the personnel and materiel, and coordinate its diverse components. For ancient Egypt, a bureaucracy was needed to develop the Nile River. In more modern times a bureaucracy was essential to produce the atom bomb.

The major growth in the bureaucracy, however, has been in the past two centuries. To a large extent, it is the product of an increasingly complicated economy. The Industrial Revolution, with its specialization of labor, consumption of many raw materials from distant countries, and use of technicians skilled in engineering, chemistry, mathematics, and physics, required a greater talent in managerial skills than called for in a less developed economic system. Modern capitalism, then, was a major factor in requiring administrative skills. Later, however, government played a more positive role in the bureaucratization of the world.

The past two centuries have been marked by a growth in government, both in expenditures and in the number of people employed by government. There has been variation in expenditures and in the size of the bureaucracy within specific periods, but the trend has generally been upward in both elements. We should note, however, that it is not necessarily the case that an increase in government expenditures automatically means a corresponding increase in the size of the bureaucracy, since some government programs require minimal administrative needs.

Government has grown for many reasons. Most important have been the demands of the economy, the role of national security, the claims of the welfare state, and the pressures exerted by the bureaucracy itself.

Economy

To many capitalists, the essence of the good society is one in which government plays only a small role (see Chapter 5). The leading proponent of free enterprise, Adam Smith, attacked government and principally the mercantile system, which involved massive government intervention in the economy.

Some capitalists remained true to the faith by advocating weak government. Others, however, called for government intervention to protect and strengthen economic expansion. As United States secretary of the treasury, Alexander Hamilton proposed a system of tariffs to protect American industry, for example. In fact, customs officials constituted one big bureaucratic unit in the first century of the American republic. Capitalism, too, received government assistance in building railroads and digging canals. Government subsidies were given to capitalists in the eighteenth century to encourage inventions and to stimulate industry, moreover.

In the twentieth century government

growth has been further stimulated by the appeals of capitalists in many areas. Subsidies are demanded and given to those in the agricultural sector, representing not the yeoman farmer but rather big corporations. Tariffs rise and fall depending upon the effects of competition from items produced in different countries. Technical assistance is provided to business interests through direct grants for research or through the provision of government services.

Government growth can be explained only in part by the demands of the capitalists for protection from competition and for other commercial purposes. The complexity of the economy led to government expansion. Air transport and communications are two of many examples of government intervention. In the United States private airline companies were formed during the early days of air transport. The need for air safety and the desire by the established airline companies to avoid competition in prices encouraged the development of government agencies that could achieve both goals. Traffic had to be regulated to avoid mid-air collisions, and aircraft had to be made airworthy.

In communications government agencies were established to control airwave frequencies. Radio stations, and later television stations, were given licenses to operate over specific frequencies so that they would not experience interference from other broadcasters.

Not only was the increased complexity of the economy a factor in government expansion, but so, too, were the demands from those whose interests were harmed by the rising power of industrial corporations, such as consumer and labor groups. In the nineteenth century, capitalism experienced the consolidation of firms and the rise of **monopolies** (in which one company controls the market for a product or service) and **oligopolies** (in which that power is held by a few companies). Demands were made to break up the giant industries so competitive forces would prevail. New government agencies were formed to achieve that goal.

Consumers in the twentieth century have been active in promoting government inspection of goods that have been produced by industry. To be sure, many companies in pursuing their own self-interest were concerned with producing high-quality products, but often companies were preoccupied with cutting costs— a factor that created hazards of safety and health. In more recent times, consumer groups have grown stronger in many countries and have spurred the growth of consumer-protection agencies for the purpose of providing credit opportunities and more rights for the consumer.

In addition to consumer demands, the rise of labor unions as a power in the political arena contributed to government growth. In the economic sector labor unions sought the protection of government to organize and to serve as collective bargaining agents. In the United States the National Labor Relations Board (NLRB) was established in 1935 to give labor those rights. Today, the NLRB deals with many cases involving disputes between labor and management. Labor also played an important role in the expansion of government in the welfare sector.

National Security

Protection of the country from external attack is an important element of government growth. Geographical location— a fixed component of international relations—permitted both the United States and Great Britain, as insular powers, centuries of low-level expenditures on military defense.

Some observers say that war is the most important reason for government growth. Modern war is a vast industrial operation requiring the centralized allocation of scarce resources for military purposes.

During wartime, governments establish or enlarge agencies for organizing military conscription, determining military priorities, and instituting price and wage controls. Countries often spend more on veterans' benefits than they do for the actual conduct of the wars for which the veterans fought.[4]

In the twentieth century, billions of dollars are spent each year on defense not only by the United States and Great Britain but also by other countries in the world (see Chapter 14). The defense budget of the United States constitutes a large share of the federal government's bureaucracy, although its percentage of total government expenditures has been surpassed by the welfare sector in the past several years. Totalitarian dictatorships often seek national security funds, moreover, to serve the needs of their large bureaucratic forces bent on control of other nations and people.

Welfare

In the twentieth century, the acceptance of the idea that the government has a responsibility to promote individual welfare through providing services in education, health, job security, and retirement assistance has contributed much to government growth. The welfare state is found in nearly every country in the world (see Chapter 5). In the United States it achieved its impetus from the New Deal programs of President Franklin D. Roosevelt in the 1930s. Welfare benefits have expanded in the United States during both Republican and Democratic administrations.

Today, government is engaged in furnishing welfare services to people. Government provides education not only at the elementary school level but also in high schools and colleges. Hospital and health services are furnished to needy people. People who are infirm, elderly, or sick receive benefits such as grants and direct services.

One reason why it is difficult to cut government spending is that the beneficiaries of welfare programs regard them as **entitlements**—that is to say, permanent benefits that individuals should receive when they are legally qualified to obtain them. Social Security, Medicare, unemployment compensation, and veterans' benefits are examples of entitlements. Entitlements plus other obligations of government, such as interest on the national debt, make about 80 percent of U.S. government spending "uncontrollable." Most other industrialized countries have even higher proportions of uncontrollable expenditures, because their social programs are more extensive than those of the United States.

Bureaucratic Pressures

Another cause of government growth is the government bureaucracy itself. Agencies tend to get bigger by promoting new programs and strengthening existing ones. Government agencies often seek to enlarge their size. The bigger an organization grows, the easier its chances for survival becomes. Opportunities for promotion are greater, moreover, as a government agency expands its budget. Even agencies whose original purposes seem forgotten tend to remain. In the words of a report of the Committee on Administrative Management in the administration of President Franklin D. Roosevelt, "There is among governmental agencies great need for a coroner to pronounce them dead, and for an undertaker to dispose of the remains."[5]

---

[4] See Bruce D. Porter, "Parkinson's Law Revisited: War and the Growth of American Government," *Public Interest*, no. 60 (Summer 1980): 50–68.

---

[5] *Administrative Management in the Government of*

Often the size of a bureaucracy increases not because of the impetus of new programs and greater enforcement, but rather because of a natural tendency of organizations to expand. Professor C. Northcote Parkinson suggests satirically that the reason for government growth can be explained in this manner. Parkinson analyzed the size of the British Colonial Office. He discovered that as the British Empire declined, the number of people employed in the British Colonial Office actually increased. He concludes from this and other data that **Parkinson's Law** applies to organizations, to wit: Work expands so as to fill the time available for its completion.[6] University professors have noted that Parkinson's Law applies in periods of declining student enrollment to university administrators and not to faculty members.

Some critics question the validity of Parkinson's Law. They note that although government agencies are resilient, some are not immortal.[7] They say that the size of some government organizations has been reduced, as was the case of the United States military establishment after World War II and the Vietnam War. They add that it is wrong to generalize based on superficial relationships. The British Colonial Office, for example, was given new tasks. It is no wonder, then, that it was increasing in size as Britain was losing its colonies.[8]

Government has grown, then, for many reasons. Although critics have complained about government growth, there is little likelihood that the size of the bureaucracy will decrease to any significant degree. Even many political leaders who are elected on a program of reducing government expenditures find that by the time their administrations have ended, government has grown bigger, not smaller. Ronald Reagan is a notable example. Bureaucracy seems to be a permanent feature of modern society.

HOW IS BUREAUCRACY ORGANIZED?

The huge and complex tasks of government require organization. Students of administration often refer to two different kinds of organization: formal and informal. **Formal organization** is the legal structure of a government unit. **Informal organization** is the unofficial arrangement of power that exists because of political or personal factors not related to the formal organizational structure.

Formal Organization

The principal classification of the administrative machinery of government is the department or ministry. The department is divided into agencies, bureaus, or divisions. At the top of the department are the political appointees, but the offices of the organization are staffed primarily by permanent public officials.

In describing organizations, some writers in administration make a distinction between line and staff agencies. **Line agencies** are organizations concerned with the direct performance of the functional goals of the administrative unit. **Staff agencies** are organizations that perform advisory functions. In the actual behavior of the agencies of government, however, it is difficult to distinguish the functions that line and staff agencies perform. Other kinds of agencies are **housekeeping** or **service agencies,** which engage in tasks

the United States (Washington, D.C.: Government Printing Office, 1937), p. 34.

[6] C. Northcote Parkinson, *Parkinson's Law and Other Studies in Administration* (Boston: Houghton Mifflin, 1957), p. 2.

[7] See Herbert Kaufman, *Are Government Organizations Immortal?* (Washington, D.C.: Brookings Institution, 1976).

[8] Porter, "Parkinson's Law Revisited," p. 53.

that are common to a number of agencies, such as transportation, personnel, and purchasing functions.

From a formal organizational point of view, power is at the top. Subordinates are assigned tasks throughout the hierarchy or chain of command. Each subordinate has a specific job and is responsible to his or her immediate superior.

Informal Organization

In practice, few organizations actually function according to the power relationships suggested by a model of formal organization. Often bureaucrats lower down the chain of command have more influence than their superiors. For years, for example, J. Edgar Hoover, as director of the Federal Bureau of Investigation (FBI), had so much influence and such high prestige that his superiors—the men who served as attorney general in different administrations—were restrained in dealing with him.

Bureaucrats accumulate a vast expertise and important contacts over the years. Political appointees often hold their positions for a short period of time, but career government officials work in their departments in many cases for decades. If the rank-and-file members of a bureaucracy do not agree with the policies of their political leaders, they can sometimes circumvent those leaders through manipulating informal sources of influence. The administration of Richard Nixon complained, for example, that the bureaucracy was not responsive to the administration's political commands. Nixon, consequently, enlarged the staff of the Executive Office in an attempt to get the bureaucracy to respond to his will.

Because of the system of the separation of powers in the United States, the bureaucracy is often free to play off elected officials in the legislative and executive branches against each other in a manner calculated to enhance the interests of the bureaucracy. In the United States, however, the politics of the bureaucracy is often subjected to public observation. In other political systems bureaucratic politics frequently operates beyond scrutiny by the general public.

Bureaucracies, then, are part of the political process and are not the neutral administrators that Wilson and Goodnow described. The informal ties that have developed between the bureaucracy and political leaders have helped to strengthen the bureaucracy in different political systems and made it a permanent feature of modern political systems.

THE COMPOSITION OF THE BUREAUCRACY

Governments have used different methods to staff administrative offices. In prerevolutionary eighteenth-century France, government offices were purchased and dispensed as private property. Another method of staffing government was used in the United States in the early nineteenth century: The victorious president and his party distributed government jobs to supporters. Under Andrew Jackson this system of political patronage became known as the **spoils system.** Jackson's partisans argued that the elected officials should be able to staff government departments with people committed to the principles of the victor. "To the victor belong the spoils" was the slogan of those supporting the Jacksonian method of recruiting personnel.

The systems of purchase and spoils had defects. Purchase did not provide for an equitable or effective means of administration. The spoils system made staffing too unstable, as new administrators replaced the old with the frequency of changeovers by electoral results. Both systems required no expertise for appointment, moreover.

The modern movement to create a

trained professional public service, or **civil service,** began in eighteenth-century Prussia. The Napoleonic administrative reforms in France, moreover, became a model for reforms in other countries. The civil service in Prussia and France established the principles of a professional career in civil service with protection of the status and tenure of public employees.

In Great Britain, the Trevelyan-Northcote report of 1854 led in the following year to the formation of a Civil Service Commission that set the basis for civil service reform. By 1870, entrance in the Home Civil Service was established based on open competitive examinations.

In the United States, the movement for civil service reform intensified after the Civil War. Its objective was to curb the abuses of the political "machines" from public service. The Civil Service Reform Act was passed in 1883. A Civil Service Commission was created, and a system of competitive examinations was made the basis for hiring federal government employees. The law initially covered only 10.5 percent of all federal jobs, but was gradually expanded to include more than 90 percent of federal government employees by 1986. Some government units, such as the FBI and the Central Intelligence Agency (CIA), remain outside the jurisdiction of the Office of Personnel Management (a successor agency of the Civil Service Commission) and recruit directly through their own procedures, but these government organizations, too, use merit as a criterion for selection. Most state governments use comprehensive merit systems for selecting state employees.

The character of the civil service varies among countries. For example, the American and British systems, although based on merit, differ in some respects. The American system encourages specialized backgrounds and a career service open to a wide variety of talents, while the British system opts for generalists and a closed career service. In addition, the higher offices at the assistant secretary and undersecretary level in the United States are mostly political, rather than civil service, appointees. In Great Britain, however, the corresponding positions are held by civil servants. The higher civil service in Britain, moreover, is dominated by Oxford and Cambridge graduates, whereas the American civil service leadership has a broader recruitment base.

Other characteristics of the civil service vary among countries in socioeconomic composition, honesty, and professional training. In general, however, the features of a modern civil service system remain the same: a group of professional public servants, gaining position on the basis of objective competitive examinations, promotion through seniority and merit, and protection from dismissal through party or personal considerations. This is the model that reformers have used in the past two centuries, although there are ample cases in which these standards are not applied.

ISSUE

The extent of government growth throughout the world cannot be denied. The significance of that growth and the evaluation of bureaucracy's power, however, have become controversial issues. A primary concern of students of bureaucracy is an appraisal of the effectiveness of democratic controls on the civil service.

22/YES

CAN THE BUREAUCRACY BE CONTROLLED IN A DEMOCRACY?

Democracy, by definition, is a system of government based on popular rule. Democracy, in practice, provides sufficient safeguards against bureaucracies to make them accountable to the people. Among the most significant of these safeguards are: (1) elections; (2) constitutional and political constraints imposed by the legislative, executive, and judicial branches; (3) referenda; (4) the controls that the bureaucracy exerts on itself; and (5) the impact of nongovernmental actors in the political process, such as interest groups, political parties, and the media.

Elections. A major component of democracy is free elections based on the principle of majority rule. Particularly in parliamentary systems, but in presidential ones as well, candidates and political parties put forward programs that they intend to carry out if they are elected. If the electorate is unhappy with the actions of the governing officials, it can elect a new group of leaders who will redirect the bureaucracy.

Although the electorate may be displeased with the acts of particular bureaucrats, in general it has supported the expansion of government services. There is scarcely much political support for eliminating services required for public safety, such as fire and police protection. Public education programs also have popular support, as do social security and veterans' benefits. If the bureaucracy grows, it is because people basically approve of the government services they are receiving and elect political leaders who will assure the continuation of those services.

Constitutional and Political Constraints. Democratic political systems have many safeguards against bureaucratic usurpation. Legislative, executive, and judicial institutions act to provide political direction of the bureaucracy.

Legislative controls involve laws, appropriations, appointments, investigation, and supervision. Traditionally, legislatures enact laws that control government agencies. Some of these laws establish the jurisdiction of agencies. Legislatures have even passed legislation destroying particular government units.

The lifeblood of government agencies is appropriations. Legislatures can destroy the effectiveness of an agency by reducing the amount of money it has to operate. Legislatures assure that the funding of an agency depends on how well that bureaucratic unit serves the public.

Legislatures also play a role in appointments, and the political appointees who reach high-level positions greatly influence the behavior of the government agency involved. The legislature can use the power of confirming appointments to influence how a government agency will act.

Legislatures may also use their powers of investigation to influence bureaucratic behavior. When legislative units observe and investigate government agencies, they are performing the function of **oversight.** Investigations are sometimes conducted to uncover facts that bureaucrats may be reluctant to reveal. Often, however, investigations are designed to influence public opinion and to point out to the bureaucracy that it is not moving in the direction the legislature prefers.

Finally, the legislature has at its command some bureaucratic institutions that are directly accountable to it. In the United States, the General Accounting Office (GAO) is an agent of Congress that audits administrative expenditures. Such a custodian of the nation's purse serves as a watchdog against unauthorized use of funds appropriated to different government agencies. In addition, many countries have the office of **ombudsman,** in which a troubleshooter with direct access to the legislature is appointed to remove the obstacles of red tape created by the bureaucracies in their dealings with the public (see Chapter 11).

In many democratic systems the executives have power to control the bureaucracy. The executives direct overall policy, influence legislation, and make appointments to the political positions dominating the bureaucracy.

Heads of government normally have principal administrative power. They are at the helm of state and thus can direct policy. In the United States, for example, the president heads the cabinet; and the cabinet, in turn, dominates the bureaucracy. If the president decides to pursue a particular course in foreign policy, the State Department and Defense Department bureaucracy must provide support lest disciplinary measures be taken. When General Douglas MacArthur took unauthorized actions as United States military commander in South Korea during the Korean War, his commander-in-chief, President Harry Truman, fired him. Truman's action against an insubordinate official is typical of disciplinary measures that may be taken against bureaucrats in military and nonmilitary positions.

The power of the chief executives over policy is often revealed in their role in legislation. In a system of separation of powers, they may veto bills they do not like. American presidents have, moreover, increasingly developed centralized budgetary controls that influence bureaucratic behavior. In the United States, the Office of Management and Budget (OMB) gives the president powers in this manner, and similar institutions have been established in other countries.

Heads of government have powers of appointment. Not only do they designate officials to cabinet-level positions and fire them if they do not carry out their duties according to their policy goals, but they also use their own staffs to supervise the vast bureaucracy. Both the cabinet and staff members supervise the bureaucracy carefully so that the vast government apparatus conforms to political rule. The Reagan administration provides a recent successful example of executive control of the bureaucracy (leaving aside whether one agrees or disagrees with the policies of that administration). It achieved this goal in many ways: It appointed loyal officials, committed to Reagan's philosophy, to important staff positions. It organized the functions of the executive office so that the executive staff's relations with the cabinet and subcabinet members were good. It instituted deregulation through administrative action in many cases, and it transferred personnel who were not acting as the president's advisers wanted.[9]

The courts are often the last resort for both citizens and elected officials when the bureaucracy acts in an irresponsible manner. An individual who feels that he or she has been subjected to unfair treatment by the bureaucracy is free to take a government agency to task for such unfairness.

Court records are filled with cases won by citizens against police officials who exceeded their authority, tax collectors who interpreted the tax law incorrectly, and inspectors who invaded people's privacy. The principle of the rule of law in which every act of an official must be taken according to a specific law must be obeyed by public officials if they expect their official actions to be sustained by judicial authority.

Referenda. Another important constraint on the bureaucracy is the use of the referendum (see Chapter 3). In some countries, the people can vote directly on matters that have a vital influence on the strength and policies of the bureaucracy. Voters have decided many issues in this way, including tax authorization for roads, schools, and libraries; the level of taxation in general; and the creation of police review boards. Although referenda do not exist in many parliamentary systems, they do offer a means of influencing bureaucratic behavior.

Self-Control. Although public officials are subject to legal controls, they often act in a responsible manner not because of those controls but rather because of their commitment to a code of behavior based on professional principles. The fire fighters who risk their lives to rescue invalids trapped in burning buildings, the public school teachers who zealously help their students to advance in their careers, the health officials who successfully locate the source of food poisoning—all are displaying pride in their work and the highest standards of professional conduct. Such codes of self-control often make the bureaucracy responsible as much as the more formal political controls.

---

[9] For a study of executive control of the bureaucracy in the Nixon and Reagan administrations, see Richard P. Nathan, *The Administrative Presidency*

(New York: Wiley, 1983). See also Peter M. Benda and Charles H. Levine, "Reagan and the Bureaucracy: The Bequest, the Promise and the Legacy," in *The Reagan Legacy: Promise and Performance,* ed. Charles O. Jones (Chatham, N.J.: Chatham House, 1988), pp. 102–42.

Interest Groups, the Media, and Political Parties. In democracies, bureaucracies respond to pressure from interest groups, the media, and political parties. Political interest groups exert influence in all sectors of the political process (see Chapter 9). Since the bureaucracy is important in making policy, interest groups attempt to influence its political behavior. A steel manufacturer needing protection from imports, farmers pressing for subsidies, feminists demanding support by government for affirmative action programs, and veterans insisting on educational benefits—all these are examples of the sometimes successful pleadings of interest groups in their bids to get the bureaucracy to respond to their demands.

Interest groups are strengthened by their expertise, which can challenge the expertise of the bureaucracy. When Defense Department agencies vigorously defended President Reagan's "Star War" directives for building a space defense system, they were challenged by scientific organizations such as the Union of Concerned Scientists. This group, consisting of internationally renowned scientists, some of whom were Nobel laureates, argued that the program was expensive, destabilizing with respect to U.S.-Soviet military relationships, and unworkable. Their expertise gave them credibility with some members of Congress.

In addition to interest groups, the media have come to play an effective role in influencing the bureaucracy. Investigations by journalists from the print and electronic media have resulted in changes in bureaucratic behavior in such matters as the administration of prisons and mental health institutions.

Political parties, too, play a role. The people chosen to head cabinet-level positions are often prominent members of the victorious political party. Particularly in those countries in which political parties are strong, the appointment power is important. The political appointees of the bureaucracy influence the activities of the bureaucracy and make it responsive to popular pressure.

Because the public is accustomed to notice the violations of law by the bureaucracy, it sometimes neglects to recognize the many responsible actions of the bureaucracy. Democratic systems have created adequate political safeguards to prevent the bureaucracy from acting as a "state within the state." Codes of professional conduct, moreover, help the bureaucrats to keep within proper bounds.

Critics of bureaucracy tend to describe the bureaucracy as if it were some hideous unified organization. In fact, bureaucrats are more likely to be at odds with each other than they are with the elected public officials who direct them. Air force, army, and navy contend among themselves for missions and control of a larger share of the defense budget. State universities compete with each other for research funds. Regional and national bureaucracies vie for control over administration of different projects. Bureaucracies, then, are so divided among themselves in a democracy that they permit the political leaders to pick and choose among them and, consequently, provide political direction.

Bureaucracies are not out of control of democratic forces. They are the servants of democracy, and not the masters.

22/NO   CAN THE BUREAUCRACY BE CONTROLLED IN A DEMOCRACY?

Although democracies claim to have political control of the bureaucracy, in actual fact these controls are generally ineffectual. Bureaucracies are able to circumvent the ostensible controls imposed by: (1) elections; (2) constitutional and political constraints placed by the legislative, executive, and judicial branches; and (3) referenda. Moreover, (4) bureaucratic self-controls often work to impede political

controls rather than to enhance them, and (5) the non-governmental actors that might exercise controls have been kept in check by an increasingly big and powerful government.

Elections. Elections do not have the influence they are supposed to have according to their democratic proponents. In presidential systems the separate election of executive and legislature makes it difficult, if not impossible, to hold a single political group responsible for government action (see Chapter 11). Bureaucracies are, consequently, free to manipulate the two branches of government. In many parliamentary systems political leadership is exercised by an unstable coalition of political parties, and this situation results in enhanced power for the permanent bureaucracy. Even in a stable two-party parliamentary system, such as exists in Great Britain, the ruling leaders are enormously dependent upon the bureaucracy for their expertise and their support.

Constitutional and Political Constraints. Legislative powers to make laws, establish budgets, confirm appointments, conduct investigations, audit government expenditures, and serve as watchdogs over bureaucratic dealings with citizens are inadequate instruments of political control. This was not always the case. In the nineteenth century, legislatures in democracies were powerful, but that was at a time when the tasks of government were less complicated. In the twentieth century, however, Congress and the legislatures of other countries have lost much of their power, and the unelected bureaucracy has assumed many of the powers previously belonging to the legislatures.

Bureaucratic power has risen in part because of the sheer volume of bills that legislators must consider. Even industrious legislators do not have time to read every bill, let alone understand them. So complex are the subjects dealt with by law that legislators have often written legislation in the most general terms and have given discretion to government agencies to act within certain guidelines. The amount of discretion is great, unfortunately. Bureaucrats must themselves interpret legislative mandates. A law directing an agency to act "in the public interest" is a case in point. The concept of public interest is so ambiguous as to allow agencies great leeway in acting. In making rules, consequently, many of the agencies are in fact legislating. Theoretically, there is a distinction between an administrative ruling and a law; in practice, however, agencies legislate.

The traditional power of legislatures over the budget has been much diminished, too. The influence of the executive branch has been strengthened in the preparation of the budget,

and it is difficult for the legislative branch to present an alternative budget. Budget proposals are generally prepared by the bureaucracy itself, which seeks to preserve its prerogatives. Political scientist Aaron Wildavsky observes for the United States that the largest determining factor of the size and content of this year's budget is last year's budget.[10] The system of achieving steady increases in the funding of bureaucracies—or **incrementalism** as it is called—is actually written into the French budgetary process, in which items in the *services votés* are accepted unless there is an explicit challenge and only new items *(measures nouvelles)* are given careful examination.[11] This is to say that bureaucracies generally count on a certain amount of funding from year to year and then they can bargain for more. Legislators' actual influence to alter budgets in any significant manner (except in an upward direction) is minimal, as the record of continually rising government expenditures in democracies suggests in most cases.

In theory, the legislative power of confirmation over political appointments is important in controlling the bureaucracy. In some countries the legislature does not have that power, since the executive decides on appointments. In any event, the bureaucracy can influence the confirmation process in those systems that grant legislatures a formal veto over appointments. One can be sure, for example, that the bureaucracy in the Department of Agriculture would use its political influence to assure that someone friendly to agricultural interests is selected to be secretary of agriculture in the United States. Bureaucracies in other departments would act similarly if confronted with the nomination of potentially unfriendly secretaries.

Legislative investigations are not effective safeguards against bureaucratic power. These investigations often attract public attention through the media, particularly television, but in fact they are limited in the influence they have on bureaucracies. Agencies may make cosmetic changes to get the spotlight of public

---

[10] Aaron Wildavsky, *The New Politics of the Budgetary Process* (Glenview, Ill.: Scott, Foresman, 1988), pp. 78–79.

[11] B. Guy Peters, *The Politics of Bureaucracy*, 2d ed. (New York: Longman, 1984), p. 214.

attention off them for the moment. Soon, however, they are back to their old habits. In the aftermath of the Vietnam War and Watergate, for example, the Central Intelligence Agency (CIA) was subjected to severe scrutiny by congressional investigations. These inquests revealed major wrongdoing, and congressional efforts were successfully made to restrict the powers of the CIA in covert operations abroad and in domestic surveillance. By the early 1980s, however, the CIA was regaining much of its power in these areas. Political controls were not strong enough to keep the CIA in check.

Legislative powers in auditing are after-the-fact determinations, and they have minimal influence on the bureaucracy. Although considerable publicity is generated by close observation of how bureaucracies dispense funds, audits take a long time to complete. Promises to reform are often made when wrongdoing or foolish expenditures are uncovered, but there is no remedying past sins.

Finally, although the ombudsman has been somewhat helpful, such an institution has not been established in every country. Usually, moreover, the ombudsman's success depends upon voluntary compliance by the bureaucracy. The voluntary aspect leaves many areas of bureaucratic wrongdoing beyond the control of elected legislative officials.

The executive is even less influential in dealing with the bureaucracy than is the legislature. The powers of directing overall policy, influencing legislation, and making political appointments are not strong enough to budge the entrenched bureaucracy.

In directing overall policy, the head of government is often at a greater disadvantage than is the legislature. At least many members of the legislature are in office for long periods of time and consequently develop an expertise in particular areas of public policy that are of interest to them and their constituencies. Often, however, the head of government is not in power for a long period of time and does not possess the specialized knowledge necessary to master the intricate details in which the bureaucracy revels.

The bureaucracy can insulate itself from executive controls in many ways. It possesses information that it can release or withhold as it deems necessary to strengthen its political position. It can, moreover, call on interest groups in the private sector to rally around the government organization when threatened by the executive. When a chief executive decides to close down a military installation as an economy move, for example, the military bureaucracy is assisted by all those interest groups that gain economically from the existence of that military installation. The military bureaucracy carefully cultivates private associations, and its behavior in this regard is not unlike that of other segments of the bureaucracy. Similar dominance is achieved by the welfare bureaucracy, the educational bureaucracy, and other bureaucracies for control in their areas of public policy.

In addition to facing obstacles to directing overall policy, the head of government has difficulty in getting his or her legislation adopted. Much of the legislation is written by the bureaucracy itself, and it is no wonder that bureaucrats have a vested interest in maintaining a condition of dependence on government by the poor. The welfare bureaucrats, consequently, have resisted attempts to bypass them through the creation of a negative income tax—a system which if implemented could result in reducing the number of welfare bureaucrats.

The executive's power to make appointments is limited in controlling the bureaucracy. If the executive chooses someone hostile to the department he or she is to administer, the candidate may find it difficult either to be confirmed by the legislature or, if confirmed, to actually rule the department. Informal patterns of power are maintained by the bureaucracy with the legislature. Bureaucrats, moreover, can make the head of a government agency look bad and undermine the political base of support. A new reform police chief, for example, may find that too vigorous application of new rules leads to opposition by the rank-and-file members of the police department. The police have been able to undermine the political leadership through strict enforcement of the traffic laws, for example, leading to public frustration with the police chief.

Even efforts to increase the staff of the executive have not proven successful. The executive staff, often numbering in the hundreds and in some cases the low thousands, is no match for the bureaucracy in the government agencies. The staff lacks the numbers, expertise, and influence to challenge the entrenched bureaucracy.

The judicial power to control the bureaucracy is limited both as a practical matter and because of new developments within the bureaucracy. As a practical matter, the ordinary citizen does not possess the resources to challenge bureaucrats. It takes time and money to prove that a driver was not speeding, as a police official charges. It is much easier to pay the ticket. The old adage, "You can't fight City Hall," suggests the frustration that the ordinary citizen faces when dealing with the city bureaucracy.

Yet another limitation of the judiciary is the establishment of administrative tribunals. Although higher courts are often permitted to review decisions of an administrative tribunal, in practice the courts have often preferred to let the administrative rulings stand. Courts lack the necessary expertise to deal with the technical problems examined by the specialized, administrative tribunals. To the extent that bureaucracies can adjudicate conflicts, they retain the judicial function within their own power.

Referenda. Although referenda are sometimes used in efforts to influence bureaucratic behavior, they are not generally successful in achieving those results. The referendum is not a legal device in many political systems. It is sometimes used in a nonbinding manner nationally, although it is employed in a binding manner regionally and locally. Even in those instances when it is used, the referendum can be managed to suit the needs of the bureaucracy.

One way of circumventing the will of the people through a referendum is through the phrasing of a referendum question. A question may be asked in such an obscure way that wrangling will continue for years after the results are in. The scheduling of a referendum, moreover, can affect the outcome. A referendum can be made part of the general election, which will produce a large turnout of voters. Or a referendum can be conducted at vacation time when perhaps only a small percentage of the voters—those most organized by the bureaucracies—will turn out. The notion that referenda provide a popular check on the bureaucracy, then, is false.

Self-Control. It is certainly true that the overwhelming majority of bureaucrats are hardworking and honest. Many maintain strong professional standards in their work. We should not, however, confuse commitment to professionalism with political controls. For example, military officers who are committed to the professional standards of their services often act in ways to strengthen the military services rather than subject themselves and their military organization to political control. Self-control in this fashion is the very opposite of democratic control.

Interest Groups, the Media, and Political Parties. Neither interest groups, nor the media, nor political parties provide the necessary controls of the bureaucracy. In every industrial democratic nation in the world, government has come to play a prominent role in the management of the economy. In some countries entire industries previously held in private hands are now dominated by the government. Government controls now extend in varying degrees of power to prices, wages, credit, and employment. Government subsidies to private businesses assure many a quiescent and supportive business interest group. In defense industries, in particular, government military managers direct the "private" industries.

Interest group subordination to government is not the case for economic associations alone; it also applies to other private associations. Government involvement in social equality, consumer protection, and welfare has also made "private" associations subservient to the dictates of the bureaucracy.

The media have been as ineffective as interest groups in moving the bureaucracy. Media interest is episodic. The media do not have the resources to investigate the bureaucracy thoroughly. In some areas, particularly national security, bureaucrats are forbidden by law from passing along "classified" information to the media. In some democracies, moreover, government either owns, controls, or dominates the electronic media, particularly television.

It is true that **whistleblowers** (government employees who reveal wrongdoing by government organizations) do give information to the media about government wrongdoing. The media then provide the information to the general public. Often, however, the whistleblower whistles his or her career away, as fellow workers in the agency look on him or her as a traitor. Few whistleblowers are successful in moving up the career ladder in the government agencies for which they work.

Political parties, too, cease to have much influence—at least not the influence they once had. In the United States political parties are weak (see Chapter 8). A substantial amount of political patronage is no longer in the hands of political parties but has been transferred to civil service commissions. In nearly every Western democratic country, the civil service performs functions, such as providing jobs and dispensing social services, that were previously handled by political parties.

The bureaucracy, then, has appeared in democratic countries and has grown in power. In the United States, for example, the administration of government is scarcely noted in the Constitution. Yet the bureaucracy has risen here as elsewhere. Bureaucratic power has expanded throughout the world to a point beyond the mere carrying out of the laws. It has moved into executive, legislative, and judicial areas previously held by others. It has consequently made a mockery of democracy. In this regard, it is well to recall the warning of James Madison in the *Federalist Papers:* "The accumulation of all powers legislative, executive, and judiciary in the same hands . . . may justly be pronounced the very definition of tyranny."[12] The bureaucrats in "democracy," then, have achieved what Madison and others of his time feared: the concentration of power. Having concentrated their power, they put to disbelief the notion that the people in a democracy actually rule.

----

[12] James Madison, *Federalist*, no. 47, in Alexander Hamilton, James Madison, and John Jay, *The Federalist Papers*, ed. Clinton Rossiter (New York: New American Library, 1961), p. 301.

KEY TERMS

Administration	Monopolies
Bureaucracy	Oligopolies
Civil service	Ombudsman
Entitlements	Oversight
Formal organization	Parkinson's Law
Housekeeping agencies	Service agencies
Incrementalism	Spoils system
Informal organization	Staff agencies
Line agencies	Whistleblowers

QUESTIONS

1. How would you assess the accuracy of Parkinson's Law in describing the size of the bureaucracy?
2. How would you compare the behavior of bureaucracy in democracies with its behavior in dictatorships?
3. What are the similarities and the differences between public and private bureaucracy?
4. How would you compare the behavior of the military bureaucracy with nonmilitary bureaucracies in a democracy?
5. Can government spending be cut? If Yes, how? If No, why not?
6. How can bureaucracy be made more accountable in a democracy?

RECOMMENDED READINGS

BEETHAM, DAVID. *Bureaucracy.* Minneapolis: University of Minnesota Press, 1987. A brief analysis.

BLAU, PETER M., and MARSHALL W. MEYER. *Bureaucracy in Modern Society.* 3d ed. New York: Random House, 1987. A sociological study of organizations.

BOLLIER, DAVID, and JOAN CLAYBROOK. "Regulations That Work." *Washington Monthly* 18 (April 1986): 47–54. Case studies of regulatory success.

BURKE, JOHN P. *Bureaucratic Responsibility.* Baltimore: Johns Hopkins University Press, 1986. A theory of bureaucratic responsibility.

BURNHAM, JAMES. *The Managerial Revolution.* Bloomington, Ind.: Indiana University Press, 1966. A major work predicting the rise and dominance of a managerial class.

FRIEDEN, KARL. "Public Needs and Private Wants." *Dissent* 34 (Summer 1987): 317–25. A criticism of the argument that government is inefficient.

GOODSELL, CHARLES T. *The Case for Bureaucracy: A Public Administration Polemic.* 2d ed. Chatham, N.J.: Chatham House, 1985. A defense of bureaucracy in the United States.

KAUFMAN, HERBERT. *Are Government Organizations Immortal?* Washington, D.C.: Brookings Institution, 1976. An argument that government organizations are endurable but that their death rate is not negligible.

MATEJKO, ALEXANDER J. *The Self-Defeating Organization: A Critique of Bureaucracy.* Westport, Conn.: Praeger, 1986. A plea for alternatives to bureaucracy.

PARKINSON, C. NORTHCOTE. *Parkinson's Law and Other Studies in Administration.* Boston: Houghton Mifflin, 1957. An explanation of bureaucratic expansion based not on societal needs but on the tendency of government agencies to expand.

RILEY, DENNIS T. *Controlling the Federal Bureaucracy.* Philadelphia: Temple University Press, 1987. A study of the U.S. bureaucracy.

ROSE, RICHARD. *Understanding Big Government: The Programme Approach.* London: Sage, 1984. An assessment of the problem of big government in contemporary society.

ROSEN, BERNARD. *Holding Government Bureaucracies Accountable.* New York: Praeger, 1982. An analysis of accountability in the American administrative system.

VON MISES, LUDWIG. *Bureaucracy.* New Haven: Yale University Press, 1944. An indictment of bureaucracy as a form of tyranny.

WEBER, MAX. *From Max Weber: Essays in Sociology,* ed. H.H. Gerth and C. Wright Mills. New York: Oxford University Press, 1946. Chapter 8 contains Weber's classic work on bureaucracy.

WILDAVSKY, AARON. *The New Politics of the Budgetary Process.* Glenview, Ill.: Scott, Foresman, 1988. A comprehensive analysis of the budgetary process in the United States.

part VI

INTERNATIONAL POLITICS

Politics is the study of allocation of values. In domestic politics the values may be economic, security, psychological, welfare, or ideological. International politics, which deals primarily with the relations among states, is also the study of the allocation of these values. International politics, however, is different from domestic politics because ordinarily, in the international arena, there is an expectation of violence rather than peace. The conditions essential for peace within a state—effective legal institutions, a constitutional consensus, and an expectation of justice—are lacking in a global context.

In international politics, there is a greater anticipation of violence than in domestic politics, as may be seen from the size of military budgets. Countries of the world spend more than a total of a trillion dollars each year for military purposes. Some of this money is used to maintain order at home. The bulk, however, is disbursed to protect the state

against foreign enemies. To be sure, there is much intrastate violence in the world, as the conflicts between Catholics and Protestants in Northern Ireland and between Christians and Muslims in Lebanon demonstrate.

Fear of violence, then, sets the stage for international politics in a way that it generally does not in domestic politics. Another difference between the two types of political activity involves legal institutions. Politics within a state operates frequently within a context of effective national legal institutions. Executive, legislative, and judicial powers are spelled out in the state's constitutional documents. When a violation of the law occurs, as in the case of a mugging, a witness may call the police, who, in turn, try to protect or assist the victim and apprehend the assailant for subsequent trial. The legal institutions at the international level, however, are not powerful. International institutions, such as the General Assembly of the United Nations and the International Court of Justice (ICJ), depend upon the voluntary cooperation of the states. It is literally possible for states to get away with international murder because there is no effective international police force that possesses greater power than the military forces of the states.

A reason for the absence of such international legal institutions is that constitutional consensus is more likely to characterize the communities that constitute a state than the international political system. Although states that contain diverse and conflicting ethnic and economic divisions sometimes suffer from political instability, often they do not.

A consensus is often achieved domestically rather than internationally because people expect justice from the government and are willing to abide by its laws and policies. In the domestic context, people often respect laws that they oppose because they feel that, overall, the system is just. A similar feeling toward international institutions is usually absent or weak.

Because of these considerations dealing with violence, legal institutions, constitutional consensus, and justice, self-preservation or security becomes an important goal. The study of international politics, consequently, is dominated by the quest for security, although other factors play important roles in motivating states' behavior.

Chapter 13 discusses the participants in international relations, with a focus on states. It deals with the factors motivating states in their relations with other countries. An issue involving aid to poor countries is then considered.

Chapter 14 discusses power in world politics and the methods that states use in their relations with other states. Issues of the decline of U.S. power, the effectiveness of economic sanctions, and the possibility of disarmament are considered.

chapter 13

International politics: motivations

Consider some of the major news stories in the 1980s:

- Iran and Iraq pursue a war for several years and then sue for peace.
- The United States and the Soviet Union ratify the Intermediate-range Nuclear Forces Treaty.
- The Palestine Liberation Organization (PLO) announces the creation of a Palestinian state and accepts the existence of Israel.
- Members of the Organization of Petroleum Exporting Countries (OPEC) meet in unsuccessful efforts to fix the world market price of oil.
- Pakistan is accused of secretly planning to build nuclear weapons.

Matters such as these that affect people of diverse locations across national or continental lines are often described as world politics. As the news stories indicate, world politics may affect war and peace, personal security, and economic well-being. When Iran and Iraq are at war, it is possible that neighboring states and the major powers of the world will become embroiled in the fighting. When terrorists hijack an aircraft, tourists in distant countries may cancel plans to travel abroad. When the world market price of oil plummets, the economic condition of oil-importing countries improves.

In this chapter we will study the actors who are engaged in world politics and why the principal actors behave the way they do.

THE ACTORS

Who They Are

States are the primary actors in world politics. The features of a state—people, territory, government, and sovereignty—are described in Chapter 1. The world is composed of more than 160 states varying in power, objectives, and culture. Military power, for the most part, is dominated by the state. The state collects taxes to finance armies and organizes the defense of the political community.

The state is not the only actor in the global arena, however. Groups and international organizations are other actors in that arena, and they are playing a more important role in this century than they did in the last. Among groups affecting world politics, economic, religious, subnational or ethnic, and professional organizations play the most important roles.

In the twentieth century one of the prominent economic groups is the multinational corporation (MNC), which is defined in Chapter 2 as a large enterprise with offices and/or branches in numerous countries conducting business operations across state lines. Among the more notable examples are International Telephone and Telegraph (ITT), International Business Machines (IBM), and Shell Oil Company. More than a century ago, Karl Marx noted the increasing interdependency of the global economy brought on by the rise of industrialism in the West. The twentieth-century form of that interdependency is sometimes seen in such MNCs.

Religious groups also are prominent global actors. When the pope speaks on matters of faith or politics, Catholics all over the world are interested in what he says. At times the interests of the Catholic church and the interests of the political leaders who govern Catholic countries conflict, as the cases of Poland and Cuba attest. Other religious groups—Jews, Muslims, and Protestants, for example—also play important roles in global politics.

Subnational or ethnic associations are also actors. As Chapter 2 indicates, the world is filled with states of diverse ethnic backgrounds. Some ethnic groups resent the existence of specific borders. In some cases these groups organize paramilitary units in an attempt to achieve a separate state. The PLO is perhaps the most notable example. It seeks to establish a Palestinian homeland in the Middle East and engages in military and diplomatic efforts to achieve its objectives. It is recognized by many states although it is not a state. The PLO is one of many subnational actors, and other organizations seeking independence for Puerto Rico, Armenia, and Kurdistan have also achieved some notoriety.

Professional associations often reflect professional interests that transcend national barriers. International associations concerned with psychology or medicine, for example, have asserted the need to promote professional standards when those standards were in jeopardy in various places around the world. The effectiveness of these organizations varies from group to group, however, but they are not without influence.

International organizations are also actors in the global arena. There are different types of these organizations: general international organizations, regional organizations, functional agencies, and alliances.

General international organizations involve nearly all the countries of the world and deal with a variety of international problems. In this century the League of Nations and the United Nations are examples of general international organizations.

Regional organizations are international organizations that are concerned with a specific geographic region. The Organization of American States (OAS), whose members come from the Western hemisphere, is a regional organization concerned with hemispheric problems. The Arab League is another example of a regional organization.

Functional agencies are international organizations concerned with specific social, agricultural, or health policy. The

World Health Organization (WHO), which deals with problems of health such as the eradication of small pox and cholera, is a prominent example. The Food and Agricultural Organization (FAO) and the United Nations Educational, Scientific, and Cultural Organization (UNESCO) are others.

Alliances are organizations of common defense among nations. The North Atlantic Treaty Organization (NATO), which is today composed of the United States and fifteen other countries, was established in 1949 for the purpose of mutual defense primarily against the Soviet Union. The Warsaw Pact, which today consists of the Soviet Union and six Eastern European allies, was set up in 1955 as a counter to the inclusion of the Federal Republic of Germany in the NATO alliance.

The Declining Significance of the State?

Some writers argue that the state is declining in significance. They point to military, economic, and environmental factors as evidence.

The state was founded in part to provide for greater military security, which more local institutions could not furnish in the face of technological developments in weaponry. In the age of intercontinental ballistic missiles and nuclear weapons the state can no longer assure security because there is no defense against nuclear weapons at the present level of technology.

Economic security was another reason for the creation of the state. The world, however, has become interdependent. Decisions made in a country may affect economies of different countries. New actors, such as MNCs, have come to dominate states in economic matters. The annual income of Exxon, for example, is higher than the annual income of most countries in the world.

Environmental problems, such as water pollution, air pollution, and the decline of rain forests, are increasingly perceived as global problems requiring global solutions. For example, the people living in a state may pollute its waterways. Often, however, the pollution cannot be confined to that state but affects other states, as well.

The view that states are declining is challenged. Some writers contend that the state is still the major provider of security, economic well-being, and environmental protection. Although there are problems that have transcended state boundaries, these writers say, the state has been able to solve them without relinquishing its authority.

Even most writers who see the state in decline do not regard it as extinct—like the dinosaur. Because of its preeminence, we shall focus our attention on the state in this and the next chapter. Here we shall concern ourselves with the factors motivating state behavior.

WHY DO STATES BEHAVE THE WAY THEY DO?

A psychiatrist may spend many hours, days, and months with a patient to piece together an explanation of why the patient behaves the way he or she does. Social scientists devote much more time analyzing state behavior. Because there are so many actors involved in international politics and because the historical record is always limited, the problems for social science investigation are enormous.

A variety of theories have been put forward to explain why states behave the way they do. Experts on **geopolitics,** for example, try to explain international behavior in terms of geographical relationships. Marxists have found economics to be the single motivating factor.

It is not the purpose here to analyze the validity of these or other one-cause theories. Instead, a variety of plausible explanations of state behavior are presented, including security, economics, nationalism, ideology, military considerations, prestige, and psychology.

Security

Security is one of the most important factors in explaining state behavior, as we have seen from our discussion about the difference between international politics and domestic politics. **Security** in the international context may be defined as a feeling that the territorial integrity, ruling government, or way of life of a country is safe from destruction by outsiders.

Many states live in fear of their neighbors and even of distant powers. Military forces watch warily on each side of the borders between North Korea and South Korea, the People's Republic of China and the Soviet Union, West Germany and East Germany, and Israel and Syria. The Soviet Union and the United States—separated for the most part by thousands of miles—feel as insecure about each other as some of these neighboring enemies and point nuclear-tipped intercontinental ballistic missiles at each other's heartlands.

The fact that there is so much armament along borders and facing distant rivals should not suggest that insecurity always characterizes the relations of states. The boundary line between the United States and Canada, for example, is the largest unguarded border in the world. France and Germany, which for many generations viewed each other as a military threat, no longer (as far as France and West Germany are concerned) think of each other in that way. Mexico and the United States still have differences, but the United States–Mexican border is marked by customs and immigration officers rather than brigades of armed forces. The feeling of security, then, varies from country to country and from period to period. It remains, however,

one of the most important factors influencing the behavior of states.

Economics

Economic factors—some related to security and others not—motivate state behavior. A country may need water resources that are blocked by an adversary and take military measures to achieve access to those resources. Such an action may be considered, in part at least, as economic, since the entire economy would suffer from a loss of such a fundamental need as water. A country, too, may go to war to enhance its control over mineral wealth in some disputed territory, or to assure sources of raw materials, or to guarantee markets.

Often economic causes are associated with private groups concerned with their own well-being. In the nineteenth century, for example, economic adventurers sought the support of their governments in overseas investments. The history of U.S. intervention in Latin America and European interference in Africa and Asia reveals much about the connection between private investors and imperialism, although debate persists on which were dominant—the political institutions or the private corporations. In our contemporary period, similar theories have been put forward to explain the foreign policy of Western nations in general and the United States in particular. It was charged, for example, that the reason why the United States intervened in Vietnam in the 1960s was because of its desire for rich Vietnamese offshore oil deposits, and because it wished to protect its capitalistic enterprises.

Nationalism

Nationalism is described in Chapter 2 as an ideology in which a people regardless of their race, class, or religion feel that they have more in common with each other than they do with other people and give their highest loyalty to a state or part of a state that may eventually become a separate state. Nationalism has been a factor in the enlargement of states, the contraction of states, and in the manipulations of big powers.[1]

Ideology

Nationalism is but one of many ideologies that have international significance. Liberalism, fascism, and communism are three principal ideologies with international ramifications.

Liberalism is a political philosophy that emphasizes individual liberty (see Chapter 4). In the twentieth century particularly, some political leaders—Woodrow Wilson and Jimmy Carter most notably—asserted the promotion of human rights as a foreign policy goal.[2]

Fascism, too, has its appeal. The alliance of fascist nations—Germany, Italy, and Japan—in World War II may be explained significantly by ideological similarities, although there were other factors involved in the formation of the alliance.

Communism as an ideology is a factor in state behavior. A major problem of students concerned with analyzing the political behavior of the Soviet Union is to determine to what extent Soviet foreign policy is dictated by the ideology of Marxism-Leninism and to what extent it is motivated by security interests. Some students argue that ideological considerations can be seen in the importance of communist doctrine to the Soviet political leadership. Others, however, contend that the doctrine is just a cloak for the security interests of the country.

---

[1] See Chapter 2 for a discussion of the impact of nationalism.

[2] The issue of human rights and foreign policy is discussed in Issue 10.

Military Considerations Military considerations have taken many forms. In the nineteenth century, for example, American naval leaders argued for the necessity of establishing overseas political control so that naval coaling stations could be assured to American naval vessels. With the advent of the **Cold War** (that period immediately following World War II in which the Soviet Union and the United States had intense confrontations, mostly in nonmilitary matters) American military leaders called for the leasing of overseas military air force bases to assure American air superiority over the Soviet Union.

Students of World War I, moreover, have pointed to the way in which purely military plans could influence political considerations. Conversations between British and French military authorities in the decade prior to the war linked their two countries in a way that made it likely that they would be allies in a war against Germany.

Another example of the impact of military plans on political decision making was the Schlieffen Plan, a German plan developed at the beginning of the twentieth century to defeat France in case of a war on two fronts. It involved invading France through neutral Belgium and, when implemented in 1914, assured that the war would involve those countries, such as England, that had given their pledge to support Belgian neutrality.

Prestige

Prestige is a country's reputation for power. Often, in international politics, states behave in certain ways because they wish to maintain their reputation for power. As a result of agreements entered into by the Allied Powers in World War II, for example, those powers were assured access to Berlin, which was located hundreds of miles inside the Soviet-dominated sector of Germany. The United

States and its allies had to fend off many attempts by the Soviet Union and its allies to place all Berlin under communist control. At each point, however, the West resisted. An airlift in 1948 shipped food and supplies to the people of Berlin after Soviet officials had closed off ground transit, and the Soviets soon determined to end the surface blockade. In the 1950s and 1960s, moreover, American presidents responded with a show of military strength when they felt that Berlin was being threatened by the Soviet Union.

Political actions of this kind constitute one example of the role of prestige in foreign policy, but there are many others. The program announced by President John F. Kennedy in 1961 to put a man on the moon before the decade was out was an attempt to show that America's reputation for technological leadership could be assured. In some respects the possession of nuclear weapons by an increasing number of nations is regarded by the newcomers to nuclear weapons as a symbol of prestige.

Psychology

Psychological factors play a role in explaining the behavior of states, although these are difficult to document. The phrase *state behavior* is, in truth, an abstraction. What is meant, really, is that the leaders of a state act in the name of a state. If the leaders are mad or incapable of perceiving accurately the correct condition of international political affairs, then clearly the fact that these individuals controlled the levels of power at the time may be understood, at least in part, by psychological explanations. Can the foreign policy of Adolf Hitler be studied without making an attempt to understand the psychology of this one person, particularly his personal craving for power? There is no easy Yes or No answer to this question, but there is evidence that a psychological explanation is plausible.

Psychological factors play a role in group behavior. At times, some groups are ready to go to war and at other times they wish to remain at peace. Mass hysteria has been blamed for some kinds of international political behavior.

All the above factors, then, can be motivating factors behind foreign policy.

ISSUE

The great disparity in income between advanced industrial countries in the West and many impoverished countries in the Third World has given economic development a prominent position on the global agenda. The debate below considers whether the West should redistribute its wealth to the Third World to narrow the economic gap.

23/YES
SHOULD THE WEST REDISTRIBUTE ITS WEALTH TO THIRD WORLD COUNTRIES?

For more than half the people of the world, poverty is a way of life. Their poverty is a *permanent* condition in which the fundamental minimums of food, clothing, and shelter are not assured. The horrors of mass starvation, disease, and malnutrition are brought to the world's attention from television's reporting of such disasters as the drought that decimated sub-Saharan Africa in the 1970s and 1980s. The case of Ethiopia in 1984 and 1985 is perhaps the most grim example of the death produced by economic deprivation. The everyday misery of the poor in Third World countries, however, is often unnoticed except by the statisticians who record economic indices, the relief agencies that work to alleviate it, and the wretched masses who are its victims.

What many affluent people in the West take for granted—balanced diet, decent homes, automobiles, jobs, and education—is not available to the vast majority of the world's population. The poor now demand attention, however. A **revolution of rising expectations** (in which people no longer expect a condition of poverty to be a permanent fixture of life but anticipate steady improvement in the quality of their lives) is taking hold in Third World countries. That revolution is shattering traditional institutions and even world order, and is the central concern of Third World political leaders.

To understand the wide gaps between the rich and poor countries of the world, it is essential to compare the industrialized and nonindustrialized states. For the most part the rich countries of the world are racially white, while the poor are nonwhite. The rich consist of the advanced industrialized countries of the world. Since most of these countries are located in the northern latitudes—North America and Europe—they are often referred to as the **North.** The poor include the countries that have not made advances in industrialization. Since most of these countries are located in the southern latitudes—Latin America, Africa, and Asia—they are often referred to as the **South. North-South problems,** then, usually refer to the economic ties between the **haves** and **have-nots** (the wealthy countries and the poor).

Countries with a **gross national product** (GNP, the sum of goods and services produced by a nation in a year) of $3,010 or more per capita are often described as **developed. Developing countries** (or **less-developed countries**) are states with less than $3,010 per

capita income and are seeking economic growth.[3]

The stark fact of poverty is there for all to see. The statistics, however, do not tell the story of the enormous problems facing developing countries in their quest for economic self-sufficiency. Their economic problems are often caused by high population growth, low per capita income, malnutrition, a weak ability to form capital for investment, poor health standards, illiteracy, dependence on agriculture, and cultural traditions that are hostile to economic development.

Because of the great disparity between the North and the South, the world's attention has been drawn to the necessity of raising the living standards of the South's impoverished population. A most noteworthy effort at popularizing the problem was the declaration on the establishment of a New International Economic Order (NIEO), which was adopted in May 1974 at the Sixth Special Session of the United Nations General Assembly. In that declaration a plea was made for the rich countries of the world to share their wealth with the developing countries.

Such a policy can only be beneficial to ending poverty in the Third World. Redistribution is not only essential as a matter of simple justice, but it is also owed to the Third World by the West because: (1) Western exploitation is historically responsible for Third World poverty; and (2) Western economic ties with the Third World today continue to be exploitive.

Western Exploitation. The poverty of Third World countries is owing to Western exploitation. Although imperialism, which has been defined as the expansion of one country into another, existed long before the rise of the West, its dynamic modern record stems from nineteenth-century penetration by the West into Latin America, Asia, and Africa. Great Britain, France, the United States, Holland, Belgium, and Germany were the principal exploiters, and these countries, too, were the most developed as far as capitalism and industrialism

---

[3] The figure of $3,010 is used by the World Bank to indicate the maximum per capita income a country may have (in 1986 dollars), beyond which the World Bank will no longer lend it money.

were concerned. Other Western countries, such as Spain, Portugal, and Italy, also built up their existing colonies or opened up new areas of the world hitherto sheltered from Western "civilization."

The historical record of imperialism is one of political, social, and economic exploitation. Politically, the colonial masters often ruled without adequately preparing an infrastructure of local administrators and political leaders. The case of Mozambique under Portuguese rule is a notorious example. Socially, many colonialists looked down on their charges as inferior people. Racial discrimination was often the result of such an attitude. The legacy of racism in South Africa endures to this very day.

In many cases economic exploitation had the greatest impact on the economies of both the advanced and underdeveloped areas of the world. The English liberal J. A. Hobson and the noted communist V. I. Lenin both argued that Western imperialism came about primarily from capitalist exploitation.[4] These and other writers revealed how the Western capitalists used colonies to acquire cheap raw materials and new markets for their goods. Because of such exploitation, the West achieved its economic ascendancy.

Rather than considering the needs of the peoples of Africa, Asia, and Latin America, the colonial masters distorted the Third World economies to serve Western interests. The principal instrument of that distortion was to make one or two primary products the essential element in each colony's economy. **Primary products** are crops, minerals, and fuels that are essentially taken from the earth with little processing involved. One-product economies—such as cocoa in the Gold Coast (now Ghana), rubber in Malaya, tin in Bolivia, and copper in Chile—became the economic norm for the Third World. The market for these products was in the West rather than in the Third World. The price of the commodity, consequently, was dependent upon what the West would pay, and that amount was low. Third World countries did not have the economic leverage to develop their own economies for their own needs. Not only were prices of primary products kept low, but these prices were subject to wildly fluctuating market conditions. Even after developing countries achieved their independence, they could not engage in making sound long-term plans because of such fluctuations.

Perpetuating Poverty. Imperialism has really not come to an end, although technically political rule has been transferred to local leaders. Economic dependency has been retained in the form of capital acquisition, commodity prices, and foreign aid.

With political independence, the new nations faced many of the economic problems that the West had solved at an earlier period. In order to create wealth the Third World had to increase productivity. Capital was essential to bring about this improved productivity. Much of that capital, however, was and is in private hands—in banks and big corporations. These capitalist institutions only invest in Third World countries if they are assured of enormous profits. Western capitalists, moreover, restrict credit for those economic activities that might interfere with the Western economies, and they also seek a fast and high return on investment.

Third World countries are no match for the power of these economic giants—multinational corporations with global interests. The revenues of General Motors alone exceed the gross national product of each of more than one hundred countries. The effect of such an imbalance is detrimental to the Third World. In the words of two leading scholars of multinationals, "The development track pursued by the global corporation in those years [the 1960s] contributed more to exacerbation of world poverty, world unemployment, and world inequality than to their solution."[5]

One mechanism of Western exploitation remains the control of prices of primary products. If these prices get too high, then Western consumers can switch to substitutes—tea for coffee, for example. In most cases, Third World countries have not been successful in forming **cartels** (organizations that can control the price

---

[4] See J. A. Hobson, *Imperialism* (London: Allen and Unwin, 1938); V.I. Lenin, *Imperialism* (New York: International Publishers, 1939).

[5] Richard J. Barnet and Ronald E. Müller, *Global Reach: The Power of Multinational Corporations* (New York: Simon and Schuster, 1974), p. 151.

and quantity of a product) to obtain high prices for their products.

The oil cartel—OPEC—was the exception to the rule. In 1973, the price of oil began to rise as OPEC successfully wrested control of the oil price from the big private oil companies. In a period of several years the price of oil increased tenfold. Oil was, however, unique in not being able to be substituted. Cartels of other primary products, consequently, would not have the same leverage as OPEC. Even OPEC began to recede in influence in the 1980s, as a combination of conservation, increased exploration for energy resources, alternative energy sources, differences among OPEC members, and economic recession pushed the world market price of oil down. By 1986, even OPEC was regarded as a moribund organization, no longer able to determine the production levels and price of oil.

Foreign aid is another device of Western imperialism because of the way it is dispensed. Instead of considering aid as a moral obligation of the advanced industrial states resulting from the colonial legacy of oppression, the former colonial powers regard it either as charity or as a means for further exploitation. The advanced countries should follow the recommendation of the United Nations and apply a standard of 0.7 percent of national income for economic aid to the less developed countries. None of the major industrial countries, however, have met this standard. The industrialized countries of North America, Western Europe, and Japan provide only 0.36 percent of GNP for aid—about half the recommended amount.

Aid is given in two forms: military and economic. Since the end of World War II, Western countries have armed the Third World to the detriment of the latter. The new countries have become dependent upon the West for their military security. Scarce resources that should be used for economic development, moreover, are now diverted to military purposes, thus slowing down the pace of economic development. Since the revolution in military technology consists of producing newer weapons that make the old weapons outmoded quickly, Third World countries find their expenses related to military aid constantly rising. Their dependence on the West thus becomes ever greater.

Economic aid is also designed to help the West. Domestic producers of farm products, for example, benefit when the West ships wheat and corn to Third World countries. Furthermore, aid is given only to projects that will not result in competition with Western industrialists.

Because of its bad historical record and its present exploitive actions, the West owes a debt to the Third World. Without the wealth derived from the exploitation of the nonwhite peoples of the world, the West would be poor today. Redistribution of income, according to the spirit of the New International Economic Order, is a proper way to compensate for past injustice and to promote equality among the peoples of the world.

23 / NO   SHOULD THE WEST REDISTRIBUTE ITS WEALTH TO THIRD WORLD COUNTRIES?

There is no gainsaying the fact that there is appalling poverty in Third World countries. Poverty is an evil, since most of us agree that "something should be done" to provide at least the necessities of life. What that "something" is, however, is the central issue. The *Affirmative* avoids considering the complexities of North-South relationships in its prescription of a New International Economic Order.

An analysis of North-South relationships must deal with two points: the character of the Third World and the method that should be used to eliminate poverty. On the first point, the Third World is not monolithic. Some of its countries have small populations and are rich; Kuwait and Saudi Arabia, with their immense oil resources, are cases in point. Others are large and poor: China and India, for example. Some countries are so poor that they have even been described as consisting of a special category—the **Fourth World**—in which the economic plight is almost without hope of salvation. Within Third World countries, moreover, there are rich people and poor, merchants and factory workers, aborigines and Western-educated professionals, and sheiks and peasants. To treat the Third World as a single entity, then, is to ignore an important fact necessary for analysis.

On the second point—the method used to eliminate poverty—we should stress that even if we recognize the problem, we need not agree on the solution. Transferring wealth from one group to another may lead to a waste of resources. Government programs that have been designed to transfer wealth from the affluent to the poor in the West have often been unsuccessful in achieving their objective of eliminating poverty.

Having made these initial comments, we can now present our case against the NIEO. The main points here are: (1) the West is not responsible for Third World poverty; and (2) it is not exploiting Third World countries today.

Western Exploitation. Western liberals take keen satisfaction in blaming Third World poverty on the dynamics of Western capitalism. In this appraisal, they are wrong. It is "do-gooders" who are guilty of inaccurate historical analysis. The West is not responsible for Third World economic decay but rather for its political, social, and economic progress.

Imperialism was not a necessary consequence of capitalism, as Leninists and some liberals would have us believe. Some of the most prosperous capitalist countries—Sweden and Switzerland—never acquired colonies during the nineteenth-century scramble. Portugal, which possessed a large empire, remains one of the poorest countries of Western Europe. Capitalists, moreover, often resisted the imperial ventures of political leaders.[6]

Politically, Western intervention often brought an end to tribal wars that had been going on for centuries. Colonial powers sought to maintain law and order in the territories under their control and, consequently, brought peace and stability instead of war and disorder. In some cases, moreover, they did establish an infrastructure of local government. The British, particularly, created local institu-

tions of self-government and prepared the way for independence.

In social matters the racism of Western imperialists certainly was prevalent. It would be wrong to conclude, however, that the West introduced racism to the Third World. Racial antagonism was endemic in many areas of the Third World long before nineteenth-century imperialism. Colonial governments often protected racial minorities. The fact that ethnic Chinese in Southeast Asia and Asians in East Africa have suffered discrimination in the past two decades is a reminder of the precolonial roots of racism.

Economically, the West brought more prosperity to the peoples of the Third World than they had experienced in the preceding centuries. The West had to establish an infrastructure—railroads, ports, highways, communication links—since these were prerequisites for industrial development. Karl Marx himself commented favorably on imperialism when he noted that Western imperialists were replacing feudalism with capitalism. Until the West took over, much of the Third World experienced grim poverty. The West brought science and technology, increased prosperity, eliminated endemic diseases, and often extended life expectancy.

Many of the people who criticize Western imperialism have a Leninist orientation on the world. They perceive capitalism as exploitation in any context, and especially in an imperial situation. They regard any profit as theft. The capitalists who invested in the Third World, however, often did so at great risk to their lives and capital. They created entire new industries. It is certainly true that they often built an economy based on a single product and that world market prices fluctuated. Had it not been for the West, however, these colonies would not have had a market to develop.[7] Western interests brought rubber to Malaya and tea to India. These products were not produced by those countries before the arrival of Westerners.

The charge that Western imperialism is responsible for Third World poverty can easily be dismissed when we note that those coun-

---

[6] See Raymond Aron, "The Leninist Myth of Imperialism," in his *The Century of Total War* (Boston: Beacon Press, 1954), chap. 3.

[7] See P. T. Bauer, "Western Guilt and Third World Poverty," *Commentary* 61 (January 1976): 32.

tries that were least linked to the West are among the poorest in the world. Some of the most economically underdeveloped countries, moreover, were never colonies (Afghanistan, Tibet, and Liberia). As economist P. T. Bauer notes, the areas of the Third World in which the West made the most extensive contacts with the Third World are the most prosperous: "the cash-crop–producing areas and *entrepot* ports of Southeast Asia, West Africa, and Latin America; the mineral-producing areas of Africa and the Middle East; and the cities and ports throughout Asia, Africa, the Caribbean, and Latin America."[8]

We cannot blame the West for Third World poverty, then, since without Western intervention poverty would be worse. To say that the colonies were essential for Western prosperity, moreover, is to ignore the fact that the West had achieved self-sustaining growth *before* it embarked on its major imperial adventures in the late nineteenth century.

Perpetuating Poverty. The West has an interest in making Third World countries politically stable and economically strong. It is a Marxist myth that economic relations constitute a **zero-sum game,** in which any gain from one player is automatically a loss for the other. Had American capitalists sought to maximize their economic advantages over war-torn Europe after World War II, they would never have supported a Marshall Plan (named after United States Secretary of State George C. Marshall) that rebuilt the European economies. As the Western European economies revived, they provided a market for American products. Today as in the past, trade ties are strongest among highly industrialized countries rather than between industrial countries and poor countries. The people of Bangladesh, one of the poorest countries in the world, cannot afford to purchase computers from the United States, but the people of West Germany can.

Western countries are currently helping Third World countries on the path to development. The new states of the world benefit from Western private and government assistance. The multinational corporations that invest capital in Third World countries are engines of development and not instruments of exploitation.

They tie the global economy together in a more meaningful way. Of course, they are only going to invest capital if they can be certain to make profits.

In engaging in their own business ventures, the multinationals risk their capital. The risk of investing in Third World countries is high because of wars, political instability, and potential nationalization of property. The multinationals must, then, seek high profits. Nevertheless, even with high profits, they bring new technology to the new countries; employ thousands of local personnel; stimulate the business of small, local economic interests; and spread prosperity. Often, moreover, they set examples for local business interests to follow in labor-management relations. Those countries that have permitted Western capitalists to develop their economies have done rather well. South Korea and Taiwan, for example, have had two of the highest growth rates in the world, and both of these countries have opened themselves to capitalist investment.

The notion that countries that have great dependence upon a single product must be constantly in a servile condition and impoverished is certainly not true. The non-Western world, it should be remembered, is not the only place that produces primary products. Developed countries, too, are major primary-producers, and they benefit from high prices for their commodities. In the 1970s, there was a major increase in the world market price of many primary products—silver, copper, gold, and coffee, for example—and the price rise aided producers in both advanced and developing countries. Third World countries, however, have been wise to diversify their economies so that they will be less susceptible to wide fluctuations in world market prices.

Foreign aid, too, has been offered to help Third World countries. Military aid is designed not to make Third World countries dependent upon the West but rather to allow them to satisfy their legitimate security objectives. The fact that the costs of the new military technology are spiraling is a characteristic of the new technology that affects not only the Third World but developed countries as well.

Economic aid to Third World countries has had successes and failures. That aid, overall, has not been beneficial to Third World countries. Economist P. T. Bauer and journalist

---

[8] Ibid.

John O'Sullivan have observed in this regard that Western aid is often wasted. They indicate that it goes to the upper classes and widens the gap between the local rich and poor; it increases **statism** (the use of the state rather than private associations to solve economic and social problems) that often results in government inefficiency and authoritarian rule; and it perpetuates inefficient economic operations.[9] The lessons of aid suggest that a major redistribution of wealth from the West to the Third World would be economically disastrous to Third World economies themselves.

The aid that has been forthcoming by the West has been generous indeed. Restrictions imposed by the West to assure that the aid will be used for the purposes to which it has been designated, rather than "without strings," have been called exploitation. Anti-West critics prefer the disbursement of aid through international organizations that would exercise only weak and ineffectual controls. The record of foreign aid shows that any new international economic order could only be harmful to the people whom it is intended to benefit.

We should rid ourselves, then, of both the Leninist talk about Western guilt and the cant about redistribution of wealth. The West achieved its wealth before the age of imperialism. It owes its prosperity to its political system and to a culture that encourages economic development. The Third World, too, can reach out and even, in time, surpass the West provided it creates the political and cultural setting for a similar advance. Such an advance would arise when development rather than redistribution becomes the main theme of Third World policy.

---

[9] P. T. Bauer and John O'Sullivan, "Foreign Aid for What?' *Commentary* 66 (December 1978): 41–48.

KEY TERMS

Alliances

Cartels

Cold War

Developed countries

Developing countries

Fourth World

Functional agencies

General international organizations

Geopolitics

Gross national product (GNP)

Haves

Have-nots

Less-developed countries

North

North-South problems

Prestige

Primary products

Regional organizations

Revolution of rising expectations

Security

South

Statism

Zero-sum game

QUESTIONS

International Politics: Motivations

1. Should states resort to war to maintain their prestige? What are the reasons for your answer?

2. What effect does interdependence play in the ability of states to persist as viable actors in the global arena?

3. What are the legitimate security interests of the United States?

4. What role do economic considerations play in the conduct of U.S. foreign policy?

5. What alternatives are there to a global system of independent states? Would these alternatives produce a better world than the current system?

Third World

1. Is capitalist investment in Third World countries a form of imperialism? What are the reasons for your answer?
2. If capitalism is eliminated and replaced with socialist economies, would imperialism continue to exist? What are the reasons for your answer?

3. What responsibility do communist states have in redistributing their wealth for the benefit of the Third World?
4. Why have some Third World countries been successful in economic development and others been failures?
5. How should the West promote prosperity in the Third World?

RECOMMENDED READINGS

International Politics: Motivations

CALVOCORESSI, PETER. *World Politics since 1945.* 5th ed. London: Longman, 1987. A history of world politics in the post–World War II years.

GEIGER, THEODORE. *The Future of the International System: The United States and the World Political Economy.* Boston: Unwin Hyman, 1988. An analysis of the changing character of the global economic and political system.

HIERONYMI, OTTO, ed. *Technology and International Relations.* New York: St. Martin's Press, 1987. Essays on the subject.

LEVINE, HERBERT M., ed. *World Politics Debated: Readings in Contemporary Issues.* 3d ed. New York: McGraw-Hill, 1989. Debates on issues of war and peace.

MORGENTHAU, HANS J., and KENNETH W. THOMPSON. *Politics among Nations: The Struggle for Power and Peace.* 6th ed. New York: Knopf, 1985. A realist view of international politics.

NIEBUHR, REINHOLD. *Moral Man and Immoral Society: A Study in Ethics and Politics.* New York: Scribner's, 1932. A theologian looks at conflict.

WALTZ, KENNETH N. *Man, the State, and War.* New York: Columbia University Press, 1954. An analysis of theories of international relations.

Third World

BAUER, P. T. *Equality, the Third World and Economic Delusion.* Cambridge, Mass.: Harvard University Press, 1981. A critical assessment of liberal and socialist views on Third World economic development.

GEORGE, VIC. *Wealth, Poverty and Starvation: A World Perspective.* New York: St. Martin's Press, 1988. An analysis of poverty in developed and developing countries.

HAQ, MAHBUB UL. *The Poverty Curtain: Choices for the Third World.* New York: Columbia University Press, 1976. The case for a new international economic order.

HARRIS, NIGEL. *The End of the Third World: Newly Industrializing Countries and the Decline of an Ideology.* New York: Meredith Press, 1986. A study of the idea of the Third World and the social science theories to which the idea gave rise.

HEILBRONER, ROBERT L. *The Great Ascent: The Struggle for Economic Development in Our Time.* New York: Harper and Row, 1963. A study of economic growth.

HOBSON, J. A. *Imperialism.* London: Allen and Unwin, 1938. A major work that blames capitalism for nineteenth-century imperialism.

KRAUSS, MELVYN B. *Development without Aid: Growth, Poverty and Government.* Lanham, Md.: University Press of America, 1983. An argument that the biggest obstacle to economic development in the Third World is big government.

LENIN, V. I. *Imperialism.* New York: International Publishers, 1939. A communist critique of imperialism.

ROSTOW, W. W. *Rich Countries and Poor Countries.* Boulder, Colo.: Westview Press, 1987. Essays on the world economy.

SEITZ, JOHN L. *The Politics of Development: An*

Introduction to Global Issues. New York: Basil Blackwell, 1988. A study of the role of politics in solving key problems of economic development.

WILBER, CHARLES K., ed. *The Political Economy of Development and Underdevelopment.* 4th ed. New York: Random House Business Division, 1988. Essays on economic development and underdevelopment.

chapter 14

International politics:
instruments
and constraints

In the summer of 1985 a TWA passenger aircraft was hijacked from Athens airport and taken to Beirut, Lebanon. One American on board was murdered, and others were taken hostage by Shiite terrorists. The president of the United States pondered the options open to the United States—ranging from peaceful negotiations with the Amal militia that held the hostages to using military force as part of a rescue operation.

Although most foreign policy events are not as dramatic as this one, a question posed to decision makers in the conduct of foreign policy is: What method should be used in solving a problem? The choice of response depends upon the state's power and the wisdom of the state's leaders. This chapter considers the components of power, the methods that states use in their dealings with other countries and the constraints on power. Issues of the decline of U.S. power, the effective-

ness of economic sanctions, and the possibility of disarmament are then evaluated in debate.

POWER

Power is the ability to influence people to do things they may not want to do. In this sense a teacher has power over students, a bully has power over weak people, a banker has power over potential borrowers, and a prison guard has power over inmates. States, too, have power. That power varies from country to country and depends upon many factors. The most important of these factors are: geography, population, natural resources, industrial capacity, military strength, transportation, communications, diplomatic skills, intelligence, internal cohesion, government administration, and national character.

Geography

Geography—location, topography, and frontiers—is important in determining power. Where a country is located is one of the few fixed elements of power. In the nineteenth century the fact that Prussia (and later Germany) was situated in Central Europe, with potential powerful enemies on most of its borders, meant that it would have to finance a large standing army to protect its security. The geographical reality that the United States is located thousands of miles away from the European mainland meant that any European power would face difficulty in maintaining the logistical support for an extended war against the United States.

Topography plays a role in power, too. Since Vietnam possessed so much jungle, for example, the United States could not depend upon its leadership in military technology to defeat communist Vietnamese guerrillas. Since Yugoslavia, moreover, contained mountains that could be used by a well-trained, indigenous guerrilla army, Joseph Stalin may have hesitated to send troops to put down Josip Broz Tito, when that dissident Yugoslav communist leader stood up to the Soviet Union in 1948.

There is much variation also in the character of frontiers. The Pyrenees Mountains separating Spain from France served as a natural boundary and fortification for Spain for many centuries. The Alps, too, achieved the same purpose for Switzerland. The fact that Israel has few natural boundaries, such as mountains and rivers, is a source of insecurity to its policy makers and people.

Population

The power of a country does not necessarily depend upon the size of its population; if that were true, the two most powerful countries in the world would be India and China. Large populations may be, in fact, a drain on a country's economy. What is important for power in the international arena is the demographic structure of a population, particularly the age distribution. Also important from a power point of view is the character of the population: How many people are skilled? How many can be mobilized for foreign policy purposes?

Natural Resources

Possession of resources gives a country advantages in the conduct of foreign policy because in times of crisis it is not dependent upon foreign commodities that may be denied to it. The fact that the United States was so wealthy in the possession of fertile land, agricultural products, coal, and oil contributed to its becoming a big power.

The mere possession of resources is not a prerequisite for power. Japan, with practically no natural resources, became a world power because of its ability to secure these resources from overseas suppliers and because of its tremendous economic achievements in production and technological development. Even countries that control huge natural resources may not have the capital or technological know-how to develop them. For a long period of time, Brazil was an example of such a country, although at its current rate of growth Brazil could easily be a big power by the beginning of the twenty-first century.

Industrial Capacity

Since the Industrial Revolution, the power of states has been influenced by their industrial capacity. The fact that the major powers of the world over the past century have been industrial countries—the United States, the Soviet Union, Germany, Great Britain, and Japan, for example—reveals the significance of industrial power. Modern armed forces are mighty industrial machines requiring the services of people skilled in the industrial arts—engineers and scientists, for example. Countries that cannot obtain such skilled personnel are at a disadvantage in the conduct of foreign policy.

Military Strength

Military strength is dependent upon the quality of military leadership, the supply and excellence of armaments, and the character of troops. A military leadership that devises poor plans and uses outmoded tactics could cause a powerful country to experience defeat. The military leaders of Europe at the beginning of World War I, for example, prepared for a war of frontal assaults. Millions of casualties later, new tactics relying on the tank and mobility succeeded in breaking the stalemate of trench warfare.

The amount and quality of weapons is another important factor. No matter how brave the troops, an army must have up-to-date weapons as well as food, clothing, and medicine. Victory in battle does not always depend on which side spends more, but the kinds of weapons are often a crucial matter.

Military strength is also influenced by the quality of an army. How well are the troops trained? How committed are they to the cause for which they are ostensibly fighting? Israeli forces, for example, have excellent *esprit de corps*. In contrast, the South Vietnamese forces contained many soldiers who deserted or who did not fight effectively, although there were many who did.

Transportation

From the point of view of international relations, a transportation system is good if it is set up in a way to assist the state's foreign policy and has adequate facilities. In the Franco-Prussian War, Prussia's railways allowed the Prussian general staff to move troops and supplies rapidly without wasting time on long, forced marches. The fact that the North had a developed railway system and the South did not contributed to the North's victory in the American Civil War. In modern times, air and sea transport are major transportation elements. The United States possesses enormous airlift resources in its commercial sector that can be diverted to military use in periods of national emergency.

Communications

Particularly in wartime, communications systems play a vital role. They permit commanders to keep in touch with fighting forces and to reshuffle troops and supplies as the combat situation requires. At present, the communications world has experienced a revolution, with communication satellites and high-speed computers involved in decision making. The development of such modern devices has allowed more centralized control over the armed forces.

Diplomatic Skills

Diplomacy is regarded as the brains of foreign policy. The ability of diplomats varies and depends on their education, their political freedom to report and evaluate the overseas diplomatic situation, and their wisdom. At certain times, superior diplomats have played crucial roles in the history of nations. At the time of the American Revolution and the immediate period thereafter, such outstanding diplomats as Thomas Jefferson, Benjamin Franklin, and John Adams helped the new United States. Certainly, the eminence of Otto von Bismarck in Prussia-Germany, Prince Metternich in Austria, and Lord Castlereagh in England contributed to successes in the foreign policy of the countries they represented in the nineteenth century.

Intelligence

Intelligence is the information gathered about the capabilities and intentions of other states. Most countries engage in intelligence activities, ranging from collecting official published government reports and newspaper articles to the use of spies and espionage to gather information from friends and foes alike. Intelligence services have had successes and failures. British writer Ian Fleming popularized British intelligence services with his depiction of the exploits of the fictional James Bond character. Most intelligence work is, however, of a scholarly nature. Knowing the military plans of an adversary is important; but in present-day conditions, knowledge about climate, agricultural production, and demographic factors is vital as well.

Internal Cohesion

If a country is at the brink of civil war or there is strong opposition to particular foreign policies, decision makers are less effective in exercising the power of the state. When the United States was engaged in a civil war from 1861 to 1865, it left itself vulnerable to foreign intervention and was lucky that no invasion occurred. France did interfere in the Western hemisphere, however, by creating a Mexican outpost for its empire and placing Maximilian on the throne.

All political leadership is vulnerable to internal divisiveness, and foreign policy may exacerbate the difficulties. The Russian government of Czar Nicholas II was toppled in part because of its losses in World War I. The conduct of foreign policy in the political administrations of Richard Nixon and Gerald Ford, moreover, was severely circumscribed because of widespread opposition to the war in Indochina by a large segment of the American public.

Government Administration

The quality of bureaucratic administration is a variable in the conduct of foreign policy. An entire bureaucratic apparatus must be able to collect taxes and recruit troops in times of national emergency. A corrupt bureaucracy may instill great popular distrust in government. An efficient bureaucracy can expedite the prosecution of a war.

National Character

Some scholars have argued that there are some national traits that characterize individual nations and permeate every class, region, and religion in that nation. This is often referred to as **national character.** For example, the Afghan people are believed to have a tradition that reveres independence—a quality that has led them to fight fiercely against foreign foes.

INSTRUMENTS OF POWER

States must choose from a variety of instruments of foreign policy to achieve their goals. Among the principal methods are alliances, balance of power, economic measures, military force, collective security, disarmament and arms control, diplomacy, international law, international organization, and intelligence.

Alliances

In the past few centuries, power has for the most part been distributed unevenly. States have often not been strong enough to provide for their own security. They have often, therefore, entered into alliances to better protect themselves. Sometimes alliances have been entered into for mutual expansion, as in the case of the German-Soviet Nonaggression Pact of 1939, in which Germany and the Soviet

Union secretly discussed how they might divide Poland and the Baltic republics.

Grand alliances, in which the major powers have united into different factions, have often been formed after a military situation has become clarified. The grand alliances that defeated Germany and Austria in World War I and World War II were of this variety. In both cases, however, the alliances came after the acts of aggression. The most prominent Western alliance, NATO, was formed in 1949 with the notion of organizing as a deterrent to attack by the Soviet Union. According to NATO supporters, if the Soviet Union knows in advance that an attack on one NATO member will be viewed as an attack on all, the Soviets leave all the NATO members alone. The Soviet Union established its military alliance, the Warsaw Pact, in 1955 with a warning to the West to respect the sovereignty of the Soviet Union and its allies.

Balance of Power

A key concept in international relations is the balance of power. Although it is used in different ways, **balance of power** generally implies a condition in which alliances balance each other off to maintain the peace and if one state or a group of states becomes too powerful, other states will unite to challenge the strong power. Balance of power assumes that the international political environment is always dangerous and states must take measures to preserve their security. Unless states take these measures, they risk great danger such as conquest or foreign domination.

Those who advocate the pursuit of balance of power politics advocate the approach of *Realpolitik,* or foreign policy realism, in which power considerations—as distinguished from moral ones—are the dominant factors of policy making. When British Prime Minister Winston Churchill said that to preserve the secu-

rity of his country he would make a pact with the Devil, he was asserting this "realistic" view. Realists often distinguish themselves from idealists, who place moral considerations as primary objectives of foreign policy and seek radically new solutions to foreign policy problems (see Chapter 3 and Debate 10 in Chapter 4.)

In the eighteenth and nineteenth centuries balance of power experienced its heyday. At that time, there were several important powers that were, by themselves, not strong enough to dominate Europe or the world. One country—Great Britain—used its naval superiority against a power perceived to be upsetting the balance—France under Napoleon—and restored the balance of power with the support of its allies. It was widely believed that the balance of power helped to promote peace in the world.

In the nuclear age, however, the situation is different from past centuries because of the extraordinary power of two countries—the Soviet Union and the United States. Each of these countries has enough nuclear weapons to destroy civilization as we know it. Under such circumstances, balance of power does not have the validity that it had in previous centuries, although it plays a role in limited or regional conflicts.

Economic Measures

States have at their disposal a variety of economic means to influence other nations. They may order an **embargo** on goods to or from an adversary—that is, exclude its nationals from trading with nationals of adversary countries. The raising and lowering of tariffs is another device of using economics as a weapon of foreign policy. Placing states on a **most-favored nation** list allows them to receive the lowest tariff schedules. Quota systems may restrict the amount or type of goods that are permitted to be imported into a state. States may also forbid or limit the amount of economic investment permitted by foreign nationals. During times of war, a state may take more stringent economic measures, such as freezing an enemy's assets under its control and thus prevent the enemy from using those assets.

Economic aid (the transfer of capital from one country to another) can be an instrument of foreign policy. The transfer may involve money, commodities, or goods. Foreign aid may consist of grants or loans. **Bilateral aid** is given directly from one state to another. A state may provide aid to an international organization, such as the United Nations, which would then dispense the aid to individual states. Such an "internationalization" of aid is called **multilateral aid.**

Relatively well-to-do countries have given aid for political or humanitarian purposes. When the goal is political, it is often designed to influence the policy choices of foreign decision makers. The United States has engaged actively both in political and humanitarian foreign aid. The **Marshall Plan,** which gave economic assistance to a war-ravaged Europe after World War II, was predominantly motivated by the political needs of the United States, which required a strong Western Europe as a counter to the Soviet Union. American disaster relief to the victims of earthquakes and wars is an example of humanitarian aid. It is often difficult, however, to distinguish between political and humanitarian uses of aid, since they are not necessarily mutually exclusive.

Military Force

War is an instrument of power, although not by any means the only one. At present, different kinds of war may be distinguished: total nuclear war, limited nuclear war, general conventional war, limited conventional war, guerrilla warfare, and terrorism.

Total nuclear war is a war that involves the major nuclear powers who use nuclear weapons without limit against their adversary. At present, only the United States and the Soviet Union could engage in such a war.

Limited nuclear war involves the use of some nuclear weapons in war. These weapons are, however, limited in size and perhaps in target area. It is unknown now whether limited nuclear war would escalate into total nuclear warfare or could be contained. Since the United States detonated atom bombs on Hiroshima and Nagasaki in Japan in World War II, no country has used nuclear weapons in war.

General conventional war is a World War II–type war in which the major powers would be involved but would not use nuclear weapons. It is unlikely that a general conventional war is possible in the event of military hostility between the United States and the Soviet Union, with their nuclear capacities.

Limited conventional war is a war fought between two countries in which at least one of the belligerents does not use all the resources at its command. The Korean War of 1950–53 involved primarily the United States and South Korea on one side, and North Korea and China on the other. Although the United States possessed nuclear weapons, it did not use them, nor did it bomb sanctuaries in the People's Republic of China that were used as a conduit for supplies to North Korea.

Guerrilla warfare involves the use of unconventional warfare against an established government. Although guerrilla warfare has its roots in antiquity, in contemporary times it is most associated with communist Chinese leader Mao Zedong, who waged a successful guerrilla war against the Nationalist Government of Chiang Kai-shek. By relying on hit-and-run tactics and ambushes by peasant forces, Mao was able to undermine confidence in the Nationalist Government and seize control of Mainland China in 1949. The Vietnamese communist leader Ho Chi Minh used similar tactics in the Vietnamese war against France in the 1950s, and against the South Vietnam government and United States forces in the 1960s. Afghan guerrillas waged a similar type of warfare against Soviet armed forces in Afghanistan in the 1980s.

Terrorism is an instrument of warfare that is generally conducted not by states but rather by substate actors, such as ethnic or radical groups. Often, however, terrorism is assisted through training or equipment by states. **Terrorism** is the use of force against civilian populations and includes such activities as hijacking of aircraft, bank robberies, political assassinations, and the bombing of buildings and other property for the purpose of undermining the authority of a government. It is sometimes known as **urban guerrilla warfare.**

Collective Security

Collective security is a system of organizing power in world politics in which all the states of the world join forces to repel acts of aggression by any state. Provisions of the Covenant of the League of Nations and the United Nations Charter establish the principle of collective security. The idea is to use either economic or ultimately military measures to prevent any act of aggression from succeeding.

Economic sanctions were used unsuccessfully, however, against Italy following its invasion of Ethiopia in 1935. The United Nations attempted to apply collective security in 1950 when North Korea invaded South Korea. Essentially, however, the Korean action was a United States cause, although many other states contributed troops and materiel to the U.N. campaign. The communist members of the U.N. never joined in collective security against North Korea.

Disarmament and Arms Control

Disarmament is the abolition of armed forces and weapons. **Arms control** is the regulation of armed power and weapons at a particular level to improve the security of states.

Attempts to eliminate or reduce armaments have been reflected in international agreements within the past century. Major concern with regulation, however, has been a consequence of the advent of nuclear weapons by the big powers and the proliferation of nuclear weapons to many countries.

Although states have entered into different kinds of agreements regulating armaments, such as the Partial Nuclear Test Ban Treaty of 1963 and the Nonproliferation Treaty of 1967, the amount of money spent for armaments continues to rise. The prospects for universal disarmament are bleak according to both proponents and opponents of disarmament.

Diplomacy

Diplomacy, according to one of the leading students of the subject, Harold G. Nicolson, is "the management of international relations by negotiation."[1] States send ambassadors to foreign countries to represent their interests and to ascertain the intentions of the leaders of those foreign countries. Diplomats engage in a variety of methods, the most notable of which is negotiation. Traditionally, negotiations have been undertaken in a secretive manner. In the twentieth century, however, with the rise of democracy, the expansion of new forms of media, and a desire to win the support of public opinion throughout the world, diplomacy has been more open to public attention. In the past, moreover, diplomacy was mostly undertaken between the ambassadors of a country and the foreign office officials and political leaders of a country. In the twentieth century international conferences and organizations provide for new forms of multinational diplomacy.

---

[1] Harold G. Nicholson, *Diplomacy*, 3d ed. (London: Oxford University Press, 1963), p. 15.

International Law

International law is a body of rules that states feel bound to obey. These rules have evolved over the past three centuries because of the growing interdependence of states and the need to avoid military conflict. International law has dealt with most subjects that have or could have resulted in military conflict, such as territorial jurisdiction, the law of the sea, the law of war, diplomatic protection, and the protection of nationals abroad.

International law is derived from many sources, such as customs, treaties, judicial agencies and scholars, and statutes of international organizations. Although much attention is given to the violations of international law on some of the more highly intense political issues, international law is widely accepted in many areas of policy. States do not cavalierly enter into international agreements for the purpose of violating them, and that is why they spend so much time in negotiating details.

Still, international law is not binding on most states, nor is the authority of the International Court of Justice (ICJ) supreme. States may give to the ICJ compulsory jurisdiction on some matters provided that the other party to the dispute grants the ICJ the same jurisdiction. In 1985, the United States withdrew its automatic consent to ICJ jurisdiction in some cases because the court was considering charges made by Nicaragua against the United States. No compulsion, however, exists that can force a state into presenting a case before the ICJ against its will or even accepting the decision of the court. Usually, however, once a party accepts the jurisdiction of the court, it is ready to accept the court's decision.

International Organization

International organizations are primarily a twentieth-century development. In the nineteenth century the Congress of Vienna in 1815, following the defeat of Napoleon, initiated the concert of Europe, or **concert system.** At the congress, representatives of the European powers met to redraw the map of Europe. Throughout the century thereafter, the powers convened to deal with specific matters, but their work was intermittent and they built no permanent organization.

Other early international organizations were the international unions. Some of the earliest were the European river commissions, which regulated the traffic on major rivers. The Universal Postal Union and the International Telegraphic Union were other important unions in the nineteenth century.

Finally, the Hague Peace Conferences—the first in 1899 and the second in 1907—established organizational precedents of lasting significance and dealt with some general topics of international law, such as disarmament.

The major international organizations of this century are the League of Nations and the United Nations. The League was created after World War I as a general international organization. Its hope of preventing a world war ended when Adolf Hitler attacked Poland in 1939.

The United Nations is the most prominent international organization today. In addition to the ICJ (described above), its major institutions are the Security Council, the General Assembly, the Secretariat, the Economic and Social Council, and the Trusteeship Council. Starting with a membership of 51 nations in 1945, it now has more than 150 members. The rise to independence of former Western colonies swelled the numbers of countries and altered the character of the organization. In 1945, the United States dominated the United Nations. Today, Third World countries, mostly the former colonies, play a preponderant role.

States feel no compulsion to abide by the United Nations' wishes. The principal agency to act in matters pertaining to the maintenance of international peace and security is the Security Council, which consists of ten nonpermanent members and five permanent members—United States, Soviet Union, Great Britain, France, and China. Each of the permanent members is permitted to cast a veto and, consequently, prevent a majority decision on important matters.

The General Assembly, consisting of representatives of every U.N. member, also plays a role in security matters but can only make nonbinding recommendations. With the rise of Third World states, much of the attention of the U.N. has shifted to the General Assembly.

The Secretariat, headed by the secretary-general, is the executive arm of the U.N. Its duties include administration of the U.N. complex and the carrying out of resolutions approved by the other organs of the U.N. chiefly those of the Security Council and the General Assembly.

The Economic and Social Council concerns itself with economic and social matters, as its name suggests. The Trusteeship Council has dealt with issues pertaining to the administration of political entities under colonial rule.

Both the League of Nations and the United Nations have considered matters of the greatest concern to international security and peace, such as war, racism, and economic relations. The record of both those organizations shows, however, that there is nothing along the lines of a world government in sight in this century.

Other international organizations, such as regional associations and multinational alliances, also allow countries to present their views. Whether a state uses these or general international organizations— or even no international organizations— depends on its commitments to those organizations and its perception of the outcome of international deliberations in those units.

Intelligence

States must get as accurate information as possible about the intentions and capabilities of other states. In the 1920s, an American secretary of state forbade spying on the Japanese because, he said, gentlemen don't do that kind of thing. Today, however, the intelligence networks of most countries pay less heed to gentlemanly behavior.

Intelligence activities have been described above. To the extent that a state can get accurate information about its adversary, it can make better decisions to strengthen its security. A demoralized intelligence community or one torn asunder by political infighting can only harm the conduct of a country's foreign policy.

CONSTRAINTS ON POWER

States are not free to do what they wish in international politics. States feel constrained to act because of moral, legal, or pragmatic considerations.

Moral

An examination of international behavior shows considerable diversity under similar circumstances. The legacy of British imperialism of the late nineteenth and early twentieth centuries is more favorable than, say, the Belgian legacy. When the British departed from India, they had already provided the basis of local self-government and the rule of law. The Belgians, however, had plundered the Congo.

The American war in Vietnam, moreover, was marked by attention to protecting the lives of civilians. Atrocities did occur, as the My Lai massacre revealed. Because of moral considerations and media attention, United States military and political leaders felt constrained about the kind of military action they took. Critics of United States policy, however, pointed to the deaths of innocent civilians and the impossibility of distinguishing a "purely military" target in a guerrilla-type war. Still, it is clear that limitations were imposed on the military.

Legal

The role of international law has been discussed above as an instrument of power. It is also a constraint on power. States often feel bound to follow the rules of international law.

The protection of diplomats is a case in point. Even when states go to war against each other, diplomats are permitted to return to their home countries. Prisoners of war are protected from torture by international conventions. Commercial transactions are encouraged because of legal agreements covering business relationships. Even arms control agreements are for the most part followed.

Pragmatic

States are constrained from taking certain actions for pragmatic reasons. These constraints, for example, include military and political matters.

The nonuse of nuclear weapons since the end of World War II shows the impact of military constraints. Even when the United States had a monopoly of nuclear weapons from 1945 to 1949 and a superiority for more than a decade thereafter, it did not use these weapons. It accepted a status quo arrangement in Korea in 1954 rather than use nuclear weapons, and it withdrew from Vietnam rather than use them. Both the Soviet Union and the United States have found these weapons too dangerous to use—at least so far.

States are also constrained from taking action because of political considerations. The Soviet Union has not been happy about the production of nuclear weapons by the People's Republic of China, the independence of Albania and Yugoslavia, the diplomatic discretion exercised by Romania, and the Solidarity movement in Poland. Although it has not been without influence, it probably has hesitated to act more vigorously because of the reaction of other states.

ISSUES

The rise and fall of states is a perennial feature of world history. For example, Spain and Great Britain were once major players in world politics, and now their influence is less than that of other countries—most notably the United States and the Soviet Union. But is the United States now in decline? Debate 24 considers whether the United States is in such decline that it should reduce its foreign policy commitments.

States have relied on economic methods to achieve foreign policy goals. Debate 25 assesses the effectiveness of economic sanctions in this regard.

The devastation produced by war has directed much attention to finding methods of control. Debate 26 examines one of these methods: disarmament.

24/YES

SHOULD THE UNITED STATES REDUCE ITS FOREIGN POLICY COMMITMENTS BECAUSE OF ITS DECLINING POWER?

Power in world politics is always changing. In the past five centuries, former great powers have become ordinary countries. Once Spain, the Netherlands, and Great Britain had mighty empires, but today their imperial glories are but memories. At the same time, states that were once small powers have achieved great power status. Both the United States and the Soviet Union have achieved top rank in this century, for example.

By all accounts, the United States became a superpower at the end of World War II. It is clear, however, that the United States is no longer the powerful country that it was in 1945. As the United States enters the last decade of the twentieth century, some facts are obvious: (1) U.S. economic and military power is in relative decline; (2) the United States is overextended in its foreign and military commitments; (3) in order to adjust to the new global realities as well as strengthen its economy and national security, the United States must reduce its commitments and allow other friendly countries to share the burden for maintaining security of countries that are not in the Soviet camp.

Economic and Military Decline. When World War II came to an end, the United States was the only belligerent whose economy was in good shape. European countries and Japan were devastated by the war in terms of both loss of lives and collapse of basic industrial and agricultural production. In 1945, the United States owned two-thirds of the world's gold resources. It held a dominant industrial and agricultural position in the world. It was the only country with nuclear weapons, and its military power was without equal.

The period since 1945 has seen the decline of U.S. economic strength. Today, Western Europe's economy is thriving, and the European Community is making headway toward reducing tariffs among its member countries. In the Pacific Basin, Japan, South Korea, and Taiwan are making major economic gains. So impressive have the economic accomplishments of these countries been that the next hundred years has been forecasted as the Pacific Century.

The economic decline of the United States has been steady over the past few decades and is reflected in many ways. U.S. manufactured goods are unable to compete as effectively as they did in the past. A number of business operations have moved offshore because of poor management, high labor costs, or low quality in production standards. The country that pioneered in television no longer manufactures television sets. Japanese cars have made major inroads in the U.S. market. The dollar has lost ground to other currencies. Foreign companies have bought up some of the tangible economic resources held in the United States, including real estate, hotels, and publishing houses. Foreign corporations, moreover, are building their own plants in the United States, as the cases of Toyota and Honda demonstrate.

In the early 1950s, the United States accounted for approximately 40 percent of the gross world product; by 1980, that share had declined to approximately 22 percent. In the early postwar period, the United States produced 30 percent of world manufacturing exports; by 1986, its share had dropped to only 13 percent.[2]

The economic decline of the United States became particularly obvious during the administration of President Ronald Reagan. During Reagan's campaign for the presidency in 1980, his theme was "Morning in America," a slogan he hoped would describe a new era of lower interest rates, higher employment figures, and reduced inflation, in contrast to the condition of the U.S. economy in the last year of the Jimmy Carter administration. Although the Reagan administration was able to achieve those goals in its two terms in office, it did so with a great increase in the national debt and at the expense of future generations. Reagan critics say we are now faced with a

---

[2] See Robert Gilpin, "American Policy in the Post-Reagan Era" *Daedalus* 116 (Summer 1987): 42.

new theme—"The Morning After."

The Reagan approach to economic management was to reduce the size of government. The president had hoped to achieve this goal by instituting a large tax cut in 1981. His administration put forward the view that a reduction in the tax rate would stimulate the economy to such an extent that the actual level of tax revenues would increase. That view, known as supply-side economics, turned out to be illusory. The Reagan administration started a massive rearmament program because it contended that U.S. military forces had been in need of rejuvenation after a decade of neglect. Although some cuts were made in nondefense expenditures during the Reagan years, these were not substantial in terms of reducing overall federal expenditures.

The result of the Reagan policies was a sharp rise of budget deficits. As the critics of Reagan pointed out, ultimately the debts would have to be paid, and foreign investment and loans would not be able to fund the debt indefinitely. The Reagan years saw the United States amass more debt in two terms than the United States had accumulated in its entire history. By 1988 the total budget deficit had reached $2.5 trillion. One need not blame the president alone for the debt, since Congress and most of the American people seemed unwilling to pay increased taxes and reduce government spending on popular programs.

In addition to budget deficits, the United States experienced enormous trade imbalances. The Pacific and Western European countries, among others, were exporting more to the United States than the United States was sending to them. The United States had to borrow more and more to pay the rising import debt.

Over the same period of time in which it experienced economic decay, the United States sought to maintain its military status as a superpower. Its foreign and military commitments were global. Since the early post–World War II years, the United States had followed a policy of containment against the Soviet Union, which necessitated building strong nuclear and conventional forces designed to deter the Soviet Union and its communist allies from aggression.

Today, the United States spends more than 6 percent of its gross national product (GNP) on defense. Thousands of the country's scientists work in military industries, such as in weapons research, development, and production.

Overextended Commitments. However legitimate were the reasons for the United States to make its foreign and military commitments in the early post–World War II years, it is clear that the United States is now overcommitted. It no longer has the wherewithal to sustain its huge global responsibilities.

Since 1945, the United States has built up a global alliance system. At the core of the system is the North Atlantic Treaty Organization (NATO), which currently consists of the United States, Canada, and fourteen Western European countries. The United States, moreover, formed other alliances—some on a bilateral and others on a multilateral basis. Not all of them survive, but most continue. Today, the United States maintains vast fleets and armies abroad—520,000 soldiers and 65,000 sailors.

Even with vast expenditures on defense and deployment of troops and support forces abroad, the United States has shown that it is unable to cope effectively with changes in the global environment. In 1945, the United States had a nuclear monopoly. Today, nuclear weapons are owned by several nations (see Issue 26).

The United States fought a war in Korea in 1950–53 but was unable to achieve victory even when it had more economic and military strength than its direct opponents—North Korea and the People's Republic of China. It fought the longest war in its history against North Vietnam in 1965–73, but its efforts to save South Vietnam from conquest by North Vietnam were unsuccessful.

With all its military and economic strength, moreover, the United States was unable to free its citizens held hostage in Iran for 444 days during the administration of President Jimmy Carter. U.S. hostages remained in Beirut during the Reagan administration, in some cases after years of captivity. One of Ronald Reagan's major failures was the retreat by U.S. Marines in Beirut under fire by a relative handful of Shiite militiamen in 1983.

Given the economic problems faced by the United States and the declining utility of force in international relations, it is clear that the United States is overextended. Historian Paul

Kennedy describes the U.S. role as "imperial coverstretch." In his study of the rise and fall of empires since 1500, he sees a pattern emerging reminiscent of the past. For an empire to remain strong over the long term, it must have the economic wherewithal to sustain its power. Empires in previous eras, such as those of Spain, the Netherlands, and Great Britain, declined because of imperial overreach. What Professor Kennedy finds crucial is the relative economic position of empires—that is to say, how the economy of a strong state compares to other states of the times. He finds that in general over time, overextended foreign policy commitments lead to economic decline. He warns that unless the United States takes steps to reduce its foreign policy commitments, it, too, can suffer the same consequences as other empires.[3]

Burden Sharing. Whatever arguments made sense in 1945 for the United States to become the policeman of the world, it is now time to recognize that conditions have changed. The United States no longer has to bear the kind of military and financial burden to promote security in the world that it did decades ago.

The United States must start by reducing its level of defense expenditures. There is no risk in making significant cuts in the military budget. It is now apparent to everyone that the Soviet Union is in even a worse predicament than the United States. Efforts begun by the Soviet leadership since 1985 to promote economic growth in the Soviet Union are under way but will take a long time to generate meaningful results. In addition, to achieve economic growth, the Soviets will have to divert resources from the military to the civilian sector.

The Soviets have given clear signals that their country needs a period of calm in international relations. The successful conclusion of the Intermediate-range Nuclear Forces Treaty in 1988 suggests that the United States should be prepared to enter into further agreements with the Soviet Union. A major item on the agenda of relations between the two countries is an agreement to reduce strategic nuclear weapons. Possibly, too, the United States

and other NATO members can come to terms with the Soviet Union for a reduction of ground forces in Europe. Such agreements, prepared with attention to the security needs of all parties, can be equally advantageous to the economies of those parties.

In the meantime, the United States should call upon its allies to make a greater contribution to their own security. The United States spends slightly more than 6 percent of its GNP on defense, whereas its NATO allies spend slightly more than 3 percent. NATO members are in a better financial position to make a greater effort for their defense. It is not necessary for the United States to withdraw its troops from Europe, but it can reduce the number stationed abroad. Nearly 60 percent of the Pentagon budget is devoted to NATO. The United States keeps ten divisions for NATO, five deployed in Europe and five in the United States capable of rapid deployment to Western Europe in case of need. By pursuing a policy of devolution, in which other countries gradually assume some of the responsibilities borne by U.S. forces, the United States could save up to $50 billion a year.[4]

Japan, too, should be called upon to play a part in its own security. At present, Japan is getting a "free ride." After World War II, at the inducement of the United States, Japan adopted a constitutional provision that it would only maintain self-defense forces. Consequently, Japan has relied on the United States for its security and devotes only 1 percent of its GNP to its defense. Thus funds that might be spent on defense are used instead for economic development; no wonder that the Japanese economy has done so well! It is time for Japan to increase its defense budget to a level of about 3 percent of GNP and to assume a greater role in its regional security.

With the savings produced from arms control agreements with the Soviet Union and with burden sharing by its allies, the United States would be in better economic shape. To the extent that a country's military strength is based on its economic health, the United States would be in a superb position to use its power effectively for the security of itself and its allies.

---

[3] Paul Kennedy, *The Rise and Fall of the Great Powers: Economic Change and Military Conflict from 1500 to 2000* (New York: Random House, 1987).

[4] David P. Calleo, Harold van B. Cleveland, and Leonard Silk, "The Dollar and the Defense of the West," *Foreign Affairs* 66 (Spring 1988): 858.

24/NO

SHOULD THE UNITED STATES REDUCE ITS FOREIGN POLICY COMMITMENTS BECAUSE OF ITS DECLINING POWER?

In 1987 and 1988, *decline* became a buzzword among writers commenting on the power of the United States. A number of books have achieved prominence with the gloomy theme that the American Century is over. The view of decline fits nicely with the views of liberals and left-leaning pundits who have for years resented U.S. efforts to meet the Soviet challenge. A close look at the facts indicates that the case for decline is an oversimplification of the facts. Specifically, we make the following points: (1) U.S. economic and military power is still quite strong; (2) the United States is not overextended in its foreign and military commitments; (3) any significant reduction in U.S. commitments with a devolution of responsibilities to U.S. allies could possibly produce consequences that are adverse to both U.S. economic and U.S. security interests.

Economic and Military Decline? Even advocates of the decline school agree that the United States is still a strong economic and military power. Paul Kennedy in particular has stressed *relative* decline. It is important, then, to observe that the United States remains a strong economic power.

The dollar, though weakened, is still the world's currency. For all the talk about the Pacific Century, the U.S. economy is twice the size of Japan's and 15 percent larger than that of the European Community. The U.S. standard of living is still the highest in the world. The United States is the largest exporter of manufactured goods. Between 1982 and early 1988, higher productivity raised family income by about 11 percent in the United States.[5]

Many decline theorists are making judgments about the U.S. economy based on an economic analysis using the immediate postwar years as a base period, but it is misleading to consider these years as the point of comparison because they were extraordinary. Most of the rest of the world was only beginning to recover from the ravages of World War II, and, obviously, the United States easily had a lion's share of the global economy. As production in other countries increased, the relative position of the United States economy inevitably declined.

Not only did the economies of the war-devastated countries improve, but the United States did everything possible to restore the economic health of its allies and former enemies. It provided economic assistance—most notably the Marshall Plan in 1947—and it subsequently extended assistance to developing countries. A motivating force behind such assistance was the view that the United States economy would gain with a world composed of strong trading partners. Such has been the reality, since in absolute terms the standard of living of American citizens has improved since 1945 in part because of the robust economies of other countries.

Decline theorists, moreover, are viewing the mistakes of the Reagan years as evidence of decline. As political scientist Joseph Nye notes, "But those mistakes are not indicators of long-run decline; they can be solved by cutting American consumption and raising savings for a period of a half-decade or so."[6]

The United States still maintains a dynamic system with many attractions for economic growth. It possesses vast natural resources. It has a people with entrepreneurial talents and the managerial skills to develop those talents. Due almost totally to small and midsize firms, the United States has created nearly fifteen times as many jobs in the 1980s as the more closed and controlled systems of Europe.[7]

The United States, moreover, has been a

---

[5] Robert J. Samuelson, "The Asia-Bashing Impulse," *Newsweek* 111 (February 22, 1988): 53.

[6] Joseph Nye, "Short-Term Folly, Not Long-Term Decline," *New Perspectives Quarterly* 5 (Summer 1988): 34.

[7] Joel Krotkin, "American Renaissance in the Asian Era," *New Perspectives Quarterly* 5 (Summer 1988): 4.

mecca for immigrants. Since the 1970s the United States has accepted more legal immigrants than the rest of the world combined. About half the doctoral candidates in engineering at U.S. universities are foreigners; and about twenty five thousand foreign students are studying for undergraduate engineering degrees. Although most of these students return home, many of the top students, including 60 percent of the Ph.D.'s, remain in the United States. Many U.S. companies and universities employ these people. Today about 20 percent of U.S. engineers are foreign born.[8] The U.S. economy clearly benefits from the country's open immigration policy.

It is possible, moreover, that the United States will improve its economy with respect to its Asian competitors as anticipated problems emerge in some of the Pacific Basin's greatest success stories. Although 40 percent of Japan's exports are currently sent to the U.S. market, Japan will have to address both foreign affairs and domestic difficulties to maintain that rate. American business, labor, and government leaders are pushing not only for protectionist legislation but for the elimination or reduction of Japanese protectionist obstacles to U.S. exports to Japan. Internally, Japan must deal with a rapidly aging population that will consume some of its savings. As for other Pacific Basin countries, South Korea is experiencing some instability caused by a transition to democracy. China is retreating from its market economy reforms, which were responsible for its giant gains in economic growth during the 1980s. And Hong Kong, which has been enormously successful in transforming its economy, will revert to China in 1997—as required by a treaty with Great Britain. A number of talented people have already left Hong Kong in anticipation of the transfer of power to a communist country.

Even if the economies of the Pacific Basin and European countries continue to improve, the power of the United States in world politics will not necessarily suffer a decline. For the most part the countries that have been most successful in economic growth are allied or friendly to the United States. These countries help to strengthen their own security as well

as that of the United States through their prosperity.

That the United States is encountering severe economic problems is not to be denied. What is to be questioned, however, is whether the problems are brought on by extraordinary military expenditures. In the Reagan administration military buildup of the 1980s, the United States spent approximately 6 percent of GNP on its defense budget. Under President Dwight D. Eisenhower during the 1950s, the corresponding figure was 10 percent.

The exact relationship between military expenditures and economic development, moreover, is a matter of dispute. There is no clear case for the assertion that high defense expenditures leads to economic decay. In the period of the most rapid U.S. growth—from 1948 to 1973—defense expenditures were a much larger fraction of GNP than they have been in the slow-growth period since 1973. In this earlier period, defense expenditures averaged 8.6 percent of GNP. Between 1973 and 1987, they have averaged 5.7 percent. In 1987, they were 6.6 percent.[9] South Korea, whose economy is soaring, devotes about the same percentage of its GNP to defense as does the United States. Taiwan spends even a higher percentage of its GNP on defense than the equivalent share for the United States, and yet it has a per capita rate of growth almost four times higher than that of the United States.[10] The defense expenditures of Great Britain as a percentage of its GNP declined in the years preceding 1978, at the same time that the British economy deteriorated.

Overextended Commitments. The United States has been and remains the only country strong enough to challenge the military power of the Soviet Union. U.S. defense expenditures and alliance commitments have been devised to strengthen U.S. security.

Although the United States has not always been successful in its foreign policy and military efforts, its successes far outnumber the

---

[8] Samuelson, "Asian-Bashing Impulse," p. 53.

[9] Henry Scott Stokes, "Stock Prices and Springsteen," *New Perspectives Quarterly* 5 (Summer 1988): 3.

[10] W. W. Rostow, "Beware of Historians Bearing False Analogies," *Foreign Affairs* 66 (Spring 1988): 866.

failures. The Soviet Union, for example, which has built a mighty military establishment, respects the military strength of the United States and its allies. Although it has achieved parity with the United States in nuclear weapons, it is careful not to risk a nuclear war with the United States because it knows that there will be no winner in a nuclear war. The Soviet Union seems most worried about the application of technological innovations to strategic defense weapons currently under research by the United States and has sought to diminish that superiority, most notably through a strategic defense arms control agreement.

Although the United States settled for a stalemate rather than victory in the Korean War and was unable to prevent the South Vietnamese government from being overrun by the communists, the failures in both cases were more of political will than military strength. The United States was simply not willing to risk expanding the wars because of possible political repercussions at home and abroad.

The security arrangements that the United States have made have been successful. All NATO members are free and independent, thanks in part to NATO. Other U.S. allies enjoy similar freedom and independence. U.S. military forces successfully toppled a Marxist government in Grenada. Naval operations to protect shipping in the Persian Gulf against Iranian gunboats and mines in 1987 and 1988 proved successful. U.S. military assistance to the Afghan rebels in fighting a Soviet-backed Afghanistan government may have helped turn the tide for the rebels and induced the Soviets to withdraw from Afghanistan.

Although U.S. commitments are far ranging, it is clear that the United States has never thought of fighting wars in Europe, Asia, the Persian Gulf, and Central America at the same time. Such an effort would require a much larger expenditure in defense than the United States is currently making.

Efforts to compare the experience of the United States today with that of earlier empires are misleading. Unlike other empires, the United States does not seek to dominate other countries in an imperial manner. When Great Britain built its empire, it did not possess the abundance of natural resources held by the United States. Unlike the United States, it was heavily dependent upon trade. Its imports constituted

25 percent of its GNP in contrast to a U.S. comparable figure of 10 percent in 1985. Britain's chief opponent—Germany—was a strong economic and military power, whereas the chief U.S. opponent—the Soviet Union—is strong militarily but weak economically. The situation of the United States as a world power is historically unique. The United States is not threatened by any country that combines strong military *and* economic assets.

Too much has been made of economic strength as a measure of power in world politics. The Soviet Union itself is an example of how a country with a weak economic base can become a global power to be reckoned with. The Soviet leaders have been willing to devote a heavy expenditure on defense. As political scientist Jeane J. Kirkpatrick notes, the Soviet Union's power has been overextended since Lenin's day. Yet its record shows that "there is no reliable correlation between economic power and military power except at the extremes, and no reliable correlation between percent of GNP spent on defense and the level of economic growth."[11] Although there are signs that Moscow needs breathing space to care for its economy, the Soviet Union continues to play a global role in world politics, as it has most prominently since 1945.

Burden Sharing. One can readily support the view that the allies of the United States should bear a heavier burden in assuming the costs of defense. It is true that our allies—particularly in Europe and parts of Asia—are in a stronger economic position than they were decades ago. But calls for burden sharing ignore aspects of Western Europe's defense contributions as well as the consequences of a devolution of the U.S. role in the world.

It is true that NATO members spend for defense about 3 percent of their GNP, compared to 6 percent of GNP by the United States. But the aggregate figures ignore the different commitments of each party. The United States has global commitments,

---

[11] Testimony of Jeane J. Kirkpatrick, in U.S. Congress, Senate, *Concurrent Resolution on the Budget for Fiscal Year 1989: Defense Burden-Sharing,* Hearings before the Committee on the Budget, 100th Congress, 2d Sess., 1988, 1:41.

whereas NATO members for the most part spend their defense funds for the defense of Europe. In these terms, the United States and Western Europe carry an equal burden in the defense of NATO.

We must also ask about the consequences of a declining role for the United States in its global commitments. If the United States either disengages from Europe or devolves responsibilities to NATO members, then it is possible that the ultimate goal of NATO—the preservation of Western security—will be jeopardized. U.S. retrenchment in Europe might encourage the forces of pacifism and neutralism in Europe, resulting in reduced defense efforts by NATO members.

Another consequence of a smaller U.S. role in NATO would be the encouragement of European NATO states to "go their own way" in fashioning an independent security apparatus. Such a policy raises the question of nuclear weapons for West Germany as part of an independent European force. A nuclear West Germany might destabilize relations in Europe with the Soviet Union.

Burden sharing would have consequences in Asia, too. If Japan raises its defense outlays and plays a greater political and military role in Asia, it is possible that other countries in the Pacific Basin might feel threatened and begin an arms race. For historic reasons, China, South Korea, Taiwan, and other Asian countries fear a militarized Japan, and those fears would be exacerbated by Japanese rearmament.

Moreover, there is no evidence that the countries of Asia favor a reduction by the United States of its Asian commitments. China, in particular, seems content with U.S. military presence in Asia as a possible counter to the military power of the Soviet Union.

In general, a reduction of U.S. support for its foreign policy commitments will result in a decline of U.S. influence. The United States will be less able to assert its priorities in such matters as nuclear proliferation, managing regional balances, and coping with terrorism. Such a development would pose dangers to world peace.

The United States, then, should not reduce its overseas commitments because of a fear that is in relative decline. Such a reduction might harm the U.S. economy and, equally important, damage the security interests of the United States and its allies. Moreover, the assumption that the United States is declining as a world power is false.

25/YES ARE ECONOMIC SANCTIONS AN EFFECTIVE INSTRUMENT OF FOREIGN POLICY?

States and international organizations use a variety of methods in the conduct of foreign policy. Economic sanctions have proven to be one such effective method. If seen in a proper and limited context, the case for sanctions is based on four principal considerations: (1) the historical evidence shows that sanctions can be successful; (2) efficient implementation of sanctions is possible; (3) sanctions can undermine the ability of targeted governments to maintain the support of their people; and (4) sanctions offer a useful instrument of diplomacy, particularly in the nuclear age.

Historical Evidence. Economic sanctions have a long history that can be traced back to ancient times. For the most part, however, sanctions have become a major means of influencing state behavior in the twentieth century. The United States has been a principal user of sanctions, as have countries that are allied with the United States. But sanctions have also been used by the Soviet Union, and even Third World countries have relied on them. International organizations, such as the League of Nations and the United Nations, have resorted to sanctions, too.

It is essential to mention at the outset that the label *success* in evaluating sanctions must be carefully circumscribed. Under optimum conditions, success means that sanctions get a target country to completely reverse course and, consequently, change policy. But success can also be achieved under minimum conditions in that the target country is required to pay a price for its behavior.

Because it is often difficult to isolate factors that contribute to a country's political behavior, one cannot say with absolute certainty that sanctions produced a particular result. In many cases, sanctions are an important contributory factor in bringing about a policy sought by the targeting country. A number of examples may be cited to prove the point.

The United States imposed sanctions on the Marxist government of Salvador Allende in Chile in the early 1970s. These sanctions helped to promote the economic decay that undermined the government and led to Allende's overthrow.

Countries institute sanctions not only against their enemies, but also against their friends. In 1956, the United States threatened to impose economic sanctions against Great Britain and France during the Suez crisis in which those countries, along with Israel, went to war against Egypt. Both the British and the French withdrew their forces from the Sinai in part because of U.S. restrictions on oil deliveries and trade credits to Great Britain and France.

Sanctions by the United States against South Korea and Taiwan from 1975 to 1977 deterred those countries from building nuclear reprocessing plants, which might have made them capable of becoming nuclear-weapons states. President Jimmy Carter's use of sanctions against the regime of Anastasio Somoza in Nicaragua from 1977 to 1979 helped bring down that government.

In 1973 Arab oil-exporting countries imposed an embargo against the United States and Western Europe and threatened to extend that embargo to other countries that supported Israel. Israel's sovereignty and strength were not, as a consequence, impaired, but the embargo did achieve some important consequences. The very threat of the embargo helped to encourage hoarding of oil and drove up oil prices around the world, thus contributing to an inflationary spiral. Many governments in Europe and elsewhere adopted a more hostile policy toward Israel in response to the pressure of the embargo.

The United Nations instituted economic sanctions against the white-ruled government of Rhodesia in 1965 in the hope of undermining the government and allowing for black majority rule. These measures did help to undermine the economic strength of the Rho-

desian government, which in 1980 transferred power to a black-majority government that renamed its country Zimbabwe.

Great Britain and other European Community countries imposed sanctions on Argentina when the British and Argentines went to war over control of the Falkland Islands in 1982. Had the war been inconclusive rather than a British victory, the sanctions would no doubt have contributed to disrupting the Argentinian economy.

Implementation. Critics of sanctions often point to the failure of sanctions to be comprehensive or to the inability of a targeting country, group of countries, or international organizations to win universal support for applying sanctions. To be sure, if sanctions are evaluated according to such extreme standards, then one could argue that they are not successful. But sanctions are more often designed to make the targeted country pay a price for its action, and often they do take a slow but steady toll.

After Soviet forces moved into Afghanistan in 1979, President Jimmy Carter imposed a partial grain embargo against the Soviet Union, which has had a continuing problem producing enough agricultural products to meet its needs. It is true that Moscow sought and obtained alternative sources of grain from countries such as Argentina and Canada. Nevertheless, the Soviets could not make up shortfalls in feed-quality grains and, consequently, suffered a shortage of meat in 1979 and 1980. According to an analysis of the U.S. Department of Agriculture, that shortage helped to spark the Solidarity uprising in Poland.[12]

The Rhodesian government paid a price as a result of the sanctions imposed first by Great Britain and then by the United Nations. Ultimately, the white-ruled government gave way to the black majority.

Much attention has been given of late to the imposition of economic sanctions against South Africa because of its policies of *apartheid* and minority-white rule. The United Nations imposed an arms embargo against South Africa in 1977. Many countries, including the United States, have enacted economic sanc-

---

[12] See Gregory A. Fossedal, "Sanctions for Beginners," *New Republic* 193 (October 21, 1985): 19.

tions that curbed new investments, loans, and trade with South Africa. If, as some critics contend, the South African government has been able to circumvent many of the economic penalties imposed from without, one wonders why that government is so vociferous in denouncing the sanctions. The reason is not surprising. The arms embargo has meant that South Africa cannot obtain many new weapons manufactured in advanced industrial societies. Circumvention of the embargoes has meant it has to pay higher prices for blacklisted items. The result of the sanctions may not be the immediate toppling of the South African government, but nevertheless, as with Rhodesia, there is a slow but steady toll: the bleeding of the South African economy.

Popular Support. Economic sanctions help undermine government support in targeted countries. They send a message to the government and people of the targeted state as well as to the rest of the world. In the case of **divestment** (the disposal of investments once held by private organizations) and sanctions imposed by the United States against South Africa, for example, the white voters of South Africa are singled out for condemnation as supporting a policy that is beyond the world's moral pale. The black majority of South Africa are, consequently, encouraged to carry on their struggle for freedom and equal political rights. Blacks in South Africa thus continue to engage in acts of protest, thereby requiring the South African government to expend more funds on maintaining law and order.

Moreover, foreign investors lose confidence in a country that has become a pariah state in the world community and is in social and economic turmoil. Their withdrawal undermines popular support even further. In Rhodesia in the 1960s and 1970s and South Africa in the 1980s, antigovernment guerrilla operations increased after international sanctions were imposed. In both countries, many white people left their homeland in search of physical safety and political stability. Sanctions, then, also took their toll in terms of undermining internal support for the government.

Diplomacy. In the twentieth century, economic sanctions are not seen as a cause of war and are therefore seen as safer than military means to obtain objectives. Considering the fact that the world lives in a nuclear age, many nuclear-weapons states regard military means as too dangerous, since wars can escalate beyond the intentions of the governing officials who make decisions of war and peace.

In a diplomatic sense economic sanctions give a signal that a country regards an issue to be important. When the United States instituted the partial grain embargo against the Soviet Union in 1979, it gave a signal to Moscow that it was willing to bear the costs to an important U.S. industry to show its condemnation of the Soviet military move that placed Soviet forces closer to the Persian Gulf. When the United States imposed economic sanctions on Nicaragua in 1985, U.S. policy makers were very much aware that the immediate economic effect would not be significant. Still, the embargo served as a signal to Nicaragua and its major supporters—the Soviet Union and Cuba—that the United States regarded expansion of Nicaraguan military power into Central America as a threat to U.S. security.

Economic sanctions offer an effective instrument of power to political leaders in another way. Particularly in democracies, leaders may be under popular pressure to take some kind of action. When military action may be deemed too dangerous, economic sanctions offer leaders a device that can give them some flexibility while retaining some political initiative. Such may have been the case with the partial grain embargo of 1979.

How and when economic sanctions are to be instituted is a matter of political judgment. Effectiveness depends in part on the vulnerability of a country to such sanctions as well as the resolve of the government and people of a targeted country.

Though sanctions are often portrayed as a policy that cannot work, the record shows that states should rely on them from time to time.

25 / NO ARE ECONOMIC SANCTIONS AN EFFECTIVE INSTRUMENT OF FOREIGN POLICY?

The case against using economic sanctions is based on many considerations. The most important are the following: (1) the historical evidence shows that sanctions are for the most part unsuccessful; (2) sanctions cannot be well implemented because they are rarely comprehensive and too easily circumvented; (3) they serve to unify the people behind the targeted government; and (4) they signify a failure of diplomacy.

Historical Evidence. For the most part, economic sanctions have not achieved their goals, and in some cases they have even been counterproductive. When the League of Nations imposed sanctions against Italy for its invasion of Ethiopia in 1935, Italy did not withdraw from that African country. In fact, the failure of sanctions against Italy accelerated the decline of the League because of a loss of prestige.

The Soviet Union was no more successful than the League of Nations when it imposed economic sanctions against Yugoslavia in 1948 to protest Yugoslavia's move for independence from Soviet domination. In spite of the fact that Yugoslavia was a communist country at the time that Joseph Stalin was the leader of both the Soviet Union and the world communist movement, Yugoslavia was able to continue on its independent course, redirecting its economic ties to Western countries and away from the Soviet Union and its allies.

Nor did the Arab oil boycott beginning in 1973 last for long. None of the three goals set by the Arab members of the Organization of Petroleum Exporting Countries (Israeli withdrawal from territories seized in the Middle East War of 1967, self-determination for the Palestinians, and a change in the status of Jerusalem) was achieved. When seventeen Arab countries imposed sanctions against Egypt after it made peace with Israel in 1978, the Egyptians did not renege on the peace achievements agreed to at Camp David in the United States.

Much has been made of the sanctions against Rhodesia and South Africa. The British imposed sanctions against Rhodesia in 1965 when the white-ruled Rhodesian colonial government announced it would become independent. British Prime Minister Harold Wilson said at the time that measures taken by his government would restore legality in Rhodesia "within a matter of weeks rather than months."[13] It took fifteen years and thirty thousand deaths before the white-ruled government of Rhodesia agreed to a peace settlement. Factors other than sanctions, such as guerrilla warfare and white emigration, contributed more significantly to the demise of the government than did sanctions.

When the United Nations decided on an arms embargo against South Africa in 1977, South Africa built its own arms industry. Today, it is the tenth largest arms producer in the world. Efforts by many countries, including the United States, to use sanctions as a way of punishing the South African government for denying majority rule have failed to bring about the desired result. South Africa continues to have the most dynamic economy in all of Africa.

The U.S. partial grain embargo against the Soviet Union in 1979 did not bring about the removal of Soviet forces in Afghanistan. The embargo, which became an issue in the presidential election campaign of 1980, was ended by Ronald Reagan in April 1981. When Soviet forces began their withdrawal from Afghanistan in 1988, they were reacting to the casualties they had suffered as a result of continuing resistance by Afghan guerrilla forces— supplied in part by the United States—and not to economic sanctions.

Another example of the failure of sanctions is Cuba. The United States imposed trade sanctions on Cuba in 1960 in the hope of toppling the communist government of Fidel Castro. The Cuban leader has remained in power and become strongly tied to the Soviet Union in spite of the sanctions. He has, moreover, played a role in aiding communist and

---

[13] Commonwealth Prime Ministers' Meeting in Lagos 1966: *Final Communique,* Cmnd. 2890 (London: HMSO, 1966), p. 5, as cited in Margaret P. Doxey, *International Sanctions in Contemporary Perspective* (Houndmills, England: Macmillan, 1987), p. 38.

anti-American forces in this hemisphere as well as in Africa.

The historical evidence is conclusive: Economic sanctions do not work.

Implementation. Economic sanctions are easily circumvented. One reason for the facility at circumvention is that sanctions are rarely universal. Another reason is that targeted countries can easily take countermeasures to offset the penalties of sanctions.

The sanctions instituted by the League of Nations against Italy failed in part because not every country in the world was a member of that international organization. The League, moreover, refused to embargo vital raw materials or to cut communications with Italy. The U.S. grain embargo against the Soviet Union in 1979 did not have the support of many countries. The Soviet Union was able to purchase grain in large quantities from Argentina and Canada. And the embargo itself was only partial, since Washington agreed to meet its contractual obligations for grain shipments to the Soviet Union.

The oil embargo of 1973 provides another example of the difficulties countries experience in achieving universal support for sanctions. Non-Arab members of the Organization of Petroleum Exporting Countries did not join the embargo. Major oil companies could still sell to countries that had been targeted for the oil ban. The Arabs, moreover, did not control the world supply of tankers or refineries.

Targeted countries can find many ways to circumvent sanctions. Their agricultural products and minerals, for example, can be exported to a country not complying with the sanctions and then transshipped as though not associated with the targeted country.

South Africa has been particularly successful in finding ways to get around sanctions. It has received enough oil and has stockpiled what is estimated as a several years' supply. Private companies have been set up in the West to serve as dummy corporations ready to buy what is necessary for ultimate South African destination and to sell South African products abroad. African countries that have been the most vocal critics of South Africa—Zimbabwe, Tanzania, and Mozambique—have a vigorous economic relationship with South Africa.

Indeed, South Africa has taken steps to become economically self-sufficient. It has a strong industrial capacity, vital food supplies, and rich minerals, and has been able to find substitutes for some items that are in short supply because of sanctions.

Another method of circumventing sanctions is through the use of multinational corporations (MNCs). With offices in many countries, these organizations can make deals that a corporation based in one country may not be able to make because of a government's decision to impose sanctions. In 1982, President Ronald Reagan sought to prevent oil-pipeline machinery from being sold to the Soviet Union. Western European allies of the United States did not agree with the U.S.-imposed sanctions, however, and encouraged and even allowed MNCs with offices in Western Europe to sell that equipment to the Soviet Union.

Popular Support. The effect of economic sanctions is generally to rally people around the government in time of stress. Nationalism is so powerful a force in the world that a leader of a targeted country can easily whip up nationalist feeling against an enemy.

Soviet sanctions against Yugoslavia brought the several nationality groups in that country together in their support of Yugoslav leader Marshal Josip Broz Tito. Castro was able to mobilize anti-American feeling in Cuba in part because of the sanctions.

In response to the taking of U.S. hostages from the American Embassy in Teheran, the United States instituted sanctions against Iran. Hostage taking was seen in many countries as a clear violation of international law. Nevertheless, the Iranian government was able to work Iranian public opinion into an anti-American frenzy.

The whites in South Africa have taken a circle-the-wagons approach against the world. Indeed, there is evidence that they are giving greater electoral support to political candidates who are committed to a stronger resistance to countries pushing sanctions.

One of the reasons that governments often become more popular when their countries are targeted for sanctions is that, ultimately, it is impossible to penalize a government without harming a people. The case of South Africa is particularly illustrative of this point.

The first group to be hurt by sanctions in South Africa is blacks. When U.S. college campuses rallied for the divestment of stocks in companies doing business with South Africa, enormous pressure was exerted for U.S. corporations with factories in South Africa to end their operations there. Many of those companies had the best records for hiring blacks and promoting them to top positions. Such action was taken in part in response to a movement headed by Leon Sullivan, a Baptist minister from Philadelphia. Once the U.S. companies withdrew from South Africa, their companies increasingly came under the control of white South Africans, who did not feel committed to abide by the Sullivan Principles, which improved conditions of blacks in these companies. The result of divestment meant that conditions for blacks became worse.

Indeed, the argument has been put forward that the best way to end white rule and the last vestiges of *apartheid* in South Africa is to promote more trade and a stronger economy in that country. According to this view, greater economic development would bring more jobs and higher income to black South Africans. Trade unions, consequently, would increase in power. Then, boycotts and strikes could be used effectively to bring pressure for racial change and political equality. As it is, economic sanctions have served to impede economic development and, consequently, hinder racial progress.[14]

Diplomacy. Economic sanctions are a failure as a diplomatic tool. First, they do not work. Second, even if they could work, domestic opposition often forces a government to drop its sanction program. The U.S. grain embargo of the Soviet Union is a case in point. Wheat producers in the United States were hurt by the embargo, and Ronald Reagan championed their cause. When he became president, he ended the embargo.

Third, countries imposing sanctions often antagonize their allies, as allies do not always hold similar interests on every issue. The pipeline controversy of 1982, for example, opened a wedge between the United States and its Western European allies. Similar conflict occurred over U.S. sanctions on Cuba, Iran, and Nicaragua.

Support for sanctions has no ideological base. Many liberals call for sanctions against South Africa and for other countries that violate human rights. Many conservatives oppose sanctions against South Africa but favor them against communist countries, such as Cuba and Nicaragua. Sanctions may make some people feel morally virtuous, but evidence indicates that they fail as an instrument of foreign policy.

---

[14] For such a view, see Helen Suzman, "What America Should Do about South Africa," *New York Times Magazine*, August 3, 1986, pp. 14–17.

26/YES   IS DISARMAMENT POSSIBLE?

Disarmament is at the forefront of the world agenda. It is possible to have a world characterized by disarmament because: (1) the world has already experienced examples of disarmament; (2) the world is more aware of the danger of nuclear war than ever before; and (3) a number of technological developments are working to promote disarmament.

Historical Experience. The world has known both war and peace. It is wrong to think that the history of the world is a history of war alone. The problem for those concerned with the well-being of humanity is how to eliminate war. The way to do that is to eliminate the weapons of war, or at least to maximize the restraints on war.

The historical record shows that disarmament has worked in many cases to promote an easing of tension and ultimately to bring peace. The Rush-Bagot agreement was one of the foremost cases of a successful approach to disarmament. That agreement, concluded in 1817 between Great Britain and the United States, provided for the naval demilitarization of the Great Lakes. For its time, too, the Washington Naval Disarmament Conference of 1921–22 was a success because it did serve to restrain the buildup of naval armaments among the signatory powers—although for a short period and for certain types of ships.

In one sense, too, we can look at the development of the laws of war as a recognition that the nations of the world are at least aware of the necessity to impose restraints on warfare. In ancient times the victors would take the spoils of war, and the vanquished would lose their freedom, property, and perhaps their lives. In modern times the application of the Industrial Revolution to military affairs has also coincided with the development of international law governing the laws of war. Soldiers are not given unrestricted freedom to treat civilians as they might choose but must respect the rights of civilian noncombatants of a hostile state. Prisoners of war, moreover, must be accorded rights and cannot legally be subjected to torture. To be sure, these restraints on power are often violated, but millions of lives have been saved because these rules have been followed.

Awareness. In the past it was feasible to agree with the Prussian military theorist Karl von Clausewitz, who argued in the nineteenth century that war is an instrument of policy. A nation could, consequently, contemplate the use of war for limited objectives. In the period between 1815 and 1914, for example, many small wars were conducted without permanent scars on the entire world political landscape.

The experience of World War I, however, demonstrated the dangers of miscalculation in war in modern times. None of the military staffs of the major European powers correctly gauged the character of the war they were about to enter. Had they known, they would have not gone to war. All the military staffs believed that the war would be short. By the time the war was over, however, the prewar governments of Russia, Austria-Hungary, and Germany had toppled. A communist government in Russia, moreover, created a revolutionary force that has transformed world politics.

The world today is aware of the danger of nuclear warfare. It is significant that although both the United States and the Soviet Union have possessed nuclear weapons since 1949, neither side has resorted to using them. At times, such as in the Hungarian uprising of 1956, the Suez crisis of 1956, the Cuban missile crisis of 1962, and the October War of 1973, one side or the other threatened the use of these weapons; but since the defeat of Japan in World War II, neither side has used these weapons. So anxious have the United States and the Soviet Union been to prevent an accidental war from occurring that they have instituted a "hot line" that is a direct communications link between the leaders of the two countries to make certain that nuclear war will not come about as a result of a misunderstanding between the two powers.

Small powers, too, are aware of the dangers. In fact, they have been in the forefront of the movement to reduce the prospects of nuclear warfare. Small powers put pressure on big powers to conclude the Partial Nuclear Test Ban Treaty in 1963, for example. The leaders of the world are not fools and are not anxious to commit either suicide for their own countries or murder against the world.

Technology. It is often assumed that technological innovations do not permit disarmament since a country must keep up with the latest military armaments of its adversary. Measure versus countermeasure fuels the arms race, according to this view. Some writers contend that as soon as the 1972 Strategic Arms Limitation Treaty (SALT), which limited certain nuclear weapons systems of the Soviet Union and the United States, was approved, new inventions negated its provisions.

What is often overlooked, however, is that technological innovations are not always detrimental to arms control and disarmament. In fact, they may enhance prospects for the control of the instruments of violence. Satellites and seismic detection devices illustrate this point.

A major difficulty in bringing about arms control agreements in the post–World War II period has been the issue of inspection. The United States insisted from the beginning of the nuclear age that on-site inspection be a prerequisite for any agreements. The Soviets resisted any such American efforts, and agreements were held up for years on this point. Advances in seismic detection and in "spy satellites" made agreement possible. The seismic devices placed in the United States or in countries friendly to the United States could detect a nuclear explosion in the Soviet Union down to small yields in the low kiloton range. The Soviets could use similar devices to check on the United States. Satellites could monitor agreements, too, to the satisfaction of both superpowers. Here were two technological innovations that improved prospects for arms control. Are there not others that can also be helpful? Would not the killer satellites developed by both sides at the same time be beneficial to arms control since they would negate

the huge expenditures on the current strategic arsenal? Surely the evidence is clear that technology can benefit the prospect for disarmament.

Disarmament, then, is not a dream of the idealists. It is a practical option that the world should choose.

26/NO IS DISARMAMENT POSSIBLE?

People who advocate disarmament are probably going to produce the very world situation that they dread. That is, they will, first, undermine the military strength of their own countries to the extent that they influence significant segments of public opinion to focus on "peace" and, consequently, put their own states into weak positions—so weak, in fact, as to make them vulnerable to attack. Second, they will encourage a nonviolent pacifist philosophy, a factor that weakens national security. Effective disarmament is utopian because: (1) wars are a constant element in the history of the world; (2) internal order requires weapons, and it is sometimes difficult to distinguish internal from external weapons; and (3) the technical problems of disarmament are insurmountable in the nuclear age.

War and History. It is wildly optimistic to believe that a world that has known war since the beginning of history will reform its ways. There is no evidence that war is abating in the nuclear era. The marquee of contemporary war features the names of Korea, Vietnam, Cambodia, Pakistan, India, Israel, Syria, Hungary, Iraq, Iran, Afghanistan, and many others.

It is true that the record of disarmament has some successes, and Rush-Bagot and the Washington Naval Disarmament Conference are two stars in what otherwise is a very dark sky. More often than not, however, disarmament agreements end in failure. At the Versailles Peace Conference in 1919, for example, disarmament was imposed on Germany. Germany was limited to 100,000 officers and men for its army, and it was not permitted to manufacture weapons of war. Germany was able to circumvent these restrictions in a variety of

ways. German weapons makers entered into agreements with other countries, such as Sweden and the Soviet Union, to produce armaments in those countries. Germany hid its own military production facilities from the inspectors of other countries. It secretly trained soldiers in organizations set up outside the formal military establishment, such as flying clubs and scout organizations.

The record of arms control agreements shows that countries have been ingenious in circumventing the provisions of disarmament treaties. In fact, the record shows that the most successful disarmament occurs when countries act unilaterally rather than seek accords. At the conclusion of World War II, for example, the world witnessed the most massive voluntary disarmament program in modern history when the United States drastically reduced the size of the armed forces. The United States Army, which had 8,020,000 men on the day Japan was defeated in August 1945, was reduced to 1,889,690 men by July 1946.[15] No international agreement forced this move. The United States acted in this manner because it sought to end its wartime mobilized state and to get on with the business of building its peacetime economy. Soon, however, it became apparent that the United States could not return to its prewar isolationist position, and it rearmed to meet a perceived Soviet danger.

The record of history, then, shows that no modern country can afford to disarm. Even

---

[15] Samuel P. Huntington, *The Common Defense: Strategic Programs in National Politics* (New York: Columbia University Press, 1961), p. 35.

countries that are neutral, such as Switzerland and Sweden, have strong military establishments. The familiar picture of the Swiss and the Swedes as peaceful people often overlooks the fact that both peoples devote a considerable amount of their gross national product to defense. Swiss citizens, in fact, have enormous military obligations. No doubt it was because the Swiss were able to mobilize an impressive citizen-army within a twenty-four-hour period that Switzerland was able to maintain its neutrality during World War II.

The nuclear age makes it even easier for states to convert to weapons of war. More states than ever are relying on nuclear energy. It is estimated that, by the year 2000, 20 to 25 percent of the world's energy will be nuclear, thus making it easy for countries to convert to nuclear weapons. The nuclear-weapons states of the world have shown that they are willing to educate the scientists of the non-nuclear-weapons states in nuclear technology. They have been willing, moreover, to sell the machinery and the expertise by which nuclear weapons could be built. It is foolish to believe that the world will show restraint when temptation is so strong for states to develop their own nuclear weapons systems.

Internal Order. Major conflicts exist in the world within states as well as between them. There is considerable evidence that intrastate violence is greater than interstate violence. In recent years Northern Ireland, Indonesia, Lebanon, Vietnam, Iran, Nigeria, and Zimbabwe have suffered civil wars costing thousands, even millions of lives. States need weapons to maintain internal order. It is sometimes difficult to distinguish weapons of internal order from weapons of external disorder. Even the Treaty of Versailles permitted a German military establishment to exist to maintain internal order; and once this kind of necessity is admitted, then the existence of any army is also allowed. Who, then, can prevent staff officers from thinking of noninternal affairs?

If states are not permitted police forces to maintain internal order, then power will go to those elements who possess weapons illegally. A state must have overwhelming military power within its own borders if it is to enforce its laws against those who violate them. Even if weapons are outlawed, then nonweapons

will be used as weapons. Gasoline, which can fuel a sports car, can also be used in a Molotov cocktail. A butcher's knife can also kill people. Dynamite, which can be used to dig tunnels, can also be used to destroy them. It is unrealistic to think that disarmament is possible without anarchy. To be sure, some anarchists who are opposed to any state would applaud disarmament. There is no evidence to indicate, however, that all human beings in a large, complex industrial society would behave in a peaceful manner in the absence of armed police or military forces.

The Technical Problem. Nuclear weapons are different from conventional weapons. Even if mutual trust characterizes the relations between the United States and the Soviet Union, it is unlikely that the mutual trust would be so pervasive as to lead to complete trust.

Technical problems make disarmament impossible. No one regards inspection systems as so foolproof that they can detect *all* weapons. In spite of all the inspection and search points set up by the British Army in Northern Ireland, for example, bombs are frequently detonated by terrorists. These are conventional bombs that take a constant toll of human life.

Nuclear inspection devices are also imperfect. Inspection must deal with the manufacture and storage of enriched uranium and plutonium—the two key ingredients for nuclear weapons. Since there is and will continue to be large amounts of these components in existence, it will be difficult to locate all of them. It takes just about one pound of enriched uranium for every kiloton of nuclear explosives. With the best inspection devices, it is not possible to account for each and every ounce of this material. It would be possible to steal it or even hide its existence from inspection devices if it were stolen in small amounts.

Then there is the problem of getting rid of existing stockpiles of nuclear weapons if nuclear disarmament is to occur. Both the Soviet Union and the United States have thousands of nuclear weapons in their arsenals. Suppose both sides agree to destroy their own arsenals, but one side successfully hides one hundred bombs of megaton capability. Such a force would be capable of obliterating a country. So devastating is each bomb that the risks of complete nuclear disarmament would be worse than the present step-by-step approach of arms control. In the real world of the 1990s, it is foolish to think about nuclear disarmament. It is unlikely, moreover, that even if some countries would agree to nuclear disarmament, all countries of the world would approve of inspection devices and give up that part of their sovereignty that would allow international inspection.

In addition to verification problems, there are two other, more traditional problems of disarmament: ratios and convertibility of weapons. Assuming for the moment that the countries of the world agree that disarmament is a good thing, how will the ratios of armaments among the states be apportioned? The Washington Naval Disarmament Conference attempted to deal with this problem with just five principal naval powers. Trying to deal with setting ratios for more than 160 countries would be a virtual impossibility.

Even if ratios could be established, how will the different weapons systems of states be counted? How many nuclear submarines of one country equal how many intercontinental ballistic missiles of another? The mind boggles at the complicated efforts to reach agreement under these conditions. It takes a great deal of time to reach a consensus in the policy-making institutions of every country in the world. Technological innovations, moreover, proceed more rapidly than the ability of states to cope with them.

Even if nuclear disarmament were possible, all that the elimination of nuclear weapons would do is promote the use of nonnuclear weapons, which can take millions of lives. In the fratricidal fighting in Indonesia in 1965, for example, it is estimated that up to half a million lives were taken. The civil war in Nigeria, moreover, may have claimed a million Ibo lives— all without nuclear weapons. The twenty-four-hour saturation bombing of Dresden in World War II took more lives than the bombing of Hiroshima. Conventional methods of destruction may be as grim as nuclear weapons.

Disarmament, then, is the pipedream of idealists. At best, we can hope to regulate weapons, but not to eliminate them.

KEY TERMS

Arms control	Grand alliances
Balance of power	Guerrilla warfare
Bilateral aid	International law
Collective security	Limited conventional war
Concert system	Limited nuclear war
Diplomacy	Marshall Plan
Disarmament	Most-favored nation
Divestment	Multilateral aid
Economic aid	National character
Embargo	Terrorism
General conventional war	Total nuclear war
	Urban guerrilla warfare

QUESTIONS

International Politics: Instruments and Constraints

1. Take a foreign policy matter currently in the news and study the instruments of power used by a state involved. Analyze those instruments and evaluate the difficulties of using alternative measures.

2. Who will be the big powers fifty years from now? Why?

3. Do nuclear weapons make collective security obsolete? What are the reasons for your answer?

4. Under what conditions should foreign aid be used as an instrument of foreign policy?

5. What relevance does balance of power have in the nuclear age?

The United States in Decline?

1. What should be the method of determining how much the United States should spend on defense?

2. What pressures can the United States bring to bear on its allies in order to get them to spend more on their own defense?

3. What criteria should be used in determining whether the United States should make a commitment to defend another country?

4. What would be the consequences of a reduction in U.S. commitments abroad on Soviet foreign policy? on the foreign policy of U.S. allies?

5. What effect would a reduction of 50 percent in annual defense spending have on the U.S. economy?

Economic Sanctions

1. What effect do international economic sanctions have on the condition of blacks in South Africa?

2. Under what conditions would sanctions be the most effective? Under what conditions would they be the least effective?

3. What criteria should be used in determining whether a country should apply sanctions? What are the reasons for your answer?

4. What are the difficulties in getting countries to impose economic sanctions against governments that have an extremely brutal record on human rights?

5. What is the best way to bring about political democracy in South Africa? What are the reasons for your answer?

Disarmament

1. Do arms control agreements strengthen or weaken the prospects for disarmament? What are the reasons for your answer?

2. What is the relationship between arms races and war?

3. How can arms control agreements dealing with nuclear weapons be verified?

4. What effect would a nuclear freeze have on the arms race?

5. What effect would the proliferation of nuclear weapons to more countries have on world peace and security?

RECOMMENDED READINGS

International Politics: Instruments and Constraints

CASSESE, ANONIO. *International Law in a Divided World.* Oxford, England: Clarendon Press, 1986. An introduction to the role of law in the world community.

CLAUDE, INIS L., JR. *Power and International Relations.* New York: Random House, 1962. An analysis of balance of power, collective security, and world government.

DEHIO, LUDWIG. *The Precarious Balance: Four Centuries of European Power Struggle.* New York: Knopf, 1962. A historical description of balance of power.

FALK, RICHARD A. *The Promise of World Order: Essays in Normative International Relations.* Philadelphia: Temple University Press, 1987. Essays on international relations.

KIPNIS, KENNETH, and DIANA T. MEYERS, eds. *Political Realism and International Morality: Ethics in the Nuclear Age.* Boulder, Colo.: Westview Press, 1987. Articles on the tension between security and morality in foreign policy.

NICOLSON, HAROLD G. *Diplomacy.* 3d ed. London: Oxford University Press, 1963. An analysis of diplomacy.

ROBERTS, ADAM, and BENEDICT KINGSBURY, eds. *United Nations, Divided World: The UN's Roles in International Relations.* New York:

Oxford University Press, 1988. An analysis of the United Nations.

SCOTT, ANDREW M. *The Dynamics of Interdependence.* Chapel Hill, N.C.: University of North Carolina Press, 1982. A study of the interdependence of states.

SMITH, MICHAEL JOSEPH. *Realist Thought from Weber to Kissinger.* Baton Rouge, La.: Louisiana State University Press, 1986. A study of modern realists.

The United States in Decline?

CALLEO, DAVID P. *Beyond American Hegemony: The Future of the Western Alliance.* New York: Basic Books, 1987. An argument in defense of a U.S. policy of devolution for NATO.

GILPIN, ROBERT. "American Policy in the Post-Reagan Era." *Daedalus* 116 (Summer 1987): 33–67. An argument that the United States will have to reduce its military commitments because of economic difficulties.

KENNEDY, PAUL. *The Rise and Fall of the Great Powers: Economic Change and Military Conflict from 1500 to 2000.* New York: Random House, 1987. An examination of the role of economic strength in the rise and fall of great powers.

MEAD, WALTER RUSSELL. *Mortal Splendor: The American Empire in Transition.* Boston: Houghton Mifflin, 1987. An argument that the United States is in decline.

MOYNIHAN, DANIEL PATRICK "Debunking the Myth of Decline." *New York Times Magazine,* June 19, 1988, pp. 34, 52–53. An argument that the Reagan administration's economic policies should be reversed so that the United States can play its proper role in world affairs.

NYE, JOSEPH S., JR. "Understanding U.S. Strength." *Foreign Policy,* no. 72 (Fall 1988): 105–29. An argument that the United States is not in real economic or military decline but that the international political and economic environment is changing.

SCHLESINGER, JAMES R. "Debunking the Myth of Decline." *New York Times Magazine,* June 18, 1988, pp. 35–36. An argument that the United States is in relatively good shape.

SCHMEISSER, PETER. "Is America in Decline?" *New York Times Magazine,* April 17, 1988, pp. 24–27, 66–68, 96. An overview of the controversy about a declining United States.

STEIN, HERBERT. "America Is Rich Enough to Be Strong." *AEI Economist,* February 1988, pp. 1–7. An argument that the United States is economically strong enough to meet its military and overseas commitments.

U.S. CONGRESS, SENATE. *Concurrent Resolution on the Budget for Fiscal Year 1989: Defense Burden-Sharing.* Hearings before the Committee on the Budget, 100th Congress, 2d Sess., 1988. 1: 1–59. A presentation and assessment of the views of Paul Kennedy about U.S. decline.

Economic Sanctions

BARTLETT, BRUCE. "What's Wrong with Trade Sanctions?" *USA Today* (Magazine) 114 (May 1986): 22–25. A case against sanctions.

BECKER, CHARLES M. "Economic Sanctions against South Africa." *World Politics* 39 (January 1987): 147–73. A refutation of the view that all effective sanctions in South Africa would greatly hurt poor blacks there.

BRIMELOW, PETER. "Why South Africa Shrugs at Sanctions." *Forbes* 139 (March 9, 1987): 100–104. A description of how South Africa is able to circumvent sanctions.

DOXEY, MARGARET P. *International Sanctions in Contemporary Perspective.* Houndmills, England: Macmillan, 1987. An analysis of recent state practice to elucidate problems of sanctions application and impact.

ELLINGS, RICHARD J. *Embargoes and World Power: Lessons from American Foreign Policy.* Boulder, Colo.: Westview Press, 1985. An analysis of the changing structure of the international system and the use of economic instruments of power.

FOSSEDAL, GREGORY A. "Sanctions for Beginners." *New Republic* 193 (October 21, 1985): 18–21. An argument that sanctions can be effective.

HUFBAUER, GARY CLYDE, and JEFFREY J. SCHOTT, with KIMBERLY ANN ELLIOTT. *Economic Sanctions in Support of Foreign Policy Goals.* Washington, D.C.: Institute for International Economics, 1983. An analysis.

LEYTON-BROWN, DAVID, ed. *The Utility of International Economic Sanctions.* New York: St.

Martin's Press, 1987. Essays on the subject with case studies.

MINTER, WILLIAM. "South Africa: Straight Talk on Sanctions." *Foreign Policy,* no. 65 (Winter 1986/1987): 43–63. An argument that sanctions may help bring about an end to *apartheid* in South Africa.

NINCIC, MIROSLAV, and PETER WALLENSTEEN, eds. *Dilemmas of Economic Coercion: Sanctions in World Politics.* New York: Praeger, 1983. Essays on the subject.

SUZMAN, HELEN. "What America Should Do about South Africa." *New York Times Magazine,* August 3, 1986, pp. 14–17. An argument that sanctions impede an end to *apartheid.*

Disarmament

BARASH, DAVID P. *The Arms Race and Nuclear War.* Belmont, Calif.: Wadsworth Publishing Co., 1987. An introduction to the subject.

BERKOWITZ, BRUCE D. *Calculated Risks: A Century of Arms Control—Why It Has Failed and How It Can Be Made to Work.* New York: Simon and Schuster, 1987. An analysis of arms control.

EBERSTADT, MARY TEDESCHI. "Arms Control and Its Casualties." *Commentary* 85 (April 1988): 39–46. An analysis of U.S. arms control efforts.

GRAY, COLIN S. "Nuclear Delusions: Six Arms Control Fallacies." *Policy Review,* no. 37 (Summer 1986): 48–53. An analysis of assumptions about the effectiveness of arms control agreements.

HARVARD NUCLEAR STUDY GROUP. *Living with Nuclear Weapons.* Cambridge, Mass.: Harvard University Press, 1983. A discussion of nuclear weapons and arms control.

LAMB, CHRISTOPHER J. *How to Think about Arms Control, Disarmament and Defense.* Engelwood Cliffs, N.J.: Prentice Hall, 1988. An introduction to the subject.

PERRY, THOMAS L., and JAMES G. FOULKS, eds. *End the Arms Race—Fund Human Needs: Proceedings of the 1986 Vancouver Centennial Peace and Disarmament Symposium.* West Vancouver, Canada: Gordon Soules, 1986. A plea for disarmament.

SCHELL, JONATHAN. *The Fate of the Earth.* New York: Knopf, 1982. An examination of the nuclear predicament.

WALLOP, MALCOLM, and ANGELO CODEVILLA. *The Arms Control Delusion.* San Francisco: ICS Press, 1987. A critique of arms control.

Index